Predictably Rational?

Richard B. McKenzie

Predictably Rational?

In Search of Defenses for Rational Behavior
in Economics

 Springer

Prof. Richard B. McKenzie
The Paul Merage School of Business
University of California
Irvine, CA 92697-3125
USA
mckenzie@uci.edu

ISBN 978-3-642-01585-4   e-ISBN 978-3-642-01586-1
DOI 10.1007/978-3-642-01586-1
Springer Heidelberg Dordrecht London New York

Library of Congress Control Number: 2009928778

Cover design: WMXDesign GmbH, Heidelberg, Germany

Printed on acid-free paper

Springer is part of Springer Science+Business Media (www.springer.com)

It is somewhat unusual to begin the treatment of a subject with a warning against attaching too much importance to it; but in the case of economics, such an injunction is quite as much needed as explanation and emphasis of the importance it really has. It is characteristic of the age in which we live to think too much in terms of economics, to see things too predominantly in their economic aspect... There is no more important prerequisite to clear thinking in regard to economics itself than is recognition of its limited place among human interests at large.

The Economic Organization   Frank H. Knight
(1933, p. 1)

Preface

In this book, I undertake a reexamination of *rationality*, or *rational behavior*, in the history of economic thought, review strands of scholarly criticisms of rationality, and develop defenses for the continued use of rationality in economic analysis. The emphasis will be on how economists have employed the rationality premise in the post-World War II era, during which time the premise became widely recognized for being at the core of fully formed neoclassical economics and during which time the premise has come under ever more serious attacks that, in no small way, have undermined the credibility of economics as a scientific endeavor (at least according to many behavioral psychologists and behavioral economists whose work will be reviewed later in this book).

Economists are a diverse group, which means my reexamination of rationality must be confined. I have chosen to adopt the perspective on rationality that is generally represented by mainstream or (what I equate with) neoclassical economics, widely adopted in modern intermediate microeconomic theory textbooks. I give special attention to two methodological perspectives on rationality that have emanated from the modern Chicago school identified by history of thought economist Steven Medema (2008): The first Chicago perspective is best represented in Milton Friedman's classic methodological essay (1953) and his textbook (1962), with Friedman focusing on the motivational force of rationality, or just self-interest, within market settings. The other perspective is best represented by George Stigler's and Gary Becker's textbooks written separately (Stigler 1952, last published in 1987 with significant evolved changes in the treatment of rationality; and Becker 1971a) and their joint methodological essay (1977), with Stigler and Becker accepting much of Friedman's methodology but untying the rational behavior premise from narrowly confined market analysis and using the premise as the founding motivational force undergirding a method of thinking, with the application of the method no longer contained by subject matter (for example, business or markets outcomes).

In giving shape to mainstream, neoclassical economics for purposes of this volume, I remain fully aware that any school of thought has boundaries that are fuzzy and changing, with adherents within the loosely defined school of thought differing significantly on many details of analysis (which is especially true of neoclassical economics that took shape in the relatively recent past, after World War II). Nevertheless, I focus on the work of Friedman, Stigler, and Becker because the perspectives on rationality they represent have been, in recent decades, at the core of intense scholarly scrutiny, especially from behavioral psychologists and behavioral economists (although the critics, who have become advocates of a behavioral premise of irrationality, have not fully recognized the divergence of methodological views within the Chicago sector of neoclassical economics, or the importance of the divergence).

Clearly, I must assume people possess some level of rationality in the development of this book. Otherwise, it is hard for me to understand how we economists and others can have thoughtful, purposeful discussions about the concept of rationality and human behavior spawned by human decision making, as well as pursue the development of a deductive science. A question that guides (and dogs) this investigation is whether an assumption of human rationality – and, more specifically, perfect rationality (to be defined with care as the book develops) – will advance our understanding of human behavior, and the *science* of economics, more than some other more descriptively accurate behavioral premises. That is to say, the question at the heart of the book is whether an assumption of human rationality, imbued with imperfections, that melds better with credible evidence on how people actually make economic and other decisions will actually better serve an important goal of economic analysis, which is to generate insights and testable hypotheses relating to the way people behave, individually and collectively, as they seek to improve their stations in life.

The Economics of the Human Brain and Rationality

The rationality premise frames a great deal of mainstream economists' discussions of a wide-range of human choices under conditions of scarcity, normally conceived as human wants far outstretching people's capacity to fulfill them. I devote several chapters to the intellectual history of the motivational foundations of economic analysis, covering the methodological thinking of notable economists from Adam Smith to Alfred Marshall to Frank Knight and Becker, and others, but with some emphasis on the methodological position of Friedman. I review the discipline's history of thought because that history reveals an evolution of the motivational foundations of economic analysis, from an expansive to a fairly narrow motivational foundation. This history reveals that behavioral economists are not the first disciplinary insiders to take issue with the descriptive accuracy of the rationality premise.

In this book, I take the discussion of rationality where few economists have, recognizing that there also must be an economics of rationality, given that all human decisions are ultimately constrained, not so much by scarcity in the external physical world – the familiar domain for economic analysis – as by the more pressing constraints of human beings' mental faculties to cope with the virtually unlimited volume of sensory information flowing daily to and through the human brain. The ever increasing flow of sensory information in modern sophisticated societies, enhanced by the growing reach of markets (and nonmarket forms of collaborations), is no doubt taxing people's rational capacities as never before, pressing them to find heuristics to manage the flow within the limits of their mental abilities.

In the economics of the human brain lie potential explanations for why people are not, and cannot be – and would not want to be – as rational as so many economists assume. After all, economists widely presume that the economic actors in their behavioral models carefully, if not precisely, weigh virtually all costs and benefits of all decisions, always appropriately discounting raw costs and gains for time and risk and always equalizing marginal discounted values and optimizing their expected net gain. Hence, any conceptual or empirical demonstration that real humans fall short of economists' behavioral premise is hardly a surprising or notable philosophical and scientific achievement, apart from the fact that some economists themselves might write as if they seem oblivious to the prospect that their behavioral premise is not descriptive of how people actually make decisions and behave.

In the economics of the human brain also lie potential explanations for why many human choices that may deviate from rationality are nothing more than calculated and expected mistakes that people make when struggling to economize as best they can on their mental faculties. Ironically, in the economics of the brain, as well as the economics of doing science, lies a potential explanation for why economists will likely continue to assume that the actors in their models have rational capacities well beyond real people's acknowledged rational limits, and well beyond the rational limits of economists themselves who pursue science as a matter of model-building and hypothesis-testing. After all, if the subjects of economic analysis have demonstrated mental faculties and rational limitations, economists, who are drawn from the general population, also must harbor those same limitations, more or less. By assuming their subjects are more rational than economists know them to be, economists may simply be seeking a means of containing the complexity of their theories in order to gain more understanding of the complex social interactions of their subjects within the limits of economists' own mental faculties. In a sense, if people were in fact perfectly rational, as well as had perfect information (as many economists are prone to assume in their models), there would be no point to the analysis, which means no purpose for assuming people are perfectly rational. Ironically, only when people, including economists, have analytical limitations does it make sense to simplify and sterilize the underlying behavioral assumption regarding human motivations, or so I will argue in some detail at various points in this book.

Besides, when economists' analytics are static, organized around changes in equilibrium, given changes in key variables, the process by which people adjust from one equilibrium to the next is obscured (if not totally obliterated). To the extent that the embedded adjustment process permits, or presses, people to correct their own and others' errant and irrational decisions and behaviors, then a rationality assumption descriptive of people's innate rational tendencies at the start of the process would lose some of its predictive capacity about how the process can be expected to unfold. This is to say that any embedded corrective feedback loops on decision making in real-world settings, such as those in competitive markets (or, for that matter, those corrective feedback mechanisms embedded in the human brain), require economists to assume a level of rationality, for the purpose of enhancing their theories' predictive accuracy, that is greater than what people are known to possess in laboratory and survey experiments where the feedback competitive pressures are absent or weak and that is greater than what people process at the start of any economic process with built-in feedback loops.

People's rational capacities have, of course, been shaped by eons of evolutionary forces, with many human decision propensities having been shaped and constrained as much by environmental and group dynamic forces extant in the Pleistocene Epoch, 10,000 years ago and more, as by the particular costs and benefits associated with people's contemporary choices. Indeed, as evolutionary biologists and evolutionary psychologists advise, an individual's current subjective assessment of costs and benefits must still be influenced by long-ago environmental conditions and group dynamics that are as alien to modern decision-makers as their influences are unrecognized by the broad swath of practicing economists. These ancient influences necessarily remain entrenched in many contemporary decisions because of how they continue to shape the allocation of the brain's hundred billion or so neurons and the untold number of synapses and their unifying neural circuits.

The Growing Critiques of Rationality

In undertaking this reexamination and organizing defenses of rationality in economic theory, I am well aware of the intensifying, and often caustic, critiques of rationality by many non-economists (cognitive psychologists, sociologists, political scientists, evolutionary biologists, and neurobiologists) and some economists (mainly behavioral and experimental economists and neuroeconomists). The critics point to an array of "decision-making biases," which lead to a host of observed "irrationalities" (or decisions and behaviors not consistent in form and consequence with those expected from the standard of perfect rationality). I cover a representative share of this scholarly evidence coming from behavioral economists and psychologists in this book (full coverage is not practical or economic). Indeed, these critiques have motivated the development of this book because they have elevated to scholarly prominence a question that goes to the heart of what mainstream economists do: "If irrationalities pervade human decision making and behaviors as extensively as the critics maintain, how can mainstream economists continue to justify reliance on the premise of perfect rationality in their models?"

The critics of neoclassical economics insist people are so pervasively irrational that they are systematically and "predictably irrational" (Ariely 2008). I have

chosen my main title, *Predictably Rational?*, to stand in contrast with the critics'
thesis in two regards. First, the obvious, the use of "rational" and second, the
insertion of the question mark. Have the critics settled the debate to the extent
they seem to suggest with the absence of a question mark after "predictably
irrational"? Might not economic theory, devised with the intent of deducing
tentative hypotheses subject to testing, require people to be more rational than
neoclassical economists know them to be? Might people be more predictably
rational than they are naturally inclined to be when people can correct their own
and others' decision-making ways in social processes in which feedback loops
affect eventual outcomes?

My subtitle, *In Search of Defenses for Rational Behavior in Economics*, was
chosen with equal care. I began writing this book years back when a prominent
university colleague in cognitive psychology challenged me in a casual conversation over some topic of mutual interest, "Richard, do you really believe in this
rationality crap?" My only response at the time was a quip, "If I did not believe it to
some extent, I do not know how we can have a meaningful discussion over your
question." At the time, I had only a nodding acquaintance with the vast scholarly
and popular literature challenging economists' rationality premise that my colleague had in mind. I began this book as a true exploration for better answers, if
any unflawed ones could be found, to my colleague's implied suggestion that economists (including me) were delusional. Might there be defenses for the continued
use of the rationality premise that goes beyond Friedman's seminal defense more
than a half-century ago (1953), especially since Friedman's (and Stigler's and
Becker's) methodological defense has been found wanting by behavioralists?
Might there be defenses that the critics would take seriously, if not shake their
confidence in their own caustic assessments of what mainstream economists do?
The writing of this book has been a true search with strictly academic and personal
intentions in mind, which means at the start I truly did not know how the book
would evolve (although I had to believe that there were defenses to be found, given
the success that so many neoclassical economists seem to have had with their
methods over the past half century or more). And as with all intellectual explorations, undertaken honestly and with care, discoveries were inevitable, with one or
more of the defenses uncovered surprisingly straightforward.

Criticisms of mainstream economists' methodological approach are hardly new.
Throughout the history of the discipline, non-economists have continually charged
that any theory founded on a premise as demonstrably false as fully rational
behavior must be grossly misleading, if not totally empty and useless. Even
economists, as far back as Adam Smith, the much heralded founder of the discipline, have recognized that self-interest-directed and maximizing behavior (Smith
never uses "rationality," "rational," or "maximizing" behavior in his two classic
treatises on moral philosophy and political economy (1759 and 1776)) is necessarily
an incomplete view of human behavior. Observed, real-world decisions and
behaviors are founded on many motivations and group and cooperative dynamics,
with market forces being a group dynamic of primary concern to Smith and almost
all subsequent classical and neoclassical economists.

The Old and New Worlds of Economics

What is new to the modern debate concerning the premise of full human rationality are two scholarly forces set afoot during the past half-century. The first is the growing body of credible scientific evidence that casts doubt on the premise that human decisions are guided by anything close to perfect rationality. People just do not seem to make their decisions with anywhere near the care, accuracy, and consistency – or rationality – that economists have long presumed. Although economists, generally, have understood that people are imperfectly rational, they have probably been surprised at the extent of the deficiencies in human rationality, when the implications for choices have been empirically tested. No doubt, some have begun to worry about whether economists' fallback position on rationality – that a premise of full rationality is a reasonable approximation for how people do in fact behave – is sustainable.

The second scholarly force that has been gaining momentum in recent decades has been economists' inclination to apply their models of human decision making and hypothesis testing to topics further and further removed from strictly market arenas, crossing the disciplinary boundaries of psychology, sociology, political science, and neuroscience. James Buchanan won the Nobel Prize in Economics for modeling the behavior of rational, self-interest-directed constitutional decision makers and politicians.[1] Becker subsequently won his Nobel for greatly expanding the array of research topics – from human capital to discrimination to family life to addiction – all investigated with mainstream models of behavior, grounded in fully rational decision making guiding the analysis and with the implications of the theories often tested with progressively more sophisticated econometric techniques.[2]

As a matter of full disclosure, I assumed this book project as an economist, who has spent a career following in the Buchanan and Becker traditions, researching and writing about a variety of personal and public policy topics – from the economics of lying, panics, donor exploitation, sex, and dying, covered in *The New World of Economics* (McKenzie and Tullock 1976) to the likely ineffectiveness of minimum wage laws (1995) to a frontal assault on conventional monopoly theory (McKenzie and Lee 2008). At every step in my career, I have employed economic models fully grounded in rational precepts (with these precepts being laid out with care in Chap. 1).

As we will see, at the turn of the twentieth century, British economic luminary Alfred Marshall preferred to relegate the study of economics to the study "of men as they live and move and think in the ordinary business of life" (1890, Sect. I.II.1). During the last half of the twentieth century, economics gradually became defined

---

[1]Of Buchanan's many writings see, for example, Buchanan and Tullock (1962); Buchanan (1975); and Brennan and Buchanan (1985).
[2]Of Becker's many writings see, for example, 1994, 1996, 1997; Becker and Murphy (1988); and Becker and Becker (1997).

not so much by the arenas studied (markets and businesses) as by the method of inquiry, which is anchored in the constructs of rationality, optimization and equilibrium, and statistical testing of hypotheses. Indeed, some casual observers might now mistakenly see the discipline as having become totally unbounded by subject matter and constrained only by its methods, given the recent publication of a spate of academic and popular economics books dealing with topics, which one or two generations before would have been considered unusual, if not bizarre. Becker is renowned for his economic imperialism, or academic forays into the economics of discrimination and the family (1971b and 1993). The more popular new books include the runaway best seller (for an economics book!) *Freakonomics: A Rogue Economist Explores the Hidden Side of Everything* that takes up, among other topics (all tied to academic journal articles), the impact of legalized abortion in the United States in the early 1970s on the decline in the country's crime rates in the 1990s (Levitt and Dubner 2005) and *More Sex is Safer Sex* (Landsburg 2007) with the topic in the book's title explained with reference to a tragedy of the (dating market) commons attributable to rational and suboptimally coordinated individual decision making.

Other recent and widely read books suggest that the economic way of thinking about everything is more or less natural. Consider two popular books released as I began developing this book: *Discover Your Inner Economist: Use Incentives to Fall in Love, Survive Your Next Meeting, and Motivate Your Dentist* (Cowen 2007) and *The Economic Naturalist: In Search of Explanations for Everyday Enigmas* (Frank 2007). Implicit (if not explicit) in these books is the admonition that economic thinking is a natural but latent skill that has the potential for improvement. Readers of such books are advised that they can hone their economic thinking skills by considering an array of questions and puzzles that can be unraveled by uncovering embedded costs, benefits, and incentives (and misguided incentives) in observed behaviors. I have since followed with a book covering popular topics with an academic thrust of my own, *Why Popcorn Costs So Much at the Movies, and Other Pricing Puzzles* (2008) that gives rational explanations for the high price of theater popcorn, as well as for why queues can be seen everywhere, ink cartridges can cost as much as printers, all movies (no matter how popular) carry the same ticket prices, and so many prices end with "9."

From my varied writings, I obviously have a personal and professional stake in the debate over rationality in economics, as do a substantial majority of all economists. At the same time, I hasten to add that for much of my career, I have had an abiding interest in the limits of economics as a science (McKenzie 1982). This book project gave me an opportunity to update and refine my thinking on just how expansive economists can be in the topics they consider before their analyses amount to so much formalized academic gibberish that is detached from real-world human behavior. The most fundamental issue in the growing critiques of rational precepts from both inside and outside the economics discipline is whether the research models and evaluative techniques of economics (or of other disciplines subject to economic imperialism) generate better, more useful insights into human behavior than other disciplines using different methodologies, or whether the methodologies of economics and those of other disciplines are complementary. But, to address such an issue, we must first appreciate a point Frank Knight made with force (1924), that economics is necessarily a partial and limited view of life (made intentionally so by the static, partial equilibrium approach to analysis). But then a partial view cannot be all bad, since, as widely recognized among economists, a theory that is sufficiently complete to explain everything will not be very useful in making predictions of anything. Readers should not be surprised that neoclassical and behavioral economists have much to inform the other groups because of the partial views of decision making they necessarily bring to the academic table.

The Ironies of Economic Education

As I develop my arguments on rationality, I return time and again to two unheralded, if not altogether unrecognized, and unaddressed ironies in economics:

- First, if people are as fully rational as economists assume in their model building, why do economists have to teach students that people are rational? Should students not know that people are rational and understand all the implications of rational behavior laid out in economics courses?
- Second, if markets do what Adam Smith says they do – lead people, as if by an "invisible hand" – to societal ends that buyers and sellers do not seek and cannot know absent the interplay of market forces through time, can people be (and do they need to be) as rational as economists presume? If people are led by an invisible hand as Smith suggests, can the outcomes of market processes, at any time, be known to market participants and, hence, can be in their choice sets, at least not during much of the time that market processes work their magic?

To answer: If people were as rational as economists assume, students need not be taught economics, unless the goal goes beyond the professed chief purpose of most economics instruction, which is to evaluate people's behavior as it *is*, not as it *should be*. I conclude that, as conventionally argued, economics is useful because it can lead to testable hypotheses and that, as not conventionally recognized, economics can be instructive on how people can improve their thinking and decision making, and their rationality – precisely because people are not as innately rational as economists assume them to be. Moreover, people cannot be fully rational in market processes when they are led as if by an invisible hand towards ends that they can only imagine beforehand in terms of their broad "patterns of outcomes" (to use an expression favored by Austrian economist and Nobel Laureate Friedrich Hayek), but not in terms of the patterns' detailed contents. Paradoxically, people's inability to be fully rational is all the more reason economists, who seek the development of a deductive science devoted to static model building and hypothesis testing, need to assume their subjects are far more rational than they really are. Moreover,

I stress that economists can assume people are more rational than they are, at least in market settings, because irrationalities will, in varying degrees, be corrected by competitive pressures that are assumed to be at work underneath the static, equilibrium-focused analyses. Without such corrective pressures, the full rationality premise may indeed lose its impact, which can be a reason critics of mainstream economics have emerged in force as economists have applied their methods further and further afield from market settings and in settings where corrective pressures on decision making can be less intense than in competitive market settings. The absence of such corrective pressures can also help explain why subjects exhibit the varieties and levels of irrationalities in surveys and laboratory settings as often as they do. This argument suggests that as economists take up topics further and further removed from social arenas, such as markets, in which competitive pressures can correct decisions and behaviors, the value of the perfect rationality premise can lose its value as a foundation for making predictions.

Plan for the Book

My interdisciplinary reexamination of rationality is wide ranging but is organized along the following lines: I first describe the mainstream, neoclassical position on rational behavior, reviewing the intellectual history of the motivational construct, and then explore the criticisms. I then respond to criticisms, using understandings developed from a review of the burgeoning literature in evolutionary biology and neurobiology. Finally, I develop my own defenses of continued use of the construct that, paradoxically, rely heavily on the proposition that human decision making and behavior cannot be as rational as mainstream economists assume.

More specifically, the book is arranged as follows:

- In the first chapter, I describe the conventional way in which economists understand rational behavior and the implications of that behavior, mainly following construction of markets underlying motivational force in Friedman's work. I also explain how the pursuit of *scientific* knowledge imposes requirements on the premises underlying behavioral models.
- Chapter 2 describes four additional analytical functions (other than as a foundation for the conduct of *science*) that a premise of rationality serves in economics. I argue that the exact nature of the rationality premise economists use depends on their theory of knowledge and the methods (e.g., mathematics) and technology (e.g., regression analysis and computers) employed. Along the way, I explain how perfect rationality, as portrayed in much basic microeconomic theory, amounts to a form of "hyperrationality," which is irrational in rationality's own terms.
- In Chapter 3, I review how Adam Smith relied on self-interest and self-love in his analyses. However, I emphasize Smith's expansive view of human motivations that affected people's decision making inside and outside of markets.

- Chapters 4 and 5 examine the views on rationality of Thomas Robert Malthus, Stanley Jevons, Alfred Marshall, Frank Knight, Friedrich Hayek and more modern scientists, such as Stigler, Becker, and Buchanan, emphasizing the evolution and refinement of the concept of rational behavior during the past 200 years.
- Chapter 6 provides a broad (but hardly comprehensive) review of the criticisms of rational behavior that have emerged from inside and outside the economics discipline, most notably from Herbert Simon, Daniel Kahneman, Richard Thaler, Cass Sunstein, Dan Ariely, and Robert Shiller – to name just several of a rapidly growing cadre of modern critics.
- Chapters 7 and 8 present findings on the limits of human rationality developed by evolutionary biologists and psychologists, on the one hand, and neurobiologists, on the other hand. From the perspective of evolutionary forces, perfect rationality is all but impossible. From the perspective of neurobiology, perfect rationality is not to be expected or even desired, given the economizing problem that the brain itself faces. Perfect rationality would be irrational, even if perfect rationality was achievable. The brain is likely to seek a rational level of rationality, as well as a rational level of irrationalities (concepts to be developed with some care in these chapters). Indeed, the brain can operate more rationality by accepting decision-making processes that lead to some irrationalities.
- In Chapter 9, I examine the Chicago defense of the premise of rationality, again with emphasis on the methodological positions taken by Friedman, Stigler, and Becker.
- In Chapter 10, I press problems with the methodologies and findings of behavioral economics and psychology, from which one of my own defenses of the rational-behavior premise in economics will emerge. All the while, I acknowledge the (rational) limits to rationality. Nevertheless, I argue that the modern findings relating to people's limited ability to behave rationally make the presumption of rationality all the more necessary, if economics is to remain a deductive science.
- In Chapter 11, I develop the argument that markets can press people to act more rationally than they might naturally be because of the costs people would incur from irrationalities, causing systematically irrational people to fail and withdraw from markets. This is to say that more competitive and efficient markets likely will lead people, as if by an invisible hand, to a level of rationality that they would not otherwise be inclined to exhibit. I explain how economics, founded on perfect rationality, can be instructive. When people are not fully rational, they can become more rational with the aid of heuristics that can emerge from learning about decision-making deficiencies and about the type of decision making that could be expected from fully rational people. With people less than fully rational, economics as a discipline of study can have a normative intent, to improve people's thinking and decision making and, hence, to make them more rational and more competitive, and make markets more efficient, than they would otherwise be. That is, competitive markets do more than induce an efficient allocation of resources among *given* wants. Market also can expand and redefine people's wants and press market participants to be more rational.

As a consequence, people can benefit from taking courses in mainstream economics because of their limited rationality; they can avoid the waste of resources that can occur from flawed decisions that have to be corrected because of competitive market pressures.

Again, throughout this book, I acknowledge the many imperfections in economists' rationality premise. But then, all methodologies intended to further our understanding of complex human behavior will have deficiencies. Just as all garden tools have deficiencies – because of the constraining influence of the economics of achieving greater perfection in garden tools – we should not be surprised that analytical tools are imperfect in varying degrees. The relevant question for me is one that Friedman stressed long ago, whether greater insight about human behavior can be acquired by efficiently using the analytical tools of economics or of other disciplines.

During my academic career, I have observed much success emerging from the work of economists toiling in the mainstream, neoclassical microeconomic tradition. The development of substantial literatures in human capital/education, information, and public choice economics, as well as the fields of law and economics had their intellectual genesis before I began my career, but those fields have certainly flourished in recent decades. Likewise, professional appreciation for the importance of property rights and residual claimants in efficient market systems has grown substantially. Forty years ago, no economist talked of network, experience, and addictive goods. Before the mid-1960s, discussion of organizational issues was far more limited than it is today. Virtually, all meaningful competition that constrained firms was in resource and final product markets, not in the competition for the firms themselves. Virtually, all meaningful monopolies were outside firms and in markets, not inside firms in the form of departments, with few economists applying their monopoly models to governmental bureaucracies and governments more broadly. Now, all of these issues (and numerous other issues), many of which have coalesced into subdisciplines, have worked their way into conventional economics, and into most textbooks.

Moreover, during my career, there has been a revolution in thinking that reversed the reliance on governments in the 1950s and 1960s and has broken down the regulatory regimes of a variety of industries (airlines, trucking, securities, banking, etc.) and privatized many government services, beginning in the 1970s and extending through the publication of this book. And all of these changes in economic paradigms have emerged in large measure, but hardly exclusively, through a war of ideas with economists – following in the Chicago price-theory traditions set by Friedman, Stigler, and Becker and in the Virginia political economy tradition founded by Buchanan and Gordon Tullock – often dominating many intellectual and policy battles with their work firmly grounded in rational/maximizing behavior (with a reversal of regulatory thinking underway as this book was being finalized in 2009, because of the housing price bubble and burst in the early 2000s). The methodological foundations of mainstream economics may rightfully be deemed imperfect, shaky, and subject to dispute, but it is also hardly reasonable to damn any methodological approach for having flaws. The test of a methodological approach, it would seem to me, lies in the generated insights. And I have hardly exhausted the categories of economic insights that have been generated from – to paraphrase Becker – pursuing topics "relentlessly and unflinchingly" by using the methodological trinity of "maximizing behavior, market equilibrium, and stable preferences" (1976, p. 5).

Now, with the advent of behavioral economics, there has been a return of proposals to correct people's errant decision making through various "nudges" and mandates, which almost always involve greater government intrusions in people's lives. This intellectual trend makes this study of rationality in economics all the more timely and important.

This volume has been an ambitious scholarly effort for me, given the range of the disciplinary boundaries crossed. I have done my best to represent various scholarly positions on rational behavior, but I have not sought to make the study exhaustive or definitive. If an exhaustive study had been intended, there is no way it could have been finished, and no way anyone would have wanted to read such a study. I have had to impose limits on coverage of the various major figures in the history of economic thought and various separate literatures on this ever-expanding subject. My regrets to readers who notice major gaps in this study.

In completing this work, I am indebted to a number of people. I have had the good fortune of having Daniel Hammond, Steven Medema, and Mark Skousen review the book in its entirety and offer detailed and incisive criticisms and comments for improvement. James Buchanan, David Hirshleifer, Robin Keller, Dwight Lee, Mort Pincus, and Paul Zak read and commented on portions of the manuscript of greatest interest to them, always adding improvements and pointing out oversights. Neurobiology is a terribly intense and complex discipline for me to fathom adequately in the time I had to work on this book. I am pleased that Paul Zak, a neuroeconomist, and Jessica Turner, a neuroscientist, joined me as coauthors on Chap. 8 on "The Neuroeconomics of Rational Behavior." They added details and cogency to the limited arguments I could make on the subject. My research assistant Sarah Hajizadeh made a heroic effort to review the penultimate draft in search of errors in spelling and grammar and arguments that crept into the book as I revised it. She also made sure that all quotations, citations, and bibliographical entries were correct, knotty, and frustrating problems that bedevil all authors. I have also had the considerable advantage of having Laura Long edit the manuscript more than once and offer substantial improvements in the flow of the narrative.

Irvine, California   Richard McKenzie
March 19, 2009

Contents

Chapter 1
Economists' "Irrational Passion for Dispassionate Rationality"

Economists have sometimes described themselves as having an "irrational passion for dispassionate rationality," a sentiment widely attributed to the late antitrust economist John Maurice Clark (with the original source, to my knowledge, not traceable).[1] Indeed, few would dispute that rationality is firmly lodged at the core of contemporary neoclassical microeconomic theory and in neo-Keynesian macroeconomics and financial economics through the premises of rational expectations and the efficient-market hypotheses. By *rationality*, economists generally accept three levels of meaning.

The first level is the simplest and least constrained: rational people act purposefully. People who do not act with a preconceived purpose – that is, who behave as they do because they have no other options or because their actions are determined by external, genetic, and historical influences (as was assumed by, say, the late Harvard behavioral psychologist B.F. Skinner and his followers) – can be said to be *nonrational* (which describes actions that are mere chemical and mechanical responses with no guiding evaluations of conditions or consequences), if not *irrational* (which describes actions that are contrary to welfare-enhancing cost–benefit calculations of people making considered judgments[2]). Otherwise, people who make decisions consciously with some sense of purpose or intent are *rational*

---

[1] As will be noted later, the pat phrase, "irrational passion," is often used in ways that Clark did not really intend.

[2] Psychologist Stuart Sutherland develops what most mainstream economists would deem to be an appropriate characterization of irrationality: "......[W]e treat as irrational any thought process that leads to a conclusion or a decision that is not the best that could have been reached in light of the evidence, given the time constraints that apply" (Sutherland 2007, p.7). Still, even excluding "mistakes" from his irrationality category, Sutherland finds so much evidence of the extent of people's irrational behaviors that he worries that the arguments he makes are themselves "irrational" (2007, p.4).

R.B. McKenzie, *Predictably Rational?*,
DOI 10.1007/978-3-642-01586-1_1, © Springer-Verlag Berlin Heidelberg 2010

(which describes actions made with deliberate, conscious, and careful consideration of the relative value, or the costs and benefits, of alternative courses of action).[3]

This second level of meaning is commonly shared by all people who seek thoughtful discussions. Rationality connotes a predisposition to reasoning, which can include an inclination to follow rules of logic, implicitly or explicitly agreed upon, in devising arguments that are subject to dispute, improvement, and possible refutation or resolution. Rational arguments can be questioned, unsettled, and possibly refuted by revealed flaws in the basic premises from which all logical arguments follow or flaws in the sequence of logical steps in argument. If the arguments speak to real-world behaviors and events, then references to external, empirical observations, and evidence may call the arguments into question, if not cause them to be set aside altogether.

From this perspective, a person can be said to be *rational* simply by, at a minimum, demonstrating a "susceptibility to reason" (to defer to Webster's definition). Persons unwilling to entertain objections at any level of discourse, no matter how incisive the argument or convincing the evidence, would not be deemed *rational*, and even could be deemed *irrational*. Religious fanatics – or even unbending disciplinary ideologues – who are unwilling or unable to submit their religious beliefs to argument and objective tests would not be viewed as *rational*.

No doubt, economists generally have a reputation for an "irrational passion for dispassionate rationality" partially because so much of their analysis – whether involving the rational foundations of marriage and divorce (Becker, 1993) or even of "irrationality" (as in "irrational exuberance," which supposedly fueled the stock bubble of the 1990s and housing boom of the 2000s, documented by Robert Shiller [2005, 2008]) – is often founded on narrow postulates without any explicit recognition of other motivations. In particular, Milton Friedman (1953), a leader of the modern Chicago school of price theory, has argued forcefully that whether people are rational in the same way and to the same degree that so many mainstream economists (mainly those who come to their analytics from the neoclassical price-theory tradition) assume is not really a relevant issue, a rather hardnosed methodological position that the discipline's critics maintain is itself void of a rational foundation (Hollis and Nell, 1975). It should be stressed, however, that premises for deductive theories cannot have a fully rational foundation. At some point, deductive theories must have a beginning that needs to be more or less asserted. Otherwise, an infinite regress lurks in the flow of the backward logic. (However, there is a distinction between the assumed rationality of subjects in theory and people's real-world rationality. The former can be a matter of choice and a matter of theoretical, or thinking, convenience, and effectiveness. The latter could be the product of and bounded by evolved physiological and neurological human constraints and subject to variation across people, a topic discussed in Chap. 7).

---

[3] However, as will be argued in Chap.8 on *The Neuroeconomics of Rational Behavior*, not all of rational decision-making processes need to be fully conscious and deliberate; efficient rational decision making can involve the consideration of sensory data inflows to the brain that engage neural networks that operate below awareness. The brain simply does not have the neural capacity to process all sensory data at the conscious level.

Few scholars would dispute these first two levels of meaning of rationality simply because they are necessarily the foundation of all academic endeavors. What would be the point of writing a book about rationality in economics without the presumption that readers and I share an appreciation for the rules of logic, the foundations for acquiring knowledge, and the give-and-take argumentation of all scholarship? This book is clearly a call for scholars from several disciplines to reason together about the productive role of rationality throughout the history of economic thought, as well as the limits of rationality in economic or any other disciplinary inquiry.

The third level of meaning to rationality subsumes the first two levels and sets mainstream economists and their methods of thinking, and doing "science," apart from those of scholars in other disciplines. Here, *rationality* is not simply a reasoning process, but is also a set of precisely cast presumptions, or premises, about human motivation, decision making, and behavior from which all logical steps in argument and the resulting deductions flow.

Many economists use *rationality* to connote purpose-driven behavior, the objective of which is welfare improvement, which often does – but need not – connote the exact maximization of net welfare gains (gains minus pains) of decisions and actions. Adam Smith seems to adopt this view of the economic behavior in his masterpiece *The Wealth of Nations* (1776), although he did from time-to-time use language that suggested maximizing behavior, as in merchants seeking the "greatest profit."[4]

---

[4]On extolling the benefits to consumers of merchants seeking the greatest profits, Smith wrote,

If by not raising the price high enough he discourages the consumption so little that the supply of the season is likely to fall short of the consumption of the season, he not only loses a part of the profit which he might otherwise have made, but he exposes the people to suffer before the end of the season, instead of the hardships of a dearth, the dreadful horrors of a famine. It is the interest of the people that their daily, weekly, and monthly consumption should be proportioned as exactly as possible to the supply of the season. The interest of the inland corn dealer is the same. By supplying them, as nearly as he can judge, in this proportion, he is likely to sell all his corn for the highest price, and with the greatest profit; and his knowledge of the state of the crop, and of his daily, weekly, and monthly sales, enable him to judge, with more or less accuracy, how far they really are supplied in this manner. Without intending the interest of the people, he is necessarily led, by a regard to his own interest, to treat them, even in years of scarcity, pretty much in the same manner as the prudent master of a vessel is sometimes obliged to treat his crew. When he foresees that provisions are likely to run short, he puts them upon short allowance. Though from excess of caution he should sometimes do this without any real necessity, yet all the inconveniences which his crew can thereby suffer are inconsiderable in comparison of the danger, misery, and ruin to which they might sometimes be exposed by a less provident conduct. Though from excess of avarice, in the same manner, the inland corn merchant should sometimes raise the price of his corn somewhat higher than the scarcity of the season requires, yet all the inconveniences which the people can suffer from this conduct, which effectually secures them from a famine in the end of the season, are inconsiderable in comparison of what they might have been exposed to by a more liberal way of dealing in the beginning of it. The corn merchant himself is likely to suffer the most by this excess of avarice; not only from the indignation which it generally excites against him, but, though he should escape the effects of this indignation, from the quantity of corn which it necessarily leaves upon his hands in the end of the season, and which, if the next season happens to prove favourable, he must always sell for a much lower price than he might otherwise have had (Smith 1776; IV.5.42).

In contrast, most mainstream, neoclassical economists today, despite considering Smith as one of their professional forbearers, treat *rationality* as a specific, perhaps narrowly constrained form of purpose-driven *maximizing behavior*. Indeed, authors of leading textbooks in economics through history – for example, Adam Smith's *Wealth of Nations* (1776), Alfred Marshall's *Principles of Economics* (1890), and Friedman's *Price Theory* (1962) – often sidestep altogether the use of the terms "rationality" or "rational behavior." In the 1952 edition of his *The Theory of Price* (1952), George Stigler also does not mention explicitly "rational behavior," but made the concept central to his utility theory in the 1966 edition, a shift in approach that reflected the growing importance and formalization of rational behavior to economic theory in the 1950s and 1960s.

The closest Smith comes to explicitly premising his arguments on rationality or rational behavior is when on five occasions he uses "rational creatures," "sensible creatures," "rational beings," and "sensible beings" in his *Theory of Moral Sentiments* (1790, II.II.13; III.I.11; III.I.106; VI.II.49; and VII.II.25) and when he refers to "rational conversation" and "rational religion" in his *Wealth of Nations* (1776, V.1.178 and V.1.197).[5] In all seven citings, Smith seems to give "rational" one or both of rationality's first two levels of meaning considered above. Clearly, he never explicitly limits "rational" to the narrow definition the modern economists now give to rationality or rational behavior (to be developed shortly), although he was free with derogatory descriptors for behavior. For example, he described landlords as being slothful and political leaders as being driven by vanity and self-importance, positions discussed in detail in Chap. 3. (See Smith, 1776; III.4.16, and 1776; IV.7.161). Smith's references to "rational creatures" rather than explicitly limiting the expression to "rational humans" or "rational people" may lead us to infer that he was willing to include nonhuman species as *possibly* having *some* rational capacity to make purpose-driven decisions with some intent to improve their position in life, as they defined improvement through their own subjective assessments, as highly constrained as they might be.

Instead of employing "rationality" or "rational behavior" as the discipline's distinguishing core premise, Marshall and Friedman preferred to found their theorizing in their textbooks, explicitly or implicitly, on "maximizing behavior" directed by some form of self-interest, always broadly defined. For example, the only time Friedman, a staunch advocate of rational precepts in theorizing, explicitly mentions rationality in the 1962 edition of his *Price Theory* is when he briefly defends the then emerging theory of "rational expectations" in macroeconomics (Friedman, 1962, pp. 230–231).

---

[5]Throughout this volume, I use what might seem to many readers an odd form of in-text citation, for example, "(1776, V.1.178 and V.1.197)." I use this form because the reference is to an online source for the publication that is best cited in terms of the author, year of original publication, and the exact paragraph in the publication (pages in the printed version of the publication is not given). The online source for the digital library used is the Library of Economics and Liberty (http://www.econlib.org/library/).

Gary Becker, a student in Friedman's microeconomics classes at the University of Chicago and a long-time dedicated and relentless follower of Friedman's methodology, sums up the neoclassical perspective on economics: "The combined assumptions of maximizing behavior, market equilibrium, and stable preferences, used relentlessly and unflinchingly, form the heart of the economic approach" (1976, p. 5).

However, it needs to be noted that Steven Medema (2008) has perceptibly argued that Friedman and Becker represent divergent Chicago schools of economic methodologies. Friedman remains Marshallian in his approach, defining economics as "the science of how a particular society solves its economic problems," delimited by the notion of scarcity (1962, p. 6) and with his analyses remaining confined to maximizing behavior within markets, or what Alfred Marshall considered "the ordinary business of life" (1890, I.II.1). Friedman maintained that his "conception of an economic problem is a very general one and goes beyond matters ordinarily thought of as belonging to economics," but then cites the allocation of leisure time as an example of the kind of expansive topic he had in mind, which Medema suggests is "hardly a topic that someone in the 1970s (to say nothing of today) would consider other than straightforwardly 'economic'" (2008, p. 5).

In the 1952 edition of his *The Theory of Price*, Stigler confined economics to the "study of the operation of economic organizations, and economic organizations are the social (and rarely, individual) arrangements to deal with the production and distribution of economic goods and services" (1952, p. 1). However, over following editions, Stigler gradually embraced the application of economic methods to noneconomic goods and services, with growing references in later editions to Becker's work on discrimination, education, politics, and household production (1966 and 1987).

More than anyone else, Becker broke ranks with Friedman, stressing that economics was not so much confined by topics as by its analytical approach to unbounded nonmarket, as well as market, topics, defining economics to the study of "the allocation of scarce means to satisfy competing ends," which makes choices the foundation of economics, and choices could involve the "choice of a car, a marriage mate, and a religion; the allocation of resources within a family; and political decisions about how much to spend on education or on fighting a Vietnam war" (1971a, p. 1) and which makes economics "essential for understanding much of the behavior traditionally studied by sociologists, anthropologists, and other social scientists" (1971a, p. 2).

The Axioms of Rationality

Rational behavior is normally understood among economists to mean that people know what they want and understand that they must make choices, given the pressing constraint of scarcity in the physical world. Rational people identify and order their wants from most preferred to least preferred, with more being preferred

to less of things that have positive value and less being preferred to more of things
that have negative value. Finally, rational people consistently choose among their
orderings or wants with the goal of maximizing their welfare, or subjective utility.
Becker suggests that the essence of rational behavior can be reduced to just two
axioms

> Each consumer has an ordered set of preferences, and he chooses the most preferred
> position available to him. Ordering includes transitivity and implies that he could rank
> any three baskets of goods, $\acute{a}$, β, γ, such that if he prefers $\acute{a}$ to β and β to γ, then (by
> transitivity) he necessarily prefers $\acute{a}$ to γ. When he neither prefers $\acute{a}$ to β nor β to γ, he is said
> to be indifferent between them (that is, he would be willing to let the toss of a coin
> determine his choice), and indifference is also transitive" (1971a, p. 26).

Almost all contemporary textbook authors define rational behavior in a similar
way, laying out verbally and mathematically, with more or less precision, the
underlying axioms. For example, in their widely used intermediate microeconomic
theory textbook, Robert Pindyck and Daniel Rubinfeld specify the axioms this way:

- Completeness of preferences with all "goods" and the subjective values placed
  on each unit are known.
- Transitive preferences, which imply that consumers do not intentionally make
  mistakes in their choices across all options.
- More is preferred to less of "goods," which have positive value and prefer less to
  more of "bads," which have negative values (Pindyck and Rubinfeld, 2004).

As noted in *Price Theory*, Friedman couches his theoretical apparatus on the
presumption that either people make choices to maximize their gain or they can be
assumed to act *as if* they do: "Accordingly, we shall suppose that the individual in
making these decisions acts *as if* he were pursuing and attempting to maximize a
single end," using subjective utility as the means of comparing alternatives available in choices (1962, p. 35; emphasis in the original). Friedman goes on to stress
that "the emphasis on 'alternative' ends, which introduces [relative] *value judgments,* distinguishes it [economics] from the technological and physical sciences,
which are concerned with the relation between scarce resources and single ends.
The acceptance of the ends as *given* distinguishes it from psychology, which deals
with the formation of preferences, and from ethics, which deals with the evaluation
of preferences" (1962, p. 2; emphasis in the original).

Rationality, as a methodological construction, serves at least five functions in
economics:

- First, rationality permits the conceptualization of precise and unique *equilibriums* which are a cornerstone of testable predictions primarily regarding the
  directional changes (but not their magnitudes) in market outcomes with the
  possible intent of recommending policy controls (or decontrols) of institutional
  (most often, market) settings. In this regard, rationality allows economists to do
  science, with the predictions made about very narrowly defined behavioral
  outcomes involving production and consumption decisions about specified
  goods, not just the broad outlines of *patterns of outcomes* within which the

content of the patterns is left undefined or ill-defined. A key issue here in assessing the value of rationality lies with the extent to which predictions regarding directional changes are confirmed or rejected with empirical evidence, often requiring sophisticated statistical techniques to be deemed compelling. This use of rationality leads to strictly *positive* (or "what is") economics, which offers economists opportunities to comment on the alignment of consequences of specific existing or proposed policies with their backers' professed intentions.

- Second, the concept of rationality permits economists to discuss choices as a process by which economic opportunities are exploited in movements toward equilibrium. A key issue from this perspective is the extent to which group dynamics, market imperfections, and institutional and policy constraints prevent or encourage the exploitation of economic opportunities and lead to welfare enhancements or detriments. In this way, rationality serves to explain how improvements are realized (as in discussions of trade flows that follow the law of comparative advantage), but can also lead to testable predictions (for example, the assignment of property rights can boost incomes through improvements in the creation, care, and maintenance of resources).

- Third, rationality is a means by which rules for maximization of utility or profit can be deduced. Rationality functions as instruction on how people who are, perhaps, innately inclined to be less than fully or perfectly rational can become *more* rational; they can make decisions *more* efficiently (but not with perfectly efficiency), or can *better* (not perfectly) *advance* their utility and profit interests. Thus, rationality has, in this regard, a strictly *normative* intent; it advises people (students, consumers, and business managers and owners) on what they *should do* or how they *should act* in competitive market settings where their decisions can affect their costs and revenue through time, their market survival, and their assets' long-term value. This function of rationality helps explain why economists spend so much time laying out the axioms of rationality, and their implications, to their students and why their lectures and writings take on a tone of advocacy for the adoption of the economic way of thinking. (If people, including economics students, were as rational as economists assume, there would be no need for economics instruction, an issue discussed with greater care in Chap. 11).

- Fourth, rationality confined to maximization of self-interest narrowly defined (without regard for the welfare of others) is a means by which institutions and policies can be devised to promote the general societal welfare, with the intent of protecting people from the others' narrow self-interest-directed behavior. (This is a perspective on rationality developed at greater length in Chap. 5, drawing on the work of Geoffrey Brennan and James Buchanan [1985]). For example, markets grounded on enforced property rights can be seen as institutional settings for directing the energies of self-interested individuals toward the promotion of societal welfare. Constraints on governments (the majority decision-making rule, for example) can be used to protect people generally from the self-interest-directed efforts of political operatives' misuse of government power. Likewise, terms of private contracts can be used to protect people from others' exclusively self-interest-directed, opportunistic behavior.

- Fifth, rationality can be used for deducing what Friedrich Hayek (1967, pp. 17–18) characterized as "patterns of outcomes" or "ranges of possibilities" within which the detailed content (for example, the exact goods consumed) would not and, for that matter, could not be known: "Although such theories do not tell us precisely what to expect, it will still make the world around us a more familiar world in which we can move with greater confidence, that we will not be disappointed because we can at least exclude certain eventualities. It makes it a more orderly world in which events make sense because we can say in general terms how they hang together or are able to form a coherent picture of them" (Hayek, 1967, p. 18). The details of the content of these patterns are unknown because economic values have subjective foundations and because outcomes must emerge from a multitude of people interacting in ways that can be known only to the people doing the interacting who themselves do not always know what they want until they see how others are acting and responding to the interactions. Besides, economic actors do not seek to maximize the *goods* bought and sold in market places, which can have objective, measurable dimensions, but rather, the more elusive and subjective *ends*, subjectively evaluated goals that require goods as inputs.

The first three functions of rationality in economic theory, mainly those that afford opportunities for some level of testable predictions, will be the focus of the rest of this chapter. The last two functions of rationality will emerge from our discussions of rationality in the history of economic thought in later chapters, especially Chap. 5.

The Rationale for Given Wants

Wants and preferences are *given* and *fixed* under most neoclassical constructions of rational behavior. Wants and preferences are *given* in the sense that their determination is exogenous to the static analysis; they are *fixed* not in the sense that the quantity is unchanged (variation in output and consumption is a common feature of most mainstream, neoclassical models), but rather in the sense that the basic nature of the goods themselves is not allowed to vary within the confines of the models. Given the defined and fixed wants, deductions/predictions are drawn following the rules of logic, and their relevance remains limited by how long the wants remain tolerably stable.

Friedman seems comfortable with the assumption of given and fixed wants on several grounds, two of which can be mentioned briefly here (a longer treatment of Friedman's defense of conventional neoclassical methodology will be reserved for Chap. 9). First, Friedman believes in the benefits of disciplinary specialization, with economists being narrowly concerned with and achieving disciplinary research economies from limiting their analytical efforts to tracing out "the consequences of any given sets of wants," along with the consequences of changes in external, environmental constraints on choices, principally changes in the prices and costs of the goods, as well as changes in people's incomes and wealth (1962, p. 13). Never mind if people are not as fully or perfectly rational as economists assume. Friedman posits, as a matter of scientific necessity, that "the legitimacy of and justification for this abstraction (that people maximize or act fully rationally) must rest ultimately, as with any other abstraction, on the light shed and the power to predict what is yielded by the abstraction" (1962, p. 13).

While hardly matching Stigler's and Becker's enthusiasm for human rationality, Friedman's view of economic science exhibits an *element* of an "irrational passion for dispassionate rationality," at least partially because he does not consider analytically internal, evolutionary or neurobiological constraints on people's ability to act rationally, other than to dismiss, or not be sidetracked by, such constraints. But then Friedman's view of the best scientific method must itself be grounded in some form of actual rational, maximizing behavior on the part of real-world people. Otherwise, his focus on "as if" behavior would appear to be arbitrary and to disconnect any testable hypotheses from any real human motivation. If we can assume that people have some rational capacity, Friedman argues that economists might as well use a simple, precise, and well-understood behavioral premise, or one that can be construed as "sufficiently good approximations" of human behavior, when it works "for the purpose at hand" rather than a more imprecise and complex one that might not improve predictions even when the complexity adds considerable analytical costs (1962, p. 15). Besides, science is a process of first deducing a hypothesis and testing it. If the hypothesis is not rejected by evidence (hypotheses can never be proved), then it is accepted until some better hypothesis is put forward. As Friedman explains in his Nobel lecture (in his discussion of the initial acceptance of the Phillips curve hypothesis and its eventual rejection), "[T]he body of positive knowledge grows by the failure of a tentative hypothesis to predict phenomena the hypothesis professes to explain; by patching up of that hypothesis until someone suggests a new hypothesis that more elegantly or simply embodies the troublesome phenomena, and so on ad infinitum" (Friedman, 1976, p. 267).

Second, perhaps, in contrast with some microeconomic theorists, Friedman is not so much concerned with understanding individual behavior as with understanding the collective outcomes of those behaviors as individuals interact with others and respond to market forces (again, a point that Medema [2008] stresses separates Friedman from other Chicago price theorists, most notably Stigler and Becker). Friedman suggests that some people's nonrational and irrational decisions and behaviors in markets can be a form of self-canceling "noise" that, on balance, does not materially alter the directional changes in market outcomes in response to changed constraints:

> Economics, by our definition, is not concerned with all economic problems. It is a *social* science, and is therefore concerned primarily with economic problems whose solutions

involve cooperation and interaction of different individuals. It is concerned with problems involving a single individual only insofar as the individual's behavior has implications for or effects upon other individuals" (1962, p. 2; emphasis in the original).

Friedman would probably accept the prospects that markets can have predictable (even rational) outcomes without all (or maybe any) participants being fully rational, at least not initially. Market forces can press people to be more rational than they naturally would be. Alternately, markets will have outcomes that are closely or "sufficiently" similar (but hardly identical) to outcomes that would be expected *if* all participants were fully rational at all times. At the very least, Friedman seems to adopt the position that unfettered competitive markets could do a good job of pressing people *toward* (but not necessarily exactly to) equilibrium positions that are approximately similar to those expected from fully rational participants. Perhaps, outside of market settings, people might not be as rational as Friedman assumes, but market pressures can lead people, as if by an "invisible hand," to a level of rationality that is a "sufficiently good approximation," which means the assumption of *full* rationality does not significantly undercut the credibility of theory or the accuracy of predictions, especially, when the central concern is mainly predicting the directional changes of key variables (that is, the signs of key coefficients, and their statistical significance, in regression equations is of greater importance than the magnitude of the coefficient itself). Friedman wrote in his seminal methodological paper:

> Confidence in the maximization-of-returns hypothesis is justified by evidence of a very different character. This evidence is in part similar to that adduced on behalf of the billiard-player hypothesis [that he shoots *as if* he can perform complicated calculations] – unless the behavior of businessmen in some way or other approximated behavior consistent with the maximization of returns, it seems unlikely that they would remain in business for long (Friedman, 1953, p. 20).

Those business people who do not act rationally will lose access to resources; those who do will "prosper": "The process of 'natural selection' thus helps to validate the hypothesis – or, rather, given natural selection, acceptance of the hypothesis can be based largely on the judgment that it summarizes appropriately the conditions for survival" (Friedman, 1953, p. 20).

Even though equilibrium might never be precisely achieved, it, nevertheless, can be a conceptualized reference point from which directional changes in market variables (price and quantity, for example) can be predicted, given the changes in the constraints facing the participants. And, again, it is the predicted *directional changes* in equilibriums, not the exact equilibriums per se (which may never be attained), that are the focus of neoclassical economics as science. In the sense that people can be pressed by market pressures to upgrade their rationality – either through weighing costs and benefits of decisions before they are made or through correcting their own and other's errant decisions in search of gains – people can be said to be *predictably rational* (or just more rational than otherwise).

Then, again, the static nature of mainstream, neoclassical analysis presents economists with a dilemma because of the underlying presumption of some process that drives the market from some initial equilibrium to some new equilibrium, with corrections in misguided, mistaken, irrational behaviors occurring along the way. If the static analysis commenced based on an accurate description of people's initial rationality, the subsequent equilibrium would not capture the corrections in decision making and behaviors induced by the underlying market process that causes the shift in equilibrium. Equilibrium analysis would thus be misleading, and could lack considerable predictive accuracy. Complicating the model by starting with descriptive rationality and by allowing for the corrective process can heap complexity on the model, making it unwieldy, perhaps of little value, since economists must work within their own limited mental (and rational) faculties. The alternative is to assume a level of rationality that economists know subjects do not and cannot have, at least not initially and absent a process incorporating some level of correction. By taking the second alternative (assuming participants have a level of rationally that is not descriptive), which economists effectively do and which Friedman recommends (and many other mainstream economists recommend), the realism of the corrective premise may suffer, but modeling (and thinking) is eased and no harm is done to the predictive power of the theory (so Friedman argues), especially, when the magnitudes of the predicted changes take a back seat to the statistical significance of the direction of the changes.

Stigler and Becker make Friedman's point with even stronger claims about the fixity of preferences in positive economic theory, which implies fixity of goods, perhaps, with the goal of seeing how much can be learned about observed behavior from changes in external constraints – prices, incomes, and wealth – without relying on internal changes in tastes. Like Friedman, Stigler and Becker's main focus is on conceptualized equilibriums and on how equilibrium can *change*, predictably, with *changes* in choice constraints. In the process, for analytical purposes, they seem to strip "goods" of any subjective origins, and/or give "goods" a totally objective reality on par with observable real-world physical objects:

> [T]astes neither change capriciously nor differ importantly between people. On this interpretation one does not argue over tastes for the same reason that one does not argue over the Rocky Mountains – both are there, will be there next year, too, and are the same to all men........On the traditional view [of tastes], an explanation of economic phenomena that reaches a difference in tastes between people or times is the terminus of the argument: the problem is abandoned *at this point* to whoever studies and explains tastes (Psychologists? Anthropologists? Phrenologists? Sociologists?). On our preferred interpretation, one never reaches this impasse: the economist continues to search for differences in prices or incomes to explain any differences or changes in behavior (1977, p. 76).

Clearly, for Stigler and Becker, rational behavior has a nonrational foundation, perhaps, grounded in intuition or in what they see as the self-evident objective reality of the equivalence of subjective preferences and goods (and bads). Becker, especially, is renowned for recognizing that many purchased goods are inputs into household production functions (1993). But then, Stigler, Becker, and Friedman can not help but give goods an objective reality. There is really no point in trying to do *science* (with economic science having any claim of being even remotely similar to physical science), as a predictive endeavor, if subjective preferences do not have objective counterparts in the external physical world in the form of identified "goods," "prices," and "incomes" that can be observed and measured with tolerable accuracy. Again, Friedman, Stigler, and Becker appear not to acknowledge a need for considering how internal, evolutionary, and neurobiological, constraints affect just exactly *how* rational people can be, although I gather they would not object to extending economic models to allow for maximization under such constraints, given how many different and new directions they have taken economic analysis. Becker introduced "home-produced goods" to his "household production function," and Stigler assumed "information" on prices is a "good." They have built their esteemed careers on the assumption, with flexibility, of rational behavior variously constrained by specified utility functions in which the "goods" are identified for the research topic at hand.

The Equality of Rational and Maximizing Behavior

Maximizing behavior must, to modern economists who use the phrase, be largely comparable to (although not necessarily exactly the same as) *rational behavior* (which implies some optimum organization of behavior). If one is not able to choose consistently among known and ordered wants, then it is hard to see how "maximum" and "optimum" have meaning. Both rational behavior and maximizing behavior mean that people cannot have everything they want, which means that more is preferred to less of things that have positive value and less is preferred to more of things that have negative values. Thus, rational/maximizing behavior implies that people make conscious choices emerging from deliberations over the values and relative benefits of alternatives, deliberations that typically have been more or less completed when economists commence tracing out "the consequences of any given set of wants." This position suggests, again, that what is often of central concern to economists in the Friedman, Stigler, and Becker methodological traditions are the testable predictions involved in the directional changes in equilibrium. From this perspective, rationality is useful as a *tool* of analysis – for thinking through how and why people get to equilibrium and then, when constraints change, how they reestablish equilibrium in a predictable and testable manner.

In moving to equilibrium, cost–benefit analysis is essential and unavoidable. To economists, the *cost* of doing, buying or consuming one thing, A, is the value of the alternative, B, which would have been taken had A not been available. Rational behavior, then, implies that the value of the alternative taken is always greater than the cost, until equilibrium is reached. At that point, the marginal cost of the last unit produced equals (or comes as close as possible to equaling) its marginal value.[6] Given that *cost* is defined as the value of the highest valued option not taken, then to say that the value of A is greater than its cost can be restated to mean that the value of A is greater than the value of B.[7] If the value of A is truly known to be more than the value of B, with both subjective assessments at the volition of the chooser, and A and B are the only two goods available, it is hard to imagine circumstances under which B would be chosen.

Experimental economics does strongly suggest that animals, even rats and pigeons, will tend to consume preferred goods over less preferred goods.[8] Field evidence has shown that ants and termites appear capable of minimizing and maximizing behavior, within their limited capabilities. Although "scout" ants might search for food in something of a random pattern as they seek to discover food sources, the following ants going to and from any discovered food source tend to make the path as straight as practical, cutting corners and taking short-cuts when they can detect at a distance the chemical trails on the routes to the food sources (Tullock, 1994).

Alternatives are never known with clarity and certainty, but such decision-making difficulties can easily be dealt with in theory. Before choices are made, a perfectly rational, maximizing person will discount the values of alternatives (measured, say, in dollars) to account for the timing of the perceived benefits received. Delayed gains and pains will be appraised as having lower subjective values than current gains and pains.

The alternatives' values also must be discounted for their associated risks. More risky options are worth less than less risky options (equal in all ways except their riskiness) simply because risk implies that some options taken will not measure up to their time-discounted worth. Over a range of risk-laden options, the expected values should be, on average, less than their values discounted only for time.

Moreover, choosers also must discount, or weight, the expected value of the options for the variance in the realized values of options. Options with high variance in risk and timing of benefits should have a lower expected value than

---

[6]Stigler, who does not use "rationality" or "rational behavior" in his textbook, *The Theory of Price*, still defines the basic axioms of consumer theory in much the same way that Becker does, perhaps, because Becker studied under Stigler at the University of Chicago:

> Each individual, we believe, is able, when confronted with a choice between two combinations of goods, to express either a preference for one of the combinations or indifference as to which he acquires. Moreover, the choices will be well ordered and consistent (except when tastes change): if combination *A* is preferred to combination *B*, then *B* is not preferred to *A*; and if *A* is preferred to *B*, but *B* and *C* are indifferently chosen, than *A* is preferred to *C* (1952, pp.68–69).

[7]Interestingly, while cost can be felt at the time of a choice decision, cost is really something – subjective value – that can never be realized once the decision is made. Cost cannot be recouped; it no longer exists after a choice has been made. In this sense, all costs are sunk, a point stressed by Buchanan (1969).

[8]For a review of this literature, see McKenzie and Tullock's *The New World of Economics* (1976 or 1994).

options with low variance because the variance can be seen as a form of risk associated with setting and using appropriate time and risk discount rates. More specifically, if there are two options with the same expected time- and risk-discounted value, the option with the lower variance will be preferred (Lee, 1969).

Exactly how choosers come to know the appropriate discount rates and make the required calculations is widely left unspecified (other than in the case of interest rates on largely risk-free government securities), which means rational choice analysis has an inherent element of mystery. However, in maximization discussions, choosers are assumed to have access to the required discount rates, or have the requisite experience and make the required calculations with precision. Critical to maximizing behavior is the assumption that the requisite calculations will be made without error, or that the comparative assessments of alternatives will account for the prospect of calculation errors. Moreover, the discount rates for gains received and pains incurred are typically assumed to be the same for all years going forward (one source of criticism from behavioral psychologists and behavioral economists, as we will see in Chap. 6).

Clearly, not all behavior outside of rationality-based models can be grounded in the type of rational calculations assumed inside the models, because outside the models the "goods" are being determined or cannot be sufficiently known to make these types of cost–benefit comparisons. Hence, rationality-based models can be only a partial view of human behavior – and, perhaps, a minor portion of behavior, a point that key economic luminaries make, especially those from the strictly subjectivists schools of thought covered in Chaps. 4–6.

Why make such extreme assumptions about the precision of decision making? Thomas Sargent (1993), a founder of the rational expectations school of macroeconomics, insists that, for methodological reasons, in equilibrium "perceptions" must be treated as "optimally chosen." Any less-than-optimally chosen perceptions will leave "unexploited utility- or profit-generating possibilities," which suggests a form of disequilibrium. Such unexploited opportunities necessarily will have been exploited in equilibrium, or else equilibrium would not exist, with equilibrium being, again, the crucial starting point of much economic analysis.[9] If there are errors in the choice of discount rates or calculations, equilibrium will not have been attained. There will be those who exploit those errors, correcting the assessed values and the decision making of others and moving outcomes toward equilibrium where no further corrections are available.

---

[9]Sargent's exact words are:

> Another reason for defending rational expectations is that the consistency condition can be interpreted as describing the outcome of a process in which people have optimally *chosen* their perceptions. That is, if perceptions were not consistent, then there would exist unexploited utility- and profit-generating possibilities within the system. Insisting on the disappearance of all such exploited possibilities is a feature of all definitions of equilibrium in economics (1993, p. 7).

Again, it is conceptualized *equilibrium* – not so much the underlying rational tenets – that is the ultimate concern to many mainstream, neoclassical economists who seek to do *science* because it is *equilibrium* (a balancing of forces – where all exploitable gains are exploited, given extant constraints) that permits analysis of expected *directional* changes when constraints are altered. Put differently, it is an analysis of comparative equilibriums that is central and crucial to the work that many (but not all) economists see themselves doing as scientists.

Rational Deductions and Predictions

From the twin claims of scarcity in the external physical world and rationality in the internal subjective world of the mind, economists are able to draw a number of *positive* (as distinguished from normative) deductions, including this short, representative sample:

- The omnipresence of scarcity implies choices, which, in turn, implies that every option taken has a cost, summarized in two widely repeated quips: "There is no such thing as a free lunch," and "Tradeoffs are ever-present in all of life."
- "Perfection" is not a viable economic option in the real world, or, put differently, the best that can be done is......., well, the best that can be done.
- Consumers will maximize their utility only when they equate at the margin, or distribute their incomes in such ways that their marginal utility-to-price ratios of the goods they consume are equal. In other words, consumers will buy the combination of goods that is exactly at the tangency of their budget lines with their indifference curves.
- Firms will maximize profits by expanding production until the marginal revenue of the last unit produced equals its marginal cost.
- Firms will continue to produce in the short-run as long as their revenues exceed their variable costs, and they will shut down only when the price falls below average variable cost.
- Expectations relating to risks, timing, and variance of gains and losses will influence choices, and choices can be expected to be made based on the expected costs and expected benefits of the available options, which is to say that discounting of gains and losses is required for full optimization of consumption and production.
- Sunk costs will be ignored.
- Demand curves slope downward.
- Trades will be mutually beneficial, or, conversely, tariffs and quotas will prevent mutually beneficial trades.
- And buyers and sellers who are driven by their own self-interest will tend (possibly unbeknownst to them) to generate societal benefits.

Economists are familiar with the kind of testable predictions that can be made through equilibrium analysis, including the following:

- If trade restrictions are imposed on imported goods, the price of domestically produced substitutes will rise.
- If a minimum wage is imposed on competitive labor markets for low-skilled workers, the available jobs for the covered workers will shrink, leading to reductions in nonmoney payments to the workers.
- If a percentage of the *economic* profit of a monopoly is taxed away, the monopoly's output level and price will be unaffected.[10]

The list of predictions could be continued at some length, given that economists have spent a great deal of their professional energies deriving and testing such predications. Their formal modeling of decision making and behavior in graphical and mathematical form, complete with exacting first and second order conditions for optimization, can be found in any of numerous economic theory textbooks, my favorite being Gary Becker's *Economic Theory* (1971a). Becker and Kevin Murphy apply their equilibrium-grounded model, founded on perfect rationality, in their article *A Rational Theory of Addiction* (1988), which is notable for its three forms of argumentation – graphical, mathematical, and narrative. They draw a counter-intuitive and counter-conventional hypothesis from the model, validated with empirical tests, that the long-run demand for addictive goods is, assuming fully rational decision making, more elastic than would be surmised by considering only the effects of chemical dependency on the consumption of street drugs. Another favorite illustration of the neoclassical approach, grounded in full rationality, is Gordon Tullock's *Toward a Mathematics of Politics* (1967), in which the rationality of voter ignorance is developed.

Perfections in the Analysis of Scarcity

Ironically, conventional treatments of rational behavior in textbooks and lectures are conceptually replete with elements of perfection, even though the implicit presumption of all-pervasive scarcity precludes perfection in any line of economic activity in the external physical world. Elements of perfection in rational decision making show up in several key ways:

- There is the presumption that the "goods" subject to choice – for example, A and B noted above – and their raw subjective values, if not explicitly given, are known to actors within models with ease and clarity, and A and B can be used as clearly identified labels on the Y and X axes of indifference curve graphs. Implicitly, the goods subject to choice are assumed into existence with well-defined clarity, fall like manna from the heavens, or come to be known by choosers with zero information and transaction costs. If there is any lack of

---

[10]However, because taxation of monopoly profits must be applied, as a practical matter, to *book* profits, the monopoly's price can be expected to rise as the monopoly curbs production to restore profit maximization subject to the profits tax.

clarity in the identification of the goods subject to choice, then consumers know the appropriate probabilities (and their distributions) by which to appropriately discount utilities they attach to goods and consumers can make the required calculations with perfection.

- Similarly, elements of analytical perfection show up in how precisely and completely consumers can define their preferences. Indifference curves are finely drawn in the preference space that is "everywhere dense" with the combinations of goods that are, or could be, chosen and with all combinations of goods given relative, if not absolute, values conceptualized as having various "utilities." Again, the information and transaction costs associated with preference formation are often assumed to be zero, or the information costs are exogenous to the model's theoretical scope. Indeed, indifference curve mappings contain another irony, that of a budget constraint on the combinations of goods A and B that can be chosen, but no constraint on the choosers' subjective evaluations of all conceivable combinations. One has to wonder why anyone would, in anything other than an imagined perfect world, go to the trouble of valuing combinations of goods A and B without limit, when in fact the vast majority of the combinations on any complete mapping are necessarily unattainable. Embedded in such analysis is a presumption of what can, and has been, called *hyperrationality*, which in the real world would be construed as a form of *irrationality*, when there are costs to making evaluations of options, as Jon Elster has pointed out (1990).

- An element of perfection is also transparent in the presumption that people will continue to consume a good up *to the limit* or boundary set by carefully and accurately calculating marginal costs and benefits, as if there are no costs to ferreting out the actual marginal values and the exact point of their equality. Similarly, firms are presumed to compute the values for marginal revenues and costs and can be counted on to produce up *to the exact* point at which those relevant marginal values are equal, a presumption that, economists surely know, sidesteps the practical accounting constraints most (especially, multiproduct) firms face.

- An element of perfection is evident in the fact that when choosers really know the goods and their values, in all their myriad dimensions and with the precision implied by the absence of information costs, and when the design of the model dictates utility (or profit) maximization, meaningful choices are, paradoxically, excluded altogether from the so-called choice model itself, as James Buchanan (1969a) noted decades ago. In a fully rational behavior model, consumers and producers actually do nothing, and can do nothing – they do not and cannot choose in any meaningful sense – because the model's static nature presumes a total absence of a time dimension, or if any time is given to the choice process, it is infinitesimally short. In economists' models, consumers and producers effectively find themselves at their equilibriums. Ironically, if there is any actual choosing and maximizing behavior, it occurs before economists determine the initial equilibrium, and such behavior remains outside of any effort economists make to trace the changes in equilibriums, in response to changes in prices, incomes, and other constraints.

Granted, economists have extended the rational choice model by adding acknowledged real-world choice constraints. For example, in his seminal paper on information economics, Stigler (1962) introduced costs from the acquisition of information on prices across markets in time and space as an ever-present constraint on utility maximization.[11] Still, as in all such constrained optimization versions of rational choice models, there are necessary elements of perfection. In Stigler's extension of the basic choice model, consumers are assumed to know going into their information searches the structure of the costs (and the appropriate discount rates and the underlying probability distributions) associated with acquiring information on the prices and qualities of goods across markets, a presumption that allows buyers to optimize on their information searches – all without having to incur any costs (within the context of the model) to ferret out the structure of information costs.

Therefore, some element of perfection must remain in such constrained, static modeling (especially when explored with mathematics), because of the ever-present prospect of an infinite regress in seeking to expunge every trace of perfection. If Stigler did not assume a known structure to information costs, he would have had to extend his analysis backward to capture the gains and costs of searching for search-cost information, and then to capture the gains and costs of extending the information search another step removed, and so on – leading to an unending information-gathering process and a resulting infinite regress with market participants, in any conceptualized model at least, having no time left to make choices between options.

Economists-as-model-builders would then have no time to consider what is crucial to the analytical process – predicting directional changes in equilibriums, given changes in constraints. But, static models start with a zero-time constraint for making choices. Ironically, constrained optimization models, such as Stigler's, can add, not reduce, complexities into subjects' choices, which can further tax the calculating capabilities of market participants beyond what is required when all information on goods and their prices are known without information searches, a point Gerd Gigerenzer and Peter Todd have stressed (1999b, pp. 8–9).

Nevertheless, some level of constrained optimization is essential if choice models are to have any hope of generating useful insights and testable predictions on directional changes relating to the concrete content of patterns of market outcomes. This is a central "justification for this abstraction," meaning the assumption of rational/maximizing behavior (Friedman, 1962, p. 13). Without some constraint on maximizing behavior in the form, say, of clear definitions of the *goods* (with identified objective proxies) over which choices are to be made (A and B in our simple two-good choice setting) or on information costs, the analytics remain totally a priori, which means there can be no deduced empirically *testable* hypotheses. Without specification of the exact nature of the goods to be maximized, within some identified constraints that is, maximization amounts to whatever people do.

---

[11] See also Sargent (1993) and Anderson and Milson (1989).

Hence, the acceptance of *science* as the *reason d'être* for economic analysis itself imposes methodological requirements on the exact nature of the underlying behavioral premises. The economist-qua-scientist must *presume* to know something of what the consumers know, or are assumed to know, perhaps by revealed preferences (they buy good A instead of good B) or by sheer personal reflection of assumption (buying anything that can explode unexpectedly is not a valued "good" because explosions are painful). This means that in economists' behavioral models, the choosers cannot be totally free to imagine their choice options and then to impose without bound their subjective evaluations on their choice options. Put another way, choosers cannot – in scientific endeavors – be left completely "free to choose" (a phrase that Milton and Rose Friedman made famous in their book [1980], based on a PBS documentary series Milton Friedman hosted in the early 1980s [Friedman, 1980]). People can be totally free to choose in ordinary life, but they cannot be assumed to be that free when their behavior is to be predicted within the scope of *science*. Living, on the one hand, and doing science, on the other hand, are separate endeavors. In some economic models, the required constraint shows up in identified goods subject to choice and/or a presumption that rational choosers follow *homo economicus*; that is, they are exclusively concerned with their own narrow interests, such as profit maximization, without regard for others, apart from how the welfare of others affects the welfare of the rational choosers. (For this volume, *homo economicus* is a subset of rational behavior).

As we will see in the following chapter, the Austrian school of economics parts ways with neoclassical economics because of the neoclassicalists' methodological leap of faith that no harm is done to the credibility of the science when subjective evaluations emanating within individual consciousness (themselves individualized by their local circumstances) are readily and unthinkingly converted to objective "goods" used for hypotheses testing.

Concluding Comments

Rational behavior is an explicit premise on which economists found their science. Another implicit premise underlying economics as a science is that objective data are available and can be reasonably used to test theories grounded exclusively in subjective, individual-eccentric evaluations; however, that may not always be the case. Most people, including Friedman, acknowledge that the premise of full rationality may not at times be a "sufficiently good" approximation of people's motivations. The same can be said for the data. Physical science starts with the presumption that objective data do not have a subjective origin. But that is not the case with economics, which necessarily sets economics apart from the hard sciences like physics, astronomy, and molecular biology, a point that Frank Knight, Ludwig von Mises, and James Buchanan make again and again and that is explored in Chap. 5 (a criticism that Friedman explicitly rejected in his Nobel lecture [1976, pp. 267–269]). Ultimately, economics is often as much art as science, founded on what are seen as reasonable "fits" between people's constellation of motivations and the full rationality premise and between perception and evaluation of "goods" and the particular data series used to represent the goods in empirical tests.

Discussions of rationality are often framed as discussion of the appropriate choices of methodologies, as if choices over such matters are unconstrained. Yet, as argued later, the evolutionary forces long ago have constrained our behaviors, if not our methodological choices for understanding human behavior. The human brain very well may be structured so that we (individual actors in markets and economists who study people in markets) seek to find some semblance of order when apparent disorder or nonorder, if not chaos, appears pervasive in everyday life. The presumption of rational/maximizing behavior may be one evolved method we use to ferret out order amidst all the behavioral noise we observe for the purpose of making predictions. As we will see in Chap. 8, the human brain has evolved to continuously update its neural networks for the purposes of improving its predictive power, given the continuous inflow of sensory data.

Rational behavior, to one degree or another, often appears natural. After all, we can detect ourselves often making the kinds of cost–benefit/maximizing decisions that the actors in economic models are assumed to be making. And there is a reason we behave in such a manner: We do live in a world of external scarcity. Moreover, as argued in more detail later in this book, our brains largely evolved in an environment in which scarcity was a far more pressing consideration than it is today. Then, cutting through the behavioral noise and doing cost–benefit calculations with some degree of success could have been a survival strategy that has been encoded in our DNA through procreation, a line of argument we will return to in Chap. 7.

Chapter 2
The Methodological Constraints on the Rationality Premise

The last chapter described how modern neoclassical economic theorists (mainly those who have an allegiance to the Chicago price-theory traditions) choose to define rationality in economics. That is, in that chapter, I considered the basic rationality premise without any consideration for how that premise might square with the theorists' more broadly conceived philosophy of knowledge and without consideration of how that premise is influenced by the methodologies and technologies theorists use in their inquiries. This chapter explains more explicitly and formally how the methodologies that theorists employ in their inquiries more or less constrain the assumed nature of the rationality premise and how the assumption of rationality connects with their theory of knowledge.

The Constraints of Model Building and Hypothesis Testing on the Conception of Rationality

Positive economic science is almost always presented as a two-step process, with each step taken independently of the other – the underlying premises used in building and analyzing models, on the one hand, and in testing methods, on the other hand. An economist-qua-scientist develops a model as she sees fit without regard to the available techniques for drawing out hypotheses and running empirical tests. Accordingly, rational-behavior models can be justified on the grounds of simplicity and facility. Why use a complex and more costly behavioral assumption when a simpler, less costly one will do just as well? Or the behavioral assumptions are justified on the grounds that all theories are readily acknowledged abstractions, intended reduced-form parodies of how people actually do behave, which necessarily means that all theories are, to some degree, unreal. The importance of the realism of models is not a debate likely to be settled, a point Milton Friedman made with force (Friedman 1953, pp. 14–15), as noted in Chap. 1. We might as well assume people act "as if" they are fully rational, and test the usefulness of the

R.B. McKenzie, *Predictably Rational?*,
DOI 10.1007/978-3-642-01586-1_2, © Springer-Verlag Berlin Heidelberg 2010

underlying model not by the accuracy of the as-if premise, but rather by what the premise and theory are supposed to do: generate useful insights and testable (empirically falsifiable) predictions.

However, such a perspective on scientific conduct fails to recognize how the methodology and technology of model building and empirical testing necessarily influence the choice of abstractions at the level of behavioral premises, which, in our case, is the extent to which people are assumed to be rational (fully rational or some degree less than fully rational). Use of mathematics constrains theorists' choice of rational premises because mathematically grounded models necessarily limit the complexity of the choices available to choosers and the variety of motivations that can be activating them.[1]

An example of the reduction in complexity of theory required by mathematics is the assumptions of independent utility functions and given preferences. Granted, mathematical economic models using interdependent utility functions have been developed to allow for actors who are motivated by concern for others as well as themselves. However, one can imagine the considerable complexity of a model of human behavior energized not only by self-interest, but also by various degrees of love for others, as well as altruism, patriotism, and religious faith (to name just a few possible distinguishable motivations), with the complexity further increasing with the inclusion of potential changes in the separate motivations and in the intensity of motivations in the context of different groups and in different institutional and physical environments. Such a model would surely be far too unwieldy to handle over time for even the most accomplished mathematicians. The use of mathematics – whether to clarify functional relationships, to find flaws in intuitive logic, or to check the validity of deductions from less precise methods of reasoning – must impose constraints on the behavioral model. To keep the equations sufficiently simple to be manipulated and understood, mathematically grounded analyses must be far simpler than the reality of behavior might suggest they should be. For example, one cost-effective model includes economic actors who are assumed to be fully and exclusively rational, making their choices with complete clairvoyance and precision.[2]

The growing application of mathematics to economic models during the past century surely has provided gains for economists in any number of ways that need not be identified here. Just as surely, mathematics restricts the assumptions about the rationality of people within economic models, as we will see in the following chapters which review the evolution of the rational/self-interested premise from the works of selected classical to modern neoclassical economists – that is, from Adam Smith all the way to Alfred Marshall and then on to Milton Friedman, George Stigler, and Gary Becker, plus those forebearers and contemporaries, who used

---

[1] Graphical analytics ever more tightly constrain the choice of options and the motivations for choice than does mathematics because of the limited dimensions available for graphing.

[2] The more limited the math skills of theorists, I suggest, the greater the tendency of theorists to sterilize and purify the motivations of economic actors.

some variant of Chicago price theory – Aaron Director, Ronald Coase, Richard Posner, and William Landes who sought to study law with economic methods (Medema 2008). (Indeed, mathematics may have given rise to advancements in economic theory *because* its use has forced a sterilization of the underlying behavioral assumptions that are far from being descriptively accurate of people's decision making).

Similarly, econometric techniques are, by their nature, limited in what they can handle in conducting empirical tests. Complicated models of behavior involving decision makers who are less than fully rational or have several and varying motivations across people and time can lead to predictions that are inconsequential to economists of the positive neoclassical tradition because they cannot be tested, or cannot be tested without great, efficiency-impairing costs. As discussed in Chap. 1, Thomas Sargent made this point indirectly when he conceded that actors in rational expectation models know – and must be assumed to know – far more about their circumstances than economists or economic decision makers can know. However, he maintained that macroeconomists in their model building have generally preferred to use *rational expectations,* which assume fully rational actors, rather than actors whose rationality is bounded because rational expectations offer simplification in model building. *Bounded rationality,* as conceived by Herbert Simon (1957, 1982), encompasses "satisfying," not "maximizing," behavior, being a form of imperfect rationality – but, imperfect only in the sense that people do not have the mental wherewithal to make the kind of flawless decisions implied in perfect rationality (an observation that is at the heart of Chaps. 7 and 8).

Bounded rationality has failed to be widely adopted for model building, Sargent argues, because of "its unfulfilled promise as a device for specifying and understanding out-of-equilibrium dynamics; and its failure thus far to suggest new and fruitful specifications of expectation formation. There has been no rush to use bounded rationality models for guiding macroeconomic empirical work, maybe for the reason that many macroeconomists are in the market for methods for reducing the number of parameters to explain data, and a reduction is not what bounded rationality promises" (1993, pp. 4–5). Surely, Sargent and many other mathematically predisposed economists would have grave difficulty in seeing an assumption of varying bounded rationality across economic actors (which is altogether plausibly realistic, especially once bounded rationality is introduced into economic analytics) as offering the prospect of "reducing the number of parameters to explain data." Varying bounded rationality across economic actors would surely muck up mathematical models, a point that reveals just how "unreal" bounded-rationality models remain even when touted for their added realism over the neoclassical full rationality premise. To follow on Sargent's point, the relevant question is again one that Friedman pressed (Friedman 1953): How much is gained in moving from models employing the unreal perfect rationality premise to models employing the unreal bounded rationality premise, at least for the purposes Friedman had in mind?

Again, the techniques of model building and manipulation and hypothesis testing sterilize *homo economicus,* opening economic analytics to criticisms that the behavioral foundations of economic models are unreal and seriously, if not fatally, flawed. Such attacks can acquire undue credibility when the discipline's rationality premise is considered separately from the rest of economists' scientific enterprise, with model building necessarily dedicated to simplifying the analytics. The critics (many of whom are the behavioral economists and psychologists discussed in Chap. 6) can easily fail to consider the interplay of exact behavioral premises and methodologies employed, or rather that engaging in deductive science requires the sterilization of the rationality premise, at least to some consequential degree, for progress to be made in economics. On the other hand, such criticisms can press economists to minimize the damage by focusing empirical tests on the statistical significance of the variables' signs and coefficients rather than on the magnitude that the predicted changes in critical independent variables (say, price) may have on the dependent variables (say, quantity demanded).

Theory of Knowledge and Rationality

Many economists, including Friedman, his followers, and his teachers (other than Frank Knight, as we will see in a later chapter) give great weight to knowledge that emerges exclusively from empirical tests that meet scientific standards for statistical rigor. Such predilections on how knowledge is acquired puts demands on the scope and fullness of the presumed rationality of the actors whose behavior is being predicted and tested. Economists, generally, have not recognized that scientific methods profoundly influence the presumptive motivations of actors in economic models. The process of science demands testable hypotheses that are, eventually, subject to empirical tests. But science, as pursued in the physical sciences and in economics, will not allow all people full freedom (or even limited freedom) of choice, nor consider any and all empirical, real-world observations. Stories of real-world happenings and anecdotal evidence, which can be subject to observers' biases, are generally unacceptable for hypothesis testing within the ranks of those who consider themselves scientists.

Hypotheses testing, generally, demands very exacting standards for the types of data considered, how the data are collected, and how the data are used and manipulated in tests, with all such dictates generally eliminating simple comparisons of total and average values for key variables. Hypothesis testing also requires sophisticated econometric regression techniques to disentangle the effects of various variables introduced into the equations of the underlying behavioral models. Then, to have full credibility, the tests must be repeatable. At every step, the scientific process imposes serious constraints on how human behavior can be modeled. According to Sargent, scientific investigation can become so taxing that practitioners necessarily seek to simplify the process with models that may reduce the parameters used to generate hypotheses and then sterilize the parameters (1993, pp. 4–5).

Paradoxically, economists are bound in their own scientific work to leave the rationality of the actors in their models unbounded. Like the actors in their models, economists do not have a whole lot of choice in the matter once they declare their intentions to do *science* of the sort that insists on empirical testing of hypotheses. As we will see in following chapters, economists as far back as Adam Smith and as contemporary as Frank Knight, Ludwig von Mises, Friedrich Hayek, and James Buchanan could pursue their economic analyses with full recognition of substantial bounds on their subjects' rationality, but such economists openly professed to be more engaged in economic philosophy. And they have often been openly hostile to demands that science is the only means to insights about human behavior because of the great difficulties objective measures of the driving force of subjectively conceived wants or ends.

As model building and hypotheses testing have become more formalized during the past two centuries, we should not be surprised that economists have progressively narrowed the range of motivations for choosers in their models and relied more heavily on extreme, or more perfect, forms of rational behavior. As advancing computer and software technologies have reduced the costs of hypotheses testing, more and more economists have moved from philosophical discussions of economic behavior (grounded more or less on the perceived truthfulness of the premises and logical deductions) to empirical tests that meet the exacting standards of statistical validation (relying on narrower views of human motivation, including the as-if perspective on rational/maximizing behavior). Hence, through time, we should expect progressively greater reliance on exacting mathematical model building that presumes more perfect, sterilized forms of behavioral premises, and, not all that surprisingly, growing criticism of neoclassical economics' behavioral foundations. This criticism may be leveled, especially, at model builders who do not understand the connection between their theory of knowledge and methodologies and their rationality premise and who may have begun to believe that economic actors are as rational as they, the theorists, declare them to be and, in a knee-jerk way, assume their rationality premise to be as descriptive of human motivations as it is useful, for scientific purposes, in modeling human behavior.

Indeed, economists as model builders can open themselves to criticism when they allow the predictive usefulness of their models to determine the descriptiveness of their behavioral premises. As we will see in Chap. 7, a cottage industry in behavioral economics has arisen that is organized mainly to demonstrate that, by the neoclassical economists' standard of perfect rationality, irrationalities in decision making and behavior abound (as might have been expected). But then, the behavioralists largely abandon deductive reasoning in favor of allowing experiments to reveal how people, do in actuality, make decisions and behave (an approach that has its own inherent problems, as we will see in Chap. 10).

Of course, a theory of knowledge grounded in empirical tests has to be founded on the presumption that the data selected are actually useful for the intended tests, which requires a presumption that, say, one apple is the equivalent of another apple, which is equivalent to a third apple, which is to say that the addition of three different apples bought by the same person or different people leads to a meaningful count of three apples that can be used as valid data in regression tests. The presumption that hypotheses testers can meaningfully sum apples (or anything else) to develop data for statistical analysis is crucial to economics as a scientific endeavor, even if fraught with fundamental conceptual problems, which economic luminaries of the past questioned aggressively, as we will see in the following three chapters.

Few economists would agree to add a banana, an apple, and an orange to get a statistically useful sum for scientific purposes. They are transparently three different fruit, and different "goods." However, the summing of apples could have the same inherent problem, given that different "apples" can also be different goods, used for substantially different purposes, and evaluated by their buyers in radically different ways for radically different ends, all with different quantitative and qualitative values. An apple can be a food item for one buyer, a missile for another, and a decor object for another. Such an observation means that the need for data testing can have feedback effects on what constitutes acceptable premises and on the choice of behavioral and market models, such as the presumption that the market for apples need not be split according to uses, or the apple market is unified, perfectly competitive (or tolerably so) and that people are fully rational and have identical preferences in terms of apples or whatever else is involved in constrained optimization models. The conduct of science requires that the rationality of the actors is directed at goods that are bought, or rather can be counted, whereas in reality the goods (which have inherent variability, as is the case with apples) that are counted for the purposes of science may be only means (or inputs) to higher and varied ends (a satisfying home-cooked meal or apple-bobbing contest at a birthday party) to which the techniques of science cannot be applied because the ends are not knowable or observable, and much less countable.

Friedman, for example, rejected monopolistic or imperfect competitive models, not because he denied their greater realism (he acknowledged that to be the case), but *because* of that market models' great realism. According to Friedman, in their efforts to achieve greater "realism" in descriptions of market structures, Edward Chamberlin and Joan Robinson effectively destroyed the conception of an "industry," apart from having every differentiated product defined as an "industry" unto itself, which undercuts its usefulness as a model to pursue the kind of science, and sense of knowing, that Friedman held dear:

> Definition in terms of "close" substitutes or a "substantial" gap in cross-elasticities evades the issue, introduces fuzziness and undefinable terms into the abstract model where they have no place, and serves only to make the theory analytically meaningless – "close" and "substantial" are in the same category as a "small" air pressure......The theory of monopolistic competition offers no tools for the analysis of an industry and so no stopping place between the firm at one extreme and general equilibrium at the other. It is therefore incompetent to contribute to the analysis of a host of important problems: the one extreme is too narrow to be of great interest; the other, too broad to permit meaningful generalizations (Friedman 1953, pp. 38–39).

To study economics using scientific methodology that will yield knowledge of detailed behavioral outcomes in specific market contexts (say, how rent controls can affect the quantities and qualities of rental units in given geographical areas), rather than simply knowledge of the broad pattern of market outcomes (say, how markets can coordinate disparate human interests and abilities), Friedman, as well as Stigler and Becker, was willing to make the conceptual leap and practical analytical concession that "firms can be treated *as if* they were perfect competitors" (Friedman 1953, p. 38, emphasis in original). And since Friedman wrote those words, experimental economists have added credibility to Friedman's position by demonstrating that although two assumed market conditions – (1) the existence, or potential existence, of numerous producers in the market and (2) the pervasiveness of perfect information held by all market participants – can ensure that the efficiency of perfect competition will be achieved, imperfectly competitive markets also may generate almost all of the efficiency gains that, in theory, perfectly competitive ones will achieve, a point supported time and again by the laboratory work of Vernon Smith and other experimental economists and to which we will return later in the book (Smith 1962, 2008a, citing numerous experimental studies).

For similar reasons, Friedman was willing to give an objective reality to goods, a significant concession that allows for the empirical testing needed to judge the presumption that people act as if they are fully rational. Economics as science, in other words, is full of conceptual and epistemological compromises – such has been done with a clearly identified objective function – to deduce testable insights that can lead to improved (not perfect) understandings of the human predicament. In constraining their laboratory experiments and surveys and in defining acceptable results, behavioralists make no fewer compromises that, perhaps, are as important as the compromises Friedman and other neoclassical economists make, except in a different methodological way.

As Chap. 5 will clarify, Austrian economists, such as Ludwig von Mises and Friedrich Hayek, rejected the neoclassical methodology, which demands that economic knowledge can only be validated and acquired through science, or empirical testing, because they could not accept the proposition that the objective physical reality of goods can be meaningfully disentangled from their subjective origins and content. Besides, Austrian economists are more concerned with understanding the implications of *human action* (as they conceive of the term), which presupposes a sense of individually conceived improvement necessarily independent of any goods that economic actors might seek to buy or sell. The conception of improvement must occur before action is taken, which suggests some newness to every action and which leaves the process of human action beyond the methods of empirical science, according to Mises and Hayek (as will be documented extensively in Chap. 5).

A science such as physics can rely on empirical tests because its subjects (gases, solids, and stars) do have an objective reality and do not have (as far as anyone knows) a capacity to attribute value to other objects in the world around them. The objects of the physical sciences have no presumed means of self-activation in the pursuit of maximizing internally generated utility functions, the end goals of which might be indirectly related to what people do or buy in the marketplace. By contrast, the subjects of economic analysis are people from whom the basic data – preferences, wants, and ends – do not necessarily have an objective reality apart from their subjective values, which are known only to the people who create them, hold them, change them, and act upon them. As we will see, Austrian economists (as well as Frank Knight and James Buchanan) insist that the internal, subjective nature of economic data limits economists' ability to do science in the same mold and with the same types of tests as physical sciences. But then, Austrian economists do not need to make the practical concessions, or seek to equate economics' scientific nature or goals with physical sciences, as Friedman has done (1953, p. 18).[3] Unlike neoclassical economists, those of the Austrian school do not seek to develop the kind of detailed knowledge of outcomes of the interactions of people, say, through markets, but rather seek only to discover the broad patterns of outcomes, with the details within those patterns left undefined or ill-defined, a major point fully documented in Chap. 5.

Hence, Austrian economists do not have to be as careful as neoclassical economists in presuming that people are exclusively rational or only act as if they are fully or perfectly rational. Rather, they have only to presume that people seek to improve their lots (with precise maximization of objective functions unnecessary) through their individual efforts made, perhaps, in cooperation with others, and to show, as Adam Smith and Friedrich Hayek have shown, patterns of outcomes (mainly through market settings) among people and societies.

For example, Smith wrote that people, whatever their level of imperfect rationality, are "led by an invisible hand to make nearly the same distribution of the necessaries of life, which would have been made, had the earth been divided into equal portions among all its inhabitants, and thus without intending it, without knowing it, advance the interest of the society, and afford means to the multiplication of the species," which suggests that Smith viewed whatever rationality, or maximization, is achieved had to emerge from their interaction with others, given the institutional constraints (Smith 1776, IV.I.10). As we will see in the next chapter, Smith in no way required his subjects to be motivated exclusively by "self-love" that is unbounded by concern for morality and social norms and by concern for others. Smith wove a tale of social improvement – growth in wealth – that actually had three invisible hands at work, one market based, one based on morality, and other based on constitutional governance and the rule of law.

---

[3]In his *Essay on Positive Economics*, Friedman does make the useful point that physicists often make calculations about the speed of falling objects on the Earth, using the rate of decent for objects in a vacuum. The assumption about the acceleration of falling objects often works "well enough" because the "extra accuracy it (a more general theory that takes account of air resistance) yields may not justify the extra cost of using it" (Friedman 1953, p. 18). While economics may strive to be like physics in using a simplified premise on rational behavior, it is categorically different when it comes to the objects of the empirical tests. The falling ball does not have a mind of its own that would allow the ball to assess the value of the fall, and even if it did, the ball rate of decent would not be materially affected. In the case of economics, the ball, and what is done with it, depends critically on how people appraise the ball and rate of descent and how their appraisals will cause them to intervene and change the rate of descent or not allow the ball to fall in the first place. There is the added complication in economics that "balls" can be different things to different people, as well as have different evaluations by different people.

Interestingly, Smith's invisible hands and neoclassical economists' rationality premise serve a similar methodological and practical function, which is facilitating a narrative about how people interact and how markets work, and when they will not work very well.

Austrians can accept that people are not motivated exclusively by self-interest mainly because Austrians do not stake their professional positions on their mathematical and hypothesis-testing, empirical skills. Neoclassical economists typically assume that supply and demand curves are market constraints that really exist "out there," or can be treated as if they are out there, mainly because they see them as devices for undertaking comparative statics. By way of contrast, Hayek argued that markets are demand- and supply-revealing processes. If supply and demand emerge as people interact in markets, then it is hardly possible for people to know and order their wants and consistently choose among their wants in some perfect way before or outside the information-revealing process. But then neoclassical economists in Friedman's camp want to understand the end-result – or more accurately, the directional changes in the equilibrium outcomes (given, for example, an imposed minimum wage) – of market processes while those in Hayek's camp want to understand the patterns of outcomes in the market process (for example, undirected "spontaneous order" that yields welfare improvements with minimum wages being a contrived intrusion) and not the detailed content of the patterns.

Obviously, different goals require different methods, and different behavioral premises. The behavioralists are simply more interested, as we will see in Chap. 6, in devising "nudges" (changes in decision-making environments) that will lead to personal and societal improvements – as the behavioralists determine that people see "improvement," a radically different goal from what neoclassical and Austrian economists have in mind. Neoclassical economists, generally, spurn the temptation to divined improvements for others (a position that denies the rationality premise one of its chief methodological defenses, as we will see in Chap. 11).

Rationality as a Foundation for Process and Institution Analysis

An analytical perspective grounded in rational/maximizing behavior also can be used to recommend institutions needed to ensure maximum exploitation of unexploited economic opportunities, and to explain how various public policies and private collusive arrangements may prevent market participants from exploiting unexploited opportunities.

Accordingly,

- Since the days of Adam Smith, economists have long made the case against restricted trade of all kinds on the grounds that the restrictions lead to unexploited economic opportunities and denial of potential welfare gains and have made the case for unfettered prices, which can guide people toward equilibrium or maximum societal gains from trade.

- Economists also have argued for the establishment of tolerably well-defined and enforced property rights on the grounds that they can ameliorate, if not eliminate, "tragedies of the commons," which means that property rights encourage people to create new economic opportunities and to exploit other opportunities that would otherwise be lost in the overuse of resources (Hardin 1968).
- Economists have elevated the importance of "residual claimants" who have the requisite incentives to find and exploit unexploited economic opportunities, and they have stressed how the growing mobility of resources across markets and improved incentive structures within firms can enhance the exploitation of unexploited opportunities.
- Economists have stressed how problems of asymmetric information can lead to unexploited gains from trade, and to lowering the values of certain goods in trades (Akerlof 1970; Spense 1973; Rothchild and Stiglitz 1976). For example, new cars lose a significant portion of their selling price as soon as they are driven off dealer lots, not from wear-and-tear but from the public's presumption that cars on used-car markets are heavily weighted toward "lemons," those with not-so-easy-to-detect mechanical problems (Akerlof 1970). But then economists, such as John Lott (2007), have explained that the so-called "lemon problem" has been greatly exaggerated because with time people will seek to exploit the unexploited profitable opportunities in any persistence of the lemon problem.

The relevance of these rationality postulates depends to a significant extent on market participants being able to operate within an institutional setting that allows and encourages – even presses – exploitation of unexploited economic opportunities.[4] The rationality postulates would have been of much less (perhaps little) use in understanding much economic activity within the former Soviet Union because for six-plus decades choices were fettered and prices were uninformative of underlying economic realities. People were not allowed (for the most part) to use their localized information to find and exploit opportunities and to change the societal pattern of outcomes not dictated by the Soviet planning authorities.

Although the issue of people's level of rationality is a lesser concern to economists seeking to do science, it is crucial to economists who seek to design institutional/constitutional settings within which people are encouraged to find and exploit unexploited economic opportunities. If people have no (or very limited) rational capacity to search for and exploit unexploited economic opportunities (as followers of B.F. Skinner believed and all too often behave much like "goslings," as one behavioral economist has suggested), then institutional/constitutional design is irrelevant and a waste. For that matter, all science and economics is irrelevant and of no consequence. The critical issue, as Friedman recognized explicitly, is whether or not people's likely imperfect rational capacities are "good enough" on which to found predictions regarding the *directional* changes in behavior, given market

---

[4]Experimental researchers have found that market institutions do influence the extent to which people are rational, exploit unexploited opportunities, and achieve the known potential market efficiency gains (V. Smith 2008).

pressures to correct errors and given changes in constraints. Neoclassical economists seem to have great confidence, derived from experience with employing rationality-based models, that the rationality-based models pass scientific muster. The success of neoclassical economics in applying their methods to a variety of novel areas of human behavior – from human capital to information to law and economics to public decision making – has been substantial over the past half century. The rationality premise might be flawed, but still useful.

Concluding Comments

Rational behavior is an explicit premise on which economists found their science; however, another implicit premise is that objective data are available and can be used to test theories that are grounded exclusively in subjective evaluations. These premises may not always be valid. Most people, including Friedman, agree that the premise of full rationality may not at times be a "sufficiently good" approximation of people's motivations. The same can be said for the data premise. Economics is not like a physical science that starts with the presumption that objective data has no subjective origin. Such concerns ultimately mean that economics is often as much art as science, founded on reasonable "fits" among people's constellation of motivations, the rationality premise, perception, and evaluation of "goods" and the particular data series used to represent goods.

Throughout this book, I can be more accommodating of multiple motivations than working neoclassical economists because here I do not seek to do science and generate testable hypotheses. Rather, this book seeks to understand both the advantages and limitations of economics as a science, and why economists might be attracted to the premise of rational behavior to understand the world around them, in spite of its descriptive flaws.

As it is argued in Chaps. 7 and 8, discussions of rationality are often focused on the appropriate choices of methodologies, *as if* peoples' and economists' choices over such matters are unconstrained. Actually, as will be seen, evolutionary forces of long ago have seriously constrained our methodological choices for understanding human behavior as well as the alternatives that we consider viable choices. The human brain now may very well be structured so that we (individual actors in market and nonmarket settings and economists who study people in such settings) seek to find some semblance of order amid the pervasive apparent disorder or nonorder, if not chaos, of everyday life. Through evolution, human beings may have developed the presumption of rational/maximizing behavior as one method to ferret out a sense of order from all the behavioral noise we observe, with the methods having fitness and survival value. After all, we can detect ourselves often making the kinds of cost–benefit/maximizing decisions that the actors in economic models are assumed to make.

In earlier evolutionary epochs, people did not have computers or the statistical and laboratory methods by which to undertake meaningful inductive, scientific research to determine how and why people do, what they do, and nor did they have the time to undertake such studies. Deductive, rationality-based reasoning was then far more cost-effective, and rationality may have developed as an effective heuristic by which people could develop a sense of order to behavior.

There is something of a quasi-scientific hypothesis that has emerged in our discussion of the methodological constraints on the rationality premise: Any evolution in economic methodology toward formalization, as revealed in the progressively greater use of mathematics and graphical devises, can be expected to be accompanied by a narrowing and growing sterilization of the presumed underlying human motivation toward, if not to, a premise of full or perfect rationality across all analytical subjects. We can also expect (with some understandable delay) growing criticisms from inside and outside the economics discipline over how a variety of human behaviors observed in laboratory experiments and surveys diverge in stark ways from what would be predicted from economists' assumed full or perfect rationality.[5] I describe my hypothesis as quasi-scientific because while I do seek to test the hypothesis, I do not use strictly scientific methods to do so. That is, I do not try to devise numerical counts to be used in regression equations.

Instead, in the next three chapters, through a review of the ways in which leading economists have conceived of buyers' and sellers' behavioral motivations, I examine how the concept of rational behavior has evolved throughout the intellectual history of the discipline. This review tends to support my methodological hypothesis. Early economists, including Adam Smith, who did not use formalized methods of argument – that is, graphs and equations – generally, took an expansive view of their subjects' motivations. Even Alfred Marshall, who introduced graphical analysis into economics, followed Smith in assuming that people were activated by motivations other than self-interest, but then Marshall saw graphs and mathematics as devices for checking the logical flow of key points, not a substitute for broadly conceived logical arguments constructed in words. Similarly, Frank Knight, Ludwig von Mises, Friedrich Hayek, and James Buchanan openly acknowledge that the economic view of behavior founded on rationality and self-interest is only a partial view, but then, again, they largely spurn the use of mathematics and lament the growing focus of the profession on mathematical methods founded to a growing degree on full rationality.

In Chaps. 6 through 8, I will take up burgeoning major strands of criticisms of rational behavior from inside and outside the economics profession. Along the way, I will show how an assumption of full or perfect rationality, as a presumed

---

[5] As we will see, critics of standard economics have made an academic sport of revealing human decision frailties and "irrationalities," all with a growing fan base within disciplines outside of economics and within the educated public (as evident by the growth in the count and sales of trade books describing economic "anomalies" and "irrationalities" (consider, for example, books by Thaler and Sunstein, *Nudge*, 2008 and by Ariely, *Predictably Irrational*, 2008, both cited in Chaps. 6 and 10 on behavioral economics). In key ways, the research agendas of behavioral economists and others have all the markings of shooting fish in a barrel.

Concluding Comments   33

description of human motivations, does not make sense from the perspectives of evolutionary biology and neurobiology nor does it make economic sense.

Nevertheless, my ultimate intent, somewhat paradoxically, in undertaking these critical reviews is the development of defenses for full rational behavior's continued use in economic analysis, despite acknowledged logical and empirical problems. Those defenses, however, will be accompanied by a plea for economists to remember the intellectual roots and function of the full rationality premise. I seek a return of professional thinking to the view, held by many of the discipline's luminaries covered in chapters to come, that the economic way of thinking provides only a partial view of the behavioral forces that motivate and activate life as modern human beings are capable of experiencing it.

Chapter 3
Human Motivation and Adam Smith's "Invisible Hands"

The foundation for the eventual emergence of economics as a distinct discipline was laid with the publication of Adam Smith's *Wealth of Nations* in 1776. The potential power of competitive market economies became widely recognized over the following 100 years through the works of David Ricardo, Thomas Malthus, Frederick Bastiat, and Karl Marx, among others. The discipline went through a revolution in the last third of that century when "marginalists" William Stanley Jevons in England, Leon Walras in France, and Carl Menger in Austria separately recognized how *marginal* values (as distinct from the prior focus on total or average values) carried great weight in determining the levels of consumption, production, and price levels. David Ricardo in the first quarter of the nineteenth century began formalizing economics as a deductive science, relying heavily on simplifying assumptions, with the publication of his *On the Principles of Political Economy and Taxation* in 1817. Alfred Marshall institutionalized the discipline's graphical techniques for generations of budding economists with the publication of his widely and long-adopted textbook, *Principles of Economics*, in 1890.

Through this history, some form of self-interest, if not less narrowly constrained rational behavior, remained embedded in economic discussions. This chapter will be concerned with the motivational foundations of Adam Smith's political economy. I devote a separate chapter to human motivations in Smith's writings not only because he is now recognized (but not in his own time) as a founding father of economics, but also because Smith's construction of human motivations was far more complex and comprehensive than most of his supporters and detractors seem to believe.

In the following chapter, I trace the development of human motivation in economists' thinking through the major writings of several luminaries: Thomas Robert Malthus, David Ricardo, Jeremy Bentham, John Stuart Mill, and Alfred Marshall. We will see that Marshall had much more in common with Smith in terms of the recognized breadth and complexity of human motivations than key economists who dominated economic discourse in between Smith and Marshall. (Obviously, time and space limitations prevent this historical review from being anywhere close to exhaustive).

R.B. McKenzie, *Predictably Rational?*,
DOI 10.1007/978-3-642-01586-1_3, © Springer-Verlag Berlin Heidelberg 2010

As noted in the first chapter, the venerable Adam Smith never explicitly used "rationality," "rational behavior," or even "maximizing behavior" in his extensive discussion of how minimally fettered market transactions can lead to an increase in the wealth of nations. Most economists associate Smith with having stressed how the invisible hand of markets improves societal welfare. Few seem to understand that Smith was actually ambidextrous (at least), methodologically speaking, or rather had a decided second invisible hand at work within and on markets, which is the one that created societal benefits through the moral behavior of many market participants. People's "impartial spectator," who rendered personal judgments on behaviors, fortified certain innate predispositions to be concerned about their fellowmen. Fear of God, as well as the pressures of the rule of law, emerging from constitutional order, also restrained and, at the same time, reinforced Smith's invisible hand of competitive markets and directed the generation of gains from trade. The unheralded invisible hand of people's consent to laws, backed up by visible enforcement of laws, largely made the gains from invisible hand of markets possible. Smith, in other words, articulated a theory of bounded self-interest and self-love.

Smith's Invisible Hand of Markets

Smith's analysis is heavily founded on people's seeking everywhere to achieve greater (if not the greatest) net gains for themselves.[1] Throughout the development of economics, Smith has been both gloriously praised and severely damned for narrowly focusing his treatment of people's behavior within markets on the unheralded guiding force in pursuit of "self-interest" and "self-love" that can lead buyers and sellers to work ultimately and, often as not, unknowingly, for the greater good of

---

[1] Consider these four instances in which Smith used "greatest":

The greatest improvement[*17] in the productive powers of labor, and the greater part of the skill, dexterity, and judgment with which it is any where directed, or applied, seem to have been the effects of the division of labor (1776, Sect. I.1.1).

The stock of the country not being sufficient for the whole accession of business, which such acquisitions present to the different people among whom it is divided, is applied to those particular branches only which afford the greatest profit (1776, Sect. I.9.12).

By supplying them, as nearly as he can judge, in this proportion, he is likely to sell all his corn for the highest price, and with the greatest profit; and his knowledge of the state of the crop, and of his daily, weekly, and monthly sales, enable[*70] him to judge, with more or less accuracy, how far they really are supplied in this manner. Without intending the interest of the people, he is necessarily led, by a regard to his own interest, to treat them, even in years of scarcity, pretty much in the same manner as the prudent master of a vessel is sometimes obliged to treat his crew (1776, Sect. IV.5.42).

The capital of all the individuals of a nation is increased in the same manner as that of a single individual by their continually accumulating and adding to it whatever they save out of their revenue. It is likely to increase the fastest, therefore, when it is employed in the way that affords the greatest revenue to all the inhabitants of the country, as they will thus be enabled to make the greatest savings (1776, Sect. III.4.16).

society. But Smith did not seem to equate the pursuit of self-interest with rational or maximizing behavior in the modern sense of those phrases. He did not foresee that people could optimize their consumption and production decisions exactly and with complete foresight, with all current and future gains and costs discounted for time and risk. Rather, he seemed to hold that people pursued the "great purpose of human life," that of "bettering" (not necessarily maximizing or optimizing, or not even "satisficing") their own individual and collective conditions (1776, Sects. I.III.16 and IV.5.82). His celebrated passage in his *Wealth of Nations* is worth repeating here.

> As every individual, therefore, endeavors as much as he can both to employ his capital in the support of domestic industry, and so to direct that industry that its produce may be of the greatest value; every individual necessarily labors to render the annual revenue of the society as great as he can. He generally, indeed, neither intends to promote the public interest, nor knows how much he is promoting it. By preferring the support of domestic to that of foreign industry, he intends only his own security; and by directing that industry in such a manner as its produce may be of the greatest value, he intends only his own gain, and he is in this, as in many other cases, led by an invisible hand to promote an end which was no part of his intention. Nor is it always the worse for the society that it was no part of it. By pursuing his own interest he frequently promotes that of the society more effectually than when he really intends to promote it. I have never known much good done by those who affected to trade for the public good. It is an affectation, indeed, not very common among merchants, and very few words need be employed in dissuading them from it (1776, Sect. IV.2.9).

Clearly, the people in Smith's analytics were not omniscient and did not try to be, given that he suggested that people collectively, through markets, often achieved societal goals unknowingly and unintentionally.

In his *Theory of Moral Sentiments* – published in 1759 and which can reasonably be interpreted as the moral/philosophical backdrop to his market-focused arguments in the subsequent publication of his *Wealth of Nations* – Smith wrote, "We are not ready to suspect any person of being defective in selfishness" (1759, Sect. VII.II.87). In *Wealth of Nations,* he famously adds that people do not expect their dinners to be provided by "the butcher, the brewer, or the baker" out of "benevolence," but rather out of their own interest: "We address ourselves, not to their humanity but to their self-love, and never talk to them of our own necessities but of their advantages. Nobody but a beggar chooses to depend chiefly upon the benevolence of his fellow-citizens. Even a beggar does not depend upon it entirely" (1776, Sect. I.2.2).

Smith's Invisible Hand of Morality

With Smith's *Theory of Moral Sentiments* and *Wealth of Nations* having become classics, his admirers and critics can be forgiven if they have concluded that Smith had a narrow view of the motivational foundations for the broad swath of human behavior, perhaps, no less narrow than modern-day neoclassical economists' construction of rational/maximizing behavior discussed in Chap. 1. According to many critics' interpretations, one's own welfare was for Smith *the* controlling, if not the *only,* economic motivation and guiding force in markets. Critics have surmised that

Smith held that if people can understand the critical roles of self-interest and self-love in the economy, then they can understand a great deal (but hardly all) about the operational dynamics of market economies. Because such motivations press the invisible hand of the market to do good for all people, one should not want to disrupt those market dynamics with government regulations or other constraints – except minimally in the form of the provision of national defense, administration of justice, stable money, and "certain public works," in the main, canals, "high roads," and some basic education (1776, Sect. IV.9.51).[2]

Laudable Principles of Action

But such a generalization of Smith's views on human motivations could not be further from the truth of how he assessed human behavior and the breadth of "the nature and causes of the wealth of nations." He extolled "the man of the most perfect virtue" as worthy of admiration and emulation, at least to a point.[3] He saw the pursuit of self-interest as often having virtuous, yet not always intended

---

[2]Smith wrote on the emergence of the "system of natural liberty," which in no way is a system without personal restraints on individuals, in *Wealth of Nations*

> All systems either of preference or of restraint, therefore, being thus completely taken away, the obvious and simple system of natural liberty establishes itself of its own accord. Every man, as long as he does not violate the laws of justice, is left perfectly free to pursue his own interest his own way, and to bring both his industry and capital into competition with those of any other man, or order of men. The sovereign is completely discharged from a duty, in the attempting to perform which he must always be exposed to innumerable delusions, and for the proper performance of which no human wisdom or knowledge could ever be sufficient; the duty of superintending the industry of private people, and of directing it towards the employments most suitable to the interest of the society. According to the system of natural liberty, the sovereign has only three duties to attend to; three duties of great importance, indeed, but plain and intelligible to common understandings: first, the duty of protecting the society from violence and invasion of other independent societies; secondly, the duty of protecting, as far as possible, every member of the society from the injustice or oppression of every other member of it, or the duty of establishing an exact administration of justice; and, thirdly, the duty of erecting and maintaining certain public works and certain public institutions which it can never be for the interest of any individual, or small number of individuals, to erect and maintain; because the profit could never repay the expense to any individual or small number of individuals, though it may frequently do much more than repay it to a great society (1776, Sect. IV.9.51).

[3]On people's reverence for virtuous people, Smith wrote,

> The man of the most perfect virtue, the man whom we naturally love and revere the most, is he who joins, to the most perfect command of his own original and selfish feelings, the most exquisite sensibility both to the original and sympathetic feelings of others. The man who, to all the soft, the amiable, and the gentle virtues, joins all the great, the awful, and the respectable, must surely be the natural and proper object of our highest love and admiration (1759, Sect. III.I.77).

consequences: "Regard to our own private happiness and interest, too, appear upon many occasions very laudable principles of action. The habits of economy, industry, discretion, attention, and application of thought, are generally supposed to be cultivated from self-interested motives, and at the same time are apprehended to be very praise-worthy qualities, which deserve the esteem and approbation of every body. The mixture of a selfish motive, it is true, seems often to sully the beauty of those actions which ought to arise from a benevolent affection" (1759, Sect. VII. II.87). But then, Smith acknowledged that the pursuit of self-interest was an imperfect process, given that people do not always know with clarity what their self-interests are.[4]

In short, Smith seems to be saying that pursuit of self-interest is an interactive *process* in which constraining personal attributes were "cultivated," not taken as totally natural or innate – or *given*. Put another way, pursuit of self-interest had feedback loops in which self-interest led people (perhaps, by an invisible and/or visible hand) to acquire attributes that positively affected the way people behaved and pursued their own interests (which has to be construed as an improvement in outcomes for markets that is superior to that which can emerge from people merely allocating known resources among given wants). People can gain from markets not only because markets improve the efficiency with which scarce and given resources are allocated among given wants, but also because markets improve the identification of wants.

And, it needs to be stressed that Smith agreed with Aristotle that people need a balance among their self-interest and other-regarding inclinations. As Smith put it:

> Virtue, according to Aristotle, consists in the habit of mediocrity according to right reason. Every particular virtue, according to him, lies in a kind of middle between two opposite vices, of which the one offends from being too much, the other from being too little affected by a particular species of objects. Thus, the virtue of fortitude or courage lies in the middle between the opposite vices of cowardice and of presumptuous rashness, of which the one offends from being too much, and the other from being too little affected by the objects of fear. Thus too the virtue of frugality lies in a middle between avarice and profusion, of which the one consists in an excess, the other in a defect of the proper attention to the objects of self-interest. Magnanimity, in the same manner, lies in a middle between the excess of arrogance and the defect of pusillanimity, of which the one consists in too extravagant, the other in too weak a sentiment of our own worth and dignity. It is unnecessary to observe that this account of virtue corresponds too pretty exactly with what has been said above concerning the propriety and impropriety of conduct (1759, Sect. VII.II.16).

Indeed, for Smith self-interest and self-love, in order to work their magic through the market's invisible hand, *required* checking by other motivational forces developed largely external to markets, not the least of which were

- A widely adopted sense of beneficence (1776, Sect. VI.III.55);

---

[4]For example, Smith writes that "profusion" and "magnanimity" may be the result of a "defect of the proper attention to the objects of self-interest" and "magnanimity" could be due to "too weak a sentiment of our own worth and dignity" (1759, Sect. VII.II.16).

- People's self-assessments of what is good and right through their individually devised and/or culturally or religiously imposed "impartial spectators," or internal personal judges, who accompany all individuals throughout life, with their impartial spectators critically evaluating the rightness of many, if not, all of their individual decisions (1776, Sect. III.I.46); and
- People's fear of the "author of nature," or deity, who kept his own behavioral scorecard and threatened people with eternal damnation if they pursued their self-interest and self-love too narrowly (1759, Sect. III.I.106).

The points in *Theory of Moral Sentiments* and *Wealth of Nations* at which Smith cites the importance of human motivations other than self-love are numerous, but consider this selection from *Theory of Moral Sentiments*:

> How selfish soever man may be supposed, there are evidently some principles in his nature, which interest him in the fortune of others, and render their happiness necessary to him, though he derives nothing from it except the pleasure of seeing it. Of this kind is pity or compassion, the emotion which we feel for the misery of others, when we either see it, or are made to conceive it in a very lively manner. That we often derive sorrow from the sorrow of others, is a matter of fact too obvious to require any instances to prove it; for this sentiment, like all the other original passions of human nature, is by no means confined to the virtuous and humane, though they perhaps may feel it with the most exquisite sensibility. The greatest ruffian, the most hardened violator of the laws of society, is not altogether without it (1776, Sect. I.I.1).

And, it needs to be stressed, while Smith understood how people were "shocked" at behavior that was founded on motivations other than self-interest and self-love, he did not believe that all such action could be derived by "any such self-interested consideration" alone, contrary to what many of his critics might like to think.[5] Smith mentions vanity, pride, and compassion close to 100 times in *Wealth of Nations* and *Theory of Moral Sentiments*. For instance, on vanity, Smith wrote,

---

[5] Smith's words in quotations were derived from this passage in *Theory of Moral Sentiments*:

> But whatever may be the cause of sympathy, or however it may be excited, nothing pleases us more than to observe in other men a fellow-feeling with all the emotions of our own breast; nor are we ever so much shocked as by the appearance of the contrary. Those who are fond of deducing all our sentiments from certain refinements of self-love, think themselves at no loss to account, according to their own principles, both for this pleasure and this pain. Man, say they, conscious of his own weakness, and of the need which he has for the assistance of others, rejoices whenever he observes that they adopt his own passions, because he is then assured of that assistance; and grieves whenever he observes the contrary, because he is then assured of their opposition. But both the pleasure and the pain are always felt so instantaneously, and often upon such frivolous occasions, that it seems evident that neither of them can be derived from any such self-interested consideration. A man is mortified when, after having endeavored to divert the company, he looks round and sees that nobody laughs at his jests but himself. On the contrary, the mirth of the company is highly agreeable to him, and he regards this correspondence of their sentiments with his own as the greatest applause (1759, Sect. I.I.14).

In countries where a rich man can spend his revenue in no other way than by maintaining as many people as it can maintain, he is not apt to run out, and his benevolence it seems is seldom so violent as to attempt to maintain more than he can afford. But where he can spend the greatest revenue upon his own person, he frequently has no bounds to his expence, because he frequently has no bounds to his vanity or to his affection for his own person. In commercial countries, therefore, riches, in spite of the most violent regulations of law to prevent their dissipation, very seldom remain long in the same family. Among simple nations, on the contrary, they frequently do without any regulations of law, for among nations of shepherds, such as the Tartars and Arabs, the consumable nature of their property necessarily renders all such regulations impossible (Smith 1776; Sect. III.4.16).

Smith is widely recognized for having built his market theory on people's propensity to "truck, barter, and exchange" (1776, Sect. I.2.4). In popular discussions of his supposed narrowly focused free-market economics, Smith is not widely recognized for his belief that much of life is directed by concern for others:

In the same manner, to the selfish and original passions of human nature, the loss or gain of a very small interest of our own appears to be of vastly more importance, excites a much more passionate joy or sorrow, a much more ardent desire or aversion, than the greatest concern of another with whom we have no particular connexion. His interests, as long as they are surveyed from this station, can never be put into the balance with our own, can never restrain us from doing whatever may tend to promote our own, how ruinous soever to him. Before we can make any proper comparison of those opposite interests, we must change our position. We must view them, neither from our own place nor yet from his, neither with our own eyes nor yet with his, but from the place and with the eyes of a third person, who has no particular connexion with either, and who judges with impartiality between us. Here, too, habit and experience have taught us to do this so easily and so readily, that we are scarce sensible that we do it; and it requires, in this case too, some degree of reflection, and even of philosophy, to convince us, how little interest we should take in the greatest concerns of our neighbor, how little we should be affected by whatever relates to him, if the sense of propriety and justice did not correct the otherwise natural inequality of our sentiments (1759, Sect. III.I.45).

Smith appears to have been a sincerely religious person (although he was hardly willing to follow blindly the teachings of churches and their "high priests"), founding his moral philosophy on something akin to the golden rule. As he put it, "And hence it is, that to feel much for others and little for ourselves, that to restrain our selfish, and to indulge our benevolent affections, constitutes the perfection of human nature; and can alone produce among mankind that harmony of sentiments and passions in which consists their whole grace and propriety. As to love our neighbor as we love ourselves is the great law of Christianity, so it is the great precept of nature to love ourselves only as we love our neighbor, or what comes to the same thing, as our neighbor is capable of loving us" (1776, Sect. I.I.44). This suggests that he believed in the rule of tit-for-tat governing close-at-hand, personal relationships.

The Economic Role of the "Impartial Spectator"

Smith was more than willing to concede that for many people their personal stake in human interactions was of far greater importance than their concern for others with whom they "have no particular connection." But he thought such natural inclinations would be corrected by people's "sense of propriety and justice" (1776, Sect. III.I.45). After all, people must always consult and reconcile their decisions and actions with their internal impartial spectator who stands ready at all times to call their hosts to task for miscalculations and misdeeds.

> Nature has lighted up in the human heart, that is thus capable of counteracting the strongest impulses of self-love. It is a stronger power, a more forcible motive, which exerts itself upon such occasions. It is reason, principle, conscience, the inhabitant of the breast, the man within, the great judge and arbiter of our conduct. It is he who, whenever we are about to act so as to affect the happiness of others, calls to us, with a voice capable of astonishing the most presumptuous of our passions, that we are but one of the multitude, in no respect better than any other in it; and that when we prefer ourselves so shamefully and so blindly to others, we become the proper objects of resentment, abhorrence, and execration. It is from him only that we learn the real littleness of ourselves, and of whatever relates to ourselves, and the natural misrepresentations of self-love can be corrected only by the eye of this impartial spectator. It is he who shows us the propriety of generosity and the deformity of injustice; the propriety of resigning the greatest interests of our own, for the yet greater interests of others, and the deformity of doing the smallest injury to another, in order to obtain the greatest benefit to ourselves. It is not the love of our neighbor, it is not the love of mankind, which upon many occasions prompts us to the practice of those divine virtues. It is a stronger love, a more powerful affection, which generally takes place upon such occasions; the love of what is honorable and noble, of the grandeur, and dignity, and superiority of our own characters (1776, Sect. III.I.46).

Smith's "Logic of Collective Action"

Most modern-day economists are familiar with the late Mancur Olson's *The Logic of Collective Action*, under which small groups are able to cohere and cooperate in pursuit of their common interests and under which large groups are not able to do the same, or not with the same cost-effectiveness as small groups (1965, Chap. 2). This is the case because the actions, or inactions, of each *individual* within small groups is consequential and, therefore, detectible by the individual and his or her cohorts in the group (say, a family or circle of close friends), which permits in-group mutual monitoring.

In contrast, the actions or inactions of individuals within large groups are more or less inconsequential and undetectable to acting individual group members. Individuals in large groups cannot be inspired to pursue the group's common interests because even they cannot see detectable gains or losses from doing so; therefore, focused incentives (in the form of, say, pay for performance or threats of firings or actual firings for nonperformance) are necessary to encourage people in large groups to cohere and cooperate. The difficulty large groups have in cohering in pursuit of their common objectives is one explanation for why highly competitive markets remain competitive, with producer groups unable to cartelize the supply side of markets to extract higher than competitive prices and with consumer groups unable to cartelize their side of markets to extract lower than competitive prices.

Although unrecognized by Olson, Smith seems to have harbored a similar view regarding people's motivations in different size groups, stating that people stand "at all times in need of the cooperation and assistance of great multitudes, while his whole life is scarce sufficient to gain the friendship of a few persons" (1776, Sect. I.2.2). In *Theory of Moral Sentiments,* Smith wrote:

> Let us suppose that the great empire of China, with all its myriads of inhabitants, was suddenly swallowed up by an earthquake, and let us consider how a man of humanity in Europe, who had no sort of connexion with that part of the world, would be affected upon receiving intelligence of this dreadful calamity. He would, I imagine, first of all, express very strongly his sorrow for the misfortune of that unhappy people, he would make many melancholy reflections upon the precariousness of human life, and the vanity of all the labors of man, which could thus be annihilated in a moment. He would too, perhaps, if he was a man of speculation, enter into many reasonings concerning the effects which this disaster might produce upon the commerce of Europe, and the trade and business of the world in general. And when all this fine philosophy was over, when all these humane sentiments had been once fairly expressed, he would pursue his business or his pleasure, take his repose or his diversion, with the same ease and tranquility, as if no such accident had happened. The most frivolous disaster which could befall himself would occasion a more real disturbance. If he was to lose his little finger tomorrow, he would not sleep tonight; but, provided he never saw them, he will snore with the most profound security over the ruin of a hundred millions of his brethren, and the destruction of that immense multitude seems plainly an object less interesting to him, than this paltry misfortune of his own (1759, Sect. III.I.46).

Smith pointed to exceptional instances in which social discipline and consideration of others could extend the range, perhaps considerably, of group sizes in which shared interests could remain operational and tolerably effective in directing group behavior (independent of the invisible hand of markets). For example, Smith pointed to how "stocks" (taxable assets) and tax liabilities in Hamburg, Germany seemed to be faithfully reported and paid, even though there seemed to be little threat of legal penalty for not accurately reporting and paying the required taxes (as far as Smith could surmise from a distance). This was an outcome he did not consider "peculiar to the people of Hamburgh" – *provided certain conditions were met*:

> At Hamburgh every inhabitant is obliged to pay to the state one-fourth percent of all that he possesses; and as the wealth of the people of Hamburgh consists principally in stock, this tax may be considered as a tax upon stock. Every man assesses himself, and, in the presence of the magistrate, puts annually into the public coffer a certain sum of money which he declares upon oath to be one-fourth percent of all that he possesses, but without declaring what it amounts to, or being liable to any examination upon that subject. This tax is generally supposed to be paid with great fidelity. In a small republic, where the people have entire confidence in their magistrates, are convinced of the necessity of the tax for the support of the state, and believe that it will be faithfully applied to that purpose, such conscientious and voluntary payment may sometimes be expected (1776, Sect. V.2.95).

Smith did not always appear astonished at how people so often did well by their fellowmen. He seemed willing everywhere to acknowledge that love of others could motivate people within their small circles of family members and friends. Thus, when he wrote of appealing to the butcher's, brewer's, and baker's self-love, not to their humanity, he was really selecting his examples with some care. First, his examples were tradesmen with whom, presumably, people had only commercial dealings. Second, they were people who could help provide dinner but who were likely outside most buyers' "small" groups of family members and friends or relevant others. These were tradesmen who would not likely, therefore, be motivated very effectively or efficiently by appeals to beneficence and love of the buyers. Not that butchers, brewers, and bakers would lack noble concerns for humanity. Smith just thought any such appeal on behalf of far-removed others would not likely translate into effective good deeds in commercial trades on any cost-effective scale.[6] People could be motivated by concern for others, but only up to a point and mostly toward others who are personally known or with whom they share some common identity that acts as a bond.

Smith was, understandably, convinced that appeals to the butcher, baker, and brewer based on self-interest often made more economic sense and could be far

---

[6] Smith added to his comments about the "man of humanity in Europe":

To prevent, therefore, this paltry misfortune to himself, would a man of humanity be willing to sacrifice the lives of a hundred millions of his brethren, provided he had never seen them? Human nature startles with horror at the thought, and the world, in its greatest depravity and corruption, never produced such a villain as could be capable of entertaining it. But what makes this difference? When our passive feelings are almost always so sordid and so selfish, how comes it that our active principles should often be so generous and so noble? When we are always so much more deeply affected by whatever concerns ourselves, than by whatever concerns other men; what is it which prompts the generous, upon all occasions, and the mean upon many, to sacrifice their own interests to the greater interests of others? It is not the soft power of humanity, it is not that feeble spark of benevolence which Nature has lighted up in the human heart, that is thus capable of counteracting the strongest impulses of self-love. It is a stronger power, a more forcible motive, which exerts itself upon such occasions. It is reason, principle, conscience, the inhabitant of the breast, the man within, the great judge and arbiter of our conduct. It is he who, whenever we are about to act so as to affect the happiness of others, calls to us, with a voice capable of astonishing the most presumptuous of our passions, that we are but one of the multitude, in no respect better than any other in it; and that when we prefer ourselves so shamefully and so blindly to others, we become the proper objects of resentment, abhorrence, and execration. It is from him only that we learn the real littleness of ourselves, and of whatever relates to ourselves, and the natural misrepresentations of self-love can be corrected only by the eye of this impartial spectator. It is he who shows us the propriety of generosity and the deformity of injustice; the propriety of resigning the greatest interests of our own, for the yet greater interests of others, and the deformity of doing the smallest injury to another, in order to obtain the greatest benefit to ourselves. It is not the love of our neighbor, it is not the love of mankind, which upon many occasions prompts us to the practice of those divine virtues. It is a stronger love, a more powerful affection, which generally takes place upon such occasions; the love of what is honorable and noble, of the grandeur, and dignity, and superiority of our own characters (1759, Sect. III.I.46).

more cost-effective, especially, when the appeal had largely, if not exclusively, commercial ends. And it should not be forgotten that in *Wealth of Nations*, Smith was intent on pressing for reforms that affected untold number of unidentified people through an indefinite future during which a nation's wealth could be expected to grow, or stagnate or retrogress, if proposed institutional and policy reforms were not adopted.

Again, Smith may have emphasized the drives of self-interest and self-love not so much because he was convinced that these were people's sole motivations, but rather because he believed that even when people in their larger commercial realms were driven exclusively by self-interest and self-love, they could be counted on, in many places and under many market-constrained conditions, to achieve societal gains, although such gains may be unintended and unanticipated. If his readers could accept such a conclusion regarding the consequences of largely self-interest-directed people in markets, then they could surely see that even more gains might be attained from more real-world people who also had the interests of others and the larger community and country at heart.

Smith's Sense of Balance in Behavioral Motivations

Smith always seemed intent on asserting a balanced view of human behavior, with several levels of motivations at work in all spheres of people's commercial and noncommercial endeavors. If it were not for people's innate concern for others and for the impartial spectator, as well as for law enforcement and competitive market pressures, self-interest and self-love might very well govern without constraint and people's behavior might be as despicable as many would suspect. Smith himself made such a point with unrecognized force:

> But though the virtues of prudence, justice, and beneficence, may, upon different occasions, be recommended to us almost equally by two different principles; those of self-command are, upon most occasions, principally and almost entirely recommended to us by one; by the sense of propriety, by regard to the sentiments of the supposed impartial spectator. *Without the restraint which this principle imposes, every passion would, upon most occasions, rush headlong, if I may say so, to its own gratification. Anger would follow the suggestions of its own fury; fear those of its own violent agitations. Regard to no time or place would induce vanity to refrain from the loudest and most impertinent ostentation; or voluptuousness from the most open, indecent, and scandalous indulgence.* Respect for what are, or for what ought to be, or for what upon a certain condition would be, the sentiments of other people, is the sole principle which, upon most occasions, overawes all those mutinous and turbulent passions into that tone and temper which the impartial spectator can enter into and sympathize with (1776, Sect. VI.III.55; emphasis added).

But then, in Smith's moral system, the work of the law enforcers, impartial spectators, and competitive pressures, was fortified by God's potential retribution:

> When the general rules which determine the merit and demerit of actions, come thus to be regarded as the laws of an All-powerful Being, who watches over our conduct, and who, in

a life to come, will reward the observance, and punish the breach of them; they necessarily acquire a new sacredness from this consideration. That our regard to the will of the Deity ought to be the supreme rule of our conduct, can be doubted of by nobody who believes his existence. The very thought of disobedience appears to involve in it the most shocking impropriety. How vain, how absurd would it be for man, either to oppose or to neglect the commands that were laid upon him by Infinite Wisdom, and Infinite Power! How unnatural, how impiously ungrateful not to reverence the precepts that were prescribed to him by the infinite goodness of his Creator, even though no punishment was to follow their violation. The sense of propriety too is here well supported by the strongest motives of self-interest. The idea that, however we may escape the observation of man, or be placed above the reach of human punishment, yet we are always acting under the eye, and exposed to the punishment of God, the great avenger of injustice, is a motive capable of restraining the most headstrong passions, with those at least who, by constant reflection, have rendered it familiar to them (1759, Sect. III.I.111).

Respect for religious dictates activates another unheralded morality-driven and distinctly nonmarket-activated invisible hand at work in society:

But by acting according to the dictates of our moral faculties, we necessarily pursue the most effectual means for promoting the happiness of mankind, and may therefore be said, in some sense, to cooperate with the Deity, and to advance as far as in our power the plan of Providence. By acting other ways, on the contrary, we seem to obstruct, in some measure, the scheme which the Author of nature has established for the happiness and perfection of the world, and to declare ourselves, if I may say so, in some measure the enemies of God. Hence we are naturally encouraged to hope for his extraordinary favor and reward in the one case, and to dread his vengeance and punishment in the other (1759, Sect. III.I.106).

Smith's Modern Market Deductions

With his decidedly mixed and complex view of human motivations and while he drew many insights from everyday experience and from history (and relied extensively on deductive reasoning), Smith had no problem, for the most part, playing through the logic of how (bounded) self-interested people could be expected to behave within markets and other social settings, drawing what remain, for the most part, deductions congenial with modern analysis about the effects of various changes in market conditions on price and output levels. Smith mused at some length and in various places in *Wealth of Nations* about nonprice competition that comes with unfettered entrepreneurship, as well as competition over price, or how prices will tend to gravitate toward their "natural" levels, which in competitive markets means that prices would gravitate toward (but not necessarily to) covering only the costs of production, including the replacement of the "stock" of capital and a "proper," "reasonable," or "ordinary profit" (which contemporary economists would call "normal profits"): "Prices of goods depend upon the expenses, the interest of money employed, and the 'labors too, the care, attention, accounts, and correspondence about them.' Sometimes, we must 'take in also the condition of the person so employed,' since 'the expense' of his station of life must be defrayed by the price of such labors; and they deserve compensation as much as any other."[7] "Extraordinary profit" (or what economists now dub "economic profit") could definitely activate entrepreneurs but could also be expected to be eroded by competition. Smith was far more concerned about the process of competition than are modern mainstream economists whose focus, generally, is on the end-state of competition, or equilibrium, a concept nowhere to be found in Smith's major works:

> When by an increase in the effectual demand, the market price of some particular commodity happens to rise a good deal above the natural price, those who employ their stocks in supplying that market are generally careful to conceal this change. If it was commonly known, their great profit would tempt so many new rivals to employ their stocks in the same way, that, the effectual demand being fully supplied, the market price would soon be reduced to the natural price, and perhaps for some time even below it. If the market is at a great distance from the residence of those who supply it, they may sometimes be able to keep the secret for several years together, and may so long enjoy their extraordinary profits without any new rivals. Secrets of this kind, however, it must be acknowledged, can seldom be long kept; and the extraordinary profit can last very little longer than they are kept (1776, Sect. I.7.21).

Accordingly, prices in competitive markets will often differ only to the extent that production and transportation costs differ, and the introduction of money will facilitate trade "on account of their small bulk and great value" that, in turn, can enhance competition, pushing product prices toward their "natural" levels and lowering "extraordinary profits" (1776, Sect. II.5.29). At the same time, he was fully aware of obstacles to prices reaching their natural levels, not the least of which were various private and public monopolies and trade restrictions. "Rent" on any more or less fixed asset, most notably land, would not be a price-determining return to owners, but rather a derivative payment attributable only to any special advantages particular pieces of land might have, but the rent is ultimately tied to interest rates (a point David Ricardo later formalized). On the tie between land rent and the interest rate on loans, Smith writes,

> The ordinary market price of land, it is to be observed, depends everywhere upon the ordinary market rate of interest. The person who has a capital from which he wishes to derive a revenue, without taking the trouble to employ it himself, deliberates whether he should buy land with it or lend it out at interest. The superior security of land, together with some other advantages which almost everywhere attend upon this species of property, will

---

[7]On "ordinary profits," Smith wrote,

> But though it may be impossible to determine with any degree of precision, what are or were the average profits of stock, either in the present, or in ancient times, some notion may be formed of them from the interest of money.[*50] It may be laid down as a maxim, that wherever a great deal can be made by the use of money, a great deal will commonly be given for the use of it; and that wherever little can be made by it, less will commonly be given for it.[*51] According, therefore, as the usual market rate of interest varies in any country, we may be assured that the ordinary profits of stock must vary with it, must sink as it sinks, and rise as it rises. The progress of interest, therefore, may lead us to form some notion of the progress of profit (1776, Sect. I.7.22).

generally dispose him to content himself with a smaller revenue from land than what he might have by lending out his money at interest. These advantages are sufficient to compensate a certain difference of revenue; but they will compensate a certain difference only; and if the rent of land should fall short of the interest of money by a greater difference, nobody would buy land, which would soon reduce its ordinary price. On the contrary, if the advantages should much more than compensate the difference, everybody would buy land, which again would soon raise its ordinary price. When interest was at ten percent, land was commonly sold for ten and twelve years purchase. As interest sunk to six, five, and four percent, the price of land rose to twenty, five and twenty, and thirty years purchase. The market rate of interest is higher in France than in England; and the common price of land is lower. In England it commonly sells at thirty, in France at twenty years purchase (1776, Sect. II.4.17).

Smith's Political Economy

Many modern economists pride themselves in extending their neoclassical economic models into new disciplinary territories; for example, politics, education, and slavery. In fact, Smith served up his own limited form of economic imperialism that has been rediscovered by modern economists using their formal, rationality grounded models. Indeed, Smith's *inquiry* is never stronger that when he takes up matters of *political economy* (or the impact of various public or state policies on growth in the "wealth of nations"), especially, the regulation of trade under mercantilism, which, ostensibly, was orchestrated to increase the national horde of gold by encouraging exports with "bounties" (or subsidies) and discouraging imports by tariffs, quotas, and outright prohibitions. Smith saw four prominent defects in the "mercantile" arguments.

- First, the "greater part" of trade restrictions have been "imposed for the purpose, not of revenue, but of monopoly, or to give our own merchants an advantage in the home market" (1776, Sect. V.2.177).
- Second, the trade restrictions led to the accumulation of gold which in itself was unproductive and would lead to more costly sources of consumed goods, as well as divert the use of scarce resources to mining and storing gold (1776, Sect. II.3.22).
- Third, trade restrictions narrowed the breadth of markets, which, in turn, meant that they undercut the benefits of the division and specialization of labor in the production, a major source of efficiency improvement, which is to say that freer trade not only allowed trading nations to take advantage of their existing cost advantages, but also expanded the scale and scope of markets, and thus lowered costs through greater specialization of resource use (1776, Sect. I.11.165).
- Fourth, both import restrictions and export bounties were bound to encourage smuggling because they increased the rewards from smuggling. Indeed, Smith saw how bounties "have given occasion to many frauds, and to a species of smuggling more destructive of the public revenue than any other": "In order to obtain the bounty or drawback, the goods, it is well known, are sometimes

shipped and sent to sea, but soon afterwards clandestinely re-landed in some other parts of the country" (1776, Sect. V.2.173).[8]

The elimination of restrictions would, accordingly, result not only in cheaper imported goods, but also cheaper domestically produced goods. Moreover, the "mercantile system" not only fettered the invisible hand of markets, but also corrupted and weakened the invisible hand of morality, with the fettered invisible hand of morality compounding the efficiency losses from the fettered invisible hand of markets considered separately.

Smith destroyed conventional arguments for slavery for most industries and most crops within agriculture both on moral and economic grounds: It was most often more profitable (with sugar production in the West Indies being a likely notable exception) for employers to pay their workers than to incur the costs of creating the requisite threat of violence to induce slaves to work anywhere near their productive capacities (1776, Sect. Bk IV, Chap.7). He also was opposed to empire building on the grounds that empires everywhere were excessively costly to maintain, given the necessity of military controls to extract taxes and to protect the monopolies in trade. Great Britain could conserve its military resources, Smith wrote, if it were to induce the American colonial leaders to drop their revolution with an offer of seats in Parliament, an offer that would appeal to colonial leaders' sense of self-importance and something they would not likely refuse.[9]

---

[8] Smith offers this assessment of the impact of bounties on public revenues from trade:

The defalcation of the revenue of customs occasioned by the bounties and drawbacks, of which a great part are obtained fraudulently, is very great. The gross produce of the customs in the year which ended on the 5th of January 1755 amounted to 5,068,000*l*. The bounties which were paid out of this revenue, though in that year there was no bounty upon corn, amounted to 167,800*l*. The drawbacks which were paid upon debentures and certificates, to 2,156,800*l*. Bounties and drawbacks together amounted to 2,324,600*l*. In consequence of these deductions the revenue of the customs amounted only to 2,743,400*l*.: from which, deducting 287,900*l*. for the expence of management in salaries and other incidents, the net revenue of the customs for that year comes out to be 2,455,500*l*. The expence of management amounts in this manner to between five and six percent. upon the gross revenue of the customs, and to something more than ten percent upon what remains of that revenue after deducting what is paid away in bounties and drawbacks (1776, Sect. V.2.173).

[9] Smith wrote on effectively buying off colonial leaders:

Towards the declension of the Roman republic, the allies of Rome, who had borne the principal burden of defending the state and extending the empire, demanded to be admitted to all the privileges of Roman citizens. Upon being refused, the social war broke out. During the course of that war, Rome granted those privileges to the greater part of them one by one, and in proportion as they detached themselves from the general confederacy. The parliament of Great Britain insists upon taxing the colonies; and they refuse to be taxed by a Parliament in which they are not represented. If to each colony, which should detach itself from the general confederacy, Great Britain should allow such a number of representatives as suited the proportion of what is contributed to the public revenue of the empire, in consequence of its being subjected to the same taxes, and in compensation admitted to the same freedom of trade with its fellow-subjects at home; the number of its representatives to

Smith's Expansive Political Economy

Contemporary economists also pride themselves for having applied economics to an expanding array of new subdisciplines, or for having engaged in "economic imperialism" across disciplinary boundaries. However, Smith also had an expansive view of political economy, showing how basic principles, based on the presumption that people would follow their (constrained or bounded) self-interest, could be used to understand nonmarket problems and to propose public policy solutions. To no small extent, modern economists who see their work as "imperialistic" have only rediscovered many of Smith's insights, sometimes without knowing of (or acknowledging) their indebtedness. But then, in Smith's day, there were no neatly drawn boundaries around economics because the discipline had not yet coalesced and would not have clear boundaries for maybe a century, with the early boundaries emerging in the form of the core subject matter – for example, Alfred Marshall's "ordinary business of life" – not so much around the methods of analysis that seemed central to Smith's approach (and he did use various methods of analysis).

Smith's Supply-Side Economics

Smith used several books within *Wealth of Nations* to discuss how taxes affect product prices and output levels, and how taxes on, say, labor would not necessarily fall on their targeted group, because the taxes could be shifted backward to landowners in the form of lower rents and forward to consumers in the form of higher prices. He also stressed the "supply-side" (a phrase Smith never used) effects of taxes that economists have from time to time elevated in public policy discussions (most recently in the 1970s), often unaware that their supply-side points were as old as *Wealth of Nations*:

> [S]uch taxes necessarily occasion some obstruction or discouragement to certain branches of industry. As they always raise the price of the commodity taxed, they so far discourage its consumption, and consequently its production. If it is a commodity of home growth or

---

be augmented as the proportion of its contribution might afterwards augment; a new method of acquiring importance, a new and more dazzling object of ambition would be presented to the leading men of each colony. Instead of piddling for the little prizes which are to be found in what may be called the paltry raffle of colony faction; they might then hope, from the presumption which men naturally have in their own ability and good fortune, to draw some of the great prizes which sometimes come from the wheel of the great state lottery of British polities. Unless this or some other method is fallen upon, and there seems to be none more obvious than this, of preserving the importance and of gratifying the ambition of the leading men of America, it is not very probable that they will ever voluntarily submit to us; and we ought to consider that the blood which must be shed in forcing them to do so is, every drop of it, blood either of those who are, or of those whom we wish to have for our fellow-citizens (1776, Sect. IV.7.161).

manufacture, less labor comes to be employed in raising and producing it. If it is a foreign commodity of which the tax increases in this manner the price, the commodities of the same kind which are made at home may thereby, indeed, gain some advantage in the home market, and a greater quantity of domestic industry may thereby be turned toward preparing them. But though this rise of price in a foreign commodity may encourage domestic industry in one particular branch, it necessarily discourages that industry in almost every other. The dearer the Birmingham manufacturer buys his foreign wine, the cheaper he necessarily sells that part of his hardware with which, or, what comes to the same thing, with the price of which he buys it. That part of his hardware, therefore, becomes of less value to him, and he has less encouragement to work at it. The dearer the consumers in one country pay for the surplus produce of another, the cheaper they necessarily sell that part of their own surplus produce with which, or, what comes to the same thing, with the price of which they buy it. That part of their own surplus produce becomes of less value to them, and they have less encouragement to increase its quantity. All taxes upon consumable commodities, therefore, tend to reduce the quantity of productive labor below what it otherwise would be, either in preparing the commodities taxed, if they are home commodities, or in preparing those with which they are purchased, if they are foreign commodities. Such taxes, too, always alter, more or less, the natural direction of national industry, and turn it into a channel always different from, and generally less advantageous than that in which it would have run of its own accord (1776, Sect. V.2.2.208).

Smith also seems to have understood the tax-policy relevance of the "Laffer curve" long before contemporary economist Arthur Laffer famously sketched out (as legend has it) the curve on a restaurant napkin, showing that taxes could be raised so high that beyond some point the resulting curb in output and income would reduce total revenues from the tax.[10] Smith deduced much the same thing when he wrote about how tariffs on certain imports were often so high that total tariff revenues were smaller than they could be.[11] However, he clearly understood that revenues were not always the point of the tariffs. Generating monopoly prices and profits for the protected industries was the point.[12] Indeed, Smith assumed, like contemporary public choice economists have done, that politicians were also

---

[10]See Laffer (2004). Jude Wanniski (1978) popularized the "Laffer curve" in 1978.

[11]On the revenue effects of high tariffs and the potential gains from "more moderate taxes," Smith wrote, "High taxes, sometimes by diminishing the consumption of the taxed commodities, and sometimes by encouraging smuggling, frequently afford a smaller revenue to government than what might be drawn from more moderate taxes" (1776, Sect. V.2.178).

[12]On the intent of high tariffs, Smith noted,

> The taxes which at present subsist upon foreign manufactures, if you except those upon the few contained in the foregoing enumeration, have the greater part of them been imposed for the purpose, not of revenue, but of monopoly, or to give our own merchants an advantage in the home market. By removing all prohibitions, and by subjecting all foreign manufactures to such moderate taxes as it was found from experience afforded upon each article the greatest revenue to the public, our own workmen might still have a considerable advantage in the home market, and many articles, some of which at present afford no revenue to government, and others a very inconsiderable one, might afford a very great one (1776, Sect. V.2.177).

motivated by private interests and that concentrated interests of producers dominated the diffused interest of consumers.[13] Indeed, the whole of the mercantile
system seemed to be intent on serving the interests of the "rich and powerful"
(generally producers) against the "poor and powerless" (especially, "inferior" and
"unproductive" workers).[14]

Finally, Smith recognized that because capitalists were always looking for the
best rate of return on their "stock" *after taxes*, they would be inclined to move their
stock across governmental jurisdictions, even national boundaries, when they were
exposed to tax burdens that amounted to a "vexatious inquisition" (1777, Sect.
V.2.91). Landowners, however, were not so mobile, and not so able to escape the
taxes imposed on them. By implication, Smith appears to have understood that

---

[13] Smith argued that the cost to the domestic economy of import protection included not only the
cost of reduced consumption, but also cost of two wars and associated debt, given that the import
restrictions were causes of the wars:

> But in the system of laws which has been established for the management of our American
> and West Indian colonies, the interest of the home-consumer has been sacrificed to that of
> the producer with a more extravagant profusion than in all our other commercial regula-
> tions. A great empire has been established for the sole purpose of raising up a nation of
> customers who should be obliged to buy from the shops of our different producers all the
> goods with which these could supply them. For the sake of that little enhancement of price
> which this monopoly might afford our producers, the home-consumers have been burdened
> with the whole expense of maintaining and defending that empire. For this purpose, and for
> this purpose only, in the two last wars, more than two hundred millions have been spent,
> and a new debt of more than a hundred and seventy millions has been contracted over and
> above all that had been expended for the same purpose in former wars......It cannot be very
> difficult to determine who have been the contrivers of this whole mercantile system; not the
> consumers, we may believe, whose interest has been entirely neglected; but the producers,
> whose interest has been so carefully attended to; and among this latter class our merchants
> and manufacturers have been by far the principal architects. In the mercantile regulations,
> which have been taken notice of in this chapter, the interest of our manufacturers has been
> most peculiarly attended to; and the interest, not so much of the consumers, as that of some
> other sets of producers, has been sacrificed to it (1776, Sect. IV.8.53).

[14] On how the mercantile system served the interest of the "rich and powerful," Smith wrote,

> As it is their interest to sell the complete manufacture as dear, so is it to buy the materials as
> cheap as possible. By extorting from the legislature bounties upon the exportation of their
> own linen, high duties upon the importation of all foreign linen, and a total prohibition of
> the home consumption of some sorts of French linen,[*13] they endeavor to sell their own
> goods as dear as possible. By encouraging the importation of foreign linen yarn, and
> thereby bringing it into competition with that which is made by our own people, they
> endeavor to buy the work of the poor spinners as cheap as possible. They are as intent to
> keep down the wages of their own weavers as the earnings of the poor spinners, and it is by
> no means for the benefit of the workman that they endeavour either to raise the price of the
> complete work or to lower that of the rude materials. It is the industry which is carried on
> for the benefit of the rich and the powerful that is principally encouraged by our mercantile
> system. That which is carried on for the benefit of the poor and the indigent is too often
> either neglected or oppressed (1776, Sect. IV.8.4).

government taxation proclivities were constrained by the competition among governments for capital and that, accordingly, a country's tax burden would tend to be more heavily imposed on landowners than on more mobile capitalists in the manufacturing and merchant classes.[15]

Smith's Fiscal Federalism

Smith advocated a form of fiscal federalism, with many local roads and canals financed either by tolls or, if tolls were impractical or gave rise to monopoly pricing, then by local governments.[16] The financing of "high roads" should be financed at the national level because their road-use benefits were national in scope. Such roads could also

- Reduce the pricing power of local, monopoly producers,
- Extend the scope of domestic markets,

---

[15] On the taxation of immobile landowners and mobile capitalists, Smith opined,

[L]and is a subject which cannot be removed; whereas stock easily may. The proprietor of land is necessarily a citizen of the particular country in which his estate lies. The proprietor of stock is properly a citizen of the world, and is not necessarily attached to any particular country. He would be apt to abandon the country in which he was exposed to a vexatious inquisition, in order to be assessed to a burdensome tax, and would remove his stock to some other country where he could either carry on his business, or enjoy his fortune more at his ease. By removing his stock he would put an end to all the industry which it had maintained in the country which he left. Stock cultivates land; stock employs labor. A tax which tended to drive away stock from any particular country would so far tend to dry up every source of revenue both to the sovereign and to the society. Not only the profits of stock, but the rent of land and the wages of labor would necessarily be more or less diminished by its removal (1776, Sect. V.2.91).

[16] On the monopoly pricing of toll roads, Smith wrote,

In Great Britain, the abuses which the trustees have committed in the management of those tolls have in many cases been very justly complained of. At many turnpikes, it has been said, the money levied is more than double of what is necessary for executing, in the completest manner, the work which is often executed in very slovenly manner, and sometimes not executed at all. The system of repairing the high roads by tolls of this kind, it must be observed, is not of very long standing. We should not wonder, therefore, if it has not yet been brought to that degree of perfection of which it seems capable.[*36] If mean and improper persons are frequently appointed trustees, and if proper courts of inspection and account have not yet been established for controlling their conduct, and for reducing the tolls to what is barely sufficient for executing the work to be done by them, the recency of the institution both accounts and apologizes for those defects, of which, by the wisdom of parliament, the greater part may in due time be gradually remedied (1776, Sect. V.1.79).

- Increase competition across markets, and, therefore,
- Extend the benefits of the division and specialization of labor.[17]

Smith's Organizational Economics

Smith made the economies of division and specialization of labor a linchpin of his growth theory in his *Wealth of Nations*. Specialization of labor generated greater output, but the division of labor was always and everywhere limited by the size of the market. He advocated the abolition of mercantile trade controls partly because this enabled people to buy in more competitive markets where production costs were lower, but also because the elimination of trade barriers extended the scope of markets and increased the potential for economies from greater division of labor.

> As it is the power of exchanging that gives occasion to the division of labor, so the extent of this division must always be limited by the extent of that power, or, in other words, by the extent of the market. When the market is very small, no person can have any encouragement to dedicate himself entirely to one employment, for want of the power to exchange all that surplus part of the produce of his own labor, which is over and above his own consumption, for such parts of the produce of other men's labor as he has occasion for" (1776, Sect. I.3.1).

In short, to reiterate, freer trade within countries (due to public provision of "high roads") or among countries (due to lower shipping costs and/or the reduction of import and export restrictions) could give rise to increasing returns to the scale of markets and, hence, increasing returns to scale for firms, a point Allyn Young (1928), George Stigler (1951), and James Buchanan (1994a,b) resurrected at various times during the twentieth century. This is to say that provision of roads and reductions in trade restrictions had much the same beneficial effects. They both expanded the scope and scale of market that allowed for greater specialization of resources and greater efficiency, which, in turn, heightened competitive market pressures and strengthened the effects of the invisible hand of market orders.

All of Smith's glowing commentaries on economies from labor specialization notwithstanding, he fully recognized that the division of labor within firms also had nontrivial negative effects for workers, not the least of which would be to change

---

[17] On how roads could reduce the power of monopolies, Smith wrote,

> Good roads, canals, and navigable rivers, by diminishing the expense of carriage, put the remote parts of the country more nearly upon a level with those in the neighborhood of the town. They are upon that account the greatest of all improvements. They encourage the cultivation of the remote, which must always be the most extensive circle of the country. They are advantageous to the town, by breaking down the monopoly of the country in its neighborhood. They are advantageous even to that part of the country. Though they introduce some rival commodities into the old market, they open many new markets to its produce" (1776, Sect. I.11.14).

people's preferences and proclivity and to undermine the invisible hand of morality, as well as making them as "stupid and ignorant as it is possible for a human creature to become (1776, Sect. V.1.1.178).[18]

Similarly, the creation of monopolies had societal costs that supersede the inefficiency from monopolists' curbs in production and hikes in prices. "The wretched spirit of monopoly" (Smith's phrase) also undermined management efficiency:

> Monopoly, besides, is a great enemy to good management, which can never be universally established but in consequence of that free and universal competition which forces every body to have recourse to it for the sake of self-defence. It is not more than fifty years ago, that some of the counties in the neighborhood of London petitioned the parliament against the extension of the turnpike roads into the remoter counties. Those remoter counties, they pretended, from the cheapness of labor, would be able to sell their grass and corn cheaper in the London market than themselves, and would thereby reduce their rents, and ruin their cultivation. Their rents, however, have risen, and their cultivation has been improved since that time (1776, Sect. I.11.14).

Moreover, Smith constantly berated various people – whether members of the landed gentry or nobility – for their "ostentation." Indeed, an additional problem of monopoly is that market pricing power, enabled, perhaps, through import restrictions, would leave many rich producers with more income than they could spend without resort to ostentatious and wasteful consumption.

---

[18] Smith elaborated on the downside of specialization on workers' character:

> In the progress of the division of labor, the employment of the far greater part of those who live by labor, that is, of the great body of the people, comes to be confined to a few very simple operations, frequently to one or two. But the understandings of the greater part of men are necessarily formed by their ordinary employments. The man whose whole life is spent in performing a few simple operations, of which the effects are perhaps always the same, or very nearly the same, has no occasion to exert his understanding or to exercise his invention in finding out expedients for removing difficulties which never occur. He naturally loses, therefore, the habit of such exertion, and generally becomes as stupid and ignorant as it is possible for a human creature to become. The torpor of his mind renders him not only incapable of relishing or bearing a part in any rational conversation, but of conceiving any generous, noble, or tender sentiment, and consequently of forming any just judgment concerning many even of the ordinary duties of private life. Of the great and extensive interests of his country he is altogether incapable of judging, and unless very particular pains have been taken to render him otherwise, he is equally incapable of defending his country in war. The uniformity of his stationary life naturally corrupts the courage of his mind, and makes him regard with abhorrence the irregular, uncertain, and adventurous life of a soldier. It corrupts even the activity of his body, and renders him incapable of exerting his strength with vigor and perseverance in any other employment than that to which he has been bred. His dexterity at his own particular trade seems, in this manner, to be acquired at the expense of his intellectual, social, and martial virtues. But in every improved and civilized society this is the state into which the laboring poor, that is, the great body of the people, must necessarily fall, unless government takes some pains to prevent it (1776, Sect. V.1.1.178).

When neither commerce nor manufactures furnish anything for which the owner can exchange the greater part of those materials which are over and above his own consumption, he can do nothing with the surplus but feed and clothe nearly as many people as it will feed and clothe. A hospitality in which there is no luxury, and a liberality in which there is no ostentation, occasion, in this situation of things, the principal expenses of the rich and the great. But these, I have likewise endeavored to show in the same book, are expenses by which people are not very apt to ruin themselves. There is not, perhaps, any selfish pleasure so frivolous of which the pursuit has not sometimes ruined even sensible men. A passion for cock-fighting has ruined many. But the instances, I believe, are not very numerous of people who have been ruined by a hospitality or liberality of this kind, though the hospitality of luxury and the liberality of ostentation have ruined many (1776, Sect. V.3.1).

While a religious person himself, Smith was no fan of the "ostentation" and "fanaticism" of religious leaders. In effect, he pressed for the religious sector to be organized more or less like open and unfettered competitive markets, with the competing sects imposing checks on the zeal and ostentation of various sect leaders:

> The interested and active zeal of religious teachers can be dangerous and troublesome only where there is either but one sect tolerated in the society, or where the whole of a large society is divided into two or three great sects; the teachers of each[*143] acting by concert, and under a regular discipline and subordination. But that zeal must be altogether innocent where the society is divided into two or three hundred, or perhaps into as many thousand small sects, of which no one could be considerable enough to disturb the public tranquility. The teachers of each sect, seeing themselves surrounded on all sides with more adversaries than friends, would be obliged to learn that candor and moderation which is so seldom to be found among the teachers of those great sects whose tenets, being supported by the civil magistrate, are held in veneration by almost all the inhabitants of extensive kingdoms and empires, and who therefore see nothing round them but followers, disciples, and humble admirers. The teachers of each little sect, finding themselves almost alone, would be obliged to respect those of almost every other sect, and the concessions which they would mutually find it both convenient and agreeable to make to one another, might in time probably reduce the doctrine of the greater part of them to that pure and rational religion, free from every mixture of absurdity, imposture, or fanaticism, such as wise men have in all ages of the world wished to see established; but such as positive law has perhaps never yet established, and probably never will establish, in any country: because, with regard to religion, positive law always has been, and probably always will be, more or less influenced by popular superstition and enthusiasm (1776, Sect. V.1.197).

Smith on Education

Smith was not shy about presenting his own brand of the economics of education, as well as religion, although his central concern remained about the appropriate role of government and institutions in affecting trade. He opposed "long apprenticeships" because they were a form of "slavery" contrived to hold down the effective wages masters paid their apprentices.[19]

While Smith made the case for state funding of basic education, he stopped short of advocating *full* funding of education at any level, even when the societal benefits could justify the costs (absent behavioral changes). He argued that a portion of the funding of education should come from the students, or their families, only to ensure that teachers had an incentive to make their classes meaningful to the students and their parents. And Smith was indeed surprisingly harsh on his university colleagues, especially in the science departments, who were paid salaries either by the state or out of their universities' endowments for delivering uninspired and out-of-date, perhaps worthless, courses.

> If the teacher happens to be a man of sense, it must be an unpleasant thing to him to be conscious, while he is lecturing his students, that he is either speaking or reading nonsense, or what is very little better than nonsense. It must, too, be unpleasant to him to observe that the greater part of his students desert his lectures; or perhaps attend upon them with plain enough marks of neglect, contempt, and derision. If he is obliged, therefore, to give a certain number of lectures, these motives alone, without any other interest, might dispose him to take some pains to give tolerably good ones. Several different expedients, however, may be fallen upon which will effectually blunt the edge of all those incitements to diligence. The teacher, instead of explaining to his pupils himself the science in which he proposes to instruct them, may read some book upon it; and if this book is written in a foreign and dead language, by interpreting it to them into their own; or, what would give him still less trouble, by making them interpret it to him, and by now and then making an occasional remark upon it, he may flatter himself that he is giving a lecture. The slightest

---

[19] On long apprenticeships, Smith observed,

> Long apprenticeships are altogether unnecessary. The arts, which are much superior to common trades, such as those of making clocks and watches, contain no such mystery as to require a long course of instruction. The first invention of such beautiful machines, indeed, and even that of some of the instruments employed in making them, must, no doubt, have been the work of deep thought and long time, and may justly be considered as among the happiest efforts of human ingenuity. But when both have been fairly invented and are well understood, to explain to any young man, in the completest manner, how to apply the instruments and how to construct the machines, cannot well require more than the lessons of a few weeks: perhaps those of a few days might be sufficient. In the common mechanic trades, those of a few days might certainly be sufficient. The dexterity of hand, indeed, even in common trades, cannot be acquired without much practice and experience. But a young man would practise with much more diligence and attention, if from the beginning he wrought as a journeyman, being paid in proportion to the little work which he could execute, and paying in his turn for the materials which he might sometimes spoil through awkwardness and inexperience. His education would generally in this way be more effectual, and always less tedious and expensive. The master, indeed, would be a loser. He would lose all the wages of the apprentice, which he now saves, for seven years together. In the end, perhaps, the apprentice himself would be a loser. In a trade so easily learnt he would have more competitors, and his wages, when he came to be a complete workman, would be much less than at present. The same increase of competition would reduce the profits of the masters as well as the wages of the workmen. The trades, the crafts, the mysteries,[*44] would all be losers. But the public would be a gainer, the work of all artificers coming in this way much cheaper to market (1776, Sect. I.10.71).

degree of knowledge and application will enable him to do this without exposing himself to contempt or derision, or saying anything that is really foolish, absurd, or ridiculous. The discipline of the college, at the same time, may enable him to force all his pupils to the most regular attendance upon this sham-lecture, and to maintain the most decent and respectful behavior during the whole time of the performance (1776, Sect. V.1.142).

At times Smith wrote as if he thought that the only lectures given by his academic colleagues that were not out of date were given in dead-language courses.[20] Smith wrote, "The discipline of colleges and universities is in general contrived, not for the benefit of the students, but for the interest, or more properly speaking, for the ease of the masters. Its object is, in all cases, to maintain the authority of the master, and whether he neglects or performs his duty, to oblige the students in all cases to behave to him, as if he performed it with the greatest diligence and ability" (1776, Sect. V.1.143).[21]

---

[20] On out-of-date university courses and the quality-enhancing benefits of teachers being dependent on the "fees and honoraries of his scholars," Smith wrote,

> In England the public schools are much less corrupted than the universities. In the schools the youth are taught, or at least may be taught, Greek and Latin; that is, everything which the masters pretend to teach, or which, it is expected, they should teach. In the universities the youth neither are taught, nor always can find any proper means of being taught, the sciences which it is the business of those incorporated bodies to teach. The reward of the schoolmaster in most cases depends principally, in some cases almost entirely, upon the fees or honoraries of his scholars. Schools have no exclusive privileges. In order to obtain the honors of graduation, it is not necessary that a person should bring a certificate of his having studied a certain number of years at a public school. If upon examination he appears to understand what is taught there, no questions are asked about the place where he learnt it (1776, Sect. V.1.145).

[21] Smith continues his attack on what he saw as the sorry state of university instruction:

> It seems to presume perfect wisdom and virtue in the one order, and the greatest weakness and folly in the other. Where the masters, however, really perform their duty, there are no examples, I believe, that the greater part of the students ever neglect theirs. No discipline is ever requisite to force attendance upon lectures which are really worth the attending, as is well known wherever any such lectures are given. Force and restraint may, no doubt, be in some degree requisite in order to oblige children, or very young boys, to attend to those parts of education which it is thought necessary for them to acquire during that early period of life; but after twelve or thirteen years of age, provided the master does his duty, force or restraint can scarce ever be necessary to carry on any part of education. Such is the generosity of the greater part of young men, that, so far from being disposed to neglect or despise the instructions of their master, provided he shows some serious intention of being of use to them, they are generally inclined to pardon a great deal of incorrectness in the performance of his duty, and sometimes even to conceal from the public a good deal of gross negligence (1776, Sect. V.1.143).

Concluding Comments

Contrary to what his supporters and detractors might believe, Smith hardly assumed that people were motivated exclusively by their own narrow self-interest, and neither was self-interest unchecked in Smith's way of thinking about political economy. Moreover, Smith seemed to feel free to play through the logic of self-interest that motivated people everywhere because he assumed that market competition would seriously check much self-interested behavior. Even market competition, and the behavior of many, if not most, people in markets, would be checked by laws and customs, by the impact of people's impartial spectators, and by innate drives to empathize with and to do right by others. Again, self-interest and self-love – and, indeed, *homo economicus* – in Smith's worldview were severely bounded on, practically, all sides.

I can only surmise that Smith was of the opinion that if self-interest of enough people were not so sufficiently circumscribed by nonself-interest motivations, then far too many human "passions" would indeed "run headlong.....after their own gratification" (1776, Sect. VI.III.55). Markets might not work at all, much less work well, to improve societal well-being if self-interest were not bounded and directed by other motivations. Smith does write at length about the absence of economic improvement within "barbarous" groups of people where violence or threat of violence undermined people's incentive to "augment" their "stocks" of capital.[22]

Smith was hardly the fabled one-arm (or one-hand) economist. As noted, his methodology for developing market economics was decidedly two-handed (at least), with both hands – market competition and morality – being more or less

---

[22] On the connection of violence and threat of violence to capital accumulation, Smith wrote,

> Order and good government, and along with them the liberty and security of individuals, were, in this manner, established in cities at a time when the occupiers of land in the country were exposed to every sort of violence. But men in this defenseless state naturally content themselves with their necessary subsistence, because to acquire more might only tempt the injustice of their oppressors. On the contrary, when they are secure of enjoying the fruits of their industry, they naturally exert it to better their condition, and to acquire not only the necessaries, but the conveniences and elegancies of life. That industry, therefore, which aims at something more than necessary subsistence, was established in cities long before it was commonly practised by the occupiers of land in the country. If in the hands of a poor cultivator, oppressed with the servitude of villanage, some little stock should accumulate, he would naturally conceal it with great care from his master, to whom it would otherwise have belonged, and take the first opportunity of running away to a town. The law was at that time so indulgent to the inhabitants of towns, and so desirous of diminishing the authority of the lords over those of the country, that if he could conceal himself there from the pursuit of his lord for a year, he was free for ever. Whatever stock, therefore, accumulated in the hands of the industrious part of the inhabitants of the country naturally took refuge in cities as the only sanctuaries in which it could be secure to the person that acquired it (1776, Sect. III.3.12).

See also Smith (1776, Sects. II.1.31, III.2.14).

"invisible," by which he surely meant that people could not see the societal consequences of their own individual behaviors. Smith's goal in *Wealth of Nations* and *Theory of Moral Sentiments* was to make the invisible hands of markets and morality sufficiently transparent to readers and policymakers that they would be led to highly deliberate and visible reforms, principally in the form of striking down trade impediments in the mercantile system and in other ways expanding the scope and scale of markets to benefit society. He crusaded for government to become a less visible, if not invisible, hand in how resources are allocated, mainly by relegating itself to establishing the background conditions for the working of the invisible hands of markets and morality.

Hence, Smith hardly limited himself to one side of the great methodological divide contemporary economists have adopted between *positive* and *normative* economics. Neither did Smith restrict societal improvements from the interplay of his two invisible hands to simple resource allocative and wealth gains that could be induced from shifting known resources among known wants. He might even consider such gains trivial when compared with the potential far greater gains that can come from the extension of markets, leading not only to new producers and consumers, but also to additional competition from new ideas and new goods and from people's fortified propensities to do right by others. Smith seemed to believe that societal gains could be achieved only when his two invisible hands worked in concert, with each hand reinforcing the power and influence of the other. Clearly, if markets led to outcomes that could not be known beforehand by market participants, he had to believe that wants and resources could not be given and that the societal value of market outcomes superseded the elementary efficiency gains economists focus on when they write and talk about improvements from the allocation of known resources among known wants through trades.

Although Smith acknowledged the socially constructive force of nonself-interest motivations (for example, beneficence), he seemed never to feel compelled to found his analyses on a premise that people act *as if* they were guided by self-interest or self-love (and never came close to saying as much). As has been noted, Smith was obviously confident that people were not "defective of selfishness" (1759, Sect. VII. II.87), so much so that Smith understood why people were shocked when they observed others acting with concern for others they did not know with some intimacy (1759, Sect. I.I.14). Moreover, Smith was confident in the power of self-interest to override, at least within broader market contexts, natural and human-made obstacles to people's individual self- and, hence, societal-improvement.

> The natural effort of every individual to better his own condition, when suffered to exert itself with freedom and security is so powerful a principle that it is alone, and without any assistance, not only capable of carrying on the society to wealth and prosperity, but of surmounting a hundred impertinent obstructions with which the folly of human laws too often encumbers its operations (1776, Sect. IV.5.82).

It was largely through competitive market forces that, in Smith's worldview, the drive of self-interest would lead all market participants by an invisible hand to place additional competitive market checks on others who either lacked a clear understanding of their self-interest or were inclined to conduct their business outside of the dictates of the law and the broadly accepted societal norms of commerce. Markets, in other words, had built-in corrective pressures. Still, in Smith's world view, it is important to remember that motivations such as benevolence were important within families and circles of friends.

Finally, Smith never allowed his bounded view of self-interest to curb his expansive view of the scope of economic analysis. However, it seems altogether reasonable to deduce that Smith believed that the further economic analytics veered from strictly market, or commercial, interactions, the more the self-interest motivation might give way to other motivations.

Smith could easily found his economic analytics on an array of human motivations and constraints because he did not tie himself to mathematical methods and the demands of positivism. He often provided an array of anecdotal evidence and sometimes data, but he never felt compelled to support his argument with the statistical rigor used by neoclassical economics that, as was argued in Chap. 2, puts limits on the behavioral motivations of the human beings under study. Moreover, statistical analysis and data were obviously limited in Smith's era, which was reason enough for his limited faith in what he called "political arithmetic."[23]

---

[23] Smith wrote, "I have no great faith in political arithmetic, computations. I mention them only in order to show how much less consequence, in the opinion of the most judicious and experienced persons, the foreign trade of corn is than the home trade" (1776, IV.5.69).

Chapter 4
Rationality in Economic Thought: From Thomas Robert Malthus to Alfred Marshall and Philip Wicksteed

In the last chapter, Adam Smith's perspective on what, at a fundamental level, makes people tick was explored. We found that he placed great emphasis on the drives of self-interest and self-love. However, we also found that even in commercial settings in which people sought the cooperation of a multitude of others, Smith held strongly to a form of self-interest and self-love, bounded by innate and learned morality and restrained by laws and market competition.

In this chapter, my main interest will be Alfred Marshall's perspective on human motivation, especially, in commercial dealings. I offer two reasons for the focus of the chapter. First, Marshall (1842–1924) remains a towering prominence in the history of economics mainly for making key economic concepts centerpieces of the economic way of thinking, including supply and demand curves, equilibrium, consumer and producer surpluses, time periods (market period, short period, and long period), and elasticity. Toward the end of the nineteenth century, he gave coherence to the then-budding neoclassical economics, sparked by the marginal revolution in the 1870s.

Second, Marshall's treatise *Principles of Economics* (1920), first published in 1890 dominated economics instruction at the university level on both sides of the Atlantic until World War II. Although, as we will see, Marshall himself had an expansive view of human motivations (following more in the footsteps of Adam Smith than David Ricardo), Marshall's methodological refinements developed in his treatise (which supplanted in classrooms John Stuart Mill's long-used text) were instrumental in diverting economists' attention from Smith's long-term growth-oriented analytics toward shorter-term static analysis. Marshall's more formalized analytics narrowed, albeit inadvertently, economists' attention to people's behavioral goals grounded in finely drawn cost–benefit comparisons, which has led economists to drop, at least for their equilibrium-centered, static analytics, the full swath of human motivations that Smith and earlier economists/moral philosophers believed contained and directed self-interest. The nonself-interest drives provided social gains in their own right, independent of any effect they had directly or indirectly on the pursuit of self-interest. To understand Marshall's perspective, however, we need some familiarity with the key contributions of economists between

R.B. McKenzie, *Predictably Rational?*,
DOI 10.1007/978-3-642-01586-1_4, © Springer-Verlag Berlin Heidelberg 2010

Smith and Marshall, including those who fathered the marginal revolution in the last third of the nineteenth century.

At the end of this chapter, Philip Wicksteed's views on human motivation, mainly because of his insistence in his early twentieth century textbook *Common Sense of Political Economy* (1910) that economics was an expansive, if not unbounded, means of assessing, understanding, and predicting human behavior. He stressed economics was a way of thinking, not a catalogue of topics limited to business or markets, which was Marshall's perspective, a shift in emphasis that freed later economists to engage in what has come to be almost unchecked economic imperialism.

Malthusian Constraints on "Rational Beings"

In his *An Essay on the Principle of Population* (1798), the Reverend Thomas Robert Malthus (1766–1834) drew a theme from Smith's *Wealth of Nations*, conceding that it would be "inexpressibly grand and captivating" if society could count on benevolence, not self-love, as the "moving principle of society," because then "every individual is in a manner the slave of the public": "But, alas! that moment can never arrive. The whole is little better than a dream, a beautiful phantom of the imagination." These "gorgeous palaces" of happiness and immortality, these "solemn temples" of truth and virtue will dissolve, "like the baseless fabric of a vision, when we awaken to real life, and contemplate the true and genuine situation of man on earth" (1798, Sect. X.2).

Malthus also proposed that "inferior," "unproductive," and "menial" workers would always have a tough time living for very long much above subsistence, because the supply of labor in lower working classes is necessarily highly elastic with respect to real wages, and also because workers would be paid out of a fixed wage fund.[1] Malthus fully adopted the wage–fund theory of wage rates and

---

[1] In anticipating Malthus, Smith wrote on how subsistence living makes for an overabundance of available workers and a highly responsive labor supply:

> Though the wealth of a country should be very great, yet if it has been long stationary, we must not expect to find the wages of labor very high in it. The funds destined for the payment of wages, the revenue and stock of its inhabitants, may be of the greatest extent; but if they have continued for several centuries of the same, or very nearly of the same extent, the number of laborers employed every year could easily supply, and even more than supply, the number wanted the following year. There could seldom be any scarcity of hands, nor could the masters be obliged to bid against one another in order to get them. The hands, on the contrary, would, in this case, naturally multiply beyond their employment. There would be a constant scarcity of employment, and the laborers would be obliged to bid against one another in order to get it. If in such a country the wages of labor had ever been more than sufficient to maintain the laborer, and to enable him to bring up a family, the competition of the laborers and the interest of the masters would soon reduce them to this lowest rate which is consistent with common humanity. China has been long one of the richest, that is, one of

the most fertile, best cultivated, most industrious, and most populous countries in the world. It seems, however, to have been long stationary. Marco Polo, who visited it more than 500 years ago, describes its cultivation, industry, and populousness, almost in the same terms in which they are described by travelers in the present times. It had perhaps, even long before his time, acquired that full complement of riches which the nature of its laws and institutions permits it to acquire. The accounts of all travelers, inconsistent in many other respects, agree in the low wages of labor, and in the difficulty which a laborer finds in bringing up a family in China. If by digging the ground a whole day he can get what will purchase a small quantity of rice in the evening, he is contented. The condition of artificers is, if possible, still worse. Instead of waiting indolently in their work-houses, for the calls of their customers, as in Europe, they are continually running about the streets with the tools of their respective trades, offering their service, and as it were begging employment. The poverty of the lower ranks of people in China far surpasses that of the most beggarly nations in Europe. In the neighborhood of Canton many hundred, it is commonly said, many thousand families have no habitation on the land, but live constantly in little fishing boats upon the rivers and canals. The subsistence which they find there is so scanty that they are eager to fish up the nastiest garbage thrown overboard from any European ship. Any carrion, the carcass of a dead dog or cat, for example, though half putrid and stinking, is as welcome to them as the most wholesome food to the people of other countries. Marriage is encouraged in China, not by the profitableness of children, but by the liberty of destroying them. In all great towns, several are every night exposed in the street, or drowned like puppies in the water. The performance of this horrid office is even said to be the avowed business by which some people earn their subsistence (1776, Sect. I.6.5).

Smith also observed,

But it would be otherwise in a country where the funds destined for the maintenance of labor were sensibly decaying. Every year the demand for servants and laborers would, in all the different classes of employments, be less than that had been the year before. Many who had been bred in the superior classes, not being able to find employment in their own business, would be glad to seek it in the lowest. The lowest class being not only overstocked with its own workmen, but with the overflowings of all the other classes, the competition for employment would be so great in it, as to reduce the wages of labor to the most miserable and scanty subsistence of the laborer. Many would not be able to find employment even upon these hard terms, but would either starve, or be driven to seek a subsistence either by begging, or by the perpetration, perhaps, of the greatest enormities. Want, famine, and mortality would immediately prevail in that class, and from thence extend themselves to all the superior classes, till the number of inhabitants in the country was reduced to what could easily be maintained by the revenue and stock which remained in it, and which had escaped either the tyranny or calamity which had destroyed the rest. This, perhaps, is nearly the present state of Bengal, and of some other of the English settlements in the East Indies. In a fertile country which had before been much depopulated, where subsistence, consequently, should not be very difficult, and where, notwithstanding, 300,000 or 400,000 people die of hunger in 1 year, we may be assured that the funds destined for the maintenance of the laboring poor are fast decaying. The difference between the genius of the British constitution which protects and governs North America, and that of the mercantile company which oppresses and domineers in the East Indies, cannot, perhaps, be better illustrated than by the different state of those countries. The liberal reward of labor, therefore, as it is the necessary effect, so it is the natural symptom of increasing national wealth. The scanty maintenance of the laboring poor, on the other hand, is the natural symptom that things are at a stand, and their starving condition that they are going fast backwards (1776, Sect. I.8.26).

constructed a form of highly circumscribed bounded rationality (although he never used the expression) founded on two postulates, which to Malthus amounted to two of several tightly binding biological/physiological constraints on the pursuit of self-interest and rational decision making: "First, that food is necessary to the existence of man. Secondly, that the passion between the sexes is necessary and will remain nearly in its present state" (1798, Sect. I.14).

Indeed, Malthus thought that founding economic discussions on presumed "rational beings," as William Godwin (1756–1836), whom Malthus frequently used as a scholarly foil, suggested was "beautiful and engaging," but something of a philosophical snare and delusion.[2] In addition to the passion for sexes, Malthus listed other biology-based preference that effectively constrained people

> The cravings of hunger, the love of liquor, the desire of possessing a beautiful woman, will urge men to actions, of the fatal consequences of which, to the general interests of society, they are perfectly well convinced, even at the very time they commit them. Remove their bodily cravings, and they would not hesitate a moment in determining against such actions. Ask them their opinion of the same conduct in another person, and they would immediately reprobate it. But in their own case, and under all the circumstances of their situation with these bodily cravings, the decision of the compound being is different from the conviction of the rational being (1798, Sect. XIII.3).

According to Malthus, the "passion of the sexes" was difficult to control, and therefore any short-term run-up in worker wages would ultimately be suppressed by an increase in the supply of labor through population growth. Only by foregoing or delayed marriage (his preventive or "prudential" check) or "periodical pestilences or famine" and war (his "positive" check) could curb this growth (1798, Sect. VII.11).[3] Malthus has long been criticized for his giving economics a dismal twist,

---

[2] Malthus wrote about Godwin's construction of deliberative "rational beings":

> The system of equality which Mr. Godwin proposes, is, without doubt, by far the most beautiful and engaging of any that has yet appeared. An amelioration of society to be produced merely by reason and conviction, wears much more the promise of permanence, than any change effected and maintained by force. The unlimited exercise of private judgement, is a doctrine inexpressibly grand and captivating, and has a vast superiority over those systems where every individual is in a manner the slave of the public. The substitution of benevolence as the master-spring, and moving principle of society, instead of self-love, is a consummation devoutly to be wished. In short, it is impossible to contemplate the whole of this fair structure, without emotions of delight and admiration, accompanied with ardent longing for the period of its accomplishment. But, alas! that moment can never arrive. The whole is little better than a dream, a beautiful phantom of the imagination. These "gorgeous palaces" of happiness and immortality, these "solemn temples" of truth and virtue will dissolve, "like the baseless fabric of a vision," when we awaken to real life, and contemplate the true and genuine situation of man on earth (1798, Sect. X.2).

[3] Malthus wrote,

> The passion between the sexes has appeared in every age to be so nearly the same that it may always be considered, in algebraic language, as a given quantity. The great law of necessity which prevents population from increasing in any country beyond the food which

made dismal because of the presumption that an arithmetic growth in food supply would conflict with a geometric growth in population, with Malthus denying all prospects for any long-term improvement in worker wages.[4]

While Malthus may rightfully be faulted for failing to anticipate the growth in real worker wages in the nineteenth century, after the Industrial Revolution was in full swing, new historical research suggests that Malthus and his immediate followers, especially, David Ricardo, had good reason to be pessimistic about worker productivity and welfare growth ever outstripping the natural increase in labor supply attributable to improved income standards. According to University of California, Davis economic historian Gregory Clark, there was indeed a "Malthusian wage trap" through human history until the early 1800s. In humankind's hunter-gatherer days, ten thousand or more years ago, economic life for bands of 25–150 humans was largely equalitarian. On the other hand, marked class inequality in living standards was a hallmark of agrarian/market economies in England (and other European countries) in 1800. Clark figures that the annual rate of technological advance before 1800 was a scant 0.05 percent, which translates into a doubling of average worker income in about fourteen hundred years – provided there were no setbacks to technology growth due to wars, plagues, inquisitions, and famines, which, of course, there were. Clark wrote, "Jane Austen may have written about refined conversations over tea served in china cups. But for the majority of the English, as late as 1813, conditions were no better than their naked ancestors of the African savannah." Clark adds a stark observation: "So, even according to the broadest measures of material life, average welfare, if anything, declined from the Stone Age to 1800. The poor of 1800, those who lived by their unskilled labor alone, would have been better off if transferred to a hunter–gatherer band" (Clark 2007, p. 2).

A Malthusian picture of economic history of the world is stunningly portrayed, according to Clark, by the path of real income per person for all years between 1000

---

it can either produce or acquire, is a law, so open to our view, so obvious and evident to our understandings, and so completely confirmed by the experience of every age, that we cannot for a moment doubt it. The different modes which nature takes to prevent or repress a redundant population, do not appear, indeed, to us so certain and regular; but though we cannot always predict the mode, we may with certainty predict the fact. If the proportion of births to deaths for a few years, indicate an increase of numbers much beyond the proportional increased or acquired produce of the country, we may be perfectly certain, that unless an emigration takes place, the deaths will shortly exceed the births; and that the increase that had taken place for a few years cannot be the real average increase of the population of the country. Were there no other depopulating causes, every country would, without doubt, be subject to periodical pestilences or famine (1798, Sect. VII.11).

[4]Many economists believe that Thomas Carlyle dubbed economics as the "dismal science" because of Malthus' population theory. However, David Levy and Sandra Peart argue that conventional wisdom is all wrong," Carlyle's target was not Malthus, but economists such as John Stuart Mill, who argued that it was institutions, not race, that explained why some nations were rich and others poor. Carlyle attacked Mill, not for supporting Malthus's predictions about the dire consequences of population growth, but for supporting the emancipation of slaves. It was this fact – that economics assumed that people were basically all the same, and thus all entitled to liberty – that led Carlyle to label economics 'the dismal science'" (Levy 2001).

and 2000 AD relative to the real income per person in 1800. Average real income wiggles above and below the flat average real income from 1000 through the early 1800s, after which the effects of the Industrial Revolution kick in dramatically, with average real income rising almost vertically over the next two centuries. Although some economic historians have found some income growth between 1500 and 1800, most agree with Clark's assessment that average growth in real worker well-being prior to 1800 was fairly meager, falling far short of the growth rate for the 1800s, and that some of the increase in worker living standards in the 1800s can be attributable to growing industriousness of workers (meaning the length of time and intensity of effort workers applied to their jobs) during the Industrial Revolution. (The exact growth in the degree of worker industriousness is controversial, and Clark does not recognize a divergence in population growth in England and on the continent, according to other economic historians [de Vries 1994; Pomeranz 2000]).

Even though Malthus was a minister (but only to the extent that he took the holy orders as a part of accepting a Cambridge Fellowship) and could see virtue, prudence, and a sense of justice being passed from parents to children in all social strata (1798, Sect. IV.VIII.16), his population economics did not reflect the full graciousness and optimism of the human spirit evident in Smith's economics. While people might often express compassion for others, Malthus certainly was not willing to believe that human compassion could be counted on to materially relieve people's suffering from overpopulation and famine:

> The emotion which prompts us to relieve our fellow-creatures in distress is, like all our other natural passions, general, and, in some degree, indiscriminate and blind. Our feelings of compassion may be worked up to a higher pitch by a well-wrought scene in a play, or a fictitious tale in a novel, than by almost any events in real life: and if among ten petitioners we were to listen only to the first impulses of our feelings without making further inquiries, we should undoubtedly give our assistance to the best actor of the party. It is evident, therefore, that the impulse of benevolence, like the impulses of love, of anger, of ambition, the desire of eating and drinking, or any other of our natural propensities, must be regulated by experience, and frequently brought to the test of utility, or it will defeat its intended purpose (1798, Sect. IV.X.2).

Clearly, if Clark's data are correct (or even if it is just close), Malthus was a reasonably good economic historian – up to his time. On the other hand, if Clark's data are correct, Adam Smith was a poor economic historian, given that his invisible-hand model of market economies suggested that most workers, landlords, and capitalists should have been sharing in the economic gains arising from the drive of self-interest that had been around for millennia and from market institutions (legally protected property rights and norms and negotiated prices) that by 1776 had been in place for at least a couple hundred years, and maybe much longer (Clark 2007, Chap. 11). While landlords and capitalists might have been getting progressively richer prior to the publication of *Wealth of Nations*, most workers were not. Smith, however, proved to be a good prognosticator of the future of the economy, if trade restraints were abolished and markets were expanded, with the gains garnered from greater division of labor continuing apace from freer and expanded trade and technological advances. However, as is widely recognized and self-evident in wage statistics since Malthus penned his population thesis, Malthus turned out to be a poor prognosticator of long-term economic developments (as if anyone should be faulted for not predicting the upswing in average worker welfare after 1800 from the vantage point of the late 1790s).

I recount Malthus' views on population growth and worker welfare to make a point on rationality in the context of his broader view of the fate of humankind: Rationality did not play a meaningful role in Malthusian economics simply because there was very little for people to be rational about. According to Malthus, people's libidos largely controlled their economic fates as workers and consumers (although he gave people some control over births through their marriage decisions). The great masses of people lived so close to subsistence for so much of the time that there were few degrees of freedom for them (ordinary workers, not so much the nobility and landed aristocracy) to be rational about; workers had few and fleeting options in life. Clark concludes that "those scourges of failed modern states – war, violence, disorder, harvest failures, collapsed public infrastructures, bad sanitation – were the friends of mankind before 1800" – because curbed population growth and worker competition had allowed for worker wages to rise, at least temporarily, more or less exactly as Malthus surmised (Clark 2007, p. 5). In the Malthusian view of the world, the choice set facing the masses was tightly constrained. Why dwell on the rational sphere of life is a question that must have constrained the methodological musings of Malthus and his followers.

Ricardo's Methodological Shift Toward Formalized Political Economy

In the century following the publication of Smith's *Wealth of Nations*, economics took shape as a distinct discipline founded on the works of any number of economists who, to a nontrivial degree, restated and refined Smith's market principles. Several economists, including David Ricardo (1772–1823) and Karl Marx (1818–1883), adopted Malthus' population theory and iron law of wages, thus leaving the overwhelming majority of economic actors (workers) in their models with not a great deal of wiggle room for meaningful rational choices, much less choices founded on other human motivations.

Ricardo did advance trade theory in one important way in that he greatly expanded the potential for trades within and across countries' borders. Smith showed the advantages of trade based on absolute production or cost advantages, not realizing (apparently) that comparative, rather than absolute, costs were the key to determining the feasibility and direction of domestic and international trade. David Ricardo in his *On the Principles of Political Economy and Taxation* (1821, with the first edition published in 1817) refined Smith's discussion of the market source of rent, but, more importantly, filled in the gap, or oversight, in Smith's trade theory, most notably observing that trade was founded on comparative, not absolute, cost advantages.

To produce the wine in Portugal, might require only the labor of 80 men for 1 year, and to produce the cloth in the same country, might require the labor of 90 men for the same time. It would therefore be advantageous for her to export wine in exchange for cloth. This exchange might even take place, notwithstanding that the commodity imported by Portugal could be produced there with less labor than in England. Though she could make the cloth with the labor of 90 men, she would import it from a country where it required the labor of 100 men to produce it, because it would be advantageous to her rather to employ her capital in the production of wine, for which she would obtain more cloth from England, than she could produce by diverting a portion of her capital from the cultivation of vines to the manufacture of cloth (1821, Sect. 7.16).

Otherwise, Ricardo dropped Smith's broad view of human motivations, with the implied restraints on self-interest behavior, which was everywhere evident in Smith. Ricardo dispensed with interjecting his economic analytics with concerns about "vanity," "pride," "virtue," as well as "self-interest," and "self-love," which Smith frequently used. Indeed, Ricardo substantially formalized economics, turning the discipline toward a largely deductive science. With few of Smith's connections to history and real-world anecdotes, Ricardo made the behavior of the actors in his models largely deterministic. If Ricardo gives the economic actors in his models a motivation, it is limited to their employing or redeploying resources with some advantage in mind, or with the goal of seeking the "greatest advantage" (1821, Sect. 14.6). Smith does not leave his readers wondering about why people seek their greatest advantage. They do it out of self-interest or self-love or just "betterment of their condition." Readers of Ricardo are left to wonder why. Perhaps "greatest advantage" is the ultimate motivation, or perhaps "betterment of condition" is presumed because Ricardo sought to build his brand of political economy on Smith's.

Ricardo's construction of human motivation could have been narrower than Smith's, simply because Ricardo saw political economy as having a dramatically different intent than did Smith. Smith was interested in explaining how people were activated to increase their own wealth and, coincidentally, the wealth of others and the nation, an unheralded positive outcome not widely recognized before Smith. Ricardo, on the other hand, was largely, if not exclusively, concerned with the issue of income and wealth distribution, or "laws which regulate this distribution" of income among identified classes – landlords, capitalists, and workers – in the form of "rent, profit, and wages." According to Ricardo, prior economists had explored this issue with "little satisfaction" (1821, Sect. P.3). Ricardo's redirection of economic analytics later fueled Marx's critique of Smithian growth-dominated economics and capitalism more generally.

Perhaps, Ricardo focused on the distribution of income because in his view, economic forces apart from individual subjective evaluations determine the level of personal and national income and wealth, and necessarily so. Indeed, aside from a few goods, the values of which were determined by their "scarcities" ("rare statutes and pictures, scarce books and coins, wine of a peculiar quality"), subjective evaluations had, according to Ricardo, little or nothing to do with the overwhelming "mass of commodities daily exchanged in the market," which suggests no need for human motivation and evaluation to activate market exchanges (1821, Sect. 1.5, 1.6).

To Ricardo, the "exchangeable values" or "relative prices" of most goods can only temporarily be affected by the forces of supply and demand.[5] In the main, goods' relative prices, meaning their market values, are determined by their relative labor content (contributed directly by workers and indirectly by the labor embodied in capital): "In speaking then of commodities, of their exchangeable value, and of the laws which regulate their relative prices, we mean always such commodities only as can be increased in quantity by the exertion of human industry, and on the production of which competition operates without restraint" (1821, Sect. 1.7).

Prices of goods and the distribution of income are further constrained and dictated not by the abundance of goods, but rather, more perceptively, by "the difficulty or facility of production," which is always and everywhere constrained by the law of diminishing returns. Ricardo pressed the prospects of diminishing returns because he assumed that the quantity of land used in the then-dominant industry, agriculture, was also more or less fixed (1821, Sect. 20.2). Subjective evaluation was also suppressed in Ricardo's models of markets by his adoption of Malthus' view that the "passion of the sexes" would everywhere tend to drive worker wages to subsistence levels, which suggests the absence of abundant and meaningful economic choices (and any need for rational motivations) for most people.[6] At the same time, the rents of landlords would be increased by the fall in wages, but the landlords' greater rents are attributable not so much to the landlords or workers' choices, made on the basis of their own internally assessed costs and benefits, but

---

[5] On the relative unimportance of demand in influencing the market value of goods, Ricardo mused,

> It is the cost of production which must ultimately regulate the price of commodities, and not, as has been often said, the proportion between the supply and demand: the proportion between supply and demand may, indeed, for a time, affect the market value of a commodity, until it is supplied in greater or less abundance, according as the demand may have increased or diminished; but this effect will be only of temporary duration (1821, Sect. 30.1).

[6] On his admiration for Malthus' theory of population, wages, and rent, Ricardo wrote:

> Although the nature of rent has in the former pages of this work been treated on at some length, yet I consider myself bound to notice some opinions on the subject, which appear to me erroneous, and which are the more important, as they are found in the writings of one, to whom, of all men of the present day, some branches of economical science are the most indebted. Of Mr. Malthus's *Essay on Population*, I am happy in the opportunity here afforded me of expressing my admiration. The assaults of the opponents of this great work have only served to prove its strength; and I am persuaded that its just reputation will spread with the cultivation of that science of which it is so eminent an ornament. Mr. Malthus, too, has satisfactorily explained the principles of rent, and showed that it rises or falls in proportion to the relative advantages, either of fertility or situation, of the different lands in cultivation, and has thereby thrown much light on many difficult points connected with the subject of rent, which were before either unknown, or very imperfectly understood; yet he appears to me to have fallen into some errors, which his authority makes it the more necessary, while his characteristic candor renders it less unpleasing to notice. One of these errors lies in supposing rent to be a clear gain and a new creation of riches (1821, Sect. 32.1).

rather on workers' biologically grounded sexual passions that largely dictated the supply of workers, a process that is on automatic pilot. Workers' futures are bleak indeed, but then they have no choice in the matter. The iron law of wages, not evaluations, governs in the economy in much the same way that gravity governs so much of what happens in the physical world.[7] Ricardo and Malthus (and later Marx) seemed to see most people's choice sets so tightly constrained that the limited cost–benefit calculations available to ordinary people could be, for all practical purposes, ignored.

In *Wealth of Nations* (1776), Smith made a positive case for freer trade (not totally free trade): If trade barriers are reduced, markets will be expanded, resulting in increasing returns and growth in national income from increased division and specialization of labor driven by the people's constrained self-interests. Ricardo's case for freer trade in *Principles* (1821) was far less positive: If trade barriers are reduced, the prices of consumable goods will be reduced because diminishing returns will be held at bay, affected not so much by an expanded market and greater labor specialization, but by an increase in the amount of foreign land employed to produce all the imported goods consumed in the domestic economy. With the drop in the prices of provisions, domestic rents on land would fall, but also wages will, with a delay, tend to fall back to subsistence. Falling wages would allow for greater rents than otherwise for landowners and, at least temporarily, greater profits for capitalists who will invest the profits in capital goods, thus further staving off for a while the binding physical-world constraints of diminishing returns. The school of economic thought fostered by Malthus and Ricardo was, indeed, largely determin- istic and dismal.

Perhaps, Ricardo did not adopt Smith's expansive view of human motivation because he was, after all a banker, not a moralist, and because, like so many economists of the nineteenth century, he wanted to move the discipline away from philosophy and toward science, which he did indeed do. But, he was success- ful only to the extent that he employed deductive reasoning and made the relative market values of goods dependent on something that had, initially at least, all the markings of being objective and quantifiable, the quantity of labor (until it was recognized that there needed to be a common denominator for the differing qualities of labor applied to production directly and for the labor supposedly stored in capital).

Perhaps, taking a more charitable view of his economic modeling, Ricardo dropped Smith's expansive view of human nature for the same reason Frederic Bastiat (1801–1850), a French classical economist and satirist, gave for narrowing his analytical focus to the force of self-interest. Bastiat acknowledged that people could be motivated by "religious sentiments, paternal and maternal affection, filial

---

[7]On subsistence wages, Ricardo wrote, "Diminish the cost of production of hats, and their price will ultimately fall to their new natural price, although the demand should be doubled, trebled, or quadrupled. Diminish the cost of subsistence of men, by diminishing the natural price of the food and clothing, by which life is sustained, and wages will ultimately fall, notwithstanding that the demand for laborers may very greatly increase" (1821, Sect. 30.2).

devotion, love, friendship, patriotism, and politeness," but relegated the study of such motivations to the "moral realm." "Political economy," Bastiat insisted, was narrowly focused on the "cold domain of self-interest" (1850, Sect. 2.19):

> This fact is unfairly forgotten when we reproach political economy with lacking the charm and grace of moral philosophy. How could it be otherwise? Let us challenge the right of political economy to exist as a science, but let us not force it to pretend to be what it is not. If human transactions whose object is wealth are vast enough and complicated enough to constitute a special science, let us grant it its own special appeal, and not reduce it to talking of self-interest in the language of sentiment. I am personally convinced that recently we have done it no service by demanding from it a tone of enthusiastic sentimentality that from its lips can sound only like hollow declamation (1850, Sect. 2.19).

Without material damage to his argument, Bastiat felt he could exclude from consideration the nonself-interest motivations, because in the main the discipline he sought to develop was concerned with the interactions of people who stood at an emotional, social, and geographical distance from one another. As Smith had argued, to seek the cooperation of others at a distance (the butcher, the brewer, or the baker), people had to enlist the only motivation that would work cost effectively, self-interest. In Bastiat's words,

> What does it (political economy) deal with? With transactions carried on between people who do not know each other, who owe each other nothing beyond simple justice, who are defending and seeking to advance their own self-interest. It deals with claims that are restricted and limited by other claims, where self-sacrifice and unselfish dedication have no place. Take up the poet's lyre, then, to speak of these things. I would as soon see Lamartine consult a table of logarithms to sing his odes (1850, Sect. 2.19).

Marx gave birth to his theory of a workers' revolution, essentially, by recognizing and heralding the power of Smith's invisible hand of markets to create wealth and then synthesizing Malthusian and Ricardian economics and throwing in Hegel's dialectic materialism to explain how workers were effectively "chained," with really only one viable course of action for future welfare improvement – overthrow of the capitalist class. After all, "proletarians have nothing to lose but their chains" and the "whole world to win" (Marx 1848, p.81). Workers could appropriate the wealth embedded in the existing capital stock and reclaim rightfully their stored labor and their surplus value that had, under capitalism, been drained from workers by the press of population growth and the Malthusian wage trap. Marx's economics, much like Ricardo's, is largely deterministic and devoid of rational decision making among the masses grounded in incentives. As such, workers need not fear that the wealth built up under capitalism through worker exploitation would disappear. A stock of appropriate labor was like any stock with a real existence in something that was there. Accordingly, workers could appropriate the capital, which, supposedly, would not diminish or change incentives by a takeover of capital by the working class. With the emergence of the Utopian socialist society, workers would work, supposedly, according to their ability even when payments to individuals was made only for need, which suggests that people need not be expected to respond to tax rates, perhaps, reaching 100 percent on the margin, in anything approaching the rational expectations embedded in modern neoclassical economics.

Ricardo and Marx might still today be considered among the ranks of the most prescient economists were it not for an inconvenient truth of the era in which they theorized: Labor productivity and wages began to rise at unprecedented rates – eightfold faster in the 1760–1860 period than in the previous eight centuries – as they wrote their treatises.[8] With the rise in workers' welfares, it made more sense for economists to explore behavior in terms of people having meaningful choices among viable alternatives, which gave rise to a need for subjective evaluation of alternatives (or else what would choices mean?) and to the expectation that people would respond to incentives.

Twixt Adam Smith and Alfred Marshall and the Marginal Revolution

By the time Alfred Marshall first published his *Principles of Economics* in the late 1800s, Smith's expansive nature of human motivations and upbeat assessment of the fate of free-market economics had taken a beating from Ricardo, Malthus, Marx, and their followers. Nevertheless, much progress in methodology was being made on other fronts. French economist Jean-Baptiste Say (1767–1832) introduced *entrepreneur*, along with the conventional trilogy (landlords, laborers, and capitalists), as critical to the advancement of human welfare through market economies (1855).[9] Jeremy Bentham (1748–1832) directed economic inquiry toward methodological individualism under which subjective utility, which could be known only to individuals, had to be at the foundation of all human calculated motivations. As Bentham wrote, "It is in vain to talk of the interest of the community, without understanding what is the interest of the individual. A thing is said to promote the interest, or to be *for* the interest, of an individual, when it tends to add to the sum total of his pleasures: or, what comes to the same thing, to diminish the sum total of his pains" (1781, Sect. I.6, emphasis in the original). Bentham identified four principle sources for pain and pleasures: physical, political, moral, and religious (1781, Sect. III.2.) More important, Bentham insisted that exchange values, or prices, depended not on the absolute scarcity of goods, as Smith had

---

[8] According to Gregory Clark, the growth rate in "national efficiency" rose from an annual rate of 0.05 percent in the eight centuries before 1800 to an annual rate of 0.40 percent between 1760 and 1860 (Clark 2007, pp.232–233).

[9] French economist Richard Cantillon (1680–1734) had first introduced the concept of entrepreneur in his *Essay on the Nature of Trade in General* (1755).

contended,[10] or on the labor content of goods, as Ricardo had insisted, but on buyers' subjective valuations, with Bentham giving all subjective valuations a common denominator, utility. Bentham starts his *An Introduction to the Principles of Morals and Legislation* by observing that

> Nature has placed mankind under the governance of two sovereign masters, *pain* and *pleasure*. It is for them alone to point out what we ought to do, as well as to determine what we shall do. On the one hand the standard of right and wrong, on the other the chain of causes and effects, are fastened to their throne. They govern us in all we do, in all we say, in all we think: every effort we can make to throw off our subjection, will serve but to demonstrate and confirm it. In words a man may pretend to abjure their empire: but in reality he will remain subject to it all the while. The *principle of utility* recognizes this subjection, and assumes it for the foundation of that system, the object of which is to rear the fabric of felicity by the hands of reason and of law. Systems which attempt to question it, deal in sounds instead of sense, in caprice instead of reason, in darkness instead of light (1781, Sect. I.1).

Bentham's principle of utility holds whenever an action increases a person's (or community's) net happiness and holds even when "a man attempts to combat the principle of utility," because subjective utility evaluations must be at the heart of all such efforts (1781, Sect. I.14). Why else would they be undertaken?

Following Say, John Stuart Mill (1806–1873), in his *Principles of Political Economy*, first published in 1848 and widely adopted for university classes until the late nineteenth century, popularized the critical role of entrepreneurs in giving organization and direction to the other factors of production (land, labor, and capital) in market economies. Mill corrected Smith on how the diamond/water paradox could be unraveled, that a thing (diamond) cannot have a value in exchange without having a value in use (Smith had argued diamonds had "scarce any value in use" in spite of their great value in exchange [1776, Sect. I.4.13]) and that a thing's use value imposes an upper limit to the exchange value.[11] Thus, Mill turned economic discussions away from Ricardo's labor theory of market price and toward a subjective theory of price.[12] Market competition could be expected to press

---

[10] Smith wrote on how the absolute scarcity of goods determined their value in exchange: "[T]he value of metals has, in all ages and nations, arisen chiefly from their scarcity, and that their scarcity has arisen from the very small quantities of them which nature has any where deposited in one place, from the hard and intractable substance with which she has almost every where surrounded those small quantities, and consequently from the labor and expense which are every where necessary in order to penetrate and get at them." (1776, Sect. I.11.167).

[11] However, the water/diamond paradox was not finally figured out until the advent of the marginal revolutions during the last third of the nineteenth century.

[12] Mill corrected Smith on the diamond/water paradox in this manner:

> We must begin by settling our phraseology. Adam Smith, in a passage often quoted, has touched upon the most obvious ambiguity of the word value; which, in one of its senses, signifies usefulness, in another, power of purchasing; in his own language, value in use and value in exchange. But (as Mr. De Quincey has remarked) in illustrating this double meaning Adam Smith has himself fallen into another ambiguity. Things (he says) which have the greatest value in use have often little or no value in exchange; which is true, since

market prices toward the good's upper values, which allows for changes in the forces of supply and demand to change market prices (1848, Sect. III.1.9).

With utility introduced as the common denominators to all subjective evaluations and the behavioral goal of utility maximization implied in the work of Bentham and Mill, it was left to William Stanley Jevons (1835–1882), Leon Walras (1834–1910), and Carl Menger (1840–1921) to conclude separately, circa 1870, that diminishing marginal subjective values were crucial to determining market prices. These three economists independently formalized the marginal conditions for utility and profit maximization.[13] Jevons and Walras (but not Menger) reduced utility maximization to mathematical equations, with Jevons declaring that "all economic writers must be mathematical so far as they are scientific at all" (1871, p. xxi). Jevons might well have added that economists could be more mathematical with the discovery of the importance of marginal valuation (or what he called the "final degree of utility," leaving it to Philip Wicksteed to be the first to use "marginal utility" [1888]) in discussions of consumer choices.

Of course, understandably, as the goals of "economic man" in economists' analytics began to narrow to fit the needs of mathematical models, the role of the entrepreneur began to recede from economic discussions precisely because entrepreneurs, who discover unexploited opportunities and bring many new methods of production and new products to the market, were the source of much unanticipated change in market economies. Unanticipated market changes can be handled at best with great difficulty (if at all) within math-based economic models.

Alfred Marshall and the Return of Varied Motivations

With the marginalist revolution in full swing by the end of the nineteenth century, Smith's broad but bounded view of human motivation could have been left behind forever in the development of economics as a discipline were it not for the arrival of

---

that which can be obtained without labor or sacrifice will command no price, however, useful or needful it may be. But he proceeds to add, that things which have the greatest value in exchange, as a diamond for example, may have little or no value in use. This is employing the word use, not in the sense in which political economy is concerned with it, but in that other sense in which use is opposed to pleasure. Political economy has nothing to do with the comparative estimation of different uses in the judgment of a philosopher or of a moralist. The use of a thing, in political economy, means its capacity to satisfy a desire, or serve a purpose. Diamonds have this capacity in a high degree, and unless they had it, would not bear any price. Value in use, or as Mr. De Quincey calls it, *teleologic* value, is the extreme limit of value in exchange. The exchange value of a thing may fall short, to any amount, of its value in use; but that it can ever exceed the value in use implies a contradiction; it supposes that persons will give, to possess a thing, more than the utmost value which they themselves put upon it as a means of gratifying their inclinations (1848, Sect. III.1.3).

[13] Jevons published his *The Theory of Political Economy* in 1871. Walras published his *Elements of Pure Economics* in 1874, and Menger published his *Principles of Economics* in 1871.

Alfred Marshall's *Principles of Economics*. By going back to Smith for inspiration on human motivations within markets and by drawing on the then-recent work of the marginalists, Marshall codified neoclassical economics and formalized static analysis with the introduction of supply and demand curves, suggesting that both sides of the markets operated as if they each were as necessary in determining competitive market prices as the opposing blades of scissors are in making cuts (1890, Sect. V.III.27).[14]

Despite his introducing graphical and mathematical analysis to his treatise, Marshall was clearly concerned that analytical devices could unduly narrow and sterilize economic analysis, separating analysis from real-world events that were the subject of the discipline (a concern that explains, at least partially, why his supply-and-demand and other graphs were relegated to footnotes). Marshall recognized how many economists before him had attempted to make economics something of a pure abstract science by talking in terms of an economic man, who was under no "ethical influences and who pursues pecuniary gain warily and energetically, but mechanically and selfishly" (1890, Sect. P.3), only to insist, as did Smith, that human behavior, both inside and outside markets, was grounded in multiple motivations,

> But they have not been successful, nor even thoroughly carried out. For they have never really treated the economic man as perfectly selfish: no one could be relied on better to endure toil and sacrifice with the unselfish desire to make provision for his family; and his normal motives have always been tacitly assumed to include the family affections. But if they include these, why should they not include all other altruistic motives the action of which is so far uniform in any class at any time and place, that it can be reduced to general rule? (1890, Sect. P.30).

Key to Marshall's theory of human motivation (and all of his economics more generally) was the "Principle of Continuity," or the premise that everything – "the ethical quality of the motives by which a man may be influenced in choosing his ends, but also to the sagacity, the energy, and the enterprise with which he pursues those ends," as well as time and product valuations – is subject to "continuous gradation" (1890, Sects.P.3–P.4). Marshall warns his student readers of the potential "mischief" that can emerge among economists in following, with excessive fervor, the dictates of the physical sciences as they seek to investigate human actions, which requires, for analytical purposes only, the abandonment of the Principle of Continuity, including the classification of human motives, actions, time periods, goods, as well as the more general ends people pursue, into operational groupings.

---

[14] Marshall famously observed, "We might as reasonably dispute whether it is the upper or the under blade of a pair of scissors that cuts a piece of paper, as whether value is governed by utility or cost of production. It is true that when one blade is held still, and the cutting is effected by moving the other, we may say with careless brevity that the cutting is done by the second; but the statement is not strictly accurate, and is to be excused only so long as it claims to be merely a popular and not a strictly scientific account of what happens" (1890, Sect. V.III.27).

There has always been a temptation to classify economic goods in clearly defined groups, about which a number of short and sharp propositions could be made, to gratify at once the student's desire for logical precision, and the popular liking for dogmas that have the air of being profound and are yet easily handled. But great mischief seems to have been done by yielding to this temptation, and drawing broad artificial lines of division where Nature has made none. The more simple and absolute an economic doctrine is, the greater will be the confusion which it brings into attempts to apply economic doctrines to practice, if the dividing lines to which it refers cannot be found in real life. There is not in real life a clear line of division between things that are and are not Capital, or that are and are not Necessaries, or again between labor that is and is not productive (1890, Sect. P.8).

Nevertheless, any science, social or physical, has a practical side and can progress only by breaking up real-life continuums for people's motivations, goods, and time periods. Accordingly, Marshall introduced the concept of time periods for production, as well as the new concept of equilibriums for those time frames.[15] At the same time, he insisted that his Principle of Continuity held: "For the element of Time, which is the centre of the chief difficulty of almost every economic problem, is itself absolutely continuous: nature knows no absolute partition of time into long periods and short; but the two shade into one another by imperceptible gradations, and what is a short period for one problem, is a long period for another" (1890, Sect. P.5). Similarly, Marshall recognized that holding

---

[15]On time, Marshall identified four time periods:

Four classes stand out. In each, price is governed by the relations between demand and supply. As regards *market* prices, "supply" is taken to mean the stock of the commodity in question which is on hand, or at all events "in sight." As regards *normal* prices, when the term Normal is taken to relate to *short* periods of a few months or a year, Supply means broadly what can be produced for the price in question with the existing stock of plant, personal and impersonal, in the given time. As regards *normal* prices, when the term Normal is to refer to long periods of several years, supply means what can be produced by plant, which itself can be remuneratively produced and applied within the given time; while lastly, there are very gradual or secular movements of normal price, caused by the gradual growth of knowledge, of population and of capital, and the changing conditions of demand and supply from one generation to another (1890, Sect. V.V.38).

On the other side of the line of division are periods of time long enough to enable producers to adapt their production to changes in demand, in so far as that can be done with the existing provision of specialized skill, specialized capital, and industrial organization; but not long enough to enable them to make any important changes in the supplies of these factors of production. For such periods, the stock of material and personal appliances of production have to be taken in a great measure for granted; and the marginal increment of supply is determined by estimates of producers as to the amount of production it is worth their while to get out of those appliances. If trade is brisk, all energies are strained to their utmost, overtime is worked, and then the limit to production is given by want of power rather than by want of will to go further or faster. But if trade is slack, every producer has to make up his mind how near to prime cost it is worth his while to take fresh orders. And here, there is no definite law, the chief operative force is the fear of spoiling the market; and that acts in different ways and with different strengths on different individuals and different industrial groups. For the chief motive of all open combinations and of all informal silent and "customary" understandings whether among employers or employed is the need for preventing individuals from spoiling the common market by action that may bring them immediate gains, but at the cost of a greater aggregate loss to the trade (1890, Sect. V.XV.7).

"everything else the same" is another analytical convenience, made necessary because of the complexity of economists' subject matter:

> The forces [in economics] to be dealt with are however so numerous, that it is best to take a few at a time; and to work out a number of partial solutions as auxiliaries to our main study. Thus we begin by isolating the primary relations of supply, demand and price in regard to a particular commodity. We reduce to inaction all other forces by the phrase "other things being equal": we do not suppose that they are inert, but for the time we ignore their activity. This scientific device is a great deal older than science: it is the method by which, consciously or unconsciously, sensible men have dealt from time immemorial with every difficult problem of ordinary life (1890, Sect. P.20).

The principle of continuity also applies to human motivations:

> Thus stress [in economics] is laid on the fact that there is a continuous gradation from the actions of "city men," which are based on deliberate and far-reaching calculations, and are executed with vigor and ability, to those of ordinary people who have neither the power nor the will to conduct their affairs in a business-like way. The normal willingness to save, the normal willingness to undergo a certain exertion for a certain pecuniary reward, or the normal alertness to seek the best markets in which to buy and sell, or to search out the most advantageous occupation for oneself or for one's children – all these and similar phrases must be relative to the members of a particular class at a given place and time: but, when that is once understood, the theory of normal value is applicable to the actions of the unbusiness-like classes in the same way, though not with the same precision of detail, as to those of the merchant or banker (1890, Sect. P.4).

In other words, Marshall recognized that people everywhere differ in the extent to which they are influenced by their "personal affections," "conceptions of duty," and "reverence of high ideals," acknowledging also that "it is true that the best energies of the ablest inventors and organizers of improved methods and appliances are stimulated by a noble emulation more than by any love of wealth for its own sake" (1890, Sect. I.II.1). He also adopted Smith's position that the call of "higher" motives, including concern for the welfare of others, dissipated as people sought to gain the cooperation of numerous other people, especially, with commercial ends in sight, who stood apart from their families and close circles of friends.[16] But then

---

[16] Marshall wrote,

> For instance, while custom in a primitive society extends the limits of the family, and prescribes certain duties to one's neighbors which fall into disuse in a later civilization, it also prescribes an attitude of hostility to strangers. In a modern society, the obligations of family kindness become more intense, though they are concentrated on a narrower area; and neighbors are put more nearly on the same footing with strangers. In ordinary dealings, with both of them the standard of fairness and honesty is lower than in some of the dealings of a primitive people with their neighbors: but it is much higher than in their dealings with strangers. Thus, it is the ties of neighborhood alone that have been relaxed; the ties of family are in many ways stronger than before, family affection leads to much more self-sacrifice and devotion than it used to do; and sympathy with those who are strangers to us is a growing source of a kind of deliberate unselfishness, that never existed before the modern age. That country which is the birthplace of modern competition devotes a larger part of its income than any other to charitable uses, and spent 20 millions on purchasing the freedom of the slaves in the West Indies (1890, Sect. I.I.16).

Marshall, like Smith, fully appreciated that people were imperfect and that it would be foolhardy to overlook people's imperfections and inclination to pursue their own selfish ends.

> If competition is contrasted with energetic cooperation in unselfish work for the public good, then even the best forms of competition are relatively evil; while its harsher and meaner forms are hateful. And in a world in which all men were perfectly virtuous, competition would be out of place; but so also would be private property and every form of private right. Men would think only of their duties; and no one would desire to have a larger share of the comforts and luxuries of life than his neighbors. Strong producers could easily bear a touch of hardship; so they would wish that their weaker neighbors, while producing less should consume more. Happy in this thought, they would work for the general good with all the energy, the inventiveness, and the eager initiative that belonged to them; and mankind would be victorious in contests with nature at every turn. Such is the Golden Age to which poets and dreamers may look forward. But in the responsible conduct of affairs, it is worse than folly to ignore the imperfections which still cling to human nature (1890, Sect. I.I.21).

Marshall felt justified in assuming narrow human motivations partially because he understood that economics was, at its core, a partial view of human life[17] and because he repeatedly stressed how economics, for the most part, narrowly focused a study "of men as they live and move and think in the ordinary business of life" and chiefly concerned "with those motives which affect, most powerfully and most steadily, man's conduct in the business part of his life" (1890, Sect. I.II.1), with those revealed actions that most readily yield to monetary measurements,[18] and with those classes of people – business people (mainly men) – most likely to be "deliberate" in their calculations of courses of action, not to the "unbusiness-like classes" (1890, Sect. I.II.1 and P.4).

---

[17] Marshall reflected on economics as a partial view of human life in this way:

> Everyone who is worth anything carries his higher nature with him into business; and, there as elsewhere, he is influenced by his personal affections, by his conceptions of duty and his reverence for high ideals. And it is true that the best energies of the ablest inventors and organizers of improved methods and appliances are stimulated by a noble emulation more than by any love of wealth for its own sake. But, for all that, the steadiest motive to ordinary business work is the desire for the pay which is the material reward of work. The pay may be, on its way, to be spent selfishly or unselfishly, for noble or base ends; and here, the variety of human nature comes into play 1890, Sect. I.II.1).

[18] On the importance of monetary measurements to assessing economists predictions, Marshall wrote,

> But, the motive is supplied by a definite amount of money: and it is this definite and exact money measurement of the steadiest motives in business life, which has enabled economics far to outrun every other branch of the study of man. Just as the chemist's fine balance has made chemistry more exact than most other physical sciences, so as this economist's balance, rough and imperfect as it is, has made economics more exact than any other branch of social science. But, of course, economics cannot be compared with the exact physical sciences: for it deals with the ever changing and subtle forces of human nature (1890, Sect. I.II.1).

While Marshall never uses the modern terms of "rational," "rationality," or "rational behavior," his analysis, which focuses on people equating at the margin to maximize their net gain, had all the markings of modern neoclassical static analysis. However, it is equally clear that Marshall stands, in time and analytical approaches, astride the motivational methods of Smith and contemporary neoclassical economists who adhere with fervor to rational precepts. He was clearly willing to narrow the human motivations in his analytics. At the same time, his self-interest-directed analytics was constrained on all sides. The subjects' maximizing behavior was constrained not only by the forces of competition, but also by nonself-interest motivations.

Clearly, Marshall was Smithian in another important regard: Marshall insisted that as the analysis moved away from the study of commercial dealings and into the study of small groups and personal relationships, the potential contributions of economics would likely break down, partially because the underlying assumption of maximization of personal gain would dissipate and partially because behaviors would become less "regular" and money dealings among people less prominent. Hence, economic predictions, based on the "force of motives," would be less subject to testing, robbing the discipline of its claims to being a science (1890, Sects. P.3, I.III. 4, III.III.18, V.V.9).

At every step, Marshall insisted that although economics was a science, it should not be compared with physical sciences such as physics or astronomy that allowed, because of the law of gravity, very exacting predictions that could be tested with equal empirical exactness. Rather, the laws of economics should be compared with those governing the "tides," where predictions of the daily rises and falls are inexact, but tolerably acceptable, and subject to improvement with refinements in theory and statistical tests.[19]

---

[19] On the laws of economics and tides, Marshal wrote,

> The laws of economics are to be compared with the laws of the tides, rather than with the simple and exact law of gravitation. For the actions of men are so various and uncertain, that the best statement of tendencies, which we can make in a science of human conduct, must need be inexact and faulty. This might be urged as a reason against making any statements at all on the subject; but that would be almost to abandon life. Life is human conduct, and the thoughts and emotions that grow up around it. By the fundamental impulses of our nature we all – high and low, learned and unlearned – are in our several degrees constantly striving to understand the courses of human action, and to shape them for our purposes, whether selfish or unselfish, whether noble or ignoble. And since we *must* form to ourselves some notions of the tendencies of human action, our choice is between forming those notions carelessly and forming them carefully. The harder the task, the greater the need for steady patient inquiry; for turning to account the experience, that has been reaped by the more advanced physical sciences; and for framing as best we can well thought-out estimates, or provisional laws, of the tendencies of human action (1890, Sect. I.III.10).

See also Marshall (1890, Sect. App. C.10).

Philip Wicksteed's Unification of Personal and Business Decision Making

Philip Wicksteed (1844–1927) was a contemporary of Alfred Marshall, with Marshall being born two years earlier than Wicksteed and dying three years earlier. Both economists wrote important textbooks in the then nascent neoclassical tradition that incorporated the marginalists' principles of consumer choice theory and that were widely adopted for long stretches of time. Wicksteed's first effort to popularize marginalist thinking came in his *Alphabet of Economic Science* published in 1888, two years before Alfred Marshall published his *Principles of Economics* (1890). However, Wicksteed's more influential book, *The Common Sense of Political Economy*, was not published until two decades later (1910). In contrast to Marshall's treatise, which was written for professional economists and university classes, Wicksteed's text was written for lay readers. This is very likely because Wicksteed, initially, was a Unitarian minister who only later became an economics lecturer in what today would be deemed an educational extension program (although Wicksteed's writing style was far more dense than is true of popular economics books written for modern lay audiences). He was not, like Marshall, an economics professor attached to a major university, but rather made his living lecturing and writing for the general public.

Marshall was unable to bring himself to credit his countryman William Stanley Jevons (or for that matter, Carl Menger and Leon Walras) for the marginalist discoveries he developed in *Principles*. This apparently was because he thought he had come to those principles independently and was disturbed that Jevons published his views in 1871 before Marshall could go to print with his marginal analysis (Keynes 1963, p. 153). Wicksteed, on the other hand, freely credited the marginalist innovators, especially Jevons.

While Marshall stressed how marginal values were an "embellishment" (to use Lionel Robbins' characterization) to explaining downward sloping demand curves and the resulting consumer surplus (Robbins 1932, p. xvii), Wicksteed emphasized the essential role that marginal values, in conjunction with market prices, play in consumers' decisions to allocate (or "administer") their resources through time. And while Marshall adopted Smith's view that the costs underlying the supply curve were something "real and absolute," Wicksteed viewed costs subjectively, the value of opportunities not taken (Robbins 1932, p. xviii). Marshall was solidly Smithian in orientation. Wicksteed was Smithian but with an Austrian streak running through his writings.

Wicksteed and Marshall differed on other important methodological grounds, not so much as matters of emphasis and influence, as in terms of professional orientation and intent. Marshall wrote his *Principles* with the apparent intention of merely revising the direction of current economics instruction. Wicksteed seemed to be more intent on destroying Ricardo's lingering influence in the discipline, excessive formalism (dubbed the "Ricardian vice," a phrase coined much later by Joseph Schumpeter who described it as the "habit of piling a heavy load of practical conclusions upon a tenuous groundwork" (1954, p.1171)) and then replacing the classical core of the discipline, founded on Smith's work, with a totally new methodological approach. As Lionel Robbins observed in his 1932 introduction to Wicksteed's textbook,

> In intention at any rate Marshall's position was essentially revisionist. He came not to destroy, but – as he thought – to fulfill the work of the classics. Wicksteed, on the other hand, was one of those who, with Jevons and Menger, thought that "able but wrongheaded man David Ricardo" had "shunted the car of Economic Science on to the wrong line, a line on which it was further urged forward towards confusion by his equally able and wrong-headed admirer John Stuart Mill"; and that complete reconstruction was necessary. He was not a revisionist, but a revolutionary (Robbins 1932, p. xvi).

As Robbins notes, Wicksteed makes his revolutionary intentions clear in his introduction, first noting that the marginal revolution had been more profound than was widely recognized among students of economics and then adding,

> Adhesion to the traditional terminology, methods of arrangement, and classification, has disguised the revolution that has taken place. The new temple, so to speak, has been built up behind the old walls, and the old shell has been so piously preserved and respected that the very builders have often supposed themselves to be merely repairing and strengthening the ancient works and are hardly aware of the extent to which they have raised an independent edifice. I shall try to shew in this book that the time has come for a frank recognition of these facts (1910, p. 2)

Marshall treated supply and demand as distinctly separate market forces, both as conceptual devices and real-world market forces, to repeat, with each curve favorably "compared to one blade of a pair of scissors" in determining market prices (1890, Sect. App.I.21). By way of contrast, Wicksteed wrote frequently about supply and demand as distinguishable constructs, but he obviously believed that their separation in Marshall's graphical analysis obscured an important point, that the supply and demand curves were mirror images of one another. The supply curve was, in fact, a reservation demand curve, with suppliers becoming demanders when the market price dropped below their reservation price. Similarly, demanders would become suppliers when the price went above their limit price (a point Nassar Senior made in the first third of the nineteenth century), or as Wicksteed made the point in his presidential address to the British Association in 1913:

> I say it boldly and baldly: there is no such thing [as a meaningful distinction between supply and demand]. When we are speaking of marketable commodities, what is usually called the supply curve is, in reality, the demand curve of those who possess the commodity, for it shows there exact place which every successive unit of the commodity occupies in their relative scale of estimation. The so-called supply curve is, therefore, simply a part of the total demand curve. ....The separating of this portion of the demand curve and reversing in the diagram is a process which has its meaning and its legitimate function.......but it is wholly irrelevant to the determination of price (1914, p.13).[20]

---

[20]Wicksteed, then, explains how separate supply and demand curves can serve the function of showing the forces at work when the market price diverges from the equilibrium price but is misleading in showing how the equilibrium price is set:

More importantly, for purposes of this volume, while Marshall and Wicksteed both held that economics was principally concerned with understanding human behavior in markets (or in "commercial life"), they differed rather dramatically on how they perceived human motivations and decision making in commercial and personal spheres of life. As noted in the foregoing section of this chapter, Marshall (following Smith) was willing to accept the fact that people's motivations in dealing with family members and friends were different from their motivations in dealing with people in business settings. He was willing to insist that, for example, ethics and call of duty could constrain people's decisions everywhere, but more so in small group settings than in market settings. Such value systems *could* call for principles of decision making separate from those used in the "ordinary business of life." Also, Marshall was willing to posit that deliberate calculations of cost and benefits were more likely to guide the decisions of business people than people in "unbusiness-like classes" (1890, p.P4), which suggests that economics was more likely to be useful and successful in understanding and predicting people's behavior in business than all other life's spheres. Perhaps, he was willing to subscribe to a point made earlier in this book, that rationality of market participants was a function of the setting in which they operated. Business was an area of life in which people self-selected for their calculating tendencies and in which they could be pressed to be more rational than they would otherwise be inclined.

Wicksteed took a totally different tack, one far more in line with the way modern economists (with elements of Becker's expansive application of economic methods of thought) think of rational behavior (although, like Marshall, Wicksteed never used the words rational, rationality, or rational behavior). Observing that everywhere people could not have everything they wanted, the overarching goal of "personal economy" had to be "the administration of the affairs and resources of a household in such a manner as to avoid waste and secure efficiency." Similarly, the ultimate goal of political economy "would be the study of the principles on

---

The ordinary method of presenting the demand curve in two sections tells us the extent to which the present distribution of the commodity departs from that of equilibrium, and therefore the extent of the transactions that will be required to reach equilibrium. But, it is the single combined curve alone that tells us what the equilibrium price will be. The customary representation of cross curves confounds the process by which the price is discovered with the ultimate facts that determine it.

Diagrams of intersecting curves (and corresponding tables) of demand prices and supply prices are therefore profoundly misleading. They coordinate as two determinants what are really only two separated portions of one; and they conceal altogether the existence and operation of what is really the second determinant. For it will be found on a careful analysis that the construction of a diagram of intersecting demand and "supply" curves always involves, but never reveals, a definite assumption as to the amount of the total supply possessed by the supposed buyers and the supposed sellers taken together as a single homogeneous body, and that if this total is changed, the emerging price changes too; whereas a "change" in its initial distribution (if the collective curve is unaffected, while the component or intersecting curves change) will have no effect on the market, or equilibrating price itself, which will come out exactly the same. Naturally, for neither the one curve nor the one quantity which determine the price has been changed (1914, pp.13–14).

which the resources of a community should be so regulated and administered as to secure the communal ends without waste" (1910, p. 14). In both regards, there is no need for economists to rule out or narrowly focus on any particular motive or end that activates people to do what they must do, "avoid waste and secure efficiency" in doing the best they can with the limited resources at their disposal (1910, p.4).

Wicksteed did make a useful distinction (now lost on many contemporary economists) between selfish motives, which cause people to act only with their individual ends in mind, and economic motives, which drive people to enlist others to achieve their goals that can be either selfish or altruistic. (Individuals can, for example, engage in market transactions with the intent of helping their family members or relevant individuals and groups.) Hence, market transactions need not be driven at all by narrow self-interest in the sense that Smith and Marshall conceived of self-interest. The exact motivation is not necessarily the distinguishing characteristic of economic relations, except that economic relations do not, in Wicksteed's view, include concern for the other trading partner(s). Once people become concerned with the welfare of those with whom they are dealing, the relation ceases to be economic. Wicksteed stressed early in his book:

> Economic *relations* constitute a complex machine by which we seek to accomplish our purposes, whatever they may be. They do not in any direct or conclusive sense either dictate our *purposes* or supply our *motives*. We shall therefore have to consider what constitutes an economic relation rather than what constitutes an economic motive. And this does away at a stroke with the hypothetically simplified psychology of the Economic Man which figured so largely in the older books of Political Economy, and which recent writers take so much trouble to evade or qualify. We are not to begin by imagining man to be actuated by only a few simple motives, but we are to take him as we find him, and are to examine the nature of those relations into which he enters, under the stress of all his complicated impulses and desires – whether selfish or unselfish, material or spiritual, – in order to accomplish indirectly through the action of others what he cannot accomplish directly through his own (1910, p.4).

Wicksteed elaborated on how in economic relations people can be selfish or unselfish by using the biblical example of Paul making tents in Corinth. He could have been making his tents for sale for his own narrow ends (to make a living), but then he could have been in the tent business to help relevant others (or, for that matter, to please God). The point is that economists are most interested in people's efforts in which concern for the other trading partner is not dominant, and certainly not paramount, to the relationship (1910, p. 173).[21]

---

[21] On Paul the tent maker, Wicksteed wrote,

> And yet the ground on which this stubborn prejudice rests is obvious enough, and the example of the apostolic tent-maker has already suggested it. We have seen that although Paul was certainly not thinking of himself or of his own advantage when he was making tents in Corinth, yet neither was he necessarily or even probably thinking, in any disinterested or enthusiastic manner, of the advantage of those for whom he was working and whose wants he was immediately supplying. In his attitude towards himself and "others" at large, a man may be either *selfish* or un*selfish* without affecting the economic nature of any given relation, such as that of Paul to his customers; but as soon as he is moved by a direct and disinterested desire to further the purposes or consult the interests of those particular

Using Goethe's words for his book's epigraph ("We are all doing it; very few of understand what we are doing"), Wicksteed insisted that the best pedagogical way students can come to understand "economic relations" (which can be construed as commercial relationships) was first to disentangle economic relations (which is a category of human interactions that stand apart from personal relations) from economic motives, which can pervade all decision making, no matter the sphere of life. The next step is to deduce, from introspection and observation, the principles that people use in the ordinary course of their personal lives with the goal of ultimately seeing how those principles can be used to understand the business sphere of life. Wicksteed wrote,

> Accordingly, I shall try to shew that it is time frankly and decisively to abandon all attempts to rule out this or that "motive" from the consideration of the Economist, or indeed to attempt to establish any distinction whatever between the ultimate motives by which a *man* is actuated in business and those by which he is actuated in his domestic or public life. *Economic relations* constitute a complex machine by which we seek to accomplish our purposes, whatever they may be. They do not in any direct or conclusive sense either dictate our *purposes* or supply our *motives*. We shall therefore have to consider what constitutes an *economic* relation rather than what constitutes an *economic* motive. And this does away at a stroke with the hypothetically simplified psychology of the *Economic Man* which figured so largely in the older books of Political Economy, and which recent writers take so much trouble to evade or qualify. We are not to begin by imagining *man* to be actuated by only a few simple motives, but we are to take him as we find him, and are to examine the nature of those relations into which he enters, under the stress of all his complicated impulses and

---

"others" for whom he is working at the moment, then in proportion as this desire becomes an ultimate object to him (so that he is directly fulfilling one of his own purposes in supplying these wants) the transaction on his side ceases to be purely economic. No doubt Paul took conscientious pains with his tent-making. So far as this was with a view to business, it was done in obedience to an economic force. So far as it was an expression of his own personality or of his independent sympathy with his employers, it was not. If you and I are conducting a transaction which on my side is purely economic, I am furthering your purposes, partly or wholly, perhaps, for my own sake, perhaps, entirely for the sake of others, but certainly not for your sake. What makes it an economic transaction is that I am not considering you except as a link in the chain, or considering your desires except as the means by which I may gratify those of someone else – not necessarily myself. The economic relation does not exclude from my mind everyone but me; it potentially includes everyone but you. You it does indeed exclude, and therefore it emphasizes, though it does not narrow or tighten, the limitations of the altruism of the man who enters into it; for it calls our attention to the fact that, however wide his sympathies may be, they do not urge him to any particular effort or sacrifice for the sake of the person with whom he is dealing at the moment. An economic relation may be entered upon equally well from egoistic or altruistic motives; but as long as it remains purely economic, it must remind us that no man's altruism is undiscriminating to the extent of lavishing itself upon all persons or all purposes at all times. Short of this, clearly the most altruistic person may enter into a relation with another man, the purpose of which is to further the good of those who are other than himself, and also other than the person with whom he is dealing. In that case, his action is altruistic because it is inspired by a desire for the good of someone other than himself, and the relation is economic because it is entered into for the sake of someone other than his correspondent (1910, p. 173).

desires – whether selfish or unselfish, material or spiritual, – in order to accomplish indirectly through the action of others what he cannot accomplish directly through his own (1910, p. 4).

In an important respect, Wicksteed explicitly adopts and extends Marshall's principle of continuity in a way that Marshall was unwilling to do.[22] He makes the extension with regards to economic motives because

> When our conception of the nature of economic facts and relations has become clear, we shall see without difficulty that the market, in the widest sense of the term, is their field of action, and that market prices are their most characteristic expression and outcome. The individual, in administering his resources, regards market prices as phenomena which confront him independently of his own action, and which impose upon him the conditions under which he must make his selections between alternatives. But when he has arrived at a thorough comprehension of the principles of his own conduct, as he stands confronted by market prices, he will find that those market prices are themselves constituted by other people's acting precisely on the principles on which he acts; so that he is in fact himself, by his own action, contributing towards the formation of those very market prices which appear to be externally dictated to him. Because other people are doing exactly what he is doing a phenomenon arises, as the resultant of the sum of their individual actions, which presents itself to each one of them, severally, as an alien system imposed from without (1910, p. 5).

After concluding that "all successful administration, then, consists in the purposeful selection between alternative applications of resources; and the ultimate value or significance of such success depends on the nature of the objects at which the administrator aims" (1910, p. 14), Wicksteed generalizes the principle on which people's choices are made to virtually all choices, suggesting that he would have no concern, and would encourage, the kind of economic imperialism, with prices and real incomes broadly advocated in contemporary times by, say, Gary Becker and George Stigler (discussed in Chap. 1). Wicksteed concluded,

> We have thus arrived at the conclusion that all the heterogeneous impulses and objects of desire or aversion which appeal to any individual, whether material or spiritual, personal or communal, present or future, actual or ideal, may all be regarded as comparable with each other; for we are, as a matter of fact, constantly comparing them, weighing them against each other, and deciding which is the heaviest. And the question, "How much of this must I forgo to obtain so much of that?" is always relevant. If we are considering, for example, whether to live in the country or in the town, such different things as friendship and fresh air or fresh eggs may come into competition and comparison with each other. Shall I "bury myself in the country," where I shall see little of my dearest friends, but may hope for fresh eggs for breakfast, and fresh air all the day? Or shall I stay where I am, and continue to enjoy the society of my friends? I start at once thinking "how much of the society of my friends must I expect to sacrifice? Will any of them come and see me? Shall I occasionally be able to go and see some of them?" The satisfactions and benefits I anticipate from a country life will compensate me for the loss of some of their society, but not for the loss of all of it. The price may be too high. In such a case as this the terms on which the alternatives are offered are matter of more or less vague surmise and conjecture, but the apparent dissimilarity of the several satisfactions themselves does not prevent the comparison, nor

---

[22]Wicksteed uses "Principle of Continuity'" on two occasions in *Commonsense* (1910, 205–206).

does it prevent the quantitative element from affecting my decision. Using the term price then in its widest extension, we may say that all the objects of repulsion or attraction which divide my energies and resources amongst them are linked to each other by a system of ideal prices or terms of equivalence. We may conceive of a general "scale of preferences" or "relative scale of estimates" on which all objects of desire or pursuit (positive or negative) find their place, and which registers the terms on which they would be accepted as equivalents or preferred one to the other (Wicksteed 1910, Sect. I.1.28).

As intimated in the above quotation, Wicksteed fully recognized that people do not always and everywhere make careful, calculating decisions. Indeed, impulse, habits, routines, and more or less automatic decisions may be necessary to avoid a waste of time and other resources in making decisions: "Life would *be* impossible if we were always in the state of mind professed by the lady who said she liked 'to get up every morning feeling that everything was an open question.'" (1910, Sect. P. 34).[23] Nevertheless, he insisted that the "principle of price" (or the inverse relationship between quantity bought and price) holds; there is some upward movement in price that gives rise to more careful decisions:

Thus the impulse to rescue a drowning man and the dread of taking a high dive may balance themselves without reflection within certain limits, but when those limits are transgressed a deliberate choice may be made. The principle is at work on the unconscious area, and emerges into consciousness when it crosses the boundary. A man of given temperament and accomplishments, who without a moment's hesitation would take a header of 5 feet to help a drowning stranger, might be conscious of a conflict of two forces in him, though hardly of a deliberate choice, as he took off from a height of 8 feet, might nerve himself with an effort to a 10-foot throw, might refrain, though with some measure of self-contempt, if the height were 12 feet, and without any self-reproach at all if it were 20 feet. But the same man might unhesitatingly take off from 12 feet to save his friend, or from 20 feet, with a sense of desperation, but with no fear or consciousness of an open alternative, to the rescue of his wife or child; though even in this case it would not occur to him to take off from 40 feet, and at some height short of this he might go through a rapid estimate of the relative chances of a desperate plunge or a race for other means of rescue, and into this estimate his own instinctive fears might or might not, according to his temperament, enter as a recognised or unrecognised weight (1910, p.29).

Clearly, if he were pressed to invoke explicitly the modern premise of rational behavior, Wicksteed would insist the extent of people's rationality was not fixed; it could be expected to vary with people's incentive to be rational, or to consider with varying degrees of care the gains and pains of decisions faced. His concept of rationality would not be one that could be modeled mathematically, especially, since he would accept variability in rationality across people.

---

[23] In Wicksteed's words: "It would be a very great mistake to suppose that the influence of the terms on which alternatives are offered to us is confined to cases where our choice is deliberate; and a still greater mistake to confine it to cases in which that choice is rational. A great part of our conduct is *impulsive* and a great part unreflecting; and when we reflect our choice is often irrational. In all these cases, however, the principle of price is active" (1910, p. 28).

Concluding Comments

In the nineteenth century, economics became progressively more formalized as economists sought to become scientists. In the process, economic analytics became progressively more mathematical and graphical, with decision makers in economic analytics shedding the full range of motivations that Smith assumed they had and approaching the construction of what modern economists dub *homo economicus*, or someone who is "perfectly selfish" (to use Marshall's characterization).

However, by the time Marshall penned his *Principles*, the progressing sterility, unrealism, and the outright determinism of economic model building (albeit less formally than in contemporary times) must have been self-evident, and, perhaps, threatening to the discipline's relevance and future. Although Ricardo remained respected for explaining the law of comparative advantage and advocating free trade on that theoretical refinement of Smith's argument, by the last quarter of the nineteenth century, his abstract formalization of economics with emphasis on the Malthusian population imperative and the labor theory of value, was justifiably derided for its "Ricardian vice."

By the time of the publication of the 1920 edition of his *Principles*, Marshall seems to have been on two missions. The first was to show how focused construction of a class of economic behavior could be productively analyzed by constricting the motivational foundation of behavior, which would allow for narrowly relevant predictions that were quasi-scientific (that is, could be tested with some tolerable precision). In this regard, Marshall seems to have placed the assumption that economic actors exercise self-interested behavior on par with the assumption of everything else equal. That is to say, paraphrasing Marshall, other nonself-interest motivations are neither denied nor are they deemed inconsequential, but are only ignored for a time to offer the prospect of at least some tentative analytical progress. As Marshall suggested, such an approach might be unavoidable, given that setting aside some analytical complexities for a time is a "scientific device (that) is a great deal older than science: it is the method by which, consciously or unconsciously, sensible men have dealt from time immemorial with every difficult problem of ordinary life" (1890, Sect. P.20). Still, Marshall insisted – because he so severely confined economic analysis to those actions that were "deliberate" (purposeful) and mainly to those actions in "commercial life" – that predictions based on self-interest calculations needed to be empirically tested at some level.

Marshall's second mission seems to have been to demonstrate how math and graphs could be productively employed as a helpful tool of analysis and prediction, but not the entire embodiment of all analysis. His first mission leaves the impression that the motivational assumptions represent a limited view of the subjects of inquiry. It also leaves open the prospect of the behavioral assumptions being a comprehensive representation of real-world actors and suggests a good measure of professional humility on the part of economists-qua-scientists. His second mission, because of mathematical limitations in modeling human motivations, hands critics of the discipline a handy straw man that they can easily use to attack the disciplinary approach, unless the equations are carefully circumscribed. In Marshall's words:

> The chief use of pure mathematics in economic questions seems to be in helping a person to write down quickly, shortly, and exactly, some of his thoughts for his own use: and to make sure that he has enough, and only enough, premises for his conclusions (i.e., that his equations are neither more nor less in number than his unknowns). But, when a great many symbols have to be used, they become very laborious to anyone but the writer himself (1890, Sect. P. 12).

As noted, Marshall takes his own advice and relegates his mathematical and graphical analysis to appendices in his textbook. In a letter to a friend, Marshall, perhaps, more accurately revealed his true feelings on the use of mathematics in economics with six rules (in his own words):

(1)   Use mathematics as a shorthand language, rather than as an engine of inquiry.
(2)   Keep to them until you have done.
(3)   Translate into English.
(4)   Then, illustrate by examples that are important in real life.
(5)   Burn the mathematics.
(6)   If you cannot succeed in 4, burn 3.

Marshall finalized his rules by confessing to his correspondent, "This last (6) I did often" (as reported by Pigou and Fay 1926, p. 87). As we have seen, Marshall's chief contributions to economics came from his resurrecting and popularizing Smithian economics while adding the marginalists' and others' important revisions. He, then, created and introduced any number of important static analytical under-standings and devices that remain today's fixtures in microeconomic courses, most notably supply and demand curves and market equilibriums.

While firmly grounding his analytics in the same marginal principles that Marshall used, Wicksteed took a decidedly different methodological and pedagog-ical approach in two principal ways. First, he insisted that purely selfish motives on either side of transactions need not guide economic dealings, even strictly business dealings. Both buyers and sellers could have, and very likely often would have, various blends of selfish and unselfish motivations for being involved in market transactions in the first place. The key to separating commercial dealings from all other dealings was the general lack of concern that the buyers had for the welfares of suppliers, and vice versa.

Second, Wicksteed insisted that people's personal and commercial dealings could not be meaningfully separated by differences in the principles for the "administration" of resources that were everywhere scarce. People everywhere, and in all categories of life, were seeking to do the best they could to achieve their ends, whether grounded in selfishness or altruism, with the overriding end of simply trying to minimize waste and secure the efficient use of scarce resources.

Although people can have different ends, they can be expected to apply the same principles. Even altruists can be expected to do the best they can in minimizing waste and securing efficiency. Readers of Wicksteed can be excused for thinking that his retort to expressed concerns would have been, "How can they be expected to do differently, at least to the extent that their decisions are deliberate?" Even when decisions are less than deliberate, the principle of price would ultimately be at work not only on market quantities but on people's level of what we now call rationality.

Marshall's lasting methodological influence on the profession is firmly affixed to his analytical devices that economists still use. Wicksteed's lasting influence (apart from affecting Robbins) seems to be subtler and less recognized among contemporary economists (many of whom have never heard of him). For many economists, however, Wicksteed's distinction between the "economic (perhaps, strictly selfish) motives" that traders have in dealing with each other can stand apart from the constellation of motives they have for engaging in trades in the first place. The great achievement of Marshall, Wicksteed, and the marginalists of the late nineteenth and early twentieth centuries, was that they helped to expose and undermine the methodological diversion of the profession charted by Malthus, Ricardo, Mill, and Marx.

At the same time, in their different ways, both Marshall and Wicksteed reasserted Smith's position that people are various combinations of human motivations, which is to say that when taken as a whole, people are not so much rational or self-interested as they are human. In stressing this simple point, Wicksteed stands apart and above Marshall, but both in different ways greatly influenced modern luminaries in neoclassical economics. Marshall was clearly more influential in guiding the work of Milton Friedman whose major work was overwhelmingly concerned with market outcomes (not with close-at-hand personal and social outcomes).

Wicksteed's influence can be readily seen in George Stigler's and Gary Becker's view that what distinguishes economics as a discipline is not its subject matter, but rather its way of thinking. While they certainly accept Smith and Marshall's view that people work from a constellation of motivations, Stigler and Becker see the limits to the scope of the discipline's subject matter being set by whether the analytics generate useful insights that can be supported by empirical evidence (an extension of Wicksteed's methodology that is fully consistent with Friedman's methodological imperative, but not an extension that Wicksteed would necessarily accept). Both Stigler and Becker received Nobel prizes because they broke new methodological ground by applying the rationality premise to a range of non-market behavior. In doing so, they opened neoclassical economics up to the criticisms of subjectivists who harbor grave concerns about the meaning of data or evidence used to test hypotheses and to the criticisms of scholars inside and outside of economics who can easily demonstrate that people often act irrationally and that evolutionary and neurological constraints necessarily bind people's rational capacities and proclivities.

Chapter 5
Rationality in Economic Thought: Frank Knight, Ludwig von Mises, Friedrich Hayek, and James Buchanan

The discipline of economics includes severe critics of rational behavior as postulated by modern neoclassical economists. These critics, mainly among economists with a decidedly subjectivist orientation, disagree with the proposition that economics' main concern is (or should be) with the allocation of scarce and *known* means of production among essentially unlimited but *known* human wants. Generally, if subjectivists accept a role for rationality in economic inquiry, they see the analytical role as strictly, but imprecisely, limited, and they posit that the discipline's real core concern is the development of principles on the efficient allocation of scarce resources among competing wants that emerge from individuals' explorations into the field of potential values and as they interact with others (with the wants never *given* to external observers-qua-economists) and that are known only to the individuals themselves. Subjectivists reject the strictly self-interested model of human behavior captured in *homo economicus*. Such a construction of human decision making is excessively narrow and confining.

Subjectivists tend to insist that wants involve evaluations of real-world goods that are the objects of trades conducted to serve the larger and more ephemeral ends of individuals. People might participate in markets to buy goods based on evaluations not only of the goods but also the ends the goods might serve. Such evaluations of both the goods and the ends require individualized evaluative, mental processes that are extraordinarily difficult, if not totally impossible, to measure in a way that allows for scientifically valid empirical assessments of any theoretically derived predictions. Subjective evaluations, which imply the conception of some *action* (a key behavioral consideration) that results in improvement for the acting individuals, necessarily mean, according to subjectivists, that any attempt to transfer the analytical methods of the hard sciences to human behavior involves a grave misunderstanding of human behavior, including the more narrowly focused subset of human behavior, economic behavior, that emerges from *action* (as Ludwig von Mises would define action).

Moreover, any predictions of human behavior, which must be based on historical data, are likely to be of limited usefulness in predicting future behaviors that are, to one degree or another, *new* in that they give rise to improvements over past

R.B. McKenzie, *Predictably Rational?*,
DOI 10.1007/978-3-642-01586-1_5, © Springer-Verlag Berlin Heidelberg 2010

outcomes. Such predictive power, to the extent that any can be achieved, can be a threat to human freedom because such predictive power might give analysts-qua-economists the illusion of control over behavior for the purpose of improving individualized choices and market outcomes for their (the analysts') own purposes. (They would be just as concerned over claims that human behavior is "predictably irrational" [Ariely 2008], for much the same reason, that the predictability might offer the adherents of such a position the pretense of control of human action and lead to policy agendas for control, which has indeed happened, as we will see in Chaps. 6 and 10).

Even if economic predictions harbored the prospects of being meaningful, some subjectivists appear eager to decry applying scientific methods to economics – pejoratively dubbing such efforts as "scientism" – because such investigations must have very short-run applications at best and could pierce the veil of people's "constitutional ignorance" (or their lack of knowledge of the exact content of people's behaviors, contained within what subjectivist have called "pattern of outcomes" from people's social interactions). Constitutional ignorance is often, if not always, a necessary precondition for agreement on societal rules within which people can freely interact within and across the public and private sectors, social and economic. Hence, analysts' predictive power – or, perhaps, more accurately what the subjectivists worry is analysts' *illusion* of such power – can threaten the scope of human freedom, or the ability of people to do as they deem appropriate within the legal and ethical boundaries that Adam Smith recognized (see Chap. 2).

Coverage of the detailed methodological views of all subjectivists here is hardly possible, or not at all economic. In this chapter, however, I consider the views of a representative sample of subjectivists who have achieved prominence within the history of relatively modern economic thought precisely because their approaches to the study of rational behavior stand in such contrast to the approach taken by the various competing strands of economic analysis prior to World War II and the emergence and growing coherence and dominance of modern neoclassical econo-mists after the war. Accordingly, I take up the views of Frank Knight, Ludwig von Mises, Friedrich Hayek, and James Buchanan who each have developed separate and different lines of criticism of strictly rational behavior (again, especially, that narrowly defined form of rational behavior captured by the *homo economicus* model), developing in the process a different perspective on the *limited* usefulness of any premise that people, within bounds, carefully, precisely, accurately, and consistently weigh the costs and benefits of their actions.

Frank Knight and the Limits of Economic Science

University of Chicago Professor Frank Knight (1885–1972), an acknowledged precursor of the Chicago school (although he was also a critic of the type of neoclassical economics now associated with that school), was willing to accept Lionel Robbins' view that economics, to the degree that the discipline had any claim at all to being a science, was, at bottom, a study of how people individually dealt with scarcity, or the allocation of limited means of production in satisfying given, but essentially, unlimited wants (1921, Sect.II.III.23). What else could reasonable and thinking people do? Nevertheless, Knight's biggest concern within economics as a discipline was how weighing of options is largely undertaken in a social context and how people's economizing behavior fosters mutual cooperation, especially, through market exchanges. Knight also accepted Philip Wicksteed's view that people purposefully seek to minimize waste in satisfying their given wants (1935, pp. 105–147).

But then, he insisted that standard definitions of his era made the coverage of economics too expansive, spurning any definition that might suggest economics is the "science of rational activity." After all was said and done, "economics deals with the *social organization* of economic activity," by which he meant the making of the "system of free enterprise," which economists should strive to make "better" (Knight 1933, pp. 6–7, emphasis in the original). Knight would no doubt resist modern neoclassical economics that takes an expansive view of the discipline in the way Gary Becker might view the discipline, which is that economics is a method of thinking applicable to topics practically without disciplinary boundaries. He also argued that we should not make too much of scarcity because "the importance of economic provision (predominantly of the necessities of life) is chiefly that of a prerequisite to the enjoyment of the free goods of the world, the beauty of the natural scene, the intercourse of friends in 'aimless' camaraderie, the appreciation of art, discovery of truth, and communication with one's inner being and the nature of things" (1933, p. 5).

However, Knight argued that the scientific world view itself imposes necessary limits on what economists can say about human behavior as scientists, apart from what they can deduce about behavior as noneconomists without scientific methods, or with nothing more than "common sense." At its heart, science is about making predictions, or "is the *technique of* prediction," to use Knight's phrase (1935, p. 109, emphasis in the original). Because human "experience in its raw state" is a "big, buzzing, booming confusion," constantly subject to change, "the variety of things with which we have to deal is infinitely too great for our minds to become acquainted." To deal with the sensory information and calculating overload, people must think, the first step of which is the simplification of experience through classifying – "identically similar things" – and finding relationships that permit useful, albeit seriously circumscribed and provisional, predictions (1935, pp. 111–112).

Knight had a number of concerns with the discipline's scientific view of life, the most notable of which were that the things with which economists deal are goods, or as he preferred to put it, "desired ends." These desired ends require subjective assessments (with "all subjectivity being illusions" [1935, p. 105]) and raise several nontrivial methodological issues:

(1) The desired ends can be one or more steps removed from the goods people can be observed buying in markets and are thus largely poorly observed, or are outright unobservable. As Becker (1993) has proposed, food items purchased

in grocery stores are most often intermediate products intended for use in home-produced meals, the exact form, nature, and quality of which cannot be observed on any large scale in cost-effective manners (but then, to reiterate, Knight would very likely take strong exception to Becker's expansive application of economic methods to all, or practically all, human behaviors, a point that will be evident in other things Knight wrote).

(2) The desired ends need not be always, or even frequently, strictly selfish ends.
(3) The desired ends can only be fully appreciated by the individuals who make the assessments.
(4) The desired ends can be affected in myriad ways by the details of people's individual circumstances.
(5) The desired ends can continually change with changing individual circumstances.

All such considerations caused Knight to stress in varied ways: "[T]here simply is no real measurement of distinctly human or social data" (1947, p. 228).

By way of sharp contrast, according to Knight, a central problem for economics is that "science is restricted to the field within which such demonstration and verification are practicable; that is, to data which are, in fact, the same to all normal observers, and *which can be communicated* so accurately as to compel all to recognize the identity" (1935, p. 116, emphasis in the original).[1] In addition, "knowledge usable for prediction in the guidance of conduct must consist of propositions which state unchanging truth and hence can be made only with regard to data which are ultimately static," with elusive economic data is hardly static except for tightly constrained time periods (1935, p. 117). But, there is another problem with being able to recognize and communicate identities relevant to the social world: The basic data of economics – values – are individual realizations. And people learn much about values, and their worlds, largely through communications with others (1935, p. 116). Moreover, as people seek to satisfy their individual desired ends, they collectively affect market and other social outcomes that, with time, can have feedback effects on what people seek to do, which can make predictions regarding the "*content* of economic behavior" impossible and can easily (and very likely will) unsettle or make obsolete anything other than very short-run predictions (1935, p. 135, emphasis in the original).[2] Even as they are "playing the game of business, people are also moulding their own and other personalities, and

---

[1] Knight wrote, "A scientific world view has no possible place for the intuitive, or any other foresight of *new* truth, in advance of perception. Its fundamental assumption is that *truth is always the same* and is known through perception and memory. But, that truth is always the same is equivalent to saying that the world is always the same. Change is unreal, or in so far as there is real change, the world is knowable only historically, the future is unpredictable" (1935, p. 110).

[2] On the difficulty of making specific predictions, Knight wrote, "Who is to say whether a specified punishment will reduce a particular crime? Whether dropping bombs on any enemy population will weaken or strengthen their military morale? Whether raising wages will cause men to work harder or to loaf, or what the effect of a change in the price of diamonds will be upon sales? It depends" (1935, p. 122).

creating a civilization whose worthiness to endure cannot be a matter of indifference" (1935, p. 47). People can affect their circumstances by how they act to
achieve their desired ends, but the reverse can more powerfully be the case, or as
Knight observed,

> Wants are usually treated as *the* fundamental data, the ultimate driving force in economic
> activity, and in the short-run view of problems this is scientifically legitimate. But in the
> long-run it is just as clear that wants are dependent variables, that they are largely caused
> and formed by economic activity. The case is somewhat like that of a river and its channel;
> for the time being the channel locates the river, but in the long-run it is the other way (1935,
> p. 142, emphasis in the original).

Moreover, so much of human activity is creative, which means that wants and
what people seek to do, are totally new and have no history to allow for observations, if observations were ever possible in the first place, much less to allow for
sophisticated econometric manipulation of "data":

> True creation, which is a field of art, involves the invention of new ends as well as new
> means for reaching them. Science is always striving to "understand" art and produce its
> effects by the calculated application of rules; but to the extent that it succeeds in its
> endeavor the result is no longer art in the true sense. The evil is multiplied by the fact
> that because science can never explain why this is so, it tends to deny the fact (1935, p.
> 108).

Knight also reasoned that people cannot be counted on to reliably report their
desired ends because "we do not know what we want, or why, as has been
emphasized by psycho-analysts" (1935, p. 117). This is the case partially because
people do not always want to understand what they want and do since "there is more
or less conflict between understanding and enjoying (1935, p. 107)."[3] In order to
cope with the great complexity of daily experience, people often seek to routinize
their behaviors and are not always aware of what they are doing, because activities
have been relegated to the subconscious, leaving people sometimes with misunder-
standings of why they have done what they do: "In so far as the new theories (of
psycho-analysis) are sound they show that men's real motives are often quite other
than they think them to be, and extremely difficult to come at. The human propensity for 'rationalizing' of which [John] Dewey's followers have made so much, and
the distinction between 'good reasons' and 'real reasons' so generally portrayed by
James Harvey Robinson are kindred developments which emphasize the difficulty
of predicting human behavior from motives" (1935, p. 125).

Knight elaborated later in another context that in addition to errors of judgment
people make in what they want and why, "Men do not even at all accurately know their
own motives, but in 'fact' act in part experimentally, to learn what they want, and also

---

[3] On the conflict between understanding and enjoying, Knight elaborated, "We strive to understand
the how and why of our actions, to analyze the technique; and yet when this process is carried too
far and it becomes altogether a matter of routine manipulation of means to produce an effect
preconceived and foreseen, there is loss of interest in the action." For that matter, Knight continued
later, the process of analysis "centers attention on the results of the activity, weakening or
destroying the value of the process" (1935, p. 107).

deliberately change their own motivation. All this is in the nature of man as a knowing and acting entity...., or as in part 'free' or problem-solving" (1947, p. 229) – with all such points leading Knight to take a very limited view of what economists (and social scientists generally) can accomplish in the way of elevating human understanding beyond what can be accomplished from, again, mere common sense, necessarily grounded in people's attempting to hone their "intuitive powers" (1935, p. 119)[4]:

> From a rational or scientific point of view, all practically real problems are problems in economics. The problem of life is to utilize resources "economically," to make them go as far as possible in the production of desired results. The general theory of economics is therefore simply the rationale of life – in so far as it has any rationale. The first question in regard to scientific economics is the question of how far life is rational, how far its problems reduce to the form of using given means to achieve given ends. Now this, we shall contend, is not very far; the scientific view of life is a limited and partial view; life is at bottom an exploration in the field of values, an attempt to discover values, rather than on the knowledge of them to produce and enjoy them to the greatest possible extent. We strive to "know ourselves," to find our real wants, more than to get what we want. This fact sets a first and most sweeping limitation to the conception of economics as a science (1935, p. 105).

In another context, Knight observed,

> That "man is rational" is one of those interesting statements which do not have to be proved, since the subject admits it. In fact he says so himself; and the objective value of the statement is to be appraised in the light of that fact. It must also be viewed in light of other statements "man" makes about himself. By the same authority, he is also a groping ignoramus, a fool, and a miserable sinner, quite unworthy of redemption. The list of opposite characteristics could be indefinitely extended, and all the statements would be true, in varying degree and numerous interpretations. But by the same token each is false or, taken singly and alone, is an exaggeration and over-simplification (1947, p. 341).

Finally, Knight noted cryptically a key difference between economics and the physical sciences, "Physical objects are not at the same time trying to understand and use the investigator!" (1935, p. 147). In leading up to this point, Knight wrote, "In the realm of physical nature, the exact methods of science have carried understanding and control enormously farther than common sense could go. But, this was because the data are relatively stable, reducible to classes of manageable number, and especially classes with recognizable and measurable indices" (1935, p. 147). In another context, Knight mused, "Man as investigated is, like man as investigator, a being who *thinks*, and who acts on the basis of thinking, who *solves problems* of many kinds, in a way which sharply differentiates him from any other

---

[4]Knight wrote on the power of common sense, To repeat, it is possible for a good judge of human nature to form opinions with a high degree of validity as to what individuals or groups are likely to do under conditions present to observation. But none of this is done by methods of science. It is all in the field of art, and not of science, of suggestion and interpretation, and not accurate, definite, objective statement, a sphere in which common sense works and logic falls down, and where, in consequence, the way to improve our technique is not to attempt to analyze things into their elements, reduce them to measure and determine functional relations, but to educate and trim our intuitive powers (1935, p. 125).

organic species, and which we have to assume is not characteristic of other inanimate nature at all" (1947, p. 231, emphasis in the original).

Nevertheless, Knight was unwilling to discard economic science altogether:

> In spite of all the foregoing, there is a science of economics, a true, and even exact, science, which reaches laws as universal as those of mathematics and mechanics. The greatest need for the development of economics as a growing body of thought and practice is an adequate appreciation of the meaning, and the limitations, of this body of accurate premises and rigorously established conclusions. It comes about in the same general way as all science, except perhaps in a higher degree, i.e., through abstraction. There are not laws regarding the *content* of economic behavior, but there are laws universally valid as to its *form*. There is an abstract rationale of all conduct which is rational at all, and the rationale of all social relations arising through the organization of rational activity (1935, p. 135, emphasis in the original).

Knight goes on to explain that economists might never be able to predict what goods people will want or what things will be construed as wealth, but that economists can predict with some confidence that people will prefer more to less of goods and "we know quite well what must be the attitude of any sane individual toward wealth wherever a social situation exists which gives the concept meaning" (1935, p. 135). Economists can also know the "general relations" between resources used and production levels (1935, pp. 135–136), but all such understandings – or laws or principles – must be, at least to a degree, provisional – or "relatively absolute" (1935, p. 45) – with the suggested meaning being that disciplinary understandings are treated as absolute until they are proven to be demonstrably inferior to new understandings. More fundamentally, the most "fundamental law of conduct" is this:

> In the utilization of limited resources in competing fields of employment, which is the form of all rational activity in conduct, we tend to apportion our resources among alternative uses that are open in such a way that equal amounts of resource yield equivalent returns in all fields" (1921, Sect. II.III.23, emphasis in the original).

Hence, any endeavor to replicate the techniques of the physical sciences in economics without an appreciation for the techniques' applicability and limitations is naïve:

> In a limited field in economic data, due largely to the fact that exchange has reduced the factors to definite measurable quantities, we have an exact science of the general form of relations. It can tell us little in the concrete, and its chief function is negative – to offset as far as possible the stupid theorizing of the man on the street (1935, p. 147).

To summarize, Knight endorsed how Adam Smith mixed "genial humanity" with common sense in discussion of human behavior and markets. Knight still was willing to address human behavior with an assumption that decision approximates some high level of rationality, knowing that the rational dimension of life was highly circumscribed by the difficult-to-know processes by which the given ends are identified as motivating mental constructs. Knight was (or would have been, had he lived long enough) unwilling to adopt the strident methodological position that Becker and George Stigler (1977) adopted – *de gustibus non est disputandum* – i.e., that suggests tastes are not subject to serious dispute, as I described in Chap. 2. Knight observed,

In all the folk-lore to which human thinking has given rise, in connection with human beings themselves, perhaps the most false and misleading single item is the common notion that men "know what they want," or that there is no arguing about tastes. It would surely be much nearer the truth to say that there is no arguing about anything else, or specifically about "facts." The principal thing that men actually want is to find out what they do really want; and the bulk of what they want, or think they want, is wanted because they think in some sense that they "ought" to do so, that it is "right" (1947, p. 234).

No doubt, because so much economic data is subjective and individual, Knight held dim views on what could be accomplished through empirical investigations over and above what can be deduced through every day common sense.

Because of his confidence in people's and his own intuitive powers through common sense investigation, Knight was frequently willing to make assertions that he felt were indisputable in his relatively absolute sense, given that his assertions came without his own documentation or citations to the works of others. Many neoclassical economists would see Knights' assertions as just musings. For example, Knight posits in several places that the ethical content of the distribution of income is determined by ownership, which, in turn, is determined by a "complex mixture of inheritance, luck, and effort probably in that order of relative importance," and with effort being the only one of the three income-determining factors having any "ethical validity" (1935, p. 56). The same considerations can be applied to determining the income of labor, but then labor has an added complication: It can "represent either a sacrifice or a source of enjoyment," which leave labor's economic role mixed, as a factor of production and as a good subject to consumption (1935, p. 56).

For all these reasons (the chief one being the difficulty of devising useful empirical tests for predictions), Knight would have dismissed an interpretation of Milton Friedman's view that it does not matter whether or not people do in fact act rationally at all. Knight was inclined to ask, if empirical tests were of limited application and usefulness, then what is left for assessing the empirical findings other than the validity of the premises that economists employ and their adherence to accepted logical rules of inference?

Knight also stressed repeatedly the need to assess market economies on some standard apart from strict neoclassical efficiency. According to Knight, efficiency was necessarily dependent on an assumption of *given* and *fixed* wants, or more elusive desired ends, which he argued were subject to change. Knight argued that individual freedom was one such standard that should be used to assess markets and other social institutions designed to promote people's cooperation in seeking their individualized ends (1947, pp. 1–34).

Ludwig von Mises' Hostility Toward Positivism

Ludwig von Mises (1881–1973) was an Austrian economist who during the middle fifty years of the twentieth century dedicated himself to saving economics from critics (mainly from the German historical school) who attacked rational *homo economicus*. As Mises put it,

It was a fundamental mistake of the Historical School of *Wirtschaftliche Staatswissenschaften* in Germany and of Institutionalism in America to interpret economics as the characterization of the behavior of an ideal type, the *homo oeconomicus*. According to this doctrine traditional or orthodox economics does not deal with the behavior of man as he really is and acts, but with a fictitious or hypothetical image. It pictures a being driven exclusively by "economic" motives, i.e., solely by the intention of making the greatest possible material or monetary profit. Such a being, say these critics, does not have and never did have a counterpart in reality; it is a phantom of a spurious armchair philosophy. No man is exclusively motivated by the desire to become as rich as possible; many are not at all influenced by this mean craving. It is vain to refer to such an illusory homunculus in dealing with life and history (1949, Sect. 1.II.130).

Indeed, as did Knight, Mises spurned the use of strictly selfish *homo economicus* as a model of human behavior that can teach anything of consequence about human action.[5]

Although important in his system of thought, rationality was not the "ultimate given" in economics or any other discipline that sought to be a science. The ultimate given is the "nonrational fact" of reason, or the human tendency at the individual level to understand the world systematically because of some dissatisfaction "with the state of affairs as it prevails" and then to organize an improvement in the state of affairs using any means available: "Man acts because he lacks the power to render conditions fully satisfactory and must resort to appropriate means in order to render them less unsatisfactory" (1962, pp. 2–3). Like all animals, humans are everywhere pressed to yield to "the impulse that most urgently asks for satisfaction." With all reasoning (or thinking) leading to some deliberate action, they are capable of "subduing" their "instincts, emotions, and impulses": "What distinguishes man from beast is precisely that he adjusts his behavior deliberately" (1949, Sect. 1.I.22).

From Mises' perspective, human action (as well as "economic rationality"[6]), which is organized to bring about improvement as individuals conceive of improvement, "is necessarily always rational" – by definition – with the term rational action

---

[5] On human action grounded in perfect selfishness, Mises observed, "It is generally believed that economists, in dealing with the problems of a market economy, are quite unrealistic in assuming that all men are always eager to gain the highest attainable advantage. They construct, it is said, the image of a perfectly selfish and rationalistic being for whom nothing counts but profits. Such a homo economicus may be a likeness of stock jobbers and speculators. But the immense majority are very different. Nothing for the cognition of reality can be learned from the study of the conduct of this delusive image" (1949, Sect. 4.XIII.6).

[6] On the coincidence of "economic" and "rational" activity, Mises mused, "It is, therefore, illegitimate to regard the 'economic' as a definite sphere of human action which can be sharply delimited from other spheres of action. Economic activity is rational activity. And since complete satisfaction is impossible, the sphere of economic activity is coterminous with the sphere of rational action. It consists firstly in valuation of ends, and then in the valuation of the means leading to these ends. All economic activity depends, therefore, upon the existence of ends. Ends dominate economy and alone give it meaning" (1951, Sect. II.5.39).

"pleonastic," which is to say redundant (1949, Sect. 1.I.32).[7] Economics – or his preferred term, praxeology, the study of human action – is not concerned with "ultimate springs and goals of action, but with the means applied for the attainment of an end sought," and all rational actions are necessarily determined by a "consideration of expense and success" (1949, Sect. 1.II.19). "Rational conduct means that man, in face of the fact that he cannot satisfy all his impulses, and appetites, foregoes the satisfaction of those which he considers less urgent" (1949, Sect. 2. VIII.93).

The ends of human action can be anything, from money accumulation to aestheticism. Moreover, "the cult of beauty and virtue, wisdom, and the search for truth are not hindered by the rationality of the calculating and computing mind" (1949, Sect. 3.XIII.6). As Mises restated his position later:

> Economics does not assume or postulate that men aim only or first of all at what is called material well-being. Economics, as a branch of the more general theory of human action, deals with all human action, i.e., with man's purposive aiming at the attainment of ends chosen, whatever these ends may be. To apply the concept *rational* or *irrational* to the ultimate ends chosen is nonsensical. We may call irrational the ultimate given, viz., those things that our thinking can neither analyze nor reduce to other ultimately given things. Then every ultimate end chosen by any man is irrational. It is neither more nor less rational to aim at riches like Croesus than to aim at poverty like a Buddhist monk (1949, Sect. 7. XXXIX.12).

The central problem of economics is one of working out the logical consequences of people's need to behave rationally, or to seek improvement, with one such consequence being that of seeking the cooperation of others, involving "acts of exchange" (1951, Sect. II.5.9). At the same time, Mises recognized the constricted sphere within which people can actually act; that is, with "act" necessarily implying any move that is deliberate, or with a purpose.[8] Nevertheless, market prices in money that emerge from whatever level of exchanges is possible are essential to

---

[7] Mises added in another book, "The spheres of rational action and economic action are therefore coincident. All rational action is economic. All economic activity is rational action. All rational action is in the first place individual action. Only the individual thinks. Only the individual reasons. Only the individual acts. How society arises from the action of individuals will be shown in a later part of our discussion" (1951, Sect. II.5.8).

[8] Mises observes, "Hence, all talk about the primacy of irrational elements is vain. Within the universe the existence of which our reason cannot explain, analyze, or conceive, there is a narrow field left within which man is capable of removing uneasiness to some extent. This is the realm of reason and rationality, of science and purposive action. Neither its narrowness nor the scantiness of the results man can obtain within it suggests the idea of radical resignation and lethargy. No philosophical subtleties can ever restrain a healthy individual from resorting to actions which – as he thinks – can satisfy his needs. It may be true that in the deepest recesses of man's soul, there is a longing for the undisturbed peace and inactivity of a merely vegetative existence. But in living man, these desires, whatever they may be, are outweighed by the urge to act and to improve his own condition. Once the forces of resignation get the upper hand, man dies; he does not turn into a plant" (1949, Sect. 7.XXXIX.6).

rational decisions because they ease economic calculations. Indeed, when market pricing is abandoned, in concert with the views of Knight and the views of Hayek, rational decision making, and the improvement implied, is lost, as it must be under socialism:

> To suppose that a socialist community could substitute calculations in kind for calculations in terms of money is an illusion. In a community that does not practice exchange, calculations in kind can never cover more than consumption goods. They break down completely where goods of higher order are concerned. Once society abandons free pricing of production goods rational production becomes impossible. Every step that leads away from private ownership of the means of production and the use of money is a step away from rational economic activity (1951, Sect. II.5.22).
>
> And without calculation, economic activity is impossible. Since under socialism, economic calculation is impossible, under socialism there can be no economic activity in our sense of the word. In small and insignificant things, rational action might still persist. But, for the most part, it would no longer be possible to speak of rational production. In the absence of criteria of rationality, production could not be consciously economical (1951, Sect. II.5.24).

Mises' conception of science is dramatically different from the conception held by neoclassical economists who, like natural scientists, insist on predictions being subject to empirical refutation. For Mises, science is restricted to the logical progression from premises to consequences:

> Science always is and must be rational. It is the endeavor to attain a mental grasp of the phenomena of the universe by a systematic arrangement of the whole body of available knowledge. However, as has been pointed out above, the analysis of objects into their constituent elements must sooner or later necessarily reach a point beyond which it cannot go. The human mind is not even capable of conceiving a kind of knowledge not limited by an ultimate given inaccessible to further analysis and reduction. The scientific method that carries the mind up to this point is entirely rational. The ultimate given may be called an irrational fact (1949, Sect. 1.I.39).

In Mises' theory of knowledge, science is dependent on "regularities" observed in historical data that can be extended forward in time. Without regularities, prediction, and control, the hallmarks of science, are not possible. For that matter, according to Mises, thinking and reasoning are not possible. The physical sciences can and have achieved much, but only because their subject matter – physical things – do not and cannot *act*. In the external world of "natural events," the focus of physical sciences, "there is no such thing as action" (1962, p. 7). Thus, "the natural sciences are causality research; the sciences of human action are teleological" (1962, p. 7). This is to say, that the subject matter of the physical sciences does not, and cannot as far as we can know, conceive of "less unsatisfactory" states and then seek real improvement with any real intent.

By way of contrast, true human action, grounded in individually conceived perceptions of improvement, cannot be expected to extend forward in time and space, because what is to be the less unsatisfactory state has no replication in the historical data. People do not so much adopt the role of *homo economicus* as they adopt the role of "*homo agens*" (the "acting animal") (1962, p. 4). Ends of actions cannot be prespecified, because they are so individualized and subjective. Thus, the value of empirical testing of hypotheses is limited at best.[9] This means that "for science, the only relevant question is whether or not these theorems can stand the test of rational examination" (1949, Sect. 1.III.0), which means whether some better, logically tighter argument can be advanced, not whether empirical tests confirm the predictions.

Mises surmised that that it is absurd to discuss human action without referring to "ends aimed at by the actors" (1962, p. xiii), and if the ends are to be taken seriously, then, again, it is hard to see how empirical verification of the kind of positive economics advocated by, say, Friedman (see Chap. 1) can advance our understanding of human action, because measurements may be of things that do not correspond to ends. Indeed, there is, in Mises' view, a "real viciousness" to positivism when "it does not acknowledge any other way of proving a proposition than those practiced by the experimental natural sciences and qualifies as metaphysical – which, in the positivist jargon, is synonymous with nonsensical – all other methods of rational discourse" (1962, p. xii).

However, this does not mean, Mises ironically insisted, that economists should not study the physical sciences, including physics and mathematics. In fact, Mises recommended that they master such subjects, but only because they might otherwise "confuse the tasks and the methods of the theory of human action with the tasks and the methods of any of these other branches of knowledge" (1962, p. 4). In other words, economists need to study the physical sciences but only to protect themselves against the lure of becoming real scientists.

According to Mises, proponents and critics of economics, or praxeology, posit mistakenly that the basic premises – whether drawn up in the form of human action or rational behavior – are arbitrary, a matter of choice and analytical convenience (1962, p. 18): "Deductions (drawn from the premises), it teaches, cannot add anything to our knowledge of reality. It merely makes explicit what was already implicit in the premises," and are not worth much because they are not drawn from experience (1962, p. 12).

Mises argued that basic behavioral premises are hardly arbitrary or matters of choice. They are drawn from a constellation of experiences of the analysts, all constrained by evolutionary forces that in people's distant pasts "eliminated those specimens and species which developed instincts that were a liability in the struggle for survival" (1962, p. 14). Nonhuman animals need not have developed successful methods of reasoning because they have so little leeway (if any leeway at all) to make their states less unsatisfactory. But reasoning is a distinctive human trait, and

---

[9]Mises recognized the usefulness and limitations of empirical data in this way: "The *booking-office* clerk at Paddington can discover, if he chooses, what proportion of travelers from that station goes to Birmingham, what proportion to Exeter, and so on, but he knows nothing of the individual reasons that lead to one choice in one case and another in another. But, Russell has to admit that the cases are not "*wholly analogous*" because the clerk can, in his nonprofessional moments, find out things about human beings that they do not mention when they are taking tickets, while the physicist in observing atoms has no such advantage" (1962, p. 25).

just as evolutionarily adapted as tastes for foods. As with food tastes, natural and sexual selection worked on reasoning faculties, selecting out those reasoning proclivities that were a liability to survival and selecting for those that, by intention or not, furthered survival of the human-like species that adopted them, the most prominent remaining thinking species being *homo sapiens*.[10] Mises was willing to speculate that there might have been some "advanced anthropoids" that tried other methods of reasoning but failed: "Only those groups could survive whose members acted in accordance with the right categories, i.e., with those that were in conformity with reality and therefore – to use the concept of pragmatism – worked" (1962, p. 15).

All of this is to say that a theoretical presumption that people act, and do so rationally, can be seen as a theoretical predilection that has survival value not only for people as they go through their daily lives actually *acting*, but also for economists-qua-analysts as they seek to understand how humans can orchestrate meaningful, improvement-directed actions. Mises was not willing to suggest that the methods of thinking were applicable to all human behaviors. Indeed, the domain of human actions could be severely limited: "Animals are forced to adjust themselves to the natural conditions of their environment; if they do not succeed in this process of adjustment, they are wiped out. Man is the only animal that is able – within definite limits – to adjust his environment purposively to suit him better" (1962, p. 8). This point he repeated only a few pages later: "There is within the *infinite expanse* of what is called the universe or nature a small field in which man's conscious conduct can influence the course of events" (1962, p. 11, emphasis in the original).

However, it needs to be noted that such an insistence on the limited scope of economics as praxeology suggests a sphere in which human behaviors could exhibit regularities founded on external forces and that could be studied through the empirical methods of natural science, or through, perhaps, the methods of behavioral economists and psychologists that we take up in the following chapter. Nevertheless, given the admixture of human behaviors, it would be hard to determine if the behaviors are true actions or something else, using Mises' definition of actions, or mere responses.

---

[10] On the selection process for thinking, Mises wrote, "Experience is a mental act on the part of thinking and acting men. It is impossible to assign to it any role in a purely natural chain of causation the characteristic mark of which is the absence of intentional behavior. It is logically impossible to compromise between design and the absence of design. *Those primates* who had the serviceable categories survived, not because, having had the experience that their categories were serviceable, they decided to cling to them. They survived because they did not resort to other categories that would have resulted in their own extirpation. In the same way in which the evolutionary process eliminated all other groups whose individuals, because of specific properties of their bodies, were not fit for life under the special conditions of their environment, it eliminated also *those* groups whose minds developed in a way that made their use for the guidance of conduct pernicious" (1962, p. 15).

Friedrich Hayek's Concern Over the Nature
of The Economic Problem

Along with Knight, Mises, and other economists of the Austrian school, Friedrich
Hayek (1899–1992), parted ways with the insistence of economists in the preWorld
War II era and the emerging neoclassical economists in the postWorld War II era
that the assumed level and scope of people's rationality is inconsequential, or that
economists can make reasonable as-if assumptions about rational behavior as
approximations of how people make decisions. To Hayek, the economic problem
could not be what economists have said it is:

> The economic problem is thus not merely a problem of how to allocate "given" resources –
> if "given" is taken to mean given to a single mind which deliberately solves the problem set
> by these "data." It is rather a problem of how to secure the best use of resources to any of the
> members of society, for ends whose relative importance only these individuals know. Or, to
> put it differently, it is a problem of the utilization of knowledge not given to anyone in its
> totality (1945, pp. 519–520).

Hayek believed that the dominant attribute of goods is their subjective values,
which cannot really be known to other people including would-be central planners
and economists professing to do science. Therefore, it is intellectual folly to test the
implications of models based on as-if behavior with data (counts of goods and bads)
because the goods (and bads) cannot capture the central concerns of choosers who
apply subjective values and preference orderings.

With the as-if behavioral assumption and the validity of data in considerable
doubt, interpreting the test results is difficult, or so Hayek would argue. If scientifically grounded tests do not confirm hypotheses, are the behavioral predictions
wrong or are the data poor proxies for the underlying subjective values being
maximized?

Austrian economists – such as Mises, Hayek, and Israel Kirtzner – have rejected
the neoclassical methodological approach, which demands that economic knowledge be validated and acquired only through *science*, or exact empirical testing.
They have done so for several key reasons.

First, the Austrian economists have rejected the proposition that goods have an
objective, physical reality that can be disentangled in any meaningful way from the
goods' subjective origins and content. Hayek agreed with Knight and Mises that a
science such as physics can rely on empirical tests because its subjects (gases,
solids, and stars) do have an objective reality and do not have a capacity to attribute
value to other objects in the world around them (again, as far as anyone knows), and
the objects of the physical sciences have no presumed means of self-activation in
the pursuit of maximizing internally generated preference orderings.

By contrast, the subjects of economic analysis are people from whom the basic
data – preferences, wants, and goods – do not necessarily have an objective reality
apart from their subjective values, with the values known only to the people who
create them, hold them, and change them. Austrian economists have insisted that
the internal, subjective nature of economic data imposes a first and sweeping

limitation on the ability of economists to do science in the same mold, and with the same types of tests, that physics and other physical sciences do.

Second, markets are processes by which known unexploited economic opportunities are exploited, but then they are also processes by which new and previously unknown unexploited opportunities are discovered through entrepreneurial "alertness," which can take economies off in whole new directions (Kirtzner 1973). This is to say, any assumption of known given wants and resources sidesteps what markets are good at doing, which is to unsettle what was previously considered as *known* and *given*.

Third, Austrian economists have agreed that the scientific approach to the acquisition of knowledge in the hard sciences harbors a chance of being productive, but only because the phenomenon of concern is relatively simple, at least when compared with the far more complex social environments of higher order animals, especially humans. The environmental forces that affect complex human behavior are too great for the human mind to grasp in their entirety and for economists, standing apart from the mix, to analyze objectively. Add to the complexity of environmental forces the gazillions of personal interactions that produce the exact details of social, political, and market outcomes, and it is not surprising that Hayek was reluctant to accept that anything other than broad patterns of outcomes could be predicted even in theory (1967, Chap. 2). Hayek used an observation by Joseph Schumpeter to bolster his (Hayek's) point: "[E]conomic life of a nonsocialist society consists of millions of relations or flows between individual firms and households. We can establish certain theorems about them, but we can never observe them all" (as quoted by Hayek 1967, p. 35 from Schumpeter 1954, p. 241). As neoclassical economists gained confidence in the ability of statistics to ferret out regularities in complex social phenomena after World War II, Hayek and other Austrians continued to insist, perhaps with greater reason and force, that the world is far too complex for economists to develop regularities for science's required "prediction and control":

> One of the chief results so far achieved by theoretical work in these fields seems to me to be the demonstration that here individual events regularly depend on so much concrete circumstances that we shall never, in fact, be in a position to ascertain them all; and that in consequence not only the ideal of prediction and control must largely remain beyond our reach, but also the hope remain illusory that we can discover by observation regular connections between the individual events (Hayek 1967, p. 34).

Moreover, modern statistical methods are far too limited in power to help to pierce economists' veil of ignorance, although the promises of statistics and the availability of data perpetuates an illusion of sorts within the profession:

> Statistics.......deals with the problem of large numbers essentially by eliminating complexity and deliberately treating the individual elements which it counts as if they were not systematically connected. It avoids the problems of complexity by substituting for the information on the individual elements information on the frequency with which their different properties occur in classes of such elements and it deliberately disregards the fact that the relative position of the different elements in a structure may matter. In other words, it proceeds on the assumption that information on the numerical frequencies of the

different elements of a collective is enough to explain the phenomena and that no information is required on the matter in which the elements are related. The statistical method is therefore of use only where we either deliberately ignore, or are ignorant of, the relations between the individual elements with different attributes, i.e., where we ignore or are ignorant of any structure into which they are organized. Statistics in such situations enables us to regain simplicity and to make the task manageable by substituting a single attribute for the unascertainable individual attributes in the collective. It is, however, for this reason, irrelevant to the solution of the problems in which it is relations between individual elements with different attributes which matter (Hayek 1967, pp. 29–30).

Hayek further bolstered his argument by noting that "no economist has yet succeeded in making a fortune by buying and selling commodities on the basis of his scientific prediction of future prices (even though some may have done so by selling such predictions)" (1967, p. 35). Having denied that doing science is a practical goal for economists, Austrian economists like Hayek do not need to make the types of practical concessions on theories underlying behavioral premises or relevant data to test theories. They feel no compulsion to equate the scientific nature of economics with, say, physics, as Friedman has done (1952, p. 18).

In his *Essay on Positive Economics*, Friedman does make the useful point that physicists often make calculations about the speed of falling objects on Earth, using the rate of descent for objects in a vacuum. The assumption about the acceleration of falling objects often works well because the "extra accuracy it (a more general theory that takes account of air resistance) yields may not justify the extra cost of using it" (1953, p. 18). While economics may strive to be like physics in using a simplified premise of rational behavior, it is categorically different when it comes to the objects in empirical tests. The falling ball does not have a mind of its own that would allow the ball to assess the value of the fall, and even if it did, the ball's rate of descent would not be materially affected. In the case of economics, the ball, and what is done with it, depends critically on how people appraise the ball and rate of descent and how their appraisals will cause them to intervene to change the descent or not allow the ball to fall in the first place. There is the added complication in economics that balls can be different things to different people, as well as have different evaluations by different people.

But then, economists of the Austrian school do not look to establish or develop the kind of detailed knowledge of outcomes of the interactions of people through markets that neoclassical economists seek. Rather, they seek only the discovery of the broad patterns of outcomes, with the details within those patterns left undefined or incompletely defined. Indeed, Austrian economists see social advantages in people's inability to predict with scientific accuracy the detailed patterns of outcomes. As Hayek wrote,

That it is thus ignorance of the future outcome which makes possible agreement on rules which serve as a common means for a variety of purposes is recognized by the practice in many instances of deliberately making the outcome unpredictable in order to make agreement on procedure possible: whenever we agree on drawing lots we deliberately substitute equal chances of the different parties for the certainty as to which of them will benefit from the outcome (1967, p. 4).

Hence, Austrian economists do not have to be as careful as neoclassical economists in presuming that people are exclusively rational. They do not need to assume that people act *as if* they are fully or perfectly rational. Rather, they only have to presume that people seek to improve their lots through individual efforts and in cooperation with others (with the issue of exactly how individuals maximize their objective functions, if such is worthy of conceptualization, of no necessary consequence). Indeed, Austrian economists stress the power and the destabilizing influence of entrepreneurs in the economic process.

Hayek and his fellow Austrians can show, as Smith showed, patterns of outcomes. They can show, for example, that people are "led by an invisible hand to make nearly the same distribution of the necessaries of life, which would have been made, had the earth been divided into equal portions among all its inhabitants, and thus without intending it, without knowing it, advance the interest of the society, and afford means to the multiplication of the species" (1776, Sect. IV.I.10). And Austrians can accept that people are not exclusively motivated by self-interest.

As discussed in Chap. 2, Smith accepted multiple motivations for people's behavior, although he focused on self-interest as being a very important motivation among market participants who are dealing with each other at a distance, in terms of geography and social groups. Austrians have no problem with such a methodological stance. This is because the Austrian economists do not stake their professional positions on their mathematical and empirical, hypothesis-testing skills. They do not seek to predict the detailed content of the patterns of outcomes, because they see such a goal as unachievable, or as Hayek argued:

> [M]ost of the phenomena in which we are interested, such as competition, could not occur at all unless the number of distinct elements involved were fairly large, and that the overall pattern that will form itself is determined by the significantly different behavior of the different individuals so that the obstacle of obtaining the relevant data cannot be overcome by treating them as members of a statistical collective.
>
> For this reason economic theory is confined to describing kinds of patterns which will appear if certain general conditions are satisfied, but can rarely if ever be derived from this knowledge any predictions of specific phenomena. This is seen most clearly if we consider those systems of simultaneous equations which since Leon Walras have been widely used to represent the general relations between the prices and the quantities of all commodities bought and sold. They are so framed that *if* we were able to fill in all the blanks, i.e., *if* we knew all the parameters of these equations, we could calculate the prices and quantities of all the commodities. But, as at least the founders of this theory clearly understood, its purpose is not "to arrive at a numerical calculation of prices," because it would be "absurd" to assume that we can ascertain all the data (1973, p. 35, emphasis in the original).

Neoclassical economists typically assume that supply and demand curves are market constraints that really exist or can be treated *as if* they really are out there, as evident by the way they introduce demand and supply functions in their models designed to focus on markets' equilibrium conditions. In contrast, Austrian economists argue that markets are, if anything, demand- and supply-creating and revealing processes. Kirtzner observed,

> These patterns of demand, we must remember, are those entrepreneurs *anticipate* will be caused by alternative opportunities they might have placed before consumers (in a manner

capable of ensuring their awareness of the opportunities available). The only consumer wants that can be considered relevant for a discussion of the efficiency of production decisions, then, are those that are manifested *after* production decisions have placed opportunities before consumers (in a manner of securing their attention). It is the failure to perceive this which vitiates all those Galbraithian discussions of the fallacy – to which economists allegedly subject – of taking consumer wants as given, when in fact, these discussions insist, consumer wants are modified by the very process of production supposedly designed to cater to them. What vitiates these discussions is the quite incorrect belief (for which economists are certainly to blame) that the demand curves which help determine production decisions in the theory of the firm (and which thus presumably support the doctrine of consumer sovereignty) are given and known apart from the production decisions. As soon as we recognize that these are anticipated, entrepreneurially guessed curves, it becomes apparent that (except in equilibrium, where product qualities have already settled) the only sense in which we can consider production as responsive to demand is that which perceives entrepreneurs striving to anticipate the demand for what they will produce, as this demand will be manifested *after* production has taken place (1973, pp. 176–177).

If supply and demand emerge as people interact in markets, then it is hardly possible for people to know and order their wants and consistently choose among their wants in some perfect way.

James Buchanan, Rational Behavior, and Constitutional Economics

Having been greatly influenced by his acknowledged mentor Frank Knight, James Buchanan (1919-present) has been ambivalent about the undisciplined use of full rational behavior in economic analysis. He would accept both Knight's point that life is far more varied and complex than a narrowly focused pursuit of the efficient allocation of given resources among given ends, as well as the idea that life is not limited to strictly self-interested pursuits. Moreover, ends are necessarily subjective and stand apart from the goods and services people buy in the public or private spheres. Like Knight, Buchanan questions whether there could be a science of choice, given that science requires prediction and that choices, to be real choices, must have some semblance of unpredictability (1969b). Buchanan acknowledges that in the "predictive science of economics" cost is "the market value of the alternate product that might be produced by rational reallocation of resource inputs to uses other than that observed. This market value is reflected in the market prices for resource units; hence, cost is measured directly by prospective money outlays" (1969a,b, p. 42).

However, Buchanan insists, in such analysis, individuals do not really choose, given that their behavior can be predicted. Neoclassical construction of cost is not really grounded on a true theory of choice, because in any true theory of real choice, cost is something quite different from a money measure of some alternate product. The cost involved in every real choice is the subjective value of a foregone opportunity (or "anticipated utility loss upon sacrifice of a rejected alternative")

[1969a, p. 43], which necessarily means that cost is the value of something that is never actually experienced. This means that cost has to be a subjective construct because it never exists in some true, measurable form. Buchanan argued that his perspective on cost leads to these implications:

(1) Most important, cost must be borne exclusively by the decision-maker; it is not possible for cost to be shifted to and imposed on others.
(2) Cost is subjective; it exists in the mind of the decision-maker and nowhere else.
(3) Cost is based on anticipations; it is necessarily a forward-looking or ex ante concept.
(4) Cost can never be realized because of the fact of choice itself; that which is given up cannot be enjoyed.
(5) Cost cannot be measured by someone other than the decision-maker because there is no way that subjective experience can be directly observed.
(6) Finally, cost can be dated at the moment of decision or choice (1969a,b, p. 43).

Concluding Comments

This chapter has examined how economists from the subjectivist school have in various ways disputed the neoclassical premise of rational behavior. In the main, they have insisted that economics based on rational precepts is necessarily a partial view of life. After all, wants that are subject to efficient allocation must be formed in some way other than through fully rational means, or else the calculations involved in making cost–benefit analyses would leave people with no time to make choices and economists/analysts no time to ferret out the implications of choices among goods. Moreover, wants and the ends they serve are subjective and individualized. Finally, people's choices and actions must be to a degree new in the sense that they are organized to generate improvement from a less-satisfactory state, which means that economists do not have at their disposal the kind of historical data needed for science.

The next chapter discusses the largely empirical demonstrations by behavioral economists and behavioral psychologists who show that people are not as rational as neoclassical economists assume. Although neoclassical economists might agree that people cannot be as fully rational as represented in economic models, they have been surprised at the extent to which this evidence indicates people's behavior diverges from predictions assuming full rationality. The subjectivists, and may be Adam Smith, would not be so surprised. The subjectivists have all along not staked their theories on the presumption of perfect rationality, and Smith insisted that people were activated by a constellation of motivations. They all would likely agree that as economic analysis moves away from the binding corrective pressures of markets, human irrationalities might be easily documented. After all, as Knight insisted, life is largely involved in exploration into the largely unknown field of values.

Chapter 6
Behavioral Economists, and Psychologists' Challenges to Rational Behavior

Behavioral economics has emerged as a subdiscipline in economics over the last half of the twentieth century because of the work of scholars whose main contributions were outside the strict boundaries of economics, most prominently Herbert Simon and Daniel Kahneman. Simon won the 1978 Nobel prize in economics for his work on "bounded rationality" applied to firm organization, collected in his three-volume set published in 1982, and Kahneman received the 2002 Nobel prize in economics, for his work on "prospect theory" developed largely in collaboration with the late Amos Tversky (Kahneman and Tversky 1979, 2000a, among a host of citations). Behavioral economics now covers a massive scholarly literature and, more recently, a growing list of widely read trade books on the subject. In this chapter, I seek to cover only a portion of the literature, but enough to establish credibility of the formidable challenge that behavioral economics and behavioral psychology present to conventional, neoclassical economics. Mainly, reservations and criticisms regarding this literature are covered in Chap. 10.

The Overall Dimensions of the Behavioral Challenge

As this chapter was being developed, Duke University behavioral economist Dan Ariely wrote a book, *Predictably Irrational* (2008), which made *The New York Times* best sellers list. Ariely's catalogue of studies describing human irrationalities was published on the heels of a string of widely selling books on behavioral economics that are accessible to general audiences, including University of Chicago Richard Thaler's, *The Winner's Curse* (1992) and Yale University economist Robert Shiller's *Irrational Exuberance* (2005, but first published in 2000). Thaler returned to the trade market with his book, *Nudge* (2008), coauthored with his former Chicago colleague, Cass Sunstein, who is now a Harvard University law professor, which describes how insights from behavioral economics can be used to shape decisions and improved behavioral outcomes.

All of these works carry two levels of argument: On one level, behavioral research reveals that people do not exhibit the perfect rationality that the economists

R.B. McKenzie, *Predictably Rational?*,
DOI 10.1007/978-3-642-01586-1_6, © Springer-Verlag Berlin Heidelberg 2010

commonly assume. The more damning, second level of argument is that people are in so much of life "predictably irrational," because of a host of decision-making biases. Ariely concludes that "we are – goslings, after all" (Ariely 2008, p. 28). Thaler and Sunstein muse, "If you look at economics textbooks, you will learn that *homo economicus* can think like Albert Einstein, store as much memory as IBM's Big Blue, and exercise the will power of Mahatma Gandhi," which they suggest stands in stark contrast with real *homo sapiens* who readily forget birthdays, have trouble with math, and regret hangovers (2008, pp. 6–7).

While recognizing the shortcomings of behavioral findings, Thaler concluded his *The Winner's Curse* with the confession that devising accurately descriptive models of human behavior is difficult because many theorists have a "strong allergic reaction to data." Moreover, economic models based on the rationality premise are "elegant with precise predictions," while behavioral work tends to be "messy, with much vaguer predictions." He then asks, "But,... would you rather be elegant and precisely wrong, or messy and vaguely right? (Thaler 1992, p. 198).

Behavioral economists and neoclassical microeconomic theorists share the concern that any discipline worthy of being called a science must be positive, not normative, in approach. That is, science must be concerned with what is, not with what ought to be. However, contrary to Milton Friedman, Thaler stresses that economics is not so much a positive science, as it is a prescriptive one: "Setting price so that marginal cost equals marginal revenue is the right answer to the problem of how to maximize profits. Whether firms *do* that is another matter. I try to teach my MBA students that they should avoid the winner's curse and equate opportunity costs to out-of-pocket costs, but I also teach them that most people do not" (Thaler 1992, p. 197, emphasis in the original).

Behavioral economists set out an array of behavioral deductions or predictions that fully rational people can be expected to follow, if people are as rational as neoclassical economists claim. Of course, behavioral economists draw up their lists of exactly how people make their choices and how they behave in the real world, outside of economists' sterilized models. Behavioral economists' lists can include these points:

- Rational people can be expected to carefully, precisely, and accurately weigh the costs and benefits of everything they do, always appropriately discounting costs and benefits for risks and time. The only thing determining the present value of a dollar earned in a riskless venture a year from now or ten years from now is the discount rate. If the discount rate is 6 percent, the value of a dollar received a year from now is \$.94. The present value of a dollar received ten years from now is \$.58. The rational person should be willing to pay \$.94 for the dollar a year from now, and \$.58 for the same dollar 10 years out.
- Rational people can be expected always to take the most advantageous option, as defined by their present values adjusted for risk.
- If given the reward and loss and the appropriate discount rates for time and risk, external observers can predict what rational individuals will do.
- The discount rates can be expected to be the same no matter how far in the future the costs are incurred and the benefits received.

- The discount rate is not expected to change with the size of the prospective loss or gain. Economists assume constant discount rates through time with no additional effort to weight discounted values.
- Losses and opportunity costs should be valued the same. That is, losses and gains share the same continuum, which implies that a person should be willing to pay the same to avoid a given dollar loss as to acquire a given dollar gain.
- The decisions rational people make should be affected only by the expected costs and benefits, not by exactly how choices are posed or decisions are framed since the calculated difference in the discounted costs and benefits is what controls the decisions.
- The rational person can be expected to take or not take an option, depending on its value, regardless of whether he or she incurred an opportunity cost of a dollar or had to give up an out-of-pocket dollar.
- Historical costs are sunk costs, and hence are not real costs for today's decisions. They should not affect today's decisions or, for that matter, any decisions going forward.
- All demand curves slope downward based on consumer choice theory.

Behavioral economists seek to improve the realism and predictive power of economics. As Colin Camerer and George Loewenstein attest, "At the core of behavioral economics is the conviction that increasing the realism of the psychological underpinnings of economic analysis will improve the field of economics *on its own terms* – generating theoretical insights, making better predictions of field phenomena, and suggesting better policy (2004, p. 3, emphasis in original).

Moreover, behavioral economists take issue with each one of the above conventional economic propositions, including the sacred law of demand. Thaler is a proponent of what he calls "quasi-rational economics," defined as including behavior that is "purposeful, regular, and yet systematically different from the axioms of economic theory" [Thaler 1992, p. 191]). He observes "As [Gary] Becker (1962) has shown, in the aggregate demand curves will slope down even if people choose at random, so long as they have binding budget constraints. What then is the economic theory of consumer?" (Thaler 1991, p. xiii) – a question posed to suggest that empirical tests revealing inverse relationships between price and quantity do not necessarily add validity to the underlying rationality premises. And since there is no way to know preferences, there is no way to test whether consumers "equate price ratios to marginal rates of substitution" (Thaler 1991, p. xiii).[1]

Ariely goes a step further, virtually denying the validity of the downward sloping demand curve. In a chapter on "The Fallacy of Supply and Demand," Ariely quotes

---

[1] In passing, it needs to be noted that Becker's demonstration that downward sloping demand curves could be obtained from people acting randomly was a matter of intense debate between Becker and Austrian economists Israel Kirzner in the early 1960s, with Kirzner stressing that an assumption of random behavior on the part of economic actors was missing a major part of the process underlying rational behavior, which is that people are expected to revise in systematic ways their plans when confronted with new information as they interact with others who are continually revising their plans to new information. See Becker (1962; 1963) and Kirzner (1962; 1963).

Mark Twain who observed that "Tom had discovered a great law of human action, namely that in order to make a man covet a thing, it is only necessary to make it dear" (Ariely 2008, p. 25). He, then, redevelops his gosling view of human decision making and behavior: What people are willing to pay for a thing is a function of the imprinting of the first price observed for a thing, or, for that matter, any number that consumers are asked to imagine. For example, he asked his fifty-five MIT management students to write down the last two digits of their social security numbers and then asked them to indicate the maximum amount they would pay for the bottle of wine that had been given a 92-point rating by *Wine Advocate*. Those 20 percent of students with the highest last two digits of their social security numbers (80–99) gave maximum prices that were 216–346 percent higher than those 20 percent of students with the lowest last two digits (1–20). He found much the same pattern with an assortment of other products (cordless trackball and keyboard, for example) (Ariely 2008, pp. 26–29), suggesting that prices people are willing to pay may be incidentally tied to preferences. He argues that we are innately bound to seek "arbitrary coherence," a form of consistency between what we have observed in prices (or just numbers) and prices we are willing to pay. Put another way, initial numbers observed, and maybe imprinted, become *anchors* that guide our assessments of acceptable prices (Ariely 2008, p. 26).

Ariely argues that the law of demand is really unsettled when the price of a good becomes "free." A price of free presses an "emotional hot button" and gives rise to a form of "irrational excitement" on the part of consumers, which, in turn, dramatically unsettles consumption choices at prices above zero. He made this point by first offering MIT students who pass his research station on campus a thirty-cent Lindt truffle for fifteen cents and a two-cent Hershey Kiss for one cent. Seventy-three percent of the students bought the truffle. When the price of each chocolate was lowered a penny, to fourteen cents for the truffle and zero cents for the Kiss, the consumption distribution almost reversed. Sixty-nine percent of the students chose Kisses, up from 27 percent when its price was a penny (Ariely 2008, pp. 51–53).

According to Ariely, the students were freely grabbing the Kisses "not because they had made reasoned cost–benefit analysis before elbowing their way in, but simply because the Kisses were FREE!" (Ariely 2008, p. 53). And the word and concept of free has an "emotional charge" to people "because we humans are afraid of loss." One does not have to fear a loss when something is free (Ariely 2008, p. 54), a line of argument that could suggest that people can engage in a constrained form of rationality in the sense that they must be, in making decisions, at least weighing the subjective damage from a loss.[2]

---

[2]Although the thrust of my critique of the behavioral literature will be deferred until Chap. 10, I need to note a minor point here: In his report on his surveys Ariely does not report whether the two sets of prices were offered the same group or totally different groups of students and whether the number of customers was greater when the two prices were lowered, with the possibility that the greater percentage emerged largely from additional students taking the Kisses, not buyers switching from the truffle to the Kiss.

Otherwise, behavioral economists argue that the rational behavior premise is patently wrong, as demonstrated by a mountain of experimental and behavioral research. Marketing researchers Thanos Skouras, George Avlonitis, and Kostis Indounas (2005) write in their survey of the differences in approaches to research by people in marketing and economics (citing Kahneman 1994; Kahneman and Tversky 2000b; Thaler 2001):

> The weakest part (of "economists' theoretical edifice") is surely the notion of utility-maximization by rational consumers. This is not only implausible as a general description of buyers' behavior but there are many instances in everyday experience of most people that seem to contradict it. Moreover, the work of psychologists and several psychological experiments have shown beyond any doubt that rationality and utility-maximization can hardly be considered as universal and ever-present traits of consumer behavior (2005, p. 362).

Summarizing his own personal observations about how people make decisions, as well as research findings, Thaler observes, (People with some consistency) "over withhold on their income taxes in order to get a refund. They have positive balances in their savings accounts earning 5 percent and outstanding balances on their credit card for which they pay 18 percent" (1991, p. xxi). Thaler cites financial researchers findings assuming "that irrational investors will automatically go broke is incorrect. In some situations, the irrational investors actually end up with more wealth" (1991, p. xxi).

What are economists to make of such findings, and the implied challenge to the way so many economists continue to do science, especially, when the findings lead some behavioralists to declare sometimes with little to no qualification, as in "There is only one problem with this assumption of human rationality: it is wrong" (Lehrer 2009, p. xv). People may in some sense and in some limited way be rational, but the way in which they are rational often stands at odds with the kind of rationality economists conventionally assume, or so behavioralists forcefully argue. Moreover, making policy deductions based on models of conventional rationality may turn out to be inadequate, misdirected, or plain wrong.

In this chapter, I take up key findings and criticisms of behavioral economists and behavioral psychologists. I reserve for later consideration the issue of whether subjects' assumed level of rationality within economic analyses can be descriptively correct in deductive static neoclassical models. Indeed, the irrational failings of people in their decisions – which very well could expose the high degree of boundedness of their rationality capacities (as behavioral economists and psychologists stress) – might make it imperative that economists assume their subjects are more rational even than economists-qua-analysts know themselves to be, if economists seek to do deductive science within the constrained limits of their own thinking, rational, decision-making capacities. Criticisms of the behavioralists' critiques of the rationality premise at the foundation of neoclassical economics will be developed in Chap. 10.

Prospect Theory

Daniel Kahneman and the late Amos Tversky argue that conventional "utility theory, as it is commonly interpreted and applied, is not an adequate descriptive model" (Kahneman and Tversky 2000b, p. 18).[3] One of their strongest arguments is that decisions, economic or otherwise, are seldom made among known goods. Rather, when options are known at all, choices frequently involve gambles because the consequences are often not understood with the precision assumed in conventional rational models. At best, choices involve prospects, which are options with probabilities attached to various outcomes. At worst, decisions have to be made with immense uncertainties regarding the available array of options and their features. Decisions can be "orderly" without necessarily conforming to the dictates of traditional rationality.[4]

Behavioral economists argue that gambles are the "fruit flies" of experimental economics: They can be rapidly or cheaply replicated to test the various propositions of rational behavior outlined above (Kahneman and Tversky 2000a, p. 3.). For example, behavioral economists point to the pioneering work of Daniel Bernoulli who, as far back as 1738, tried to explain that people tend to be risk averse when contemplating choices involving gains, favoring sure-thing gains over gambles with expected gains. They will tend to be risk prone when contemplating choices involving losses, favoring gambles with expected loses to sure-thing losses. By implication, avoiding losses loom larger in decisions than garnering potential gains, a position that even Adam Smith also adopted in 1759 in his *Theory of Moral Sentiments*. In Smith's words,

> We suffer more, it has already been observed, when we fall from a better to a worse situation, than we ever enjoy when we rise from a worse to a better. Security, therefore, is the first and the principal object of prudence. It is averse to expose our health, our fortune, our rank, or reputation, to any sort of hazard. It is rather cautious than enterprising, and more anxious to preserve the advantages which we already possess, than forward to prompt

---

[3] Behavioral economists Jones and Cullis (2000, p. 82) observe, "Increasingly, evidence suggests that 'homo-economicus rationality' fails to describe adequately the behavior of individuals. To rely on such behavioral assumptions when evaluating social policy options may prove misleading." Nevertheless, as behavioral economist Thaler (1994, p. xvi) has noted, "No matter how strange a particular action might seem to be, some economist can usually construct a rational explanation."

[4] Tversky and Kahneman summarize their view of prospect theory: "Prospect theory departs from the tradition that assumes the rationality of economic agents; it is proposed as a descriptive, not a normative, theory. The idealized assumption of rationality in economic theory is commonly justified on two grounds: the conviction that only rational behavior can survive in a competitive environment, and the fear that any treatment that abandons rationality will be chaotic and intractable. Both arguments are questionable. First, the evidence indicates that people can spend a lifetime in a competitive environment without acquiring a general ability to avoid framing effects or to apply linear decision weights. Second, and perhaps more important, the evidence indicates that human choices are orderly, although not always rational in the traditional sense of this word" (Tversky and Kahneman 2000, p. 65).

us to the acquisition of still greater advantages. The methods of improving our fortune, which it principally recommends to us, are those which expose to no loss or hazard; real knowledge and skill in our trade or profession, assiduity and industry in the exercise of it, frugality, and even some degree of parsimony, in all our expences (1759, Sect. VI.I.7).

Kahneman and Tversky illustrate Bernoulli's point with a set of choices in a laboratory experiment from which a working rule of decision making can be drawn. Suppose you give subjects "a choice between a prospect that offers an 85 percent chance to win $1,000 (with a 15 percent chance of winning nothing) and the alternative of receiving $800 for sure" (Kahneman and Tversky 2000a, p. 2). According to conventional rational tenets, as behavioral economists present them (often implicitly equating the conventional view of rational behavior with monetary maximization), the gamble should be chosen by a "large majority," if not all, choosers, since its expected value (equal to ($1,000 × 0.85)+($0 × 0.15)] is $850. But the exact opposite is the case, a choice outcome that supports a presumption of risk aversion that represents a decision-making bias that at least constrains human rationality, if it is not evidence of a form of irrationality, according to Kahneman and Tversky (2000a, p. 2).

In an experiment involving 150 subjects, the choice was between a sure thing-option valued at $240 and a gamble with an expected value of $250 (25 percent chance to gain $1,000 and a 75 percent chance to get nothing), 84 percent of the subjects took the sure thing (Kahneman and Tversky 2000a, p. 6). In an actual experiment, when 95 subjects were presented with a choice between a guaranteed $3,000 and an 80 percent chance of a $4,000 payoff (with an expected value of $3,200), 80 percent of the subjects took the sure thing (Kahneman and Tversky 2000b, p. 21, citing Allais 1953). Kahneman and Tversky report another experiment in which the dollar values of the two options were the same as above ($4,000 and $3,000), but the probability of each were reduced by three-quarters, to 0.20 and 0.25, respectively. The equal percentage reduction in the probabilities gave rise to 65 percent of the subjects taking the first option ($4,000), up from 20 percent (Kahneman and Tversky 2000b, p. 21, citing Allais 1953). Kahneman and Tversky suggest that "over half the subjects violated expected utility theory" in that their choices were inconsistent, or were not transitive. The same general pattern of inconsistent choices was found when subjects were given non-money payoffs (weeks of tours in England) as options (Kahneman and Tversky 2000b, p. 21).

Kahneman and Tversky argue that economists have decision theory wrong. People do not evaluate alternatives, including prospects, just by discounting the monetary outcomes. Rather, people apply an additional subjective weight to the discounted value of the alternative outcomes.[5] In standard microeconomic

---

[5] According to Kahneman and Tversky, "Prospect theory distinguishes two phases in the choice process: an early phase of editing and a subsequent phase of evaluation. The editing phase consists of preliminary analysis of the offered prospects, which often yield a simpler representation of these prospects. In the second phase, the edited prospects are evaluated [with a subject weight applied to each choice option] and the highest value is chosen" (Kahneman and Tversky 2000b, p. 28, reprinted from Kahneman and Tversky 1979).

treatment of rational decisions, $100 should be evaluated the same no matter whether it is added to a gain in wealth of $100 or $1,000 or added to a loss in wealth of $100 or $1,000. But, prospect theory and laboratory experiments suggest, that is not the case. People's subjective valuations of $100 can be different, depending on the probability that the stated payoff will be received, on the weight that is applied to the discounted value, and whether the $100 is a loss or gain.[6]

Why does it matter whether a value is a loss or gain? People innately tend to be risk averse, not risk seeking, on matters involving gains (or so can be the case for a sizable majority of people).[7] What this means to behavioral economists is that losses loom larger in decisions than gains of equal monetary value. (As we will see in the next chapters, evolutionary biologists and evolutionary psychologists have their own explanations for people's innate risk aversion.) Kahneman and Tversky posit, "Loss aversion explains people's reluctance to bet on a fair coin for equal stakes. The attractiveness of the possible gain is not nearly sufficient to compensate for the aversiveness of the possible loss. For example, most respondents in a sample of undergraduates refused to stake $10 on the toss of a coin, if they stood to win less than $30" (Kahneman and Tversky 2000a, p. 3).

Prospect theory postulates that people's "hypothetical value function" spanning losses and gains has a flattened S shape to it, as described in Fig. 6.1 (which graphically illustrates the risk aversion on gains and the risk proneness on losses). The positive subjective value of a $100 gain is less than the negative subjective value of a $100 loss. Put in behavioral economic terms, people (or some ill-defined majority of people) are subject to loss aversion, which means they will favor gambles involving losses over sure-thing losses and they will incur more costs to avoid a loss of a given amount than they will incur to obtain a gain of the same amount. The observed discontinuity in people's evaluations of losses and gains is at odds with conventional rational behavior, which assumes gains and losses are mirror images of one another. In effect, behavioral economists admonish other economists to adjust, at the very least, their conception of rationality to accommo-date risk aversion on decisions involving gains and loss aversion (which implies a form of risk proneness) on decisions involving losses. This, they suggest, will lead to improved predictive power of their modeling.

People's inclination to be loss-averse also means that people are more inclined to gamble to avoid a loss than to garner a gain. When given a choice between a sure

---

[6] When sixty-six subjects were given a choice between $6,000 with a probability of 0.45 and $3,000 with a probability of 0.90, 86 percent of the subjects took the second option, even though both options have the same expected value. However, when (presumably) same sixty-six subjects were given a choice between an option of $6,000 with a probability of 0.001 and $3,000 with a probability of 0.002, with the expected values of both being the same, 73 percent took the $6,000 option – showing, according to Kahneman and Tversky that the option taken depends not just on the expected value but added weighting of the discount rate and/or the size of the payoff (Kahneman and Tversky 2000b, p. 21–22).

[7] Risk aversion occurs when people choose a sure-thing gain that is of lower monetary value than a gamble involving gains. Risk seeking is when people turn down a sure thing in favor of a gamble with a lower expected value. Again, risk seeking is observed when losses are at stake.

Fig. 6.1 A hypothetical value function

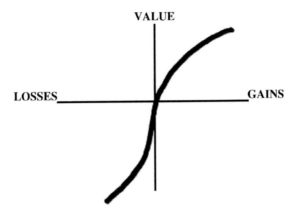

loss of $800 and a gamble with an 85 percent chance of losing $1,000 (and a 15 percent chance of no loss), a large majority of the subjects in the Kahneman and Tversky experiment took the gamble, in spite of the fact that the gamble had a higher expected loss, $850. This split of the subject's choices is the opposite of the outcome when the choice was between a sure gain of $800 and a gamble with an 85 percent chance of a $1,000 gain (Kahneman and Tversky 2000a, p. 3, citing a number of experiments and survey findings they and other behavioralists had undertaken).

Most telling, according to Kahneman and Tversky (2000a, p. 3), is the loss aversion that shows up in samples of undergraduate students who are not willing to bet $10 on the toss of a fair coin unless the potential gain is greater than $30, whereas by conventional economic theory they should be willing to bet $10 so long as the potential gain were just slightly above $20. Why? They simply do not consider the subjective value of a 50 percent chance of a gain of, say, $25 (which has an expected value of $12.50) is as great as the subjective negative value of the sure-thing loss of $10 in the bet.

Loss aversion also shows up in people's reluctance to sell losing stocks and real estate. One study found that the trading volume of stocks that have fallen in price on large exchanges is lower than the trading volume of stocks that have risen in price (Weber and Camerer 1998). Another study found that investors held stocks that rose in price for a median of 104 days; they held stocks that fell in price for a median of 124 days. Many investors might explain their unwillingness to sell losers quickly on the grounds that they expect their losers to rebound, but in one study, unsold losers yielded a return of 5 percent in the following year, whereas the gainers that were sold had a return of nearly 12 percent in the following year (Odean 1998). Similarly, homeowners who incur a capital loss on houses apparently try to avoid the loss by setting the selling price at or higher than their purchase price, only to end up delaying their sales (Genesove and Mayer 2001).

Again, one of the strong points of prospect theory is that, as illustrated by the S-shape of the value function in Fig. 6.1, behavioralists posit that people will tend to be risk averse when the choices are between potential gains and risk seeking, when the choices are between losses, not exactly the kind of consistent behavior expected of fully rational people, as rationality is conventionally presumed.

Dominance and Invariance

Behavioral economists point to two basic propositions underlying conventional constructions of rational behavior: *dominance* and *invariance*. The principle of *dominance* in decision making means that option A, which is better than option B in at least one respect and at least equal in all other respects, should always be preferred to option B. The principle of *invariance* means that the choice between A and B should not be affected by how the options are *framed*, or by how they are described or presented. What is important in choices, according to mainstream, neoclassical microeconomic theory, is the respective discounted value of the options, not so much the exact context or reference points, i.e., the choice frame. Shiller maintains that even single words such as "insurance" can frame a choice, making people more receptive to the choice, because of its "association, in our culture, of safety, good sense, integrity, and authority" (Shiller 2005, p. 83).

Kahneman and Tversky (1979) and Tversky and Kahneman (1981) point to violations of dominance and invariance in laboratory experiments. For example, 152 subjects were told that the outbreak of an unusual influenza virus was expected to kill 600 people and that there were two potential reaction programs: program A could save 200 people and program B would yield a one-third probability that 600 people would be saved and a two-thirds probability that no one would be saved. The number of expected lives saved under the two programs is exactly the same, 200, but 72 percent of the respondents chose program A.

Now, when the problem was reframed and a different set of 155 subjects were told that program C would result in 400 people dying and program D would yield a one-third chance that no one would die and a two-thirds chance that 600 people will die, 78 percent of the subjects favored program D. This is a total reversal of the vote between A/B and C/D, when, in fact, all four options are "indistinguishable in real terms"; that is, the number of people expected to die is always 200 (Kahneman and Tversky 2000a, p. 5).

Why the difference? In two words, risk aversion. The first experiment framed the problem with 600 expected deaths as a starting point and programs A and B *reducing* the deaths. Exercising risk aversion, people chose the sure thing – the saving of 200 lives under program A. In the second experiment, the problem has a starting frame in which no one dies, with the programs, C and D, causing deaths. People avoid the sure-thing option, 400 people dying, in favor of a gamble that 400 people could die.

According to Kahneman and Tversky, repeated experiments among sophisticated and unsophisticated subjects yield much the same results. Kahneman and Tversky report that when 86 subjects were given a choice between A, a sure gain of $240, or B, a 25 percent chance of gaining $1,000 and a 75 percent chance of gaining nothing,

84 percent of the subjects chose the sure gain of $240, despite the gamble having a higher expected value. When the subjects were given a choice of C, a sure loss of $750 and D, a 75 percent chance of losing $750 and a 25 percent chance of losing nothing, 87 percent of the subjects chose D, the gamble, despite the fact that the discounted monetary values of C and D are the same.

Hence, Kahneman and Tversky believe such findings, corroborated by others, support two behavioral principles: First, when gains are involved, people tend to be risk averse. Second, when losses are involved, people tend to be risk seeking. Again, the source of the difference emerges in how people subjectively evaluate expected monetary outcomes, not the monetary values of outcomes without additional weighting adjustments, with evaluations systematically affected by the reference point (Kahneman and Tversky 2000a, p. 5).

Conventionally, rational behavior often subsumes implicitly, if not explicitly, linearity in the value assessment of the chances of reaping gains and incurring losses. That is, the expected value of a prospect of reaping a $100 reward with a 5 percent probability and a 95 percent probability of reaping nothing is $5. When the probability of reaping the reward is raised fivefold to 25 percent, the expected value rises fivefold to $25. If the reward is raised to $1 million while the probability of reaping the reward is held to 5 percent, then the assessed expected value rises in line with the reward, or 10,000 times, to $50,000.

Such reassessments need not be the case, behavioral economists argue. People can apply different decision weights to different probabilities and the sizes of gains and losses, a fact that helps to explain why people buy both lottery tickets and insurance. The amount they give up in a lottery is small, but the decision weight given to the lottery's combination of a very high reward but very low probability of winning can be high, making the tickets a deal worth taking, in terms of subjective assessment or decision weights applied to the discounted values (Kahneman and Tversky 2000b and Tversky and Kahneman 2000). Kahneman and Tversky use gambles to bolster their argument that people tend to overweight choices with low probabilities and high rewards. The first involved sixty-six subjects who were given a choice between a 0.1% chance of receiving $6,000 and a 0.2 percent chance of receiving $3,000. While the expected values of both options were the same ($6), 73 percent of the subjects chose the first option, smaller probability but a much larger potential reward (Kahneman and Tversky 2000b, p. 22).

The second experiment involved a choice between a 0.1 percent chance of receiving $5,000 and a sure thing of $5. Again, both options had the exact same expected value, but 72 percent of the seventy-two subjects chose the first option (Kahneman and Tversky 2000b, p. 35). Kahneman and Tversky also point to the work of Kachelmeier and Shehata (1992), who found that if subjects were given an option with a small chance – 5 percent – of the payoff being received, the sure-thing cash option would have to be three times the expected value of the bet.

People's purchases of lottery tickets cannot be explained simply by comparing the price of the tickets with the expected monetary value of the reward. Lottery ticket purchases make no sense in present discounted terms alone, since a dollar ticket typically has a discounted value of less than one-thousandth of a cent.

Similarly, people who buy lottery tickets also buy insurance, even when they fully understand that the insurance costs more than it is worth in strictly expected value monetary terms, independent of some consideration, such as risk or loss aversion. People buy insurance, however, because of the imputed subjected value of a loss, especially a major loss, such as that of one's home.

Real people, not those whom economists model, seem to recognize their own limited control over their ability to forego close-at-hand temptations to consume now as opposed to consuming later. One hundred adult students at Chicago Museum of Science and Industry were asked to choose between three lifetime income paths that had the same total income over time with no discounting. The first income path had income starting high and declining. The second had income constant. The third path had increasing income. Obviously, in terms of their discounted value, the first path was superior to the second and third, and the second superior to the third. However, 12 percent of the subjects chose the first path and 12 percent chose the second, meaning that 76 percent of the subjects chose the path with the lowest discounted value, not exactly what neoclassical economists would surmise (at least not in real-world social and market settings). Even after the discounting of income streams was explained to the students, they stuck with the third path with the lowest discounted income by a substantial majority, 69 percent (Loewenstein and Sicherman 1991). The explanation? Perhaps, again, loss aversion. The students might have imagined that they would end their careers in an inferior position with the first and second paths because they might have saved too little, given their limited ability to control their consumption out of current income. The third income path incorporated a form of forced saving.

Mental Accounting

Thaler maintains that people's decisions are also affected by what he calls "mental accounting" – the "entire process of coding, categorizing, and evaluating events" (Thaler 2001, p. 244) – that causes people to categorize expenditures and to elevate the importance of relative prices versus absolute prices. According to standard cost–benefit analysis and the principle of invariance, a person's decision to drive from one store to another to save $5 should be founded simply and only on the balance when the $5 savings is compared with the cost and inconvenience of the drive. If the cost of the drive is greater than $5, then the drive will not be made, according to conventional cost–benefit theory. If lower, then the drive will be made.

However, behavioral researchers have found that when eighty-eight subjects were told that they could buy a hand calculator in one store for $15, but could buy it elsewhere for $10, 68 percent said they would make the drive to the store with the $10 price. When another group of ninety-three subjects were told that a calculator in one store cost $125, but that could be bought for $120 in another store, only 29 percent of the subjects said that they would make the drive to save $5 (Kahneman and Tversky 2000a, p. 12). Given these findings, behavioralists are not surprised that experiments demonstrated that shoppers did not expend more effort to save $15 on a $150 item than they expended to save $5 on a $50 item, although conventional theorists might expect greater effort to be expended to save a greater amount (Pratt et al. 1979).

The problem is reversed by other researchers who asked subjects how much they would pay for an item to avoid standing in line for forty-five minutes to purchase it. When purchasing an item that cost $45, the subjects were willing to pay, on average, twice what they were willing to pay to avoid the wait for a $15 item, suggesting to the researchers that the value subjects put on their time depends on the price of the item to be bought (Leclerc, Schmitt, and Dubé 1995).

Such findings are consistent, or so behavioral economists argue, with the so-called "Weber-Fechner principle" of psychophysics, which states that "the just noticeable difference in a stimulus is proportional to the stimulus" (Thaler 2000b, p. 279). Hence, percentage changes in prices tend to be disproportionably influential in buying decisions relative to absolute changes in prices, a point that appears to show up in the findings that price variations tend to rise almost linearly with the mean price of goods (Pratt et al. 1979).

In another study of the importance of framing choices and mental accounting, two hundred subjects were told that they had paid $10 for a ticket to attend a play, but discovered that they had lost the ticket when they arrived at the theater. When asked if they would buy a replacement ticket, less than half, 46 percent, said yes. When another group of one hundred and eighty-eight subjects were told that they had not bought a ticket before arriving at the theater, but had lost $10 on the way to the theater, 88 percent of the theatergoers said they would buy a ticket (Kahneman and Tversky 2000a).

These findings appear anomalous from the standard construction of rational behavior because in both cases the theatergoers have incurred identical $10 losses, which are sunk costs to be ignored. But if people engage in forms of mental accounting and/or are affected by the framing of the choice situation, the loss is not identical. For more than half of the theatergoers who lost their tickets, purchasing a second ticket could be viewed as increasing the price of seeing the play to $20, beyond the maximum they would have been willing to pay in their mental account. The lost ten-dollar bill, on the other hand, could be construed as a loss in one mental account, separate from the mental account for the play.

Interestingly, when both the lost ticket and lost bill scenarios were presented to the same subjects with the lost-ticket problem preceding the lost-bill problem, the subjects' answers did not change materially. However, when the lost-ticket problem followed the lost-bill problem, the percentage of the subjects willing to replace the ticket went up "significantly" (Kahneman and Tversky 2000a, pp. 12–13). In the second ordering, the subjects apparently deduced that consistency required them to see the two problems as the same, leading more people to buy the ticket, given that they had said they would buy it when they lost the bill. Hence, Kahneman and Tversky "conclude that frame invariance cannot be expected to hold and that a sense of confidence in a particular choice does not ensure that the same choice would be made in another frame" (Kahneman and Tversky 2000a, p. 7) – a position to which I return in Chap. 10 (because it raises a serious question concerning the worth of experiments in drawing out general rules since the frames for posing choices are essentially unlimited). Kahneman and Tversky do recognize the problem: "It is therefore good practice to test the robustness of preferences by deliberate attempts to frame a decision problem in more than one way (Kahneman and Tversky 2000a, p. 7, citing Fishhoff et al. 1980)." But the framing hook on which behavioralists adopt the Kahneman/Tversky position remains problematic: the research regime can be unending, if the framing position is taken with the seriousness behavioralists believe that it deserves. Neoclassical economists might rightfully worry that behavioralists' findings could be biased by the particulars of the ways their prospects have been framed.

But for the time being, we can set such matters aside and address the behavioralists' question: Why does framing affect subjects' decisions? Ariely suggests a direct and simple answer: the brain is set up to process sensory information as it is received, with bits of information like prices, put in context, with the context adding to the meaning of the information. Hence, all data is evaluated by the brain relatively, consciously and unconsciously. A price has meaning, but only in the context of other prices and arbitrary numbers – "anchors" – recently viewed or heard (Ariely 2008, pp. 26–31). Ariely's answer can be problematic to theorists who seek general principles and who rightfully can imagine a multitude of contexts for economic variables like prices. (We will return to such issues in Chap. 10.)

Endowment Effect

Mainstream, neoclassical microeconomic theory posits that rational people unwilling to pay $200 for a football ticket should be willing to sell such a ticket she is given, or has bought at a much lower price, if the ticket can be sold for at least $200. The reasoning is straightforward: people unwilling to pay $200 for the ticket are saying that they have something better to do with $200, or else they would buy the ticket. The utility of the something else is greater than the utility of seeing the game. If people have been given the ticket, then they still have something better to do with $200, unless something has changed. They should sell the ticket and do the something else that is more valuable to them.

But abundant anecdotal evidence from everyday life suggests that people's buying and selling prices often differ, sometimes markedly. I have taught at big-time sports universities with strong and popular sports rivals, especially in football. Key games between rivals are almost always sellouts, with the result being that tickets are often scalped days before the game for hundreds of dollars. Before the big games, I have asked my students if they would be willing to pay the known price for scalped tickets, which, to illustrate the point, is, say, $200. Typically, no students have raised their hands. I have then asked how many of them would be going to the game. Many hands go up. I cannot resist asking, "Why? You just said you would not pay $200 for a ticket, and you can get $200 for the 'free' student ticket you have. Why not sell your ticket and use the $200 to do what you would have done with $200 had you not received the 'free' student ticket and had not bought a ticket? Something is amiss." No doubt the students would sell their tickets at some price (as, you might remember, Wicksteed postulated a century ago), but for most, the price would clearly have to be much higher than $200.

Ariely put my anecdotal evidence to a more rigorous test. He contacted one hundred Duke University students, half of whom had won the lottery on receiving basketball tickets to a home game and half of whom had not. All one hundred students had camped out for days to be in the lottery for tickets. The students who did not have tickets were willing to pay an average of only $170 for a ticket, whereas the students who had tickets were willing to sell their tickets for an average price of $2,400. No student who had a ticket was willing to sell a ticket for a price that anyone who did not have a ticket was willing to pay (Ariely 2008, pp. 129–133).

To a conventional economist, the students' buy–sell decisions on sports tickets are puzzling. Thaler (2000b) argues that we have here is a general principle: People are commonly willing to pay less to obtain a good than they are willing to accept as payment on selling the good. He notes that income effects and transaction costs can explain the differences between people's buying and selling prices. Students who are given a ticket are, in effect, given a real income grant, which results in a higher wealth. Students' greater wealth might result in a suppression of their need to sell the ticket, which shows up in a greater price to sell their tickets than the price they would be willing to pay, absent the wealth represented by the ticket. However, Kahneman, Knetsch, and Thaler ran an experiment in which they gave coffee mugs to some subjects in the group. Those who were given the mugs set their selling prices two to three times the buying prices of those who were not given the mugs. These researchers conclude that people's difference between "willing to buy" and "willingness to pay" are "too large to be explained by income effects" alone (1990, p. 1325). The income and wealth effects involved in things like tickets must be minor, if not trivial, when compared to people's expected total lifetime wealth.

Students might not be willing to sell their tickets for the $200 specified in my anecdote because of the transaction cost of finding a willing buyer and finalizing the exchange (especially, when antiscalping laws are enforced, which introduces a risk cost as well). When the transaction costs are deducted from the $200-ticket price, the net price is lower than what the students would be willing to pay at maximum for the ticket. But, such an explanation can surely be dismissed, since the enforcement of antiscalping laws is minimal at most major college sporting events and the probability of getting caught could easily be less than a small fraction of 1 percent.

Thaler suggests a more "parsimonious" explanation for the differences between people's buying and selling prices, the "endowment effect," which is different from the wealth effect noted above (Thaler 2000b, p. 273–276). According to Thaler, the endowment effect is the inertia built into consumer choice processes due to the fact that consumers simply value goods that they hold more than the ones that they do not hold (for which I give an evolutionary explanation in Chap. 8).

Thaler traces the endowment effect to a difference (not recognized in conventional microeconomics) between opportunity costs and out-of-pocket expenditures, with the former viewed by many consumers as foregone gains and the latter as losses. Given people's observed inclination toward loss aversion (see Fig. 6.1), the pain of loss will suppress consumers' buying prices below their selling prices.

Similarly, their required selling prices can be inflated because decision weights for gains (implied in the selling price of a good received free of charge or bought at a lower price) are subjectively suppressed.

To support his endowment effect arguments, Thaler points to an experiment with MBA students by other researchers (Becker et al. 1974). The students were given a choice between two projects that differed in only one regard: One project required the students or their firms to incur an opportunity cost. The other project required that the students or their firms make out-of-pocket (or out-of-firm coffers) expenditures. "The students systematically preferred the project with the opportunity cost" (Thaler 2000b, p. 274). This finding suggests that the students should be willing to accept a lower rate of return on opportunity-cost investment projects than out-of-pocket expenditure projects of equal amounts. Similarly, researchers studying the choice of schooling in the Seattle-Denver income maintenance experiment found that changes in parents' out-of-pocket expenditures for school had a stronger effect on schooling choice than did an equivalent change in opportunity costs (Weiss et al. 1980).

If, as behavioral economists attest, buyers subjectively weigh opportunity costs as less than an equal dollar amount in out-of-pocket expenditures, then we have another explanation for the long queues in retail stores, at movies, and elsewhere.[8] When sellers curb the number of their ticket booths or checkout counters, they can curb their costs and, in turn, lower their prices, thus lowering buyers' out-of-pocket expenditures. But, the lower prices can lead to lines that impose a time cost, or opportunity cost, on buyers. According to standard analysis, sellers should continue to maintain their ticket booths and checkout counters so long as sellers can lower their prices by more than buyers incur in opportunity costs. Sellers have optimized on the length of their queues when the increase in buyers' opportunity cost (say, $1) from the last increase in the length of the queues equals the reduction in the price (say, $1).

However, if behavioralists are right on the differential weights buyers apply to opportunity costs and out-of-pocket expenditures, then the dollar equality suggested above would mean that the line is suboptimal – or too short. Firms can increase their profits and consumer welfare by increasing the length of their lines. This is because buyers would subjectively weigh the last increase in length of the queue (opportunity cost) as less than the last reduction in price (out-of-pocket expenditures). Hence, sellers should continue to curb their ticket booths and checkout counters, extending the length of their queues until the additional subjectively weighted opportunity costs equal the subjectively weighted reduction in out-of-pocket expenditures.

Acquisition and Transaction Utility

Conventional microeconomics assumes people maximize their welfare by comparing the intrinsic value of a good with its price. Once again, Thaler takes issue with conventional neoclassical economics by positing a more expansive view of the

---

[8] For a review of various explanations for queues, see McKenzie (2008).

source of utility. He argues that people choose goods because of two sources of utility, "acquisition utility" and "transaction utility" (Thaler 2000a, pp. 248–249). Acquisition utility is, in effect, the consumer surplus (total benefits minus the price paid) buyers receive from their purchases, whereas transaction utility is any perceived advantage from buyers making deals. A good in which the subjective value is greater than the price paid has acquisition utility. A purchase that is viewed by buyers as a good deal – defined as the "difference between the amount paid and the 'reference price' of the good" – has added transaction utility (Thaler 2000a, p. 248). Presumably, this means that people may buy goods when the acquisition utility is negative, but more than offset by the positive transaction utility.

Thaler posed a scenario to support his contention that people evaluate goods relative to some reference price and other qualities of the deal. He asked all subjects to imagine they were on a beach on a hot day and would like nothing better than a cold beer. He told one subset of the subjects that they could get the beer only from an expensive resort hotel. He told the remainder of the subjects that the beer could be obtained only from a "small, run-down grocery store." He then asked each group to indicate the maximum price they would pay for the beer. The subjects who were told that the beer could be bought only at the expensive resort hotel gave an average maximum price of $2.65, in 1984 dollars. The other group gave an average price of $1.50, also in 1984 dollars (Thaler 2000a, p. 248). The presumption must be, according to Thaler, that the subjects gave a higher maximum price for the resort hotel because they assumed that the "reference price" is higher than at the run-down grocery store.

Thaler concludes that "some goods are purchased primarily because they are especially good deals," as indicated by the fact that "most of us have some rarely worn items in our closets." He also concludes that "sellers make use of this penchant by emphasizing the savings relative to the regular retail price (which serves as the suggested reference price)" (Thaler 2000a, p. 249). That is, posting sale prices alongside regular prices can increase buyers' total utility and can cause additional sales, even some for which the acquisition utility might be negative. The utility value of deals can also explain the prevalence of sales, as well as pervasive use of coupons and rebates that insert wedges between the reference prices and the prices consumers actually pay.

The Matter of Sunk Costs

In conventional microeconomics, there is a common refrain: Sunk costs do not matter (or rather, should not matter) in real choice decisions. The logic of the claim is compelling to many, if not all, strictly neoclassical economists. Costs that have already been incurred cannot be recovered. They are gone forever. In a real sense, they were true costs at the time they were incurred, but not afterwards. In effect, once incurred and not subject to recovery, sunk costs are misnomers: They are no longer costs; that is, potential value that can be forgone by decisions yet to be made.

But behavioral economists point out that people certainly behave as if sunk costs do matter, at least for a while. Thaler proposes what he dubs the "sunk-cost hypothesis": "[P]aying for the right to use a good or service will increase the rate at which the good will be utilized, *ceteris paribus*" (2000b, p. 276). He points to a study by Aronson and Mills (1959) involving different levels of initiation for three groups of students wanting to join a discussion group:

- Group 1 was put through a "severe" initiation: Students were required to read aloud sexually explicit material.
- Group 2 was given a "mild" initiation: Students were required to read aloud tamer material.
- Group 3 was the control group: Students were not subjected to the initiation reading.

As predicted, the students who endured the severe initiation reported enjoying the discussion group more than the other two groups (Aronson and Mills 1959), an experiment repeated with the same findings by other researchers (Gerard and Mathewson 1966). Thaler is convinced that the best evidence of the sunk-cost effect can be easily observed among students who are resistant to learning and then believing that sunk costs do not matter.

In another experiment on the relevance of sunk costs, Lewis Broad ran an experiment at a pizza parlor, which charged $2.50 for all you can eat (as reported by Jones and Cullis 2000, pp. 75–76). The customers who paid the up-front payment, which the researcher presumed to be a sunk cost, were considered the control group. Other customers, who were randomly selected on entering, were offered a free lunch. If people were unaffected by sunk costs, then the control group would eat no more than the experiment group. But the control group consistently consumed more pizza than the experiment group, supposedly showing that sunk costs can indeed affect, positively in this case, consumption.

Apparently, the sunk-cost effect wears off, eventually, and the costs incurred no longer matter. Arkes and Blumer (1985) developed an experiment in which three groups of people were buying season tickets for an on-campus theater group. The first group paid the full season ticket price. The second group was given a 13 percent discount, and the third was given a 47 percent discount. Those in the group who paid the full price attended productions significantly more than the two groups that were given discounts, but only during the first half of the season. During the second half, the three groups attended production with more or less the same frequency, suggesting that the sunk-cost effect diminishes. This point is supported by the work of Gourville and Soman (1998) who found that attendance at health clubs charging semiannual dues increases in the month following the date for payment, only to decline during the subsequent five months. Although the sunk-cost effect wears off, the important point for behavioral economists is that sunk costs do matter, even though how much they matter tends to depreciate.

The endowment and sunk-cost effects should alter the way economists and others think about public policy, or so behavioral economists argue. Consider, for example, the policy question of whether prescription drugs are given free of charge to the elderly or are sold to them at a subsidized price. Conventional microeconomic theory suggests that the charge will cause the elderly to economize on their drug usage, taking medications at less than the recommended frequency. But the endowment and sunk-cost effects suggest that prescription charges can be expected to cause the elderly to follow more carefully their doctors' advice to take the drugs with a prescribed frequency. If following a prescribed usage plan leads to more *effective* drug use, the result can be, perhaps, less need for medical treatments (Jones and Cullis 2000).

Behavioral Finance

Behavioralists in finance, in large measure, stand in opposition to the widespread adoption among finance scholars in the last third of the twentieth century of the "efficient-market hypothesis," which University of Chicago financial economist Eugene Fama developed in his doctoral dissertation in the early 1960s. Fama's work was rewritten in two forms, for an academic audience in a journal article (1965a) and for a less technical audience in a trade publication (1965b).

In these early publications, Fama argued that stock prices were difficult to predict. With earlier scholarly work showing that professional investors could not consistently beat the market (Cowles and Jones 1937), Fama further developed his argument by positing that asset prices that were broadly traded were "information-efficient." That is, asset prices captured all relevant information on firms' prospective financial health, which helped to explain why professional investors were so hard-pressed to beat the market. To beat the market, investors either had to know something others did not know or they had to be lucky in buying stock just before new information became widely known. Otherwise, in the strong form of Fama's theoretical model of market behavior, fully rational investors, utilizing full rational expectations (or the ability to interpret and discount with perfection the value of any and all information on firms' earning streams), would, on average, act on the existing public and private information, driving stock prices to their efficiency-enhancing levels more or less instantaneously, given prospective earnings and risks, with no one being able to earn excess returns, absent the advent of new information.

While markets may never have been as information efficient as Fama's model suggests, the efficient-market hypothesis proved a shocking insight and a means of modeling market behavior and generating hypotheses (in line with Friedman's methodology) and as a means of empirically assessing the market impact of new information, or events, in the financial lives of firms. If stock prices captured all existing information and some new event, incorporating some new information, affecting firms' earning streams into the future, then stock prices can be expected to respond immediately. Fama and his coauthors published the first so-called event study in 1969. Literally, hundreds (if not thousands) of such event studies have been produced across the world over the last four decades, which explains why Fama deserves a Nobel Prize in economics.

While the efficient-market hypothesis was certainly productive in generating empirical research, many economists and financial professors inside and outside the academy greeted it with considerable skepticism. Their skepticism was grounded in casual observations of how slowly financial information flowed among investors and how difficult *information* was to pin down in data, much less interpret with tolerable accuracy. Then, there were concerns that market prices frequently seem to rise and fall for no apparent reason, with no apparent new event or no apparent change in relevant information flows. One has to wonder how some individuals could become quite wealthy from stock trading if stock markets were at all times, and everywhere, as efficient as Fama's model posited. (But then, most investors can not beat the market).

Behavioral finance scholars have attacked the efficient-market hypothesis for the same reason that behavioral economists and psychologists have criticized the perfect rationality premise: The foundation of the efficient-market hypothesis seems other worldly, given people's observed "irrationalities" in the marketplace and the economy.

Then, there are the matters of the historical reality of stock market bubbles and crashes that seem completely at odds with the efficient-market hypothesis. Much behavioral finance literature suggests that investors are often no more rational in their decision making than consumers and both are affected by biases and conditions seemingly unrelated to financial markets, such as weather.[9] I can use Robert Shiller's explanation of the stock-market bubble of the 1990s and the housing market bubble of the 2000s to illustrate the problems behavioralists have with models founded on fully rational investors. Shiller explains these bubbles in his two widely read, praised, and well-timed books, *Irrational Exuberance* (2005, first published in March 2000 as the stock market peaked, and re-released with an added chapters on the housing market bubble as housing prices peaked) and *The Subprime Solution* (published in May 2008 only a few months before the credit markets began to freeze up, the mortgage-backed security market evaporated, banks began to fail worldwide, and governments passed bailouts of their financial sectors).

Shiller sees such recent bubbles as repeats of similar stock and housing-market bubbles throughout history. Bubbles founded on investor incompetence, greed, and the tendency of people to herd. Herding describes people's proclivity to accept some "new era" common story for the continued rise in the prices of stocks and houses and to make buying decisions based on what others are doing (Shiller 2008). Shiller is fully convinced that people's – even expert investors'– financial decisions are infused with what can only be called "irrational exuberance" (a phrase Alan Greenspan, then chairman of the Federal Reserve, coined in 1996). In effect, Shiller reiterates a point neoclassical economists make with reference to prisoner-dilemma and public-good settings, that rational decision making at the individual level can give rise to outcomes that have all the markings of being irrational, i.e., outcomes that are inferior to what all – investors – would prefer.

---

[9]For an array of behavioral finance studies, see Thaler (1993 and 2005).

Shiller offers a dozen factors that made up the "skin" of the stock-market bubble of the 1990s, but that had *"an effect on the market that is not warranted by rational analysis of economic fundamentals"* (2005, p. 18; emphasis in the original). The first such factor was the opening of the Internet to the broad public by the advent of the first browser in early 1994, which led many people to believe that the economic landscape would be radically changed. One story widely accepted, to extend Shiller's theme, in the dot-com bubble and burst of the late 1990s, was that the Internet fundamentally changed the way business could be done and would continue to be done in the future. With a small investment in software and a few servers, any reasonably competent computer geek could become a seller to the world from an easily established virtual storefront.

Moreover, with the emergence of China and India as economic power houses founded on an abundance of skilled but cheap labor, markets had become global in scope with the potential for vast economies of scale and vast increases in sales (Shiller 2008, Chap. 3). With costs low and potential revenues high and with most work being done by Internet-site visitors from all over the globe, the potential for future economic profits were unlimited, which justified the dramatic escalation of stocks' price–earnings ratios to levels far removed from previous records – as the story was told and retold.

All the while, according to Shiller, irrational exuberance took hold in stock markets (2005). Few purveyors of the new-era story in the midst of the 1990s bubble may have realized that the argument for exorbitant profits was self-contradictory and defeating, given that the touted low entry costs made internet-based markets open to new entrants and highly competitive, which would eventually lead to low profitability and the high likelihood of failure for many dot-com companies.

The stock-market bubble was further expanded by other considerations, several of which were:

- The downfall of the Soviet Union and the conversion of the Russian and Chinese economies to free markets, which heightened profit expectations.
- Business moves toward downsizing and outsourcing.
- The Republican takeover of both houses of Congress in 1994, which meant that more pro-business legislation could be expected (and did result in a cut in the top capital gains tax rate in 1997).
- The movement of the Baby Boomers into midlife during which they could be expected to increase their savings and stock purchases.
- The expansion of business news reporting, which could increase the demand for stocks, because so many of the reports were optimistic.
- The expansion of defined contribution pension plans and the development of mutual funds.
- The expansion of stock trading with the development of discount brokers and internet trading, which permitted more people to "gamble" more cheaply in day trading (Shiller 2005, Chap. 2).

Along the way, there can emerge an "information cascade," with all investors in herd-like mode starting to look to the same information on the performance of stocks and looking to each other for guidance on what they should do in their financial dealings. As a result, a disconnect can develop between the actual performance records of firms and the information investors use in making their buy, hold, and sell decisions because investors are future looking (Shiller 2005, pp. 151–153, citing Bikhchandani et al 1992; Banerjee 1992). These and other considerations have a "self-fulfilling aspect" to them, which contributed to stock markets taking on attributes of one big Ponzi scheme (Shiller 2005, p. 43 and Chap. 3). Even though investors may have recognized in the late 1990s that the stock market may have been expanding through an unwarranted bubble, they need not have been deterred from submitting buy orders because of the general expectation that the market would continue its expansion – for a time – which meant that there were still gains to be had. The market took on something of a casino character with investors gambling on how far out the bubble would expand before it burst and generated a reversal information (and expectations) cascade (Shiller 2005, Chap. 3). Of course, the stock market bubble in the 1990s and the housing market bubble in the 2000s could have been fueled partially by what Federal Reserve Chairman Ben Bernanke called a "global savings glut," which could have caused investors to take greater risks just to bolster their returns on investments that were sagging because of the global savings glut, or so George Mason University economist Tyler Cowen has argued (2008).

A key element of the new-era story behind the housing bubble of the 1990s and early 2000s was, according to Shiller, that housing and the land on which houses had to sit was in short supply and would only get tighter in supply as the country's population and economy continued to expand, especially, in key charmed markets like Los Angeles, San Francisco, Las Vegas, New York City, and various cities in Florida (Shiller 2008, Chap. 4). Beginning in the 1990s, the housing bubble was fueled with various government subsidies and falling interest rates. The rising housing prices in the late 1990s validated the new era housing story, which, in turn, encouraged herding and speculation into the first five years of the 2000s. Along the way, the housing bubble was expanded with the advent in the 1970s of the securitization of home mortgages, creating a moral hazard for many bankers, who had become mortgage retailers and resellers, to induce home buyers to take on larger debt than they would likely be able to handle over the long term.

Under pressure from Congress and a string of administrations, especially, the Clinton and following Bush administrations to increase home ownership, especially, among low-income earners and minorities, with emphasis on minorities, the U.S. Department of Housing and Urban Development loosened mortgage restrictions on first-time homebuyers in the mid-1990s (Becker et al 2008). Over the three decades preceding 1995, the U.S. ownership rate remained within a fairly narrow band, 63–65 percent, but then started an upward trek during the Clinton's second term and the following Bush's first term, peaking at 69.2 percent in second quarter 2004 (and then dropping only to just under 68 percent by the third quarter of 2008).[10]

---

[10]U.S. Census Bureau historical data accessed December 22, 2008 from http://www.census.gov/hhes/www/housing/hvs/historic/index.html.

One of the major changes was that borrowers no longer had to prove five years of stable income. HUD guaranteed billions of dollars in mortgages for low-income borrowers in identified ethnic groups (Streitfeld and Morgenson 2008). Fannie Mae and Freddie Mac followed suit in 1999 by taking on the mortgage-backed securities loaded with high-risk subprime (under which interest rates were initially suppressed and then set to jump after several years) and Alt-A mortgages (mortgages granted without supporting documentation on the borrowers' income and assets). At that time, "*The New York Times* reported that African Americans borrowers constituted 18 percent of homeowners holding subprime mortgages and 5 percent of conventional mortgages" (Holmes 1999). Franklin Taines, then chairman and CEO of Fannie Mae, defended the company's action on the grounds that "Fannie Mae has expanded home ownership for millions of families in the 1990s by reducing down payment requirements. Yet, there remain too many borrowers whose credit is just a notch below what our understanding has required who have been relegated to paying significant mortgage rates in the so-called subprime market" (Holmes 1999). Accordingly, Freddie and Fannie began aggressively buying mortgage-backed securities.

Between 2004 and 2007, Freddie and Fannie bought mortgage-backed securities to the tune of $1 trillion, to "curry congressional" favor, all with private funds invested in the two organizations attracted by federal government guarantees (Calomiris et al 2008). HUD's policies and Freddie and Fannie's investments had the desired effects: U.S. home ownership rose from 64 percent in 1994 to 69 percent in 2005 (Streitfeld and Morgenson 2008), but also increased the riskiness of the securitized mortgages. Subprime and Alt-A mortgages rose from 8 percent of all mortgage originations in 2003 to 20 percent in 2006 as their investments primed the subprime mortgage pump and the housing bubble, but also of containing the risk exposure of Freddie and Fannie investors, or so they might have thought, given that they bought bonds issued by the two quasi-governmental corporations – or until the housing bubble burst (Calomiris and Wallison 2008).

The development of the risky subprime mortgage and the Alt-A mortgages boosted short-run housing demand, further pushing housing prices that, in turn, validated (for a time) the story about housing being a solid investment and the borrowers' decisions to choose subprime mortgages with delayed balloon payments. Given the continuing sharp escalation of housing prices (which rose in some areas of the country for several years at more than 20 percent), many real-estate speculators could expect to refinance their mortgages on speculative properties on more favorable terms, as their expected equity built up and before the balloon payments kicked in. Moreover, banks increased the riskiness of their mortgage portfolios in search of higher spreads between the interests rates they paid for their loanable funds and the interest rates they charged borrowers (with lowered credit standards). Their growing profitability and the continuing escalation of housing prices (which hid the growing riskiness of bank's portfolios) improved banks' credit ratings and their ability to sell off mortgage-backed securities, which, in turn, fueled the spread of subprime loans and the housing bubble.

People in power virtually denied the prospects of a truly national housing bubble. Shiller quotes Alan Greenspan, who wrote in his *Age of Turbulence,* "I would tell audiences that we were facing not a bubble but a froth – lots of little local bubbles that never grew to a scale that could threaten the health of the overall economy" (cited by Shiller 2008, p. 40).

Shiller argues that once a bubble gets started, it can take on a life of its own, with acceptance of the story spreading like a disease through what Shiller calls "social contagion of boom thinking," under which people set aside local and personal information that denies the validity of the widely adopted story of success and believe that everyone else has better information (Shiller 2008, p. 41).

The housing bubble can expand as people begin to buy based on past price increases and the prospects of greater wealth with a continued rise in prices. At some point, many people may come to understand that prices are excessively inflated but continue to fuel the bubble with added buy decisions that can be founded on little more than the belief that the story is widely believed and, thus, will be self-fulfilling – at least for a time. A bubble is then expanded by nonrational or irrational decision making – or irrational exuberance, a term that Shiller exploits to good effect (2005 and 2008).

All can be well until "bubble thinking" comes to a halt as people begin to recognize the disconnection between housing prices and potential resale values (or rental rates), given the realities of buyers' ability to pay. The housing price bubble peaked in 2006 after leveling off in 2005 as housing price increases began to taper off with the price downturn jeopardizing many subprime and Alt-A mortgages (and variations of such mortgages) that had been earlier negotiated with practically everyone – borrowers, mortgage originators, mortgage-backed security buyers, even government regulators and policy makers – believing that escalating housing prices could and would continue. As price increases tapered off, the speculative demand for houses dampened, and housing prices began to reverse course in 2006 and 2007, leaving many borrowers under water (or with mortgages larger than the resale prices of their houses). Many subprime and Alt-A (and, of course, negative amortization) borrowers were unable to refinance their way out of ballooning mortgage payments. The result was a collapse of the housing markets and escalating foreclosures on houses and personal bankruptcies (Shiller 2008, Chap. 3).

Real-estate finance professors Major Coleman, Michael LaCour-Little, and Kerry Vandell found that between 1998 and 2003, housing prices were, by and large, tied to economic fundamentals (population and income, for example), with later price increases having all the markings of pure speculation, supporting Shiller's central point. Indeed, they found that instead of subprime mortgages *causing* the housing price bubble, the housing price bubble gave rise to a surge in subprime mortgages, which were attractive because of speculation fever and which peaked at 24 percent of all mortgages originated in 2006 (2008). Of course, the emerging subprime mortgages could still have had feedback effects on the housing price bubble and, no doubt, contributed to the downward spiral of housing prices and upward spiral in foreclosures after 2006 and to the downward spiral in market evaluations of mortgage-backed securities and the freezing up of interbank credit in 2008.

In his *Subprime Solution* (2008), Shiller presciently argued that the burst in the housing bubble, not to mention the pervasive financial fraud afoot in the mortgage industry, put the country virtually on the precipice of a financial calamity, possibly on par with the 1929 collapse in the stock market. This could give rise to a second coming of the "great depression":

> The *subprime crisis* is the name for what is a historic turning point in our economy and our culture. It is, at its core, the result of a speculative bubble in the housing market that began to burst in the United States in 2006 and has now caused ruptures across many other countries in the form of financial failures and a global credit crunch. The forces unleashed by the subprime crisis will probably run rampant for years, threatening more and more collateral damage. The disruption in our credit markets is already of historic proportions and will have important economic impacts. More importantly, this crisis has set in motion fundamental societal changes – changes that affect our consumer habits, our values, our relatedness to each other (Shiller 2008, p. 1).

And as an early draft of this chapter was being finalized (mid-October 2008), the burst in the housing price bubble was patently obvious in the widespread escalation of foreclosures and bankruptcies over the months since Shiller released his book, the collapse of the investment banking firms of Bear Stearns and Lehman Brothers, the takeover of Merrill Lynch by Bank of America (which paid a share price less than half of Merrill's market price a year before), the financial precariousness and rescue of American insurance group (which was considering the selloff of some of its assets to stay afloat), the takeover of Wachovia by Wells Fargo Bank, the rising closures of a number banks, the federal takeover of Freddie and Fannie, as well as a rise in the unemployment and inflation rates to levels not seen in years. All of this was keeping high-level Bush Administration officials at work late at night and on weekends seeking ways to avert a wider financial system meltdown.[11]

Shiller was one of the first financial economists to go on record, advocating a massive bailout of banks and other financial institutions, as well as other large companies that have been described as "too big to fail" because of the potential irreparable damage to the larger economy (2008). If irrational exuberance and bubbles can take hold in financial and housing markets, then, perhaps, they can emerge with the same ease, and same effects, in policy circles. As this chapter was being finalized in early 2009, a "policy bubble" did seem underway with various politicians and policy advocates adopting "new-era" stories about how the economy was on the brink of an economic collapse that could unfold as a second great depression and that so many sectors of the economy were in retreat that the federal government was the only entity left to fuel demand. Federal Reserve Chairman Ben Bernanke supported then-Secretary of the Treasury Henry Paulsen by pressing what

---

[11] See reports in *The New York Times* (Norris and Bajaj 2008), the *Los Angeles Times* (Vikas 2008), and *The Wall Street Journal* (Mollenkamp et al. 2008).

he saw as the reasons for the urgency of approving the Treasury's initial $700-billion bailout plan, "My interest is solely for the strength and the recovery of the U.S. economy. I believe if the credit markets are not functioning, jobs will be lost, the unemployment rate will rise, more houses will be foreclosed upon, GDP will contract, the economy will just not be able to recover in a normal, healthy way, no matter what other policies are taken" (Reynolds et al. 2008). In making his case for his company's bailout, General Motors CEO Ric Wagoner exhorted his workers and suppliers to write their congressmen, arguing that "The current financial crisis goes far beyond any one industry. With each passing day without a solution, the credit market continues to freeze up, denying consumers and businesses the needed cash for home loans, car loans, small business loans, and the critical investments that grow the economy and create jobs" (Sorkin 2008).

Of course, talk of both bailout and stimulus packages activated lobbyists from all sectors of the economy – including home building, air conditioning, railways and air transportation, environment, travel and tourism, wireless telephony, fish farming, and library – began seeking their own bailout or stimulus programs, with everyone claiming damage from the economic downturn and great benefits from federal expenditures on their industries, according to news reports (Oliphant and Simon 2008).

Keynesian economics came to the economic policy forefront once again with a series of ever-higher bailout and stimulus proposals that would have "multiplier effects."[12] At this writing, the projected federal budget deficit for fiscal 2009 was closing in on $2 trillion dollars, or 12.3 percent of gross domestic product, a share not seen since the end of World War II, with another proposed $750 billion addition to the federal budget for bailout of the financial sector if that sector and the general economy deteriorated faster than was projected (Puzzanghera 2009). There seemed to be no end to the federal funds being routed to firms that seemed to be "too big to fail," including General Motors and Citi Group (Bensinger 2009; Dash 2009).

One has to wonder, given arguments and findings from behavioral research, if the prospects of a policy bubble continuing could do as much damage as the financial and housing bubbles. After all, the problem of moral hazard was at least partially responsible for the country getting into its financial and economic mess, and the proposed bailout and stimulus packages could create a major moral hazard problem for the future, as many firms and individuals begin making decisions with an eye toward their losses being "socialized" through future bailout and stimulus packages. The bailout and stimulus packages could also be translated into higher future tax rates and inflation rates, given the mounting federal debt, and in his first

---

[12] A distinguished advocate of massive federal stimulus packages (even greater than the stimulus package proposed by President Barack Obama) that would have a multiplied effect in the neighborhood of 1.5 was Nobel laureate and *New York Times* columnist Paul Krugman who insisted that the country, and world, had fallen into Keynesian "liquidity trap," reminiscent of Keynes' analysis of conditions of the 1930s (2008 and 2009).

proposed budget President Obama did include 0 major tax increases on the "rich" (those making more than $200,000 a year) (Reynolds and Nicholas 2009). At the very least, from the perspective of the new behavioralism, such a prospect cannot be summarily dismissed.[13]

Concluding Comments

Behavioral economists have developed a number of key insights about people's behavior:

- People facing real-world choices among prospects sometimes, if not often, violate the principles of dominance and invariance underlying rational behavior models (at least in laboratory and survey settings without the build-up of market consequences that can press for changes in decision making).
- People tend to be risk and loss averse, which implies that they will require payment premiums to confront prospects that involve risk, the potential for losses.
- People's buying price of an item often can be expected to be lower than their selling price because of the endowment effect.
- Opportunity costs tend to be given a lower negative subjective weight than an out-of-pocket expenditure of the same (present discounted) dollar amount. In other words, the way in which costs are incurred can matter and choosers will favor projects involving foregone opportunities to those involving out-of-pocket expenditures.
- Sunk costs can matter, meaning they can affect current and future behavior, at least for a while (and so long as market pressures do not come to bear on decision making).
- People can engage in mental accounting, which can affect their perception of the costs and benefits of different prospects.
- Stock market and housing market (as well as other asset markets, like oil) are subject to speculative fever, fueled by information cascades, that lead to price bubbles. Bubble thinking can have irrational and/or nonrational foundations, which can be the case when people do not engage in due diligence on investigating their investments. Speculative fever can be rational, given that people might rationally decide to invest when they detect others are engaging in (irrational) bubble thinking.

In general, behavioralists insist that people simply do not have the mental wherewithal to be as rational as mainstream economists theorize, a position that a

---

[13] For accounts of the unfolding policy events in late 2008, see Lewis (2008), Gosselin and Reynolds (2008), Andrews (2008), Herszenhorn et al. (2008), Solomon and Paletta (2008), Hitt et al. (2008), Anderson et al. (2008), Hitt and Solomon (2008), Herszenhorn (2008a,b), Simon and Gaouette (2008).

burgeoning behavioral literature has documented. Herbert Simon argued that the concept of bounded rationality should supplant full rationality in economics simply because "the capacity of the human mind for formulating and solving complex problems is very small compared with the size of the problems whose solution is required for objectively rational behavior in the real world – or even for a reasonable approximation to such objective rationality" (1957, p. 198). To explain in some detail what Simon had in mind, Chaps.7 and 8 will examine the literature in evolutionary biology and psychology and neurobiology, on our way to a discussion of the rationality of bounded rationality, and the development of what I like to call *rational rationality*, a conceptual step removed from *bounded rationality*.

Chapter 7
The Evolutionary Biology of Rational Behavior

Modern neoclassical microeconomics has developed in an era in which evolutionary biology and neurobiology have flourished with their many important insights on why people today behave the way they do. And the experts' explanation is fairly straightforward: There remains a great deal of noise in people's behavior (mainly because human intellectual, physical, and emotional evolution has never stopped), but when the noise is stripped away, today's people do what they do in large measure because of how their basic physiological and mental functionalities evolved long ago. Those evolved functionalities continue to constrain modern human behavior.

These insights from evolutionary theory (and neurobiology that will be considered in the following chapter) have been integrated into a number of physical and social disciplines, most notably psychology. "Evolutionary psychologists" have posited evolutionary grounds for human behaviors, not the least of which are entrenched mating behaviors that help explain male/female interactions today.[1] Although evolutionary and neurobiological theories have filtered into modern microeconomics (mainly through developments in the emerging subdisciplines of bioeconomics and neuroeconomics, initially pushed forward with the work of Rubin and Paul [1979] and Hirshleifer [1982, 1984, 1993]), standard microeconomics textbook discussions of rational behavior continue to stand largely apart from the evolutionary and neurobiological influences that must have shaped exactly how rational people can be today.

As conventionally presented in modern textbooks, economists' rationality premise has no widely acknowledged evolutionary roots and looks for the whole world to be a completely arbitrary theoretical starting point plucked from the air. This treatment of rational behavior leaves economists open to attacks. As some critics

---

[1] Even astrophysics have extended evolutionary theory backwards, given that they have established origins for the evolution of life that predates life's primordial beginnings on Earth, namely in the chemical caldrons of exploding red giant stars, if not in the Big Bang, the presumed origins of the universe as we can now know it.

might say in any number of ways, "Of course, markets can be expected to be efficient if you assume fully rational people who have perfect or costless information at their disposal all the time and who never make mistakes other than those that are calculated, given unavoidable risks that are known with perfection." Friedrich Hayek complained that the assumption that people everywhere in markets know everything at zero cost assumes away the core issue with which economists must grapple, that is, how people who know very little about what other people know, much less the risks they face, can have their activities coordinated for everyone's betterment.[2]

Also, economists rarely do base their construction of rational behavior on neurological constraints that real people must face. Indeed, as generally presented, rationality is a premise that has no neurological foundation. It exists solely by assumption, by intent. It is the mental "starting point," which, being "plucked from the thin air" of theory, cannot be contested other than through the validity of its logical deductions as established through empirical tests, or so, as noted early in the book, Milton Friedman and other neoclassical economists have argued (although, as also noted, George Stigler and Gary Becker departed company with Friedman by moving away from market-level rationality, a point Medema [2008] has stressed).

Accordingly, for theoretical purposes, the extent to which people behave rationally can be anything that is convenient for the theoretical tasks at hand. Perfect rationality is a matter of choice and convenience, or economy in thinking. Equally, bounded rationality can be construed as arbitrary, except for how people (survey and laboratory subjects) are observed to behave. Yet bounded rationality lacks generalization, since observations of people's behavior cannot be complete and can be filled with noise, even when the observations are made in laboratory experiments. The degree of boundedness is functionally related only to the external-, physical-world constraints that people may currently face, say, the array of goods from which they make their choices or the physical-world costs of decision-making.

The conventional premise of rationality does not require that rationality itself be a necessary reality or a natural occurrence. All, too often, rationality is treated as a fact or a given that has a one/zero reality: Either people are rational to a specified (or unspecified) degree or they are not. This is an odd position for economists to take since people exhibit considerable diversity and flexibility in most every other

---

[2]Hayek observed at the end of his classic essay "The Use of Knowledge in Society,"

> Any approach, such as that of much of mathematical economics with its simultaneous equations, which in effect starts from the assumption that people's *knowledge* corresponds with the objective *facts* of the situation, systematically leaves out what is our main task to explain. I am far from denying that in our system equilibrium analysis has a useful function to perform. But when it comes to the point where it misleads some of our leading thinkers into believing that the situation which it describes has direct relevance to the solution of practical problems, it is high time that we remember that it does not deal with the social process at all and that it is no more than a useful preliminary to the study of the main problem (1945, p. 291).

way – in incomes, physical endowments, skills, access to resources, desires, responsiveness to price, tastes, etc. Indeed, people's diversity and flexibility are widely touted as a source of gains from specialization and trade.

The rationality premise leads economists to derive the most important functional relationship in the discipline, the law of demand.[3] Yet, generally, rationality itself is not conceived as a logical deduction, that is in any way functionally related to anything, with the notable exceptions in Bryan Caplan's (2007) and Vernon Smith's (2008a) recent works, and among the growing group of experimental economists they cite. Rather than being a fixed human mental condition, rationality is more accurately viewed as a derived human condition that could be seen as a proclivity or propensity, given local conditions, institutional settings, and social and market pressures – all because of long-past evolutionary forces and still-intact neurological constraints.

The analysis in this chapter and the following chapter departs from standard microeconomic theorizing. In both these chapters, I develop the argument that rational behavior in some form has a reality in fact, not just theory, and is as real as people's vision, bipedalism, and sense of consciousness. An important theme of these chapters is that people's true rationality is an evolved characteristic that has proven survival value, no less so than sexual preferences and tastes for certain foods, and remains constrained by the evolutionary forces that shaped the construction of the human brain and people's human rational capacities – or proclivities, propensities and limitations – long ago. Just as is true of people's physical capacities, the degree to which people are inclined to be rational today can be attributed to the living conditions, opportunities, and constraints that hominids and early humans faced as they sought to survive and procreate (a point that Ludwig von Mises touched on [1962, p. 14]). These conditions molded people's physical and mental capacities and proclivities that today affect their abilities to assess opportunities and make choices.

Emerging from the lines of argument developed in this chapter is this strong theme: Perfect rationality makes no evolutionary sense; rational rationality does. Rationality can hardly be expected to be a fixed, immutable human condition; it is likely to be an evolving variable basis for decision making, which means that rationally rational people will vary their rationality – or the intensity with which they consciously and deliberately weigh alternative courses of action – depending on conditions, institutional settings, and social and market pressures.

While discussing rationality, it is important to distinguish between ends and means. To an economist, ends are embodied in a utility function – the relationship between human happiness and the set of goods and services that people consume. Economists typically take the utility function as arbitrary and do not examine it with much care; people have whatever preferences they have. The entire analysis of rationality (maximization of utility subject to constraints, with the geometric

---

[3] Although as Becker and Murphy (1988) and Becker (1962) write, even irrational behavior and random behavior, respectively, can also lead to the law of demand.

apparatus of indifference curves and budget constraints and the more formal mathematical analysis of consumer behavior) is predicated on maximization of an arbitrary utility function. In this sense, the economic notion of rationality in its most general form is quite weak, or exacting in terms of what people want.

One main contribution of evolutionary analysis to economics is to put some structure on this utility function. That is, rather than assuming an arbitrary utility function, we can assume that the utility function has the shape that maximized *fitness* in humans' ancestral populations (with fitness ultimately meaning the ability of a species to survive and propagate). We like fat and sweets and sex because our predecessors who liked fat and sweets and sex became our ancestors; those who did not left few or no offspring. We pursue these goals and others more or less rationally, but our rational proclivities, as well as the goals themselves, are ultimately derived from our evolutionary history.

Fitness, Variation, and Evolution

Evolutionary theory, since the work of Charles Darwin (1859), is founded on the premise that life evolved through billions of years from primordial soups of amino acids to simple, perhaps one-cell organisms, to ever more complex ones. In the mammalian realm, the progression is from some form of small rodent-type animals to monkeys to chimpanzees to protohumans to hominids and eventually *Neanderthals* (a lineage, among possibly several lineages, of primates who became extinct), and *homo sapiens*, the lineage from which modern humans evolved. Although selective pressures affected the outcomes, to the best of our scientific knowledge, no Grand Designer appears to have acted behind the scenes, deliberately making choices on which and how organisms would evolve. What happened through evolution happened without goals or intents (or so evolutionists contend and religious people contest).

The key to evolution has always been species' *fitness* to survive and to procreate in particular environments. Those organisms with attributes best suited – or fittest – for survival, given local conditions, were (and remain) most likely to procreate with greater rapidity and to have a higher percentage of their success-engendering genes spread through populations over long stretches of time (Robertson 1966; Li 1967; and Price 1970).

Likewise, those least fit organisms were and remain less likely to procreate and their genes tend to fade through successive generations. After taking the distinctly Malthusian perspective that species can – if not for checks on survival in the form of starvation, disease and pestilence, and war – multiply at "geometric rates," Charles Darwin confessed to scholars his ignorance on exactly what would cause one species to prosper and others to retreat but muses,

> All that we can do, is to keep steadily in mind that each organic is striving to increase in
> a geometrical ratio; that each at some period of its life, during some season of the year,

during each generation or at intervals, has to struggle for life and to suffer great destruction. When we reflect on this struggle, we may console ourselves with the full belief, that the war of nature is not incessant, that no fear is felt, that death is generally prompt, and the vigorous, the healthy, and the happy survive and multiply (Darwin 1859, p. 87, end of chap. 3).

The evolutionary process is propelled by two great natural conditions. The first is the Darwinian "struggle" for survival, given that "as many more individuals are produced than can possibly survive, there must in every case be a struggle for existence, either one individual with another of the same species, or with individuals of distinct species, or with the physical conditions of life" (Darwin 1859, Chap. 3). The second condition is the pervasiveness of ever-so-slight variations in species over long stretches of time, perhaps a consequence of random mutations (at the DNA level that, of course, Darwin knew nothing about), and the variations in environmental conditions in which species find themselves. These variations make the ability to adapt a foundation for survival.

The most successful species (those most likely to survive and procreate) were those possessing variations best suited for the local conditions, or the ability to adapt to changing conditions. The species' advantages – their relatively greater fitness – elevated their probability of survival and reproductive success, giving rise to a tendency for their advantages to spread, albeit ever so slowly, unless, of course, some other variation emerged and proved to be fitter. And the adaptations can be surprisingly refined for particular species. Frogs, for example, have a retina with a built-in "bug detectors," while rabbits have a retina with built-in "hawk detectors" (Marr 1982, p. 32).

Prominent evolutionary psychologists Leda Cosmides, John Tooby, and Jerome Barkow declares the logic of Darwinian national selection to be "inescapable." A species can have a "new design feature," such as a more sensitive retina:

> The new design feature causes individuals who have it to produce more offspring, on average, than individuals who have alternative designs. If offspring can inherit the new design feature from their parents, then it will increase in frequency in the population. Individuals who have the new design feature will tend to have more offspring than those who lack it... Eventually, the more sensitive retina ... will become universal in that species, typically found in every member of it (Cosmides, Tooby, and Barkow 1992, p. 9).

Darwin seems to have come to his great theory in part by juxtaposing three critical observations. First, at an early age, he observed how breeders of pigeons (among an array of domesticated animals that captured his interest) could intentionally or inadvertently select for desired traits (color, size, hunting tendency, etc.) and within a relatively short time could produce an immense array of breeds, several of which could be described, as Darwin did describe them, as "monstrosities" (Darwin 1859, pp. 41–47 and 59).

Indeed, Darwin devoted the first chapter of his *Origins of the Species* (1859) to people's selective breeding of domesticated animals. He obviously intended to lead readers to surmise that if breeders could easily produce domestic stocks with preferred variations in mind, then surely nature could create variation at a slower and undirected pace. But for Darwin's theory to have credibility, the earth would have to be far older than was widely believed among scientists and religious leaders in the middle of the nineteenth century. (One prominent minister of Darwin's era had deduced from his reading of the Bible, and convinced his many followers, that the earth had been created on a given day in 4000 BC). The theory of evolution was bolstered as the discoveries in the fossil record began to show species to be tens and hundreds of millions of years old and the age of the earth to be in the billions of years.

Second, during his famous round-the-world sailing trip on the Beagle as a young scientist in residence, Darwin observed on the Galapagos Islands, how various species of birds on the Galapagos shared many similarities with birds on the mainland of South America, but also had striking differences in key survival features, most notably in the varying sizes and shapes of finches' beaks (Darwin 1859, pp. 84–90). He inferred that those finches that had beaks ill-suited for the food sources at hand either died out or found more favorable habitats (if only by accidents in their random searches for food). Those variations of finches that had improved beaks for the food sources at hand had reproductive success, with their advantages gradually being refined and improved with further variations in later generations (an evolutionary process that continues to be observed on the Galapagos to this day).

Third, after reading a article of Thomas Robert Malthus, Darwin realized that all species had more offspring than could survive and reproduce, so that there was a struggle for existence. It was in this struggle that the first two principles operated. Indeed, Darwin's debt to Malthus was one of the first links between economics and biology, and in this case, the direction was from economics to biology.

Although Darwin himself seemed to see evolution as a process of uneven but progressive improvement in species, evolutionary theory does not necessarily imply that success is always assured for the fittest of variations within species. As paleontologist Stephen Jay Gould (1990) stressed, the fittest of species, or the fittest of variations within species, could be wiped out suddenly by an erupting volcano or at the slower pace of one of the several ice ages in the world's history. If the dinosaurs had not suffered a mass extinction 65 million years ago by a meteor striking the Yucatan Peninsular region (according to the best available theory and evidence), some species of dinosaur could have evolved into more intelligent beings than modern humans. Paleontologists widely recognize that if the dinosaurs had not gone extinct, mammals quite possibly would never have evolved into such varied life forms both on land and in the seas, and human intelligence might never have come to be what it is (with the human brain three times as large as would be expected from the brain-to-body-size ratios of all other primates, soaking up 20 percent of human energy consumption at rest [Rose 1998, p. 155]). But then, there is no reason to expect evolution to lead to the perfection of species. Some change leads to increased reproductive success but also to harmful effects in old age (Rose 1998). Moreover, evolution can only operate on what previously existed, and the outcome is a set of tradeoffs between several goals. Human childbirth is difficult because the female pelvis is an adaptation of a structure that originally evolved for four-legged horizontal movement, and is only imperfectly restructured for vertical locomotion. Childbirth is also difficult because there is a tradeoff between cranial size and maternal risks of childbirth. Moreover, diseases can show up when the species are no longer fertile, which means that life-curbing genes can be perpetuated (Rose 1998).

Natural and Sexual Selection

As did Darwin, modern evolutionary biologists posit two forms of selection that are constantly working in concert. Natural selection involves a process wherein variations in species emerge more or less randomly. Successful variations of species prosper while unsuccessful ones go extinct over millennia. The other process, described below, is sexual selection. In both cases, selection is directed toward the genes of individuals, not so much for the individuals per se. This is the "selfish-gene" theory that originated with evolutionary biologist William Hamilton (1964), who never used the phrase "selfish gene," which was later popularized by evolutionary biologist Richard Dawkins in his widely read book *The Selfish Gene* (1976).

In sexual selection, the sexes seek mates that will give them the greatest chance of having reproductive success and of having their offspring themselves surviving to reproduce. Those individuals within species that develop attractions for the opposite sex obviously can have reproductive success. Those that demonstrate relatively greater fitness, or stronger likelihood of survival, very likely are selected more frequently than those that show less survival prowess. Individuals that develop attractors that reveal the viability of their genes, whether these are directly useful in the sexual acts or not, can also be expected to enjoy reproductive success. Those that develop some aspect of physiology or behavior that is attractive to members of the opposite sex will have reproductive success even if this aspect reduces survival probabilities.

The peacock's large and brilliant tails may be an encumbrance in avoiding the attention of potential predators, but also could have developed into an attractor either because the tails caught the attention of peahens with relatively greater frequency or because peahens, recognizing that tails are encumbrances, understood that those peacocks who could make fabulous tail displays were unusually fit. Perhaps peacocks with fabulous tails had been able to evade predators despite their encumbrances. This is an example of "handicap competition" (Zahavi, Zahavi, Ely, Ely, and Balaban 1999).

The larger and more brilliant the peacocks' tails, the more likely the peacocks could have been selected for mating (regardless of whether peahens recognized peacocks' tails survival value), which is reason enough to infer that the tails of peacocks grew and became ever larger and more brilliant – at least up to a point. One can imagine that some variations of peacocks' tails were "too large," making them easy prey. Those peacocks with supersized tails do not now dominate the ancestry of living peacocks. In this manner, evolutionary forces have a way of optimizing (but hardly perfecting) fitness traits and adaptations.[4]

Growth Spurt in the Human Brain Size

Perhaps the most decisive evolutionary force for *homo sapiens* was the dramatic growth in the human brain that reached, according to dominant evolutionary theory, its full development during the Pleistocene Epoch, which lasted between approximately 1.6 million to 10,000 years before the present. At the end of the epoch, *homo sapiens* had largely converted from wandering hunter-gathers to settled farmers.

For the last 40,000 years of the Pleistocene, humans were likely intellectually modern with brains that had become dramatically larger than the brains for other primates (Rubin 2002, citing Klein 2000). Psychologist Daniel Gilbert notes that the brain appeared on earth a half billion years into our past, gradually enlarging for the next 430 million years to the size of the first primates' brains. During the next 70 million years, the brain reached the size of the first proto-humans: "Then something happened – no one knows quite what . . . and the soon-to be-human brain experienced an unprecedented growth spurt that more than doubled its mass in a little over two million years, transforming the one-and-a-quarter-pound brain of *homo habilis* to the nearly three-pound brain of *homo sapiens*" (Gilbert 2006, p. 10, citing Banyas 1999).

Although the fossil record does not record people's actual behaviors nor the reasons for the human brain's dramatic growth, evolutionary biologists and others have speculated that the growth was connected to the development of bipedalism, which freed the hands for tool-making and increased the odds that predators could be spotted at a distance; to language and oral communications that increased the potential group size and interactions of group members, increasing the demands on human mental faculties; to the increase of meat in human diets, and to competition for survival among human groups in securing prey and fending off predators (with aggression and violence playing a nontrivial role). Those humans, who experienced growth in intelligence were likely more successful on all fronts than their less capable counterparts and came to dominate the ancestors of modern humans (Aiello and Wheeler 1995; Foley 1995; and Kaplan et al. 2000; and Rubin 2002, citing in

---

[4]Sexual selection may be more important for humans than for most other species. This is because in most species males compete for females, and females choose males, so only females engage in sexual selection. However, in humans, males invest in offspring, so males desire females who will produce the most fit offspring, at least for long-term mating. This means that both sexes engage in sexual competition and are subject to sexual selection, according to Geoffrey Miller (2001). This will have important implications for the shape of human utility functions, although Miller probably goes too far in attributing human behavior to sexual selection.

various places Manson and Wrangham 1991; Wrangham and Peterson 1996; Sober and Wilson 1998; Dunbar 1998).

The Pleistocene-Conditioned Human Brain

Regardless of the exact rapidity of the brain's development, evolutionary biologists and psychologists consider it something of an article of faith – perhaps a premise – that by the end of the Pleistocene, the brain had evolved to more or less what it is today in size and functionalities. The implication is then pressed with force: The human brain takes its shape in response to the conditions, demands and limitations that prevailed way back then, with modern conditions playing a relatively minor role in the development of human's mental faculties. Prominent cognitive scientist Steven Pinker, articulating a common view among his contemporary colleagues, elaborates on the constraints that human's evolutionary history has imposed on modern human's mental faculties:

> [Natural and sexual] selection operates over thousands of generations. For ninety-nine percent of human existence, people lived as foragers in small nomadic bands. Our brains are adapted to that long-vanished way of life, not to the brand-new agricultural and industrial civilizations. They are not wired to cope with anonymous crowds, schooling, written language, government, police, courts, armies, modern medicine, formal social institutions, high technology, and other newcomers to the human experience. . . Had the Pleistocene savanna contained trees bearing birth-control pills, we might have evolved to find them as terrifying as venomous spiders (Pinker 1997, p. 42).

Cosmides, Tooby, and Barkow (as well as most other evolutionary psychologists and evolutionary biologists) maintain that because of evolutionary forces, "there is a universal human nature, but that this nature exists primarily at the level of evolved psychological mechanisms, not of expressed cultural behaviors; ... that these evolved psychological mechanisms are adaptations, constructed by natural selection over evolutionary time; ... that the evolved structure of the human mind is adapted to the way of life of Pleistocene hunter-gatherers, not necessarily to our modern circumstances" (1992, p. 5).

Evolutionary psychologists do not claim that behaviors, especially complex ones, are necessarily determined today in every detail by long-ago evolutionary forces, but only that engrained human proclivities remain entrenched and, to a degree, govern much of today's observed behavior.[5] Modern human decision making and behaviors are constrained, but not determined, by long-ago conditions and forces. Also, evolutionary psychologists do not (generally) claim that people today cannot resist, contain, and direct their behaviors – for example, their

---

[5]Much human behavior today can also be attributed to ongoing evolutionary mutations and adaptations that remain a work in process, which is to say that not all observed behaviors can be fully adapted behaviors and can be in the process of being replaced by the spread of some superior variation.

attractions to people of the opposite sex or foods that taste sweet – but they do insist that people's basic attractions to the opposite sex and sugary foods cannot be denied. To this extent, evolutionary psychologists and biologists do not deny people have some rational capacity, only that their rational capacities are necessarily bounded in terms of how they must cope with sensory data, make decisions, and organize responses largely by the way the brain was structured long ago. At the same time, some rational capacity can be expected.

According to evolutionary psychologists and biologists, the human brain has not likely evolved very much since the Pleistocene Epoch, mainly because of an apparent "evolutionary lag" of about fifty thousand years for improved mental adaptations to spread throughout the human population (Levitan 2006). Ten thousand years is simply too short a time period for more than minor meaningful mental adaptations to have pervaded the human population. As Cosmides, Tooby, and Barkow state:

> [O]ur ancestors spent the last two million years as Pleistocene hunter-gatherers, and, of course, several hundred thousand years before that as one kind of forager or another. These relative spans are important because they establish which set of environments and conditions defined the adaptive problems the mind was shaped to cope with: Pleistocene conditions, rather than modern conditions. . . Moreover, the available evidence strongly support this view of a single, universal panhuman design, stemming from our long-enduring existence as hunter-gatherers (Cosmides, Tooby, and Barkow 1992, p. 5, who cite Tooby and Cosmides 1990a and 1990b).

In short, to understand human proclivities today, we had best consider the conditions under which the brain took shape.

This does not mean that human preferences and behaviors have not, and cannot, change. They have changed and do change. Modern humans buy assortments of goods that could not have been imagined a hundred years ago, much less ten thousand years ago. One of the likely sources of the success of *homo sapiens* has been their ability to adapt to changing land structures and climates and to surprises in the form of natural (and man-made) disasters, as well as to the evolution of other species, with some important food sources and predators becoming extinct in the era in which the human brain was in a "growth spurt," as measured by evolutionary time. Indeed, human brains likely grew because humans had to adapt, with the brain's development critically dependent on early humans' developing a taste for meat and the ability to outsmart and bring down large protein-rich game that could fuel with greater efficiency the energy-guzzling human brain and reduce the amount of energy needed to digest plant food (Aiello and Wheeler 1995; Foley 1995; Kaplan et al. 2000).

Pleistocene-Conditioned Preferences for Sugar

Today, modern humans have a decided preference for foods that taste sweet and are loaded with fats, which is a source of modern obesity problems, all understandable from evolutionary selection processes. Those proto-humans and early *homo sapiens*, who developed a taste for sweet tasting and fatty foods had a bias for energy rich foods, which was no doubt important in their survival and reproductive success because of the varying availability of food sources and frequent lean times. The limited ability of early humans to store foods outside their bodies in times of abundances made scarcity all the more pressing, and life-threatening.

Those proto-humans and early humans, who had the "fat gene," or the ability to pack on pounds of body fat when food was plentiful, probably made it through times of scarcity more frequently than those with the "thin gene." Such a selection bias may be a source of modern humans' growing obesity problems (Finkelstein and Zuckerman 2008). Although modern humans understand that sugary and fatty foods can create a variety of health problems, undercut their earning powers, and even shorten their life expectancy, many people prefer the sugary and fatty foods in their diets, mainly because the technology of food production has lowered the relative prices of high-energy but sugar-laden and fat-laden foods (Burnham and Phelan 2000; Philipson and Posner 2003). The "battle of the bulge" is a real and ongoing battle for many modern humans very possibly because encoded in human DNA or mental circuitry is the rule to eat when food is available, especially fatty foods, and today fattening foods are ever present at modest costs.

Hard-Wired Mating Choices and Labor-Market Realities

Similarly, behavioral hard-wiring affects the pattern of human behaviors in mating choices. Then, mating choices can feed into gender-based labor market wage-rate differentials, the foundation of which stands apart from rank, sexist discrimination. These patterns of economic behavior might not appear to have evolutionary roots on the surface. The argument can be outlined briefly, given that I have provided a more detailed discussion elsewhere with evolutionary biologist Steven Frank (Frank and McKenzie 2008).

Females have limited reproductive capacities. Females also invest more than males in the physical reproductive process. Understandably, the human female is inclined to be selective in choosing mating partners, given her limited reproductive capacity to perpetuate her gene line (Hamilton 1964; Dawkins 1976; Browne 1995, 1998, 2002; and McKenzie 2008, Chap. 13).

In contrast, males can sire any number of babies, although individual males' reproductive success depends crucially on their access to females, which can make them less selective (Dawkins 1976). The more sexual partners males have, the greater the likelihood that their genes will survive into future generations. Understandably, research has found that males use "resource displays" much more frequently than females in attempts to attract the opposite sex (Buss 1988; Hamermesh and Biddle 1994) and that "the attractiveness of a man usually depends predominantly upon his skills and prowess rather than on his physical appearance" (Ford and Beach 1951, p. 94).[6]

Accordingly, males can be expected to exhibit sexual attractors to compete for access to females. Such attractors are holdovers of those that proved successful in earlier epochs when the brain was developing into its modern size and form.[7] In addition, given that child birth was a debilitating and life-threatening event and limited the female's ability to forage, females likely sought males, who could provide good pre- and post-partum support. Consequently, males would have competed for females on the basis of dominance and support capabilities (Dawkins 1976).

A vast literature of research findings summarized in several seminal articles authored by evolutionary psychologists David Buss and various combinations of co-authors supports the evolutionary perspective on mating behavior (Buss 1986, 1989, and 2003; Buss and Barnes 1986; and Buss et al. 1990). On one hand, females of all ethnicities and cultures across the globe continue to assess potential mates on the males' willingness and ability to provide financial and other forms of support, using age and height as markers of financial earnings and career prospects (Buss 1989).[8] On the other hand, a female's physical appearance is a marker of her fitness as a mate, with the waist-to-hip ratio as an important indicator of her fertility.[9]

The female preferences for male dominance and support opportunities can intensify males' willingness to take risks (and override an innate risk-aversion

---

[6]When the study was redone and expanded to include three hundred non-urban, non-Western societies, much the same conclusion was drawn (Gregersen 1982).

[7]Social status and relative wealth in the Pleistocene hunter-gathers greatly affect the number of mates and progeny males had. Perhaps 15 percent of the males were successful in attracting more than one mate (Geary 1998).

[8]In surveys undertaken in thirty-three countries on six continents, evolutionary psychologist David Buss found that females rated males' good financial prospects more highly than males rated females' good financial prospects. On the other hand, males rated female physical attractiveness far higher than females rated males' physical attractiveness (Buss 1989 and 1990). Other research shows that males who marry in any given year earn about 50 percent more than unmarried males of the same age, suggesting that modern females continue to select mates based on their command over resources (Trivers 1985).

[9]Psychologist Devendra Singh (1993 and 1994) showed men from the United States, Britain, Australia, India, Uganda, and several other countries line drawings of women with various waist-to-hip ratios, and most men chose the drawings with a ratio of 70 percent. He found that sculptures and paintings, dating back as much as thirty-two thousand years, had much the same proportions, as do *Playboy* magazine centerfolds have much the same proportions. During ovulation, women's hip-to-waist ratios tend to adjust toward 70 percent, giving them a greater chance of being selected for mating. And Singh found that women with the 70 percent ratios are more likely to become pregnant because of their underlying body chemistry (including the proportions of estrogen and testosterone, although such findings have not always been supported by other studies.) See, for example, Marlowe, Apicella, and Reed (2005). Physically attractive females have been found to be able to marry with greater frequency males with high occupational and social status than less attractive females (Buss 1989; Elder 1969; Taylor and Glenn 1976; Udry and Eckland 1984). The evidence on this point is so strong that one researcher concluded that females' attractiveness is the best of all predictors of their male partners' social and economic status (Elder 1969).

adaptation) in securing provisions that enable them to attract females. Today, the risk might be observed in males' propensity to drive recklessly or under the influence of alcohol and drugs or to climb sheer cliffs. If risk-taking is an evolved male trait, it can show up in modern times in the financial risks modern males are inclined to accept in pursuit of career paths with expected high pay but also high failure and termination rates. A mountain of evidence – not all of which need to be mentioned here – seems to support the evolutionary argument. But it is worth noting that males today are disproportionately descended from successful risk-takers and, accordingly, have, perhaps, an innate proclivity to take, on average, more risks than females (Rubin and Paul 1979; Rode and Wang 2000). And the relatively higher risk-taking shows up in males' higher accident rates relative to females, their more aggressive behavior towards other males, their higher rates of incarceration, and their shorter life expectancy (Browne 1998; Geary 1998). In addition, the pay distribution of males tends to exhibit higher variance than that of females, which results in more men than women suffering from alcoholism, drug addictions, and homelessness, but also with more men than women at the top of corporate ladders and among the world's richest people. By way of contrast, females who have limited reproductive capacities and are typically saddled disproportionately with nurturing young children on average have fewer stocks than men in their investment portfolios. This occurs presumably because stocks are riskier than bonds and CDs even though stocks provide a higher long-run return (Christiansen, Rangvid, Joensen 2006).

This line of argument also have been used to explain why males in all ethnic and cultural groups around the world earn *on average* more than females: males simply have greater reason to compete on salary and corporate position vectors than females, which can explain the persistent gender-based average-pay gap (Browne 1995, 1998, and 2002).[10]

The point of this digression into evolutionary-grounded male/female mating theory is that species preferences in general and human preferences in particular can be as engrained as they are unacknowledged, the sources of which may not now be well understood. Many of our contemporary likes and dislikes are not so much unalterable facts of fixed behavior as they are proclivities and propensities to act with certain expected patterns, often obscured by the noise of daily behaviors.

The engrained cost and benefit structures – or just people's perceptions of costs and benefits structures – developed eons ago that influence human choices today are not easily or entirely jettisoned. Often, we remain unaware that our behaviors have roots in the natural and sexual selections processes, and sometimes we fancy, we can remake human nature by changing institutions (or more generally environments), offering incentives, or making appeals for higher articulated goals.

---

[10]For more findings supporting the this evolutionary view of gender differences in mating attractors that could give rise to a gender average-pay gap see Harrison and Saeed 1977; Buss 2003; Green, Buchanan, and Heuer 1984; Townsend and Levy 1990a; Townsend and Levy 1990b; Sadalla, Kenrick, and Vershure 1987; Beigel 1954; Gillis and Avis 1980; Gillis 1982; Cameron, Oskamp, and Sparks 1978; Lynn and Shurgot 1984; and Townsend 1987.

Evolutionary theory suggests that we are far more constrained than economic theory suggests. Institutions, or environments, are matter, of course; but they matter in how they can cause modern humans to adjust their rationality and affect perceived and assessed costs and benefits of options.

De Gustibus Non Est Disputandum, Perhaps at Some Level

Gary Becker and George Stigler (1977) may have had a point when they argued that there is a transcendent quality to people's tastes and preferences that are guiding human decisions at some level. The evolutionarily resolved structure of people's utility functions could be more or less the same for all people, and Becker and Stigler's claimed "*De Gustibus Non Est Disputandum*" holds with force today, but perhaps only because our tastes at some fundamental level were shaped in the Pleistocene. The difference in behaviors in the two eras can be seen in the exactness of concrete predictions regarding how people's unifying utility functions precisely control their choice, given the far greater variety of goods and services available today. We may infer that ten thousand years ago, Pleistocene hunter gatherers, with great frequency, picked all, or almost all, the berries they stumbled upon. Yet modern shoppers, understandably, will not likely select with the same frequency the first berries they see at the grocery store. In addition, Stigler and Becker, no doubt, had another point: Pointing to differences in tastes, or preferences, to explain differences in behavioral outcomes across people settles very little, or can easily obscure the effects of more objective explanations, such as differences in incomes among people and differences in prices that various people face.

I make these points about human's mating and eating proclivities to make a broader point about the foundation for modern human's (economic) decision proclivities. Clearly, such a propensity to act on present opportunities can be observed in distorted discount rates, or in people's ability to calculate accurately discount rates into the future. The future – especially beyond days and months – must always have been in doubt in the Pleistocene Epoch when exacting subsistence living prevailed. What would be the point in carefully calculating the present values of future gains and pains from resisting immediate opportunities when life was often literally "nasty, brutish, and short," in Thomas Hobbes' words? Life expectancy was at best thirty years, and more likely in the mid-twenties (as estimated by the wear of teeth of fossils [Castro et al. 2003]).

From such an evolutionary perspective, it might be understandable why economists have found people to have a decided time preference – i.e., they prefer to have things sooner rather than later, and have developed a decided risk and loss aversion. Early humans must have lived under pervasive uncertainties, given that they knew little to nothing about the causes of natural forces, such as weather fronts or volcano eruptions, not to mention solar eclipses and diseases, and other bodily ailments that could easily choke off subsistence. Risk and loss aversion could have provided early humans with a survival advantage, which can explain why their progeny have a bias toward risk aversion (Rubin and Paul 1979; Rode and Wang 2000; Rogers 1994).

However, we would not expect all humans to have the same preferences. First, as discussed in many places, males and females would have different preferences. Second, preferences would change in predictable ways over the life cycle. Third, the success of a given behavior (based on a set of preferences) might vary with its frequency in the population. For example, in a population of cooperators, there is room for a certain fraction of cheaters. This sort of analysis exists in a discipline called "evolutionary game theory" that has been extended by economists (see John Maynard Smith 1982).

Evolution as the "Great Economizer"

Evolution itself has been a great taskmaster in the perpetuation of species. A major attribute of fitness has to be a proclivity of species to economize, that is, to minimize costs, either intentionally or habitually, in order to achieve maximum net gains. Economizing behavior has to be an evolved condition of members of species (not the species taken separately), because life-sustaining resources are scarce in comparison to the overwhelming reproductive capabilities of existing and potential species. Scarcity of resources must at some point constrain the advancement of particular species and possibly the emergence of additional species.

Species need not be expected always to economize rationally, that is, in some conscious, thoughtful, deliberate manner. All we know from evolutionary theory is that those species that economized very likely tended to be fittest for their environments. Hence, such economizing species would tend to be the more successful in their struggle for survival. Subsistence living conditions can be a hard taskmaster because species that are not inclined to economize can be forced below subsistence living, and out of the gene pool.

Ants might not have a rational capacity to make cost/benefit comparisons (as far as we know now); nevertheless, they do seem to minimize as best they can the cost of making round trips between their home bases (colonies or hills) and food sources by gradually straightening their paths, cutting corners as they follow the chemical trails laid down by the "scouts" and following food gatherers, and because ants tend to be more tolerable of "loafers" when food surpluses abound (Tullock 1992). Without such economizing behavior, it is hard to see how ants could have spread so completely and in such mass throughout the world.

As organisms evolved more complexity and brain sizes increased, some species developed the capacity to assess deliberately alternative courses of action in order to make the most efficient use of food and other necessities and to avoid becoming food for other species. Such mental capacity allows the species the flexibility to deal with new situations and to make improvements, or to find ways to avoid the perils of subsistence living conditions. (If nothing else, such conscious evaluations could eliminate the waste of random searches for the most cost-effective courses of action.) A capacity to make deliberate, gains-maximizing choices would give the species a survival and procreation advantage that could be expected to spread through the population with succeeding generations. One has to wonder why the prefrontal cortex – the "thinking" part – of the human brain went through the growth spurt it did, if it did not allow for a greater economizing capacity, which suggests an enhanced ability to evaluate alternative courses of action and then to weigh the costs and benefits.

And to be successful on all fronts, some early humans must have sought (or stumbled upon) a certain economical level of rationality that had superior reproductive and survival value compared with alternative inclinations toward rational behavior. Why would any species be successful if it were inclined to waste scarce energy? Very likely, some hominids and early humans probably tried levels of rationality that were either excessively or inadequately attentive to costs and benefits of alternative courses of action, giving rise to a waste of available resources. Those hominids and early humans could be expected to be dominated in the struggle for survival and procreation by their cohorts that chose levels of rationality that were less wasteful of resources.

Conservation of resources is a good reason for some decision making to be deliberately devolved to non-rational levels, because of the scarcity of neurons available for conscious, deliberate, explicitly rational decisions and the overabundance of decisions that could be made by rational methods. Indeed, it is altogether reasonable to expect that as the growing human brain was able to process sensory information in early humans' progressively more complex social environments, some mental capacity would be reserved to take ordinary common demands for assessing and decision making "off line," or below the level of conscious awareness. This unconscious rationality would be used to develop workable routines and heuristics to obviate the need for detailed analyses of every choice, freeing conscious mental powers to analyze new and surprising situations in a risky, uncertain world that could have been made ever more risky and uncertain for early humans as their brains evolved and grew, enabling them to venture forth into new and ever more complex physical and social environments. In this way, the development of a rational capacity by early humans could have provided net gains, but could have led early humans to put their rational capacities under some strain at the margin, which could have expected to lead to decisions that could appear irrational, but could also be seen as rational irrationalities (or just calculated mistakes in decision making and resulting actions). Such "irrationalities" might very well have been a part of a developmental process that was welfare enhancing, which could have spurred growth in the human brain and people's rational capacities (along with more rational irrationalities) – but on balance, and somewhat paradoxically, likely made people "smarter." Hayek fully recognized this point, and before him Alfred North Whitehead, whom Hayek quotes in his seminal article on "The Uses of Knowledge in Society": "It is a profoundly erroneous truism, repeated by all copy-books and by eminent people when they are making speeches, that we should cultivate the habit of thinking what we are doing. The precise opposite is the case. Civilization advances by extending the number of important operations, which we can perform without thinking about them" (as quoted by Hayek 1945, p. 291). To Whitehead's point, Hayek adds, "We make constant use of formulas, symbols, and rules whose meaning we do not understand and through the use of which we avail ourselves of the assistance of knowledge which individually we do not possess. We have developed these practices and institutions by building upon habits and institutions which have proved successful in their own sphere and which have in turn become the foundation of the civilization we have built up" (Hayek 1945, p. 291).

Granted, such points about the evolution of rationality have a major element of speculation, but then such speculations (since the soft brain tissue is nowhere to be found in the fossil record) have a firm evolutionarily logical foundation. After all, a brain that can economize on itself would seem to have survival value over a brain that persisted in trying to handle, futilely, the overload of sensory information at the conscious level, which can explain why experimental economist Vernon Smith reports that subjects in laboratory experiments (no matter their level of sophistication in economics) have great difficulty articulating the foundations for their market decisions (2008a, pp. xv, 5, and 9). Of course, a rational level of rationality implies that conscious and unconscious human cognition and behavior can be expected to be replete with errors. In a world full of uncertainty, even total surprises and errors can be, and should be, expected.

There is no reason people's rationality, whatever its level, could not have evolved to be a variable, being more or less utilized with more or less intensity. The extent to which people finely tune their cost/benefit comparisons must surely depend upon the current and expected availabilities of goods and on the expected payoffs from decision making, as well as the costs incurred from errors in decisions. Public choice economist Gordon Tullock (1967) stressed this point, arguing that people have considerable incentive to be informed about purchases that directly affect them but precious little incentive to be informed about public matters because their votes count for little in most elections. Rational voters, according to Tullock, would be "rationally ignorant" on public policy issues and political candidates' positions on issues. Bryan Caplan (2007) takes issue with Tullock's argument, which has been widely parroted by public-choice economists, by arguing that, in public matters, there is no reason to expect modern humans to be as rational as Tullock assumes in the first place. Caplan effectively asks why engage in conscious, deliberate cost/benefit comparisons when the resulting decisions would have no reliable, much less detectable, effects. Would not rational people exhibit variable rationality for evolutionarily sound reasons, if for no other reason? Why would the human brain have evolved to waste its scarce resources by engaging in a level of rationality – time and energy consuming decision making – with little to no gain in fitness, survivability, and procreation?

The late economist Joseph Schumpeter made the same point decades earlier: "Thus the typical citizen drops down to a lower level of mental performance as soon as he enters the political field. He argues and analyzes in a way which he would readily recognize as infantile within the sphere of his real interests. He becomes a primitive again" (1942, p. 262). More recently, Caplan (2007) has argued that the "rational voter" is a myth and should always have been expected to be so, given the virtual absence of penalties for voters to be less than fully rational, non-rational, or even irrational. He argues for recognition of "rational irrationality" (which also implies the obverse, "rational rationality"). "Rational irrationality is a modest refinement of existing (economic) models of human behavior," writes Caplan. "Assuming that all people are fully rational all the time is bad economics. It makes more sense to assume that people tailor their degree of rationality to the costs of error" (2007, p. 135), and, as we will see, rational rationality – or rational mental plasticity – has evolutionary survival value, whereas full or perfect rationality does not. Moreover, experimental research demonstrates that people are more or less rational depending on the level of reward, as well as on the particulars of the institutional setting (Vernon Smith 2008, Chap. 8, citing Fouraker and Siegel 1963; Vernon Smith 1976 and 1980; Roth and Sotomayer 1990; Vernon Smith and Walker 1993a and 1993b; Camerer and Hogarth 1999; Hertwig and Ortmann 2001; Deck and Wilson 2004; Guala 2005, pp. 231–249).[11] Schumpeter's and Caplan's points have been echoed by Vernon Smith:

> There is an interesting parallelism in the way our brains and the socioeconomic world evolve and function. Both the world and our brains have evolved problem solutions, essentially via forms of selection that are not a significant part of our formal reasoning efforts. Whereas the world of social brains have evolved institutions to solve problems, the brain has evolved internal off-line parallel processing capacities that enable us to function in daily life without continuous monitoring and conscious control, an important adaption to the emergent mind as a scarce resource (2008, p. 9).

Surely, species that developed the capacity to vary the extent to which they engaged their rational capacities – or to use Schumpeter's phrase, "mental performance" – would have a survival advantage because mental performance is a major drain on the body's metabolized energy resources and the ability to vary the engagement of rational decision making would conserve resources.

Surely successful species would not, in the conduct of life (not in the conduct of science), waste resources in defining values for units of goods that are far outside of the attainable sets of combinations of goods. The kind of *hyperrationality*, that in an earlier chapter we identified with the structure of choice, sets developed for indifference curve analysis (in which the choice space is everywhere dense with combinations of goods that have been given precise cardinal or ordinal values) would hardly be an efficient survival strategy for any species. This is to say, the kind of indifference-curve mappings economists develop in their textbooks and lectures to explore choice structures makes no Darwinian evolutionary or economic sense. Such people would have gone extinct soaking up scarce resources in making super-extensive assessments among remotely real and imagined alternatives, and leaving no time for the decision making crucial for survival.

---

[11] I must note, however, that while an assumption of full or perfect rationality may not have survival value in real-world evolutionary process, it could still have, for good reason, survival value in theory, a point to which I return in the last chapter.

To understand real-world rational behavior, we need to understand the evolutionary forces that have structured our brains and have set formidable limits on our rational capacities, including the capacity to be rationally rational. No doubt, evolutionary pressures selected for the mental capacity for people to do deductive reasoning, given that one simplifying method of managing sensory overload is to categorize similar phenomena and then to draw generalizations that could be applied to new sensory input (as Friedrich Hayek observed more than a half century ago, before the development of neuroscientists' ability to observe the operations of living brains with scanning technology).

But, as will be considered in greater detail in the following chapter, the acknowledged evolutionary limits on our innate rational capacities, ironically, can help to explain why modern economists model human behavior today as if people are more rational than they are inclined to be, or even can be. Economists-qua-analysts seek to understand extraordinarily complex social settings – markets, for example. But they, like their subjects, have limited capabilities to think rationally about rationality. Given their evolved limitations, economists-qua-analysts may have to resort to using some fabricated form of rational behavior for analytical purposes simply to make the great complexity of their subject matter manageable within deductive scientific methods, a goal of which is to pierce through the noise in human behavior and identify generalities that themselves are valuable because such generalities are themselves so scarce. Deductive reasoning capacity need not have been selected for some advantage it provided. Rather, like spandrels between arches, deductive reasoning could have been a byproduct of other selected-for benefits of human intelligence. As Gould has observed, "I don't doubt for a moment that the brain's enlargement in human evolution has an adaptive basis mediated by selection. But I would be more than mildly surprised if the specific things it now can do are the product of direct selection 'for' that particular behavior. Once you build a complex machine, it can perform many unanticipated tasks. Build a computer for processing monthly checks at the plant, and it can also perform factor analyses on human skeleton measures, play Rogerian analyst, and whip anyone's ass (or at least tie them perpetually) in tic-tac-toe" (as quoted without citation in Gazzaniga 1992, p. 88)

At the same time, a word of caution is in order: Selective evolutionary pressures "may not have conferred on the human being all possible capacities to learn all kinds of strange things" (Gazzaniga 1992, p. 95). Their limited learning capacities can show up in the greater time and thinking costs human have to incur to adapt their mental capacities to learn to do deductive science, including mathematics, physics, and economics.

It needs to be noted that economists generally assume that the brain is an all-purpose computer that can solve any problem. But it is actually unlikely that this is the mechanism designed by natural selection. Rather, the brain is likely a set of separate computational modules aimed at solving specific problems that regularly arose in the evolutionary environment. There are specialized modules for solving problems, such as "habitat selection, foraging, social exchange, competition from small armed groups, parental care, language acquisition, contagion avoidance, sexual rivalry" (Cosmides and Tooby 1994, p. 329). This is a point to which I will return in the next chapter on the neuroeconomics of rational behavior. Of course, the extent to which each of these modules is rational is subject to the same considerations discussed above.

The Unnatural Economic Way of Thinking

People may have long made cost/benefit calculations with varying degrees of precision. In that regard, rationality as practiced by individual decision makers can be an evolved natural condition, a point that calls into question claims that people's decision making is so pervasively (if not completely) fraught with irrationalities that any presumption of rationality needs to be dismissed. One has to wonder about the evolutionary survival value of pervasive irrationalities (on the order suggested by Ariely [2008] and Thaler and Sunstein [2008]). Moreover, there seems to be no point in holding an intelligent discussion over such a position, which suggests that the claim itself made in argument harbors a heavy dose of irrationality (which could be said to prove the claim itself).

Nevertheless, the economic way of thinking, as captured by neoclassical models founded on the premise of full rationality, is necessarily and deliberately unnatural. The methodology of neoclassical economics is based on abstraction – a radical simplification of the overwhelmingly complex subject matter – and requires an assumption of rationality that is not likely to exist among the subjects of the analysis, the economists who do economic analyses or the students in classrooms where the pressures to be rational are limited. The economic way of thinking must stand apart from the continual pressures existing in markets that cause people to take actions with various levels of decision making. People's innate natural rational proclivities had to be bounded by their survival conditions in a long-ago era in which selection/survival pressures dramatically limited choice strategies.

Evolutionary Conditioning and the Findings of Behavioral Economists

Evolutionary forces can help to explain several decision-making biases reviewed in the last chapter. For example, human evolutionary conditioning could very well be responsible for the "endowment effect," the tendency for modern human beings to value more heavily what they have than what they do not have and to refrain from selling what they have unless the selling price is higher than what they would pay for the same item. An endowment offers a secure prospect of the endowment holder surviving in the near term. What value people might secure in an exchange is never as certain as that which is held, given prevalent risks and uncertainties, points that Adam Smith made, along with the differential effects of gains and losses of equal value, central to his *Theory of Moral Sentiments*:

> We suffer more, it has already been observed, when we fall from a better to a worse situation, than we ever enjoy when we rise from a worse to a better. Security, therefore, is the first and the principal object of prudence. It is averse to expose our health, our fortune, our rank, or reputation, to any sort of hazard. It is rather cautious than enterprising, and more anxious to preserve the advantages which we already possess, than forward to prompt us to the acquisition of still greater advantages. The methods of improving our fortune, which it principally recommends to us, are those which expose to no loss or hazard; real knowledge and skill in our trade or profession, assiduity and industry in the exercise of it, frugality, and even some degree of parsimony, in all our expences (1759, Sect. VI.I.7).

However, there are good reasons for assuming that the endowment effect is not fixed. That is to say, the exact endowment effect depends on the particulars: the experience of consumers in buying and selling, their incomes and wealth, costs of finding and consummating trades, and the stability and competitiveness of market settings. Experimental research has affirmed that the endowment effect is variable, and can even vanish, depending on the particulars of the setting, most notably consumer experience and competitive market pressures (Vernon Smith 2008a, ch. 7; citing Plott and Agha 1983 and Plott and Turocy 1996), findings that are consistent with behavioral economists' position that the *framing* of decisions is crucial to choices that are made (see Chap. 6).

Moreover, maximizing behavior in long-ago epochs had to be subject to the constraining rule: "First, ensure survival." Those early humans who simply maximized without regard to the survival constraints may have had an overall expected mean living standard higher than those who did concern themselves with the survival constraint, but those who did not worry about survival took more risks. Although there may have been some highly successful maximizers unconstrained by the survival impulse, there were probably many risk-takers who cut their lives short. Hence, those attentive to the downside survival risks survived in greater numbers and would likely be disproportionately represented among modern humans' ancestors.[12] Consequently, evolution provides good reasons why a disproportionately large segment of modern humans demonstrate a proclivity toward risk (and loss) aversion. As discussed in Chap. 6, behavioral economists have found that subjects in surveys weigh losses of a given value greater than gains of an equal value, because of, supposedly, risk aversion. Experimental economists have found evidence of risk aversion, but they also have found the measurement of "risk aversion (the gap, as postulated in the endowment effect) depends on the procedures, or the institutional context in which risk aversion is measured," with people at times shifting from risk-averse to risk-loving behaviors (Vernon Smith 2008, p. 153, citing Plott and Zeiler 2005; Berg, Dickhaut, and McCabe 2005; and Isaac and James 2000).

---

[12] This line of argument is an adaptation of an argument Roy Radner (1998) made, pointing out that firms that survived into the long run were likely dominated by firms that did not seek to maximize profits.

Similarly, human evolution and the survival instinct might help to explain why subjects in research settings tend to favor investment projects that have opportunity costs over those with out-of-pocket expenditures (Thaler 2000b, p. 274). Opportunity costs are values that are never realized from opportunities not taken (as noted in Chap. 5; Buchanan 1969a, p. 43), while out-of-pocket expenditures require giving up part of their fungible money endowment, which could be given greater weight in choices than opportunity costs, of their survival–protection benefits. If the funds that could be used for projects have to be borrowed, then, of course, out-of-pocket expenditures are accompanied by an added liability, more highly leveraged assets and potentially greater risk, all of which company decision makers can perceive as a threat to survival.

Researchers have also shown that modern humans have a tough time dealing with the practically unlimited choices available in markets today, with many suffering consequential anxiety in trying to decide what to do and buy and then trying to limit choices. Psychologist Barry Schwartz argues that people are prone to making decision errors even when they have to deal with a limited range of choices. This is partly the case because when options rise, the pair-wise comparisons escalate. This can give rise to "mental fatigue," with decision errors escalating, perhaps because their decision-making abilities were formed eons ago when choices were highly constrained (Schwartz 2004a, pp. 73–74), which suggests a strong diminishing marginal return in decision making as the array and complexity of choices escalate.[13]

Understandably, research also has shown that beyond a point, more choices can undermine rather than elevate people's professed happiness partially because more choices can be overwhelming (Schwartz 2004b, p. 104), a consequence that Schwartz dubs the "paradox of choice": if a person has only two choices, A and B, the cost of taking the most beneficial option, A, is the value of doing B. The net gain from the decision is the difference in the two values. With only two options, the benefit gap can be significant. However, as the array of choices escalates, the gap between the two highest valued options can diminish until it becomes trivial or nonexistent, which suggests that, even if time was not a constraint in identifying choices (and *if* considered only for the sake of argument), there are rational reasons for people's limiting the array of their choices and estimates of their values. This means that, it is altogether plausible to assume evolved rational limits to rationality (Schwartz 2004b, p. 122). When consumers are faced with twenty flavors of jam, the binary comparisons reach past twelve million (which can explain why sales of jam in one study were brisker when the options were reduced from twenty to three [Swartz 2004b and Hall n.d]). That is to say, people can – maybe must – delimit the options they consider with care, intentionally leaving open the prospects that would-be better options are forgone or are not considered with the care needed to accurately compute present values (for example, any one of the gambles

---

[13]When consumers are faced with twenty flavors of jam, the binary comparisons reach past twelve million.

behavioralist have presented their subjects) – all with a form of rationality, because of evolutionary conditioning.

Moreover, the more choices we have, the greater the personal responsibility we can feel for the alternatives we take, and hence, the greater the potential feeling of regret (or "buyer's remorse") for wrong decisions (Schwartz 2004b, ch. 7; Tversky 1972). According to an array of research findings, as choices rise personal happiness can be undermined (Schwartz 2004b, Chap. 5). Herbert Simon pointed out that given the costs of settling on alternatives, satisfying behavior can be the only economical form of maximizing behavior (Simon 1956 and 1957), especially since the more maximizing (as distinguished from the less-taxing satisfying) people professed to be, the less happy and optimistic and the more depressed they reported being (Schwartz 2004b, pp. 85–86).

But in making such a concession, I emphasize that it is equally implausible that a species with a brain size that of humans would not develop some rational capacity to evaluate an array of options and to choose those that seemed to hold the greatest promise of reducing the pressing strain of subsistence living (especially since that brain has, undeniably, been used to devise incredible technological feats, many of which have required monumental calculations of one sort or another). The physical world of the Pleistocene Epoch and the social interactions of hunter-gatherers were surely too complicated and the senses of sight, smell, touch, hearing, and taste too well refined for these early humans to rely on hard-wired, preprogrammed responses to all conceivable contingencies, a line of argument Daniel Dennett develops at some length to justify the evolution of "freedom" (2003). Surely those early humans – who used some of their brains' limited neuronal capacity to think, evaluate, and take action with the intent of improvement – would have had an adaptive advantage. Evolution would likely have selected for an optimum level of rationality to fit the conditions of the times ten thousand or more years ago. Today, if people's choices appear to be irrational, or unaligned with rational precepts, the reason could be that people's engrained mental proclivities are out of sync with modern technologies, array of choices, and costs of making better decisions.

Rationality and Economic Education

If people had really evolved to be as fully rational as economists often presume, economic education for the masses of high school and college students would be a waste of resources. After all, if people can determine the timing and risks associated with various costs and benefits of a wide array of goods and services to be received through time and make the very precise and complicated expected value calculations (appropriately discounted) that economists assume they make, then students might reasonably be expected to be able to perceive and understand their own rationality.

But, of course, students must be taught basic economic principles, mainly because modern humans did not evolve to be as rational and clairvoyant as economists presume in their models. Evolutionary forces are themselves too grounded in selection for economizing behavior, even in the rationality of making choices. Moreover, although evolution may have selected people for being optimally rational (with a survival constraint in place), there is no necessary reason to believe that people evolved to consciously understand their own rational processes involved in making economizing decisions, given the critical time during which the brain was growing and adapting. All that may have been necessary was some basic understanding of decision-making processes that were and remain useful in dealing cooperatively with others.

In understanding why economists must teach the economic way of thinking and its policy implications, Emory University law and economics professor Paul Rubin (2002) has stressed four key conditions of the Pleistocene Epoch that were crucial in shaping and limiting people's mental proclivities and their public policy biases, all of which can make economic education relevant and even socially productive:

- First, when human's mental powers were being formed, the basics of life – food and shelter – were pressing scarcities. Subsistence living was pervasive. Starvation was a constant threat.
- Second, living conditions could be improved through hunting and gathering and/or through violence and forced taking, which were far more prevalent long ago than they are today (Daly and Wilson 1988; Keeley 1996). The persistence of subsistence living must have caused early humans to think that economic activity was, almost exclusively, zero sum, that the gains of one person or group came at a comparable loss to another person or group. Belief in the zero-sum nature of economic life must have been demonstrated by the intergroup raids on economic stores and fertile women.
- Third, people lived in relatively small and scattered groups with twenty-five to one hundred and fifty members, an estimate based upon the group sizes of existing primates today who have brain sizes similar to those of the human species in the pre-Pleistocene era. Rubin and other evolutionary theorists suggest that the group sizes of primates are limited by brain sizes because growth in group sizes imposes progressively greater organizational and computational problems for group members' interactions. Thus, growth in group sizes must be founded on growth in brain sizes. Based on the group sizes of primates – say, chimpanzees – today with much smaller brains, the three-pound human brain in the Pleistocene would have permitted organized bands of no more than one hundred and fifty, with typical groups sizes much smaller (Rubin 2002, p. 7, citing Dunbar 1998; Stiner et al.1998; Knauft 1991; Kelly 1995).
- Fourth, technological development moved at a snail's pace, if nonexistent, over long stretches of time. The first farmers ten thousand years ago were still using stone tools. The concept of progressive improvement in human welfare was not likely to be a matter that early humans contemplated in any carefully crafted way. Early humans lacked the technology on which to base improvement in welfare. They had limited means of storing and preserving excess food and of

accumulating capital. Their tools and possessions were limited in size and complexity to those that they could transport from place to place, as the wheel was not invented until around five thousand five hundred years ago, long after the end of the Pleistocene.

- Fifth, with little reward from work and few means of developing technology and capital goods that could make work more productive, early humans had little incentive to work longer than was required to survive. Rubin surmises that "as a result, we may not have intuitions about the productivity of capital or investment. This may explain why some religions have forbidden charging interest ..." (Rubin 2002, p. 23). Moreover, as a consequence of low productivities and the persistent absence of economic progress during and after the human brain's formative years, early humans worked only a few hours a day (maybe three or four), a work pattern that remained until the eighteenth century, perhaps also because wages for ordinary workers (not the landed gentry or educated elite), while variable, followed a flat trend between 1000 and 1800 AD (Clark 2007, Chap. 1).

Rubin argues that certain conclusions flow from the extant Pleistocene conditions: first, there were relatively few opportunities for specialization of labor, aside from those that were gender-based and related to child-rearing (which to this day have an array of implications for the differing behaviors of males and females).[14] The constrained benefits from specialization limited the opportunities and incentives for trade. Because groups were small, there were a constricted number of trading partners. Because groups were widely dispersed and crossed paths infrequently (with intergroup hostilities not uncommon), there were relatively few opportunities for early humans to trade across groups, although trades among groups were likely common long before formal competitive markets existed (Rubin 2002), and as noted, even Adam Smith recognized that the benefits achievable from specialization were limited by the size of the market, or the range of opportunities for trade (see Chapter 3).

Hence, Pleistocene people had little reason to devote their limited time and energies in understanding the law of absolute advantage that Adam Smith established as the foundation of domestic and international trade, much less the more subtle and general law of comparative advantage that David Ricardo discovered and pressed as the basis for gains from trade under almost all conditions. Early

---

[14]Citing the work of others, Rubin quotes Matt Ridley: "One man made stone tools, another knew how to find game, a third was especially good at throwing spears, a fourth could be relied upon as a strategist (1996, p. 49), but then Rubin adds, "But in a group of 50 or 150 individuals, the likely group size during much of the EEA [Environment of Evolutionary Adaptedness], there would not have been full-time work for most of these specialties. Rather, while people may have had the skills Ridley mentions, they would have been unlikely to engage in these activities on a full-time basis. That is, while there may have been some limited amount of specialization, the hunter who knew how to find game would have thrown spears at it as well, and the spear thrower might have engaged in butchering if his spear hit" (2002, pp. 19–20, also citing in other places to make this point Stiner et al. 1998; Knauft 1991; and Kelly 1995).

humans were, hence, not mentally or intellectually predisposed to see how trade restrictions (if there were any) could be welfare destroying. Accordingly, such lines of arguments, Rubin reasons, must be taught.

Understandably, with our mental faculties having evolved when trade must have been limited at best, Rubin argues that it is altogether understandable why students today often see the notion of mutually beneficial trades as counterintuitive, or difficult to grasp given hardwired neural circuits. Modern humans remain inclined to "base decisions on zero-sum thinking when other forms of analysis would be useful" (2002, p. 18), or as Rubin deduced later in his book, "Our minds are built for understanding a zero-sum society" (2002, p. 21). With such mental proclivities, people may be expected to see trade restrictions as yielding gains to the groups that impose them at the expense of would-be trading partners. If they do have such proclivities, they are hardly free to exhibit perfect rationality.

Second, small group subsistence living was no doubt productive because the group provided needed social and survival insurance, especially since incidence of aggression and death by violence long ago was far higher, as a percentage of all deaths, than it is today (Clark 2007, Chap. 6). Obviously, group living could be an effective means of spotting and warding off attacks from predators and invasions from other groups simply because there were more eyes and ears to detect predators and aggressors. Groups also could be capable of bring down larger game than could one individual, without considerable risk. Without storage capabilities for downed animals, sharing kills would have reduced the variability of food source and, thus, would have had survival value (Bowles and Gintis 2001).

Despite their cooperative living, early humans also must have honed strategies to pursue their self-interests. After all, pursuit of self-interest has survival and procreation value and those who totally neglected their own needs are not likely to be highly represented among modern human's ancestors. By the same token, early humans who were exclusively concerned with their own interests were likely to have been ostracized and banished from the protection of the group and are not likely to be represented in modern human's ancestry. Selecting group members for their proclivities to be cooperative could have reduced monitoring costs and increased the group members' probability of survival. If cooperating groups were able to increase their chance of survival, then the group members natural inclination to cooperate could have been passed down to following generations with greater frequency than would have been the case for non-cooperating group members. Thus, modern humans may be more inclined to cooperate than might be expected from a host of economists' models that suggest rampant free riding in the provision of public goods (Wilson 1993). Experimental research suggests that when subjects in one study thought they were involved in the provision of a public good in groups of four or eighty, they would contribute 40–60 percent of their expected contribution to the provision of a public good (although the contributions of subjects who were graduate students in economics, and who had learned about free-rider problems, were only 20 percent of the expected contribution) (Marwell and Ames 1981; Frank 1987).

Nevertheless, today, a similar advantageous mixture of interests – self-interest and group interest – motivates people, a point that is not only apparent from casual observation but also is supported by research (Rubin 2002, p. 14, citing Reiss 2000). Such an evolutionary perspective supports contentions of economists from Adam Smith to Frank Knight to Friedrich Hayek to even Gary Becker that economic theory founded strictly on pursuit of self-interest is necessarily a partial view of life.

The prevalence of sharing in communal living conditions is, according to Rubin, a likely source of modern humans' focus on cooperation and sharing as virtues and as more transparent sources of group gains than trade with distant people. The hardwiring of the brain during years when sharing was prevalent and a dominate source of individual and groups gains could be responsible for the emergence of reciprocity – or "reciprocal altruism" – as a coordinating rule for group members' behavior. Those early living conditions for humans also can help to explain "kin altruism" and group and ethnic identifications and associations (Hamilton 1964; Frank 1987; Rubin 2002, citing Brown 1991, p. 137; Krebs and Denton 1997; and Boyer 2001). One advantage of related people forming groups is that they share the correlate behavior of seeking the perpetuation of their shared genes, as noted previously (Hamilton 1964).

Evolutionary biologist Steven Frank (2009) argues that cooperative behavior among group members could have evolved from strictly self-interest motivated group members. As do economists, he points to the potential tragedies of the commons as being a core problem for groups, when group members compete for the largest share of the gains from common property. As is well known, commons' tragedies can be overcome if everyone restrains his or her competitive tendencies, keeping the greater gains of cooperation in mind. Group members can agree to suppress competition and then police group member behavior, imposing penalties for competitive violations. But the agreement negotiations, policing, and penalty impositions can soak up the gains from cooperation.

Some of those costs can be avoided if group members have correlate behaviors, meaning the "same behavioral level of competitiveness." This suggests that no group member can "out compete a neighbor" in individual pursuits of larger shares of the gains from common access resources (Frank 2009, p. 6). In long-ago epochs, humans who formed groups from among individuals with correlate behaviors would have had a survival advantage, with lower survival costs, over other groups: "The invisible hand may come to discover and use information about social partners without conscious knowledge of those associations. Alternately, direct and conscious information may have come into play in some cases" (Frank 2009, p. 7). Groups with members who had correlate behaviors also could have become larger in membership than other groups, giving rise to greater gains from specialization, but the source of their gains might not be known to the group members because of the way the gains evolved over long stretches of time and not always with design: "much of the cooperative structure in biology and human behavior arises from such synergetic interactions. The positive feedbacks and consistency of cooperation often become so deeply embedded that their very existence can be difficult to discern. The more cooperative and nonvarying the interaction, the less one tends to notice it" (Frank 2009, p. 12, citing Axelrod and Hamilton 1987). Hence, such correlate-behavior groups could have increased their relative numbers, making cooperation out of self-interest ever more common among their progeny.

Those early living conditions in which the brain took its final form may also help explain why in a cooperative-games tournament, among sixty-four strategies designed to overcome the free-rider problem, the most successful strategy is "tit for tat," in which parties continue to cooperate so long as they do not detect others' defections (Axelrod 1984). Tit for tat (which Adam Smith recognized as a cooperative strategy when he wrote that "kindness is the parent of kindness"[15]) could have been a dominant strategy among early humans and remain an enforced mental proclivity that explains why people do not free ride (or who do not defect from the cooperative provision of collective/community goods) as frequently as economists might expect from their behavioral models founded on *homo economicus* (a point developed with game-theory analytics by Jack Hirshleifer, who explains how affections and passions can make cooperative arrangements self-enforcing, even when individuals dominant strategy calls for their taking the non-cooperative actions [1984 and 1993]).

An engrained tit-for-tat proclivity also might explain why many people harbor disdain for people who do free ride and for economists who often suggest, with some professional pride, if not arrogance, that pursuit of self-interest should be expected in cooperative game settings where free riding is the dominant available strategy. Even in one-time games, subjects have been found to take the cooperative strategy, although they tend to take the cooperative strategy more frequently when interactions are repeated and when the interactions are subject to market pressures (Thaler 1992, Chap. 2, citing Marwell and Ames 1981; Kim and Walker 1984; Isaac, Walker, and Thomas 1984; Isaac, McCue, and Plott 1985). Understandably, in plays of ultimatum games (in which one player proposes a division of some amount of money, say, $10 or $100, to another, perhaps anonymous player, with the second player having the right to reject the division), subjects typically come close to an even split of the funds – possibly because the first player fears the second player will reject any unfair split. Still, even in one-time plays of dictator games (in which the

---

[15] Adam Smith made his kindness point when he wrote,

Of all the persons, however, whom nature points out for our peculiar beneficence, there are none to whom it seems more properly directed than to those whose beneficence we have ourselves already experienced. Nature, which formed men for that mutual kindness, so necessary for their happiness, renders every man the peculiar object of kindness, to the persons to whom he himself has been kind. Though their gratitude should not always correspond to his beneficence, yet the sense of his merit, the sympathetic gratitude of the impartial spectator, will always correspond to it. The general indignation of other people, against the baseness of their ingratitude, will even, sometimes, increase the general sense of his merit. No benevolent man ever lost altogether the fruits of his benevolence. If he does not always gather them from the persons from whom he ought to have gathered them, he seldom fails to gather them, and with a tenfold increase, from other people. Kindness is the parent of kindness; and if to be beloved by our brethren be the great object of our ambition, the surest way of obtaining it is, by our conduct to show that we really love them (1759, Sect. VI.II.22).

first player's proposed split of the funds cannot be rejected), the first player will typically propose that the second player receive nearly a quarter of the funds.

Such splits are difficult to explain unless one assumes that the subjects making the split are either hardwired to share the experiments' spoils or, as Vernon Smith suggests, they bring to the laboratory games their life experiences that make the games a presumed part and parcel of life's repeated game plays in which the rules of fairness are active, or reciprocity, is expected (Vernon Smith 2008, ch. 10 and 12, citing Camerer 2003; Crockett et al. 2006; Henrich 2000; and Henrich, et al. 2005). As Vernon Smith observes from his survey of a mountain range of laboratory experiments (including his own) on one-shot and repeated ultimatum and dictator game-theoretic experiments, people seem to carry with them everywhere their "social experience," leaving them with "deeply entrenched innate habits of cooperation" that "are so strong that they persist even under the strong contrary condition of anonymity" (Smith 2008a, p. 205).

Economic conditions, in addition to the developing human brain, were likely to have influenced the sizes of groups that formed in the Pleistocene Epoch. In small groups, members could have learned with relative ease the subtle clues in facial expressions and body language that reveal others' hostile or cooperative intentions, skills, especially valuable before complex vocabularies were developed. Within small groups, members also could monitor others' work efforts and mutual sharing with the intention of pressuring slackers to do their part and curbing cheating and free riding (Rubin 2002, citing Bowles and Gintis 2001).

The availability of monitoring behavior and the associated costs affected group sizes, and "mental modules" likely evolved for policing transactions and for detecting cheaters (Cosmides and Tooby 1992). Rubin argues that these mental modules tended to focus on how people abided by the terms of the bargains rather than on the mutual gains to the trading partners, a tendency that makes gains from trade made at a distance or mediated by money all the more counterintuitive, which suggests why economics courses are replete with lessons on the gains from trade with unknown others (Rubin 2002, p. 21, citing Wright 1999).

People's civic behavior, such as voting, giving to charity, and participating in environmental projects may also have roots in the evolution of the human brain. Economists are hard pressed to explain, within the strict confines of perfectly rational, maximizing behavior, why people vote, contribute to presidential campaigns, or make charitable contributions. In such endeavors, people's individual contributions to the outcomes are often inconsequentially small. Individual votes, for example, cannot possibly determine who will win election campaigns (except, maybe, in very local elections with low turnouts). Similarly, contributions to presidential campaigns or to charities cannot, except in rare occasions, affect the course of the elections or the good that charities do. Even becoming an informed voter can be construed, using standard rational precepts, as irrational or just outside of the pale of rational behavior. This line of argument, developed most prominently by Tullock (1967), as noted, suggests that people should not be expected to incur the personal costs that many actually do incur to vote and to become informed.

In addition, when large groups of people sweep through large areas to pick up trash, the trash picked up by *individual* participants often makes little differences to the area's overall cleanliness. Yet, people continue to participate in community trash pickups in public areas, and even more frequently hold their trash and recyclables until they reach appropriate bins.

Rubin's Darwinian perspective on politics suggests a way to unravel the paradox (for economists) involved in people's participation in elections and other civic activities. Because of their Pleistocene-era mental conditioning, people today may be predisposed to vote for the same reason they are predisposed not to free ride in cooperative efforts. The brain's hardwiring, developed when groups were relatively small so that contributions to the collective whole were indeed significant and ostracism from nonparticipation was a real threat, may still constrain rational calculations. This is to say that free riding may be a rational welfare maximizing strategy only when an individual's brain is indeed free and able to assess the probabilities and expected values of the individual's contribution, an assessment of which the brain very well may be incapable, or just lack the inclination to make the required assessments. Put in different terms, people today can be systematically predisposed to overestimate the impact of what they do in large-group settings because they cannot easily and fully shake their small-group mentality.

But then, there is a downside to group living that can give rise to the type of decision-making bias Robert Shiller has highlighted, "bubble thinking" (2008) with the emergence of benefits from group living and in deferring to the ears and eyes of their fellows, cooperation could have fed into the natural and sexual selection processes, creating in modern humans a more or less instinctive reliance on "herd" thinking and action, with "herding" in, say, fashion and social customs having both positive and negative consequences, but still often with net gains (Bikhchandani, Hirshleifer, and Welch1992). Still, Shiller (2005 and 2008) could be right in suggesting that modern human's decision bias toward herding is unlikely well adapted to some modern institutions, such as asset markets where people's herding proclivities can emerge as the type of "bubble thinking" that led to the booms and busts in the stock market in the late 1990s and the boom and bust in the housing market in the late 1990s and early 2000s, as well as the serious financial crisis of 2008 (as well as the bubble thinking on government remedies that led to escalating proposals to increase the sizes of bailout and stimulus packages in 2008 and 2009).

Concluding Comments

In conventional microeconomic theory, rational behavior is assumed, but perhaps no more firmly grounded in reality than the theorists' self-affirmations based on introspection of their own behavioral motivations. For purposes of economic theory, rational behavior can appear arbitrary, which is to say it can be anything – perhaps whatever works best for the theoretical purposes at hand. From this perspective, an assumption that people act as if they make choices with perfect rationality is no less arbitrary than an assumption that people do act with perfect rationality. Indeed, an as-if assumption might be the more credible theoretical starting point. But critics of economics, who harbor a different intuition about the foundation of human behavior, easily dismiss such a perspective, citing a mountain of scholarly evidence that people's real-world and laboratory behaviors are frequently at odds with the predictions of economic theory.

Theoretical rational behavior must not be confused with the rational behavior available to people making choices in complex social settings involving real physical, mental, and emotional world constraints. In life, the form, extent, and precision of the rational behavior people exhibit did not magically appear. Real-world rational behavior must have emerged from the same evolutionary processes that formed all other human attributes. And those long-lost evolutionary conditions and forces under which people developed their mental faculties and their rational capacities must constrain rational behavior today. An examination of the conditions of the critical period within which people's brains formed can offer potentially valuable pointers on why people tend to make the kinds of choices they do today, as well as inform us on why people have policy biases and must be taught the implications of rationality that, as Rubin has perceptibly argued, are often counterintuitive. The economic way of thinking, from an evolutionary perspective, is indeed far from natural, which might explain the difference between the thinking of real people and the thinking of those imagined subjects of economic analysis.

One of the more telling arguments from an evolutionary perspective on human rationality is that people today cannot possibly be as rational as economists assume they are. Perfect rationality makes evolutionary nonsense, since evolution is the great economizer on the selection of species and variations within species that so many evolutionary theorists have argued is the case. By the same token, it is altogether reasonable to presume that for any species that developed the level of intelligence that humans have, that species would have developed in complex environments some rational capacity, meaning some capability of *acting,* in Ludwig von Mises' meaning of the word to make circumstances "less unsatisfactory."[16]

Primitive life forms might be expected to devote their limited brains to preprogrammed responses to particular stimuli precisely because their worlds were, and, for those that did not go extinct, remain simple. However, once physical and social environments become as complex and sophisticated as human environments,

---

[16]I understand this is a claim with which some neurobiologists take issue, because they view behaviors developing from external world experience doing nothing more than activating and shaping genetically implanted neuro-circuits. What appears to be "learning" is the shaping of circuits from repeated activation. People "learn" from their experiences in much the same way that the immune system "learns" by developing particular antibodies in response to an invasion of the body by specific antigens (Gazzaniga 1992). I know of no way to settle whether this way of thinking is more correct than the economic way of thinking that presumes a capacity for value assessments. In the end, such a distinction may not make a difference, and both could be complementary ways of thinking through why people behave as they do.

we can expect that those species that developed the capacity to evaluate new and changing situations would have a survival advantage. Yet the development of human rationality is still bounded by the conditions under which it developed and by the evolutionary process by which advantageous adaptations are spread through populations. People simply cannot be more rational than evolution, as an economizing process, will allow. This does not mean that people cannot be coaxed into understanding the rules of rationality, or be driven by institutional and market pressures into becoming more rational than they otherwise would naturally be inclined to be.

Perhaps evolutionary biologists and psychologists are wrong to assume with great confidence that human rational capacities have remained more or less the same for the last ten thousand years, with no appreciable change in the brain's ability to respond to conditions differently than it did eons ago. After all, there have been documented changes over the last six thousand years in the human genome that affect mental processes (Wade 2007). Perhaps, the brain does have rational capacities today that it did not have way back then. Indeed, scholarly evidence has mounted showing that people's problem-solving abilities mounted during the last two-thirds of the twentieth century, at least as measured by a gradual rise in mean IQ scores (Flynn 1999; Nettelbeck and Wilson 2004; Blair, Baker, Gamson, Thornton 2005).

Nevertheless, the perspective that evolutionary theorists articulate should remind economists that people's rational capacities can be more than an abstract premise; rationality can be an evolved state of mind with evolved boundaries that cannot be summarily dismissed. Perhaps the boundaries of human rationality can be assumed away for the purpose of developing theories, but not when describing real-life human motivational and behavioral proclivities.

Obviously, evolutionary theorists and economists share a common approach to doing science: They seek to reduce the complexities of their theories to manageable proportions. Biologists and other physical scientists must deal with a great deal of noise in the natural world. Not all human behavior can be explained in terms of long-ago physical and social conditions under which the human brain became fully formed, because we simply do not know many of the details of the Pleistocene environment. Also, early humans made mistakes and humans continue to do so, partially because of constraints on making all the required calculations, for economic and noneconomic reasons. Those mistakes remain a part of the noise of behavior, then and now.

Social processes themselves are complex and interactive, and evolutionary, which make predictions on the correct courses of actions difficult and make corrections of behaviors inevitable. The evolutionary process, grounded in natural and sexual selection, has never stopped, and may not have altered its pace. Random mutations in species continue apace, as must adaptations, although at the pace of evolutionary time. Evolutionary theorists cut through all this added noise by a simplifying assumption, that many human proclivities today were set long ago. The presumption is that an analysis of long ago conditions (to the extent they can be known, or just surmised) can be more telling about people's behavior today than an assumption that the brain did not reach its full potential until relatively recently.

Economists do much the same thing when they adopt a simplifying premise while acknowledging the complexity of people's social interactions and the considerable noise in those interactions. Perhaps, economist's concept of full rational behavior is nothing more than a means of cutting through the noise of extant behaviors and gaining more understanding about people's behaviors than they would have gained had they allowed people's actual behaviors to clutter the analysis. The complexity of the analysis could exceed economists' evolved mental faculties and proclivities, which, like those of their subjects, were molded for a different time and set of conditions that did not include the need to understand elaborate market and social interactions in what may be for all modern humans, including economists, a strange world that requires a lot of groping their way through the intricacies.

Chapter 8
The Neuroeconomics of Rational Decision Making

with Paul Zak and Jessica Turner[1]

Economists appropriately stress the problem of scarcity of resources in the external physical world where people seek to maximize their gain from an array of individually conceived wants that far exceed their capacities to fulfill their wants. A nontrivial portion of life for almost everyone is spent making choices and tradeoffs, some made unconsciously, which is to say, automatically or by instincts, routines and habits (regardless of whether or not the routines and habits are set by rational processes). A major goal of conventional microeconomics is to understand how the particulars of alternative institutional settings will encourage people to use their scarce resources efficiently in the external physical world, given whatever rational capacities people possess. And people's rational capacities are typically viewed as fixed (more or less), not as a variable, subject to more or less activation.

The so-called "economic problem," which reduces, in conventional neoclassical microeconomics, the inherent difficulty of achieving economic efficiency in the external physical world, has been qualified in key ways throughout the discipline's intellectual history, most notably by Frank Knight and Friedrich Hayek (see Chap. 5). Knight insisted that economics was concerned with the "rationale of life," but he also recognized that a central problem for the discipline was how far life was, or even could be, rational, or (as rationality is normally conceived by neoclassical economists) as a matter of people deliberately choosing to allocate known resources among known wants. Knight mused that much time and human energy is soaked up in a life-long exploration into the field of alternatives and their evaluations in order that people can determine what ends can be and should be pursued (Knight 1935, p. 105). Hayek's major concern was that information on people's wants and the scarcities of resources is scattered among individuals who are the ultimate (and, according to Hayek, only) wellspring of wants. Moreover, subjectively conceived wants determine what physical things in the external world can, indeed, serve as resources; that is, as material and nonmaterial inputs that can be used to actually satisfy individually determined wants (Hayek 1945 and 1952b). Subjective evaluation, accordingly, is at the foundation of both sides of the scarcity dichotomy, wants and resources, the market values of which are necessarily determined interactively in social settings in the external physical world, which means

[1] Paul Zak is a professor and director of the Center for Neuroeconomics Studies at the Claremont Graduate University. Jessica Turner is a senior neuroscience researcher in the School of Medicine at the University of California, Irvine.

R.B. McKenzie, *Predictably Rational?*,
DOI 10.1007/978-3-642-01586-1_8, © Springer-Verlag Berlin Heidelberg 2010

that as a discipline, economics could not, and should not, imitate the methods of the physical sciences. Since Lionel Robbins defined the economic problem as that of coping with scarcity, Knight's and Hayek's (and other subjectivists') methodological concerns have been largely sidelined, if not dismissed, because, if taken seriously, economists' pursuit of empirical science would be seriously hobbled.

The economic problem has not, in our view, been fully recognized and explored, and deserves further modification. As important as the external physical world constraints are to the work of economists, perhaps, the more fundamental and binding economic problem with which economists as theoreticians must deal is how best to conceptualize human behavior in the external world of scarce physical resources – given the truly pressing constraints imposed on economic thinking (or any other kind of thinking) by the evolved physiological limitations of the human brain. Although rarely acknowledged, the human brain is quite possibly the scarcest resource that economists encounter, both for themselves as analysts and for their subjects who must work their way through choices and tradeoffs within the internal world of the mind. This process is essential to economists as analysts if they are to have any hope of understanding all of the choices and tradeoffs in the external physical world, with both sets of choices necessarily made interactively, or each set of choices affecting the other, often in Bayesian feedback loops.

Economists seek to understand dauntingly complex phenomena – virtually the totality of individuals' behaviors and their social interactions under alternative institutional settings – all within the confines of their own mental faculties. Economists must find ways of economizing on their limited mental faculties in order to cope with the complexity of their analytical subject matter, which involves the economizing behavior of people in the external physical world constrained by institutional settings. The problem at hand for economists (and all others who study human behavior) is akin to the "mind–body problem," which reduces to the issue of whether the mind (the totality of our mental faculties) is able to understand the base material from which it itself is constructed. Then, again, the brains of economists' subjects are equally scarce resources for managing complex activities: coping with the onslaught of data received in a multitude of intensities and combinations through the five senses (used in numerous combinations), conceiving of wants, evaluating and ordering their wants, and choosing consistently among their ordered wants with the intent of maximizing their welfare – all done within severe time constraints for economists and subjects alike and in the context of complex physical, social, and institutional settings. And to heap on complexity, the subjects' real-world social and institutional settings are forever evolving, as must surely be the case if the venerable Adam Smith was correct, that in their pursuit of their own narrow ends, market participants can be led by an invisible hand toward social ends that may not have been originally imagined by anyone and were not, necessarily, a part of anyone's original intent.

The brain imposes a first and sweeping limitation on human rationality both in the real world and in economists' deductive scenarios. People's brains, not just the people themselves with their brains activated, must engage in economizing processes. As with market participants who cannot have everything they want, the human brain itself cannot do everything demanded of it. Accordingly, the brain must somehow also make choices and tradeoffs on what is done with sensory data before individuals can make myriad choices and tradeoffs in the external physical world, the usual domain of economic analysis.

This chapter examines the neuroeconomics of rational behavior at a level once removed from typical neuroeconomic analytics, which generally involves the brain's specific reactions to specific sensory information. Data is received from the physical external world (normally laboratory settings) through the senses that in various combinations produce perceptions of the world. The brain must analyze sensory data, make decisions, and undertake responses, including those that are automatic or reflexive and those that are, to one degree or another, deliberate, with the latter being the main source of human actions. The brain must then develop feedback loops in which it assesses the effects of its decisions and orchestrated responses through analyzing additional sensory data in an iterative manner with the goal of making predictions and devising its own responses at the neural network level. The human brain must also decide, with both conscious and unconscious processes involved and intermingled, which reactions can be made automatically, routinely, or habitually, thereby economizing on caloric energy consumption and saving its limited neural resources for other more deliberate analyses. So, this chapter differs from standard neuroeconomic analytics in that we seek to initiate a discussion of how the economizing within the human brain affects the rationality of decision making.

This chapter also differs from standard neuroeconomics in that we are mainly concerned with why and how the brain must economize its activities to achieve an efficient level of rationality, given both its biological constraints and those constraints in the external environment that affect the availability of the nontrivial energy resources the brain's multifaceted and multi-level operations require. Acknowledging that the human brain cannot do everything at a conscious, deliberate level, we seek to assess the internal, neurobiological bounds on human rationality, given the comingling of conscious and unconscious mental processes involved in rational and nonrational decision making. Finally, we want to explain how the acknowledged neurobiological bounds on human rationality must constrain the assumptions economists make about their subjects' rationality for analytical purposes.

We do not seek to convey numerous neurobiological details of brain functions, but rather our intent is to describe the basic problem of scarcity that besets the human brain and then, as economists are good at doing, to draw out the implications for, in our case, the likely limits on human rationality both in reality and in economic (or any other) theory. We leave it to neurobiologists to fill in many of the missing physiological details. Our intent is to follow the lead of, say, environmental economists who theorize about the conceptual implications of externalities in the absence of well-defined property rights, but leave many of the details of the chemical causes of environmental decay to atmospheric chemists and physicists. In short, our goal is to paint the economic operations of the brain with a broad brush, but include enough details that the neurobiological limits on human rationality are fully evident. And we need to be emphatic on one point: Rational decision making need not all be conscious. Indeed, efficient rational decision making requires an admixture of mental processes that are unconscious and conscious. Deliberate conscious decision making must involve unconscious processes, given the complexity of decision making, the brain's limited neural and energy resources, and the speed with which a multitude of decisions are made (a matter of milliseconds). But then, unconscious processes can have all the efficiency attributes of routine or habitual behaviors that enable people to cope with repeated circumstances and events.

Our analysis leads to a more complete understanding of rationality, and *bounded rationality*, which will allow us to discuss rationality as a mental variable that permits the conceptualization of optimum rationality, which we prefer to call *rational rationality* (which stands apart from the conceptualization that is fixed by neurobiological constraints). We conclude that while people are, no doubt, in some sense, often irrational, the scope of human irrationalities necessarily narrows when scarcity of resources is extended to the internal workings of the human brain. Many presumed irrationalities are no more irrational than are mistakes in the external physical world where reductions in mistakes come at an escalating cost and, thus, where making the optimal number of mistakes is the only guiding economic goal. Rationality is necessarily bounded, but only in the sense that decisions must be made within the biological constraints of the human brain that, as noted in the last chapter, have evolutionary foundations, points familiar to readers of Herbert Simon and Friedrich Hayek. By the same token, rationality is not fixed. Just as emotions can be more or less invoked, so can our rational capacity.

We do not imply that all human behaviors can be defined as rational, and our arguments leave much room for true irrationalities. As discussed in Chap. 6, several behavioral psychologists and economists have effectively defined irrationality to include human decisions at odds with an assumption of perfect rationality (see Ariely 2008 and Thaler and Sunstein 2008, to mention two of the widely read trade books in the new behavioralism covered in Chap. 6). Perfection in rationality is hardly an achievable benchmark, and consequently, critics of economic rationality have found human decisions and behaviors replete with irrationalities, so much so that irrationality has begun to lose at least some of its force as a distinguishing category, as well as raise doubts about whether pervasively irrational people can engage in a meaningful rational discussion of people's irrationalities, especially, if the discussion is intended to lead to meaningful improvements in people's decisions and behaviors.

Our line of argument returns irrationality to a more confined definition: An irrational decision is a decision that is inconsistent with respect to the organism's proximate and ultimate goals. This is to say that an irrational decision is any decision or behavior that is at odds with the human brain's ability to do the best it can in processing sensory data, evaluating options, and generating responses within the constraints of its own internal resources (including the body's energy resources).

To make the argument clear, some reiteration here at the start can be useful: Not all deviations in decisions and behaviors from perfect rationality, as conventionally defined, are necessarily irrational. Even with acknowledged mistakes and irrationalities, the human brain may be doing the best it can, which is to say that many purported mistakes and irrationalities are grounded in a form of rationality, again involving the comingling of conscious and unconscious neural processes, more frequently than critics of rationality may commonly think.

Our line of argument helps to unravel theoretical conundrums that have emerged with behavioral psychologists' and behavioral economists' criticisms of the rationality premise in conventional, neoclassical microeconomics: How it is that people in so many varied ways can be deemed irrational and, at the same time, can view their own analyses as rational and can expect their readers to rationally evaluate their findings of irrationalities? How is it that people, including economists (behavioralists and neoclassicalists), can view themselves as trying to make decisions with evolving economic *ends* in mind? We suggest a relatively simple and transparent resolution to both questions: People do seek to make rational decisions, but they have to make their decisions not only within the constraints they face in the external physical world, but also within the constraints of the internal biologically driven world of the human brain. As will be argued in the next two chapters, the mental constraints described here and documented by the critics of rationality in economics, as well as by neurobiologists, force economists to assume their subjects are more rational and mentally unfettered than economists know them to be. An assumption of perfect rationality in human decision making can, thus, be seen as a means by which economists can terminate the infinite regress involved in considering the rationality of rationality, and, unavoidably, the rationality of rational rationality, ad infinitum. The human brain does not have the resources to cope with such an infinite regress, needless to say. A premise of perfect rationality in economic theory can be, simply put, a rational coping mechanism – a rationally flawed one to boot – that neoclassical economists may be required to use in the type of static analysis that they pursue – because of neuroeconomic constraints.

To see these points with clarity, we must first review economic principles and then the array of decision-making limitations that evolutionary forces have built into the biology and chemistry of the human brain.

Rationality and the Construction of the Human Brain

Scarcity in the human brain domain implies that not everything that is wanted will be produced. It implies some things will be left undone, or not even contemplated or, if contemplated, not attempted. Indeed, every biological system, including the brain, is conservative in the physical sense; it tends toward achieving its goals with minimal energy expenditure. In this regard, all biological systems are economic systems in the sense that they have evolved to handle the problems of scarcity at some level, if only scarcity of useable energy by their internal biological systems, as they seek to deal with the ever-present "exploit-or-explore" dilemmas as best they can. Cows, for instance, must decide whether to continue to exploit the grass that can be seen around them or move off to explore distant hillsides, and such decisions must mean that, because of evolutionary conditioning, they seek (at least in some rough way) to equate at the margin, or weigh the marginal gains in distant energy sources versus the additional energy expended to move to the distant energy sources. Evolution will favor those cows that, by whatever means, equate at the margin in exploit-or-explore decisions, as suggested in the last chapter.[1] Cows are hardly the brightest animals on farms. Ducks are likely dumber, but that hardly means that they could have evolved to be where they are without some rough economizing behavior, at least compared with all other decision rules that could have been tried by their direct competitors over evolutionary time (a point Ludwig von Mises made; see Chap. 5).

With pervasive scarcity, nothing will be done by any species, not even primates with the mental capacities of humans, with perfection because of cost constraints. Everything is subject to diminishing marginal utility on the demand side of the market and diminishing marginal returns on the supply side, with optimal or efficient consumption and production levels of various goods falling short of perfection. Optimality is necessarily constrained by entrepreneurs' proclivities, technologies, capital, institutional systems, and the physical and human resource base.

Many of the same implications can be drawn from an acknowledgement of scarcity within the internal world of the human brain as it performs its functions. Many irrationalities in decision making and in deliberate responses to sensory data in such a setting are likely to abound, but then should not most irrationalities be treated as forms of expected and unavoidable mistakes when the scarcity of the internal mental world is superimposed on the scarcity of the external physical world? Should not irrationalities be expected for much the same reason that baseball pitchers walk batters, that drivers have accidents, and that many products and firms fail? If for no other reason, biological systems have an irreducible stochastic quality to them, which can be described as noise that obscures the underlying economizing processes, just as mechanical processes are beset with irregularities, or noise, however small.[2]

---

[1] For extended discussions of exploit-or-explore decisions, see Zak and Denzau (2001) and Ghiselin (1974).

[2] Granted, the human brain contains far more intelligence – or capacity for thinking, reasoning, remembering, and learning – than that of any other species, including, of course, cows and ducks. The intelligence of adult chimpanzees, for example, comes close to rivaling humans' intelligence, but only for humans up to 18-months of age or so. Adult human intelligence reaches well beyond the mental capacities of chimpanzees. "By adolescence," observes neuroscientist Michael Gazzaniga, "human intelligence is uniquely human, and other primate intelligence is unique to those particular species. When circuits unique to our species click in, we leave the chimps in the trees" (Gazzaniga 1992, p. 105). Humans may be the only species capable of contemplating its own consciousness, much less the origins and fate of the universe or create complex production processes and markets to ease the scarcity problems they face, and these abilities must be traced to their mental resources unmatched by other species.

As in the external physical world, scarcity in the internal world of the brain is a matter of conflict between ends and means. The human brain encompasses roughly one hundred billion neurons, the basic cellular factories in which all of the chemicals and electrical impulses used in brain functions are produced. Each neuron has, perhaps, ten thousand synapses, or points of actual or potential connectedness with other neurons, creating a communication network that uses electrical impulses and chemical reactions to recognize, manipulate, store, and recall sensory data. The number of possible connections among the neurons for information exchange rivals "the number of molecules in the universe" (Gazzaniga 1992, p. 50), which suggests a lot of thinking/reasoning/computing power is potentially available for rational decision making.

However, that thinking/reasoning/computing power available for rational decision making is far below what might be imagined. Many of the neurons are involved, often in clusters, in operating components of the body in automatic responses, largely without conscious or deliberate thought, all with the effect of economizing on the brain's available energy reserves. The portion of the brain dedicated primarily to higher reasoning is the prefrontal cortex, but then the prefrontal cortex also acts as the "executive" part of the brain in that it draws input from other critical regions and subcortical areas. So, although our knowledge of the workings of the brain remains limited (but improving) and the number of neurons and other cells (for example, glia cells) available for information processing and rational decision making is not exactly known, the count of available neurons at any given time for rational decision making of the kind economists imagine is far fewer than might be expected, given the billions of neurons and synapses and potential trillions of combinations of neurons that can form networks. The point is not that all neurons can be used for rational decision making (any set of neurons can be enlisted). Rather, the point is that during any period of time, the brain is called upon to do so many things. Then, we hasten to stress again that rational thinking and decision making do not have to draw exclusively on conscious mental processes (as might be suggested by the way rationality is typically explored in conventional economics). Rational thinking and decision making can be, and often is, engaged by unconscious processes. And decisions, of course, are often the product of the comingling of conscious and unconscious processes in various areas of the brain.

The biological structure of the human brain constrains in a number of key ways rational decision making through whatever neurons are available, and whatever their efficiency. As psychologist Gary Marcus (2008) has stressed, the human brain is something of a "kluge," a Rube Goldberg, or an inelegant way of accomplishing assigned tasks because the component parts – lower, middle, and higher brain – may have evolved for purposes other than those for which they are now used. The higher brain (neocortex) evolved on top of the lower brain (brainstem) and middle brain (limbic) and there is no necessary reason to expect that the component parts of the brain have been optimized for all decision makers all the time (especially, in modern times). Optimization has never been a goal of evolutionary forces. At any stage of the brain's evolution, a chance augmentation or mutation in the DNA, no matter how "klugy," could have changed its construction, so long as the change was a sufficient enough improvement over previous adaptive models for the change to be spread through the human population through reproductive success of those humans who possessed the augmentation/mutation (Marcus 2008).

There are good evolutionary reasons why people's mental faculty and rationality remain circumscribed. The development of additional mental capacity had gains for early humans in their being able to survive in larger and more complex groups and against predators far stronger and faster than humans of every age. Neurons (known as "gray matter"), make up 40 percent of the brain, but consume 94 percent of the brain's oxygen (Zak 2004). As the size of the human brain developed, any additional energy the body absorbed was no longer available for alternative non-mental uses, such as being better able to fend off diseases or to run faster. The development of a larger brain along with the development of bipedalism was not accompanied by an expansion of the birth canal, requiring that newborns start life more or less helpless and inexperienced. The required learning can be costly because learning can cause the brain to absorb calories that have alternative bodily uses and can be expected to lead to thinking/reasoning/computing mistakes. At some point, the species' losses from mistakes can be less damaging to the species' survival than are the losses that can come with greater neural energy consumption that will be required to make improved decisions with a larger brain.

Again, evolution is hardly a force for the perfection of anything; it has no goal. Moreover, evolution works so slowly and works through a multitude of simultaneous and serial modifications and adaptations in a multitude of individuals that human goals for rationality are not easily conceived, much less imposed on the process.[3] Evolution is simply a process by which a species' random modifications and adaptations enhance or undermine the species' chances of survival and reproductive success. The level of intelligence represented in humans is obviously a rare evolutionary outcome. In evolutionary terms, the rarity of modern humans' intelligence is understandable because a species' intelligence can be expected to evolve to a progressively higher level only so long as the gains to the species' survival and reproductive success exceed the costs. Nevertheless, under real-world conditions over evolutionary time, species seem to reach some equilibrium between the benefits and costs of developing greater intelligence.

Evolutionary biologists Tadeusz Kawecki and Reuven Dukas have theorized that all species – including humans – may be genetically capable of being smarter than they are, but conditions in evolutionary history did not permit it, or rather greater intelligence did not make economically adaptive sense (as reported by

---

[3] It is hard to see how humans in any transient generation would be able to conceive of a more efficient, higher level of mental capacity and then institute the biological modifications required to establish the greater mental capacity throughout future generations. Any species, human or otherwise, able to pull off such a feat would not need to move to a higher mental capacity, or so it would seem. Of course, genetic engineering might eventually overcome the time constraints of evolution, enabling people in some future generation to transform human mental abilities in a matter of generations, if not during one or two generations.

Zimmer 2008, citing an article by Reuven Dukas and Tadeusz Kawecki, forthcoming in the journal *Evolution*). For example, evolutionary biologists have found that vinegar worms (which have only 302 neurons), fruit flies, and bumble bees are capable of learning at some level, but only at a survival cost beyond some point. For example, fruit flies that were induced over fifteen generations through laboratory conditions to learn food sources quickly had life spans 15 percent shorter than slower learning fruit flies. The fruit flies that evolved under laboratory conditions to live long lives were up to 40 percent less capable of learning (Zimmer 2008).

Human mental capabilities today might appear limited because human intelligence evolved under radically different environmental conditions than exist today. Life could have been simpler and shorter long ago with fewer viable options. Having fewer choices, humans could more accurately evaluate their limited options for risk and time preferences, which suggests fewer mistakes. In contrast, life today is everywhere filled with options that far exceed people's analytical capacity, forcing humans to economize more carefully. Plentiful options and a growing flood of new options can lead to "mistakes," or decisions that appear to be irrational or nonrational to outside observers. As noted in Chap. 7, people today may not be good at discounting the costs and benefits of events in their distant futures because the brain did not evolve at a time when they had anything approximating the distant futures that modern humans can contemplate.

Human rationality necessarily falls short of economists' construct, perfect rationality, and that shortfall can vary across people and their life spans simply because the physiologies of the body and brain change over people's life spans. The cortex generally develops connecting "wiring" for integrating with the rest of the brain at a slower pace than evolutionarily older parts of the brain, which explains why teenagers may be more prone than adults to emotional responses to given experiences, or find it more difficult to divert sensory data for decision making to their higher brains (Bjork et al. 2004). Also, as people age, the brain continues to change for strictly physiological reasons. As people move into "old age," their lungs' capacity to move oxygen to the blood stream begins to deteriorate, as does the capacity of red corpuscles to absorb and transmit nutrients and oxygen to the brain, and they lose both gray and white matter, as well as many other changes in cellular numbers, volume, and function (see, e.g., Sowell et al. 2004; Fraser, Khaitovitch et al. 2005; and Conde and Streit 2006). At times, both healthy teenagers and the healthy elderly may be less "rational" than others, but only in the sense that teens' and the elderly persons' decisions may be less considered because they face different physiological and neural constraints.

The brain's communication system, which is hardly as exacting as circuits within microprocessors, constrains human cognition and decision making. The error rate within the neural circuits' mishmash of electrical impulses and chemical transmitters introduces a randomness and quirkiness in neural activity that can impair the efficiency, timing, and correctness in evaluations of sensory data and decisions (Carstensen and Mikels 2006). And it is common knowledge that what people eat, drink, and inject can radically affect communication within the brain. Addictive drugs (alcohol and hallucinogens included) are, especially, effective in altering neural communications. For example, hallucinogens can increase serotonin levels that give rise to hallucinations that, of course, can substantially affect decision making.

The Human Brain's Economic Problem

One need not be a neuroscientist to recognize the human brain's fundamental economic problem: It must operate within its own cognitive, evaluative, and computing limitations while monitoring and activating a multitude of physiological functions, all of which can be affected by what the brain does or does not do. The economic decision making problem the brain faces is compounded by the fact that it very likely confronts problems of diminishing marginal returns, and eventually negative returns, that can set in fairly early as the sensory data inflow escalates. Diminishing and negative returns can show up in commonly experienced confusion and frustration when problems faced become overwhelmingly complex.

No neuroscientist has attempted to measure the gap between the potential and actual sensory data flow into the brain and the brain's potential and actual capacity to cope with the substantial inflow of sensory data, possibly hundreds of gigabytes a day, but there is little doubt that even at its most efficient operating limit, the human brain can handle only a minor portion of the potential sensory data inflow. Herbert Simon, more than a half century ago, had good reason for founding his theoretical construction of *bounded rationality* on the scarcity problem confronting the human brain, or in his words: "The capacity of the human mind for formulating and solving complex problems is very small compared with the size of the problems whose solution is required for objectively rational behavior in the real world – or even for a reasonable approximation to such objective rationality" (Simon 1957, p. 198). As described in Chap. 5, Frank Knight and Friedrich Hayek adopted similar positions.

Simon's simple point – the inherent scarcity problem within the human brain – imposes a most fundamental and sweeping limitation on how rational people *will be* and, if they have any choice in the matter, will *choose to be* (or even the brain itself would choose to be, if it had any choice in the matter). Both consciously and unconsciously, the human brain must somehow limit the sensory inflow by totally ignoring some substantial portion of all sensory data, filtering other sensory data flows, and then absorbing much sensory data in compressed form (that is, with many of the details of sensory experiences left out) (see e.g., Nuñez and Malmiera 2007). All the while, the brain must engage in the noted exploit-versus-explore decisions, many of which are done at lightning speed, which gives decision making a highly dynamic, even Bayesian, process with feedback loops that allow for continuous updating and adjusting of decisions even before decisions work their way into behaviors. All this occurs in less than a few dozen milliseconds for automatic, primal responses and a few hundred milliseconds for more considered decision making. At all times, however, the brain must economize on its available energy reserves, which is the reason the brain excludes and filters sensory data in the first place.

The brain has developed sensory filtration and compression methods to address this problem. For example, the human brain might process and store in compressed form, or not even consider the backgrounds of daily scenes (Simons and Levin 1997 and 1998). The brain might place the telephone numbers received from chance meetings of distant friends only in short-term or working memory for retrieval for perhaps the next thirty minutes, while it might decide to place the key life experience, from births and deaths, especially, those that evoke strong emotional responses, in long-term memory, with many of the details never to be forgotten and most details easily retrieved (but, perhaps, only after such memories are "relived" and consolidated during sleep). Even then, the brain might not have allowed many sensory data of key life events – for example, the actual blueness of the clear skies during key life events – to be noticed, much less stored.[4]

Although the cerebral cortex controls many emotional responses to sensory information, the basal ganglia and limbic system are primarily responsible for handling stimuli that harbor rewards and pains (thirst, hunger, and sex, for example) and dealing with fight-or-flight decisions necessary for survival and, as a consequence, procreation. Limbic structures (the thalamus and, to a lesser degree, the amygdala) often process initial sensory information, making flash judgments in less than five hundred milliseconds on whether an immediate response is required, and then, when appropriate, relaying the information to the cerebral cortex for more complex, complete, and time-consuming analyses (although information processing is often undertaken, as best we know, in all parts of the brains more or less simultaneously, with information flows sometimes going in multiple nonlinear directions among neural networks). The limbic system, in other words, is often a mental gatekeeper. For good evolutionary reasons, "risk aversion" is likely built-in, localized in the anterior insula, which is a portion of the cortex twisted toward the inside of the brain, with a focus on both feeling and recognizing in others negative emotions such as disgust and pain – because decisions for survival must be made in those gate-keeping systems and because survival decisions were crucial for the evolutionary development of the brain (Wicker et al. 2003). This bias toward emotional decisions for survival often checks human rational responses to sensory information when it is first routed through the limbic systems.

The exclusion and filtration of sensory data is self-evident when we look at and/ or talk with someone totally unaware of surrounding sights and sounds. The exclusion of much sensory input also has been documented dramatically in experiments classified under the rubric "change blindness." Subjects have been randomly stopped for interviews on the street, only to have "workmen" carrying a large panel pass between the interviewer and interviewee. In the moments of separation, the interviewer is changed. The interview can often be resumed without the interviewee

---

[4] A potential basis for this can be seen in neural responses in visual areas to the same visual stimuli being modulated by attentional states (Treue and Maunsell 1996).

realizing that the interviewer is someone different (Simons and Levin 1997 and 1998).[5]

Harvard researchers have developed an experiment involving "sustained inattentional blindness" that dramatically reveals the extent to which subjects will ignore much sensory data when they are asked to focus their attention on assigned tasks (Simons and Chabris 1999).[6] For the study, nearly two hundred undergraduate subjects were asked to watch a video of six basketball players in a tight group, with three wearing yellow jerseys and three wearing black jerseys. Half of the subjects were asked to count the passes the three players in yellow jerseys made among themselves as they moved about the group of six players, while the other half of the subjects were asked to count the passes the three players in black jerseys made among themselves as they also were on the move in the group. In the middle of the video, a research assistant dressed in a gorilla costume strolled slowly into the middle of the group of six players as they continued to make their passes. The gorilla faced the camera for a few seconds, paused, and beat her chest. At the end of the video, the subjects were asked how many passes their assigned players made. After recording their answers, the subjects were then asked if they noticed anything unusual. Typically, only 50 percent of the subjects indicated they had noticed the gorilla. The rest had no knowledge that the gorilla appeared in the video. When all subjects were shown the video again in a group setting, and were not assigned the counting task, they were, understandably, in disbelief, as are viewers of replays of the experiment posted on the internet (Simons and Chabris 1999).[7]

The point of describing the limitations of the brain, the sensory data overload and the filtration methods in place is straightforward: the human brain, before it seeks to economize on external resources, must first economize on itself, on its own internal resources. It must somehow decide (with "decide" being used loosely here and elsewhere) what sensory data will be acknowledged and absorbed and then how the data will be processed, compressed, set aside, stored, and retrieved. All the while the brain must determine the form and the relative importance of the processed data in order to use the information to make considered judgments. In a real sense, the human brain uses a form of rationality (if not perfect rationality). The human brain must be the ultimate single-minded optimizer, given its resource constraints, because it is hard to imagine that it would have evolved with any other goal, which can explain why "good enough" (not perfect) decisions can be the norm, which is to say that the human brain seeks rational rationality in a neurobiological way.

---

[5]The experiment can be better visualized by viewing a video of the interviews with the change of interviewers occurring in the midst of the interviews (http://viscog.beckman.uiuc.edu/grafs/demos/15.html).

[6]The experiment can be seen in a video of the experimental setting (http://www.youtube.com/watch?v=T0nYQEm6Ajg).

[7]In another version of the experiment involving basketball players passing the ball, a research assistant walked through the players holding an open black umbrella with the results much the same (Simons and Chabris 1999).

The scarcity of neurons available for rational decision making can press the brain to allocate its neurons with some sense of efficiency between conscious and unconscious processes, with the unconscious processes having a rational foundation, given that such processes can make decision making more efficient, and more rational, than otherwise would be possible. Specialized mental circuits maintain automatic functions and generate reflexive/conditioned responses in, for example, the heart, lungs, sweat glands, and even muscles, conserving the brain's scarce energy reserves and freeing those mental circuits from having to rely on time-consuming, calorie-burning conscious thought. Narrow assignments in some specialized mental circuits may also reduce errors in cognition and thinking, or irrationalities in decisions and behaviors because, if nothing else, the brain has reserved greater energy resources for high-thinking processes (which are the most pronounced energy guzzling components of the brain; see Scholey et al. 2001).

A primary way the brain saves resources is by automating repetitive tasks. This is why a person can drive a car as if on autopilot, and talk on the phone or listen to the radio at the same time (although maybe with impaired driving skills). The brain has stored the procedure associated with driving the car and exploits this knowledge until it is sufficiently valuable to one's goals (such as survival) to bring this task into costly conscious awareness. Being fully conscious of driving occurs, for example, when the driver of another car in front slams on his or her brakes, causing the driver behind to make an evasive maneuver. Talking on a cell phone appears to slow down this transition from unconscious to conscious because talking itself requires resources, leading to accidents that might otherwise be avoided (Jessup 2008). Using procedural memories is often the best way to perform a task, such as in sports where "not thinking" about how to do repetitive tasks (being in a certain spot on the field) is the key to quality performance.

Put another way, unconscious mental processes can enhance the brains' ability to make efficient deliberate, conscious decisions with its available and scarce energy resources, despite the fact that these unconscious mental processes may from time to time produce responses deemed to be irrational when measured against the conventional neoclassical model of perfect rationality (which does not account for the economizing, optimizing problem the brain faces). The existence of these presumed irrationalities may simply indicate that the brain is operating efficiently in achieving its own goals within the constraints of its own physiological and energy resources and is also undertaking more conscious and deliberate thought than would otherwise be possible. This is a part of our understanding of what rational rationality means. Gains can be realized from many irrationalities, or expected mistakes, from the brain automating decisions or making decisions before all available sensory data is absorbed and considered. The presence of irrationalities (such as those seen in the decision biases noted by behavioral economists who seem to think all irrationalities detract from rational decision making) may enhance and extend people's rationality beyond what would otherwise be possible in much the same way that product failures can enhance multiproduct firms' profitability in a risky and uncertain world.

Humans have developed a variety of ways outside of the brain for economizing on their mental resources for the purposes of making their decisions potentially more rational than they could otherwise be. Humans live in communities (for a variety of reasons related to their economizing on external physical resources that economists readily acknowledge), but there is also an internal economizing reason: specialization in decision making can free up neural resources. The diversity in different people's brain functions means that humans can learn from observing other's decision making, thereby lowering their energy costs and freeing energy reserves for other more deliberate decision making purposes (with the origin of the word "learn" coming from "to show" Zak and Park 2002).

The human brain is a kluge in another important way: People learn by storing memories, which require neural circuits, yet memories are not stored in specific assigned neural addresses in the way that digital files are assigned specific digital addresses in personal computers. The adult human brain learns new information by strengthening connections between existing networks of neurons through repeated encounters.[8] Memories in bits and pieces can be spread among clusters of neurons across the two halves of the brain and over regions within each half; the storage system and frequency of memory recall both affect the speed and efficacy of memory recall.

Memories also are spatially distributed throughout the brain and are stored contextually, meaning they can be recalled through various cues and associations and combinations of cues and associations, not by plugging in specific neural addresses (Kandel 2007). For example, we can recall people's names and telephone numbers by remembering the situations in which we met them (context-dependent memory). Because neurons are scarce, many details of experiences will not be stored, or will be stored in stylized and compressed form. The intensity of the situations in which memories originate can affect the strength and usefulness of memories stored and available for recall and use in conscious and unconscious decision making. Few people who watched in person or on television the horrors unfold on September 11, 2001, including the bodies dropping from high up the Twin Towers or the buildings collapsing in a rising plume of smoke and dust, may remember the clear blue sky on that day, the names of the airline on the sides of the two planes, or exactly how many deaths there were. But, only a few who read "9/11" can escape recalling a multitude of gruesome scenes, many of which will be mental collages of actual scenes recalled together along with concocted details not originally stored, partially because the brain's amygdala was activated with full force, as evidenced by brain imaging studies (Sharot et al 2006). Similarly, people who have been mugged at gunpoint are often unable to give any details of the assailants' faces or even their guns and, hence, are subject to substantial errors in identifying suspects in a police line-up (Pezdek and Blandon-Gitlin 2005). The rush of chemicals released in the primitive brain when the fear response is activated

---

[8] See the classic article by Squire (1986) and the more recent review by Bruel-Jungerman et al. 2007).

overwhelms the capacity to do higher analysis on the sensory flow, which can give rise to an immediate, perhaps, reflexive response. Such emotion-filled experiences are often stored immediately as long-term memories, which allow for later analysis but can sometimes cause post-traumatic stress disorder (McGaugh 2004).

Storage of initial experiences is thus incomplete; the accessibility of the experiences for later analysis is also uneven, often depending on varied cues and associations (with more cues and associations elevating the speed and accuracy of memory recall). In addition, repetition of the sensory input heightens the solidarity and usefulness of memory circuits. The more frequently any sensory data input is experienced, the stronger and more useful the mental circuits are for decision making. That is why names and telephone numbers can be more easily remembered and recalled if they are repeatedly encountered. As a result of the way the brain economizes on itself, when one encounters the same stimulus, or a similar stimulus, the brain is biased toward a particular decision. Behaviorally, this neuronal process manifests as heuristics, based on rational rationality (Gigerenzer and Todd 1999b).

Learning combined with rational rationality and use of heuristics means that there is a range of related stimuli that lead people to make nearly identical decisions. For example, people often order from a narrow selection of items on restaurant menus that they frequent, mainly because they have sampled and narrowed the relevant set of choices. Drawing from established neural circuits created through past experience requires less energy consumption in decision making than trying new items and dealing with new sensory information. Restaurant patrons might sometimes regret always ordering the same item, but often do so anyway, mainly because of having experienced disappointment with trying new items in their pasts. Nevertheless, occasionally people will order different dishes (often after someone else has, saving on cognitive resources required for explore-versus-exploit calculations), or drive home by a different and often longer route.[9] Individual differences in novelty-seeking behavior have been linked to the mesolimbic dopamine system (Bardo et al. 1996).

Many memories dissipate as the strength of connections between neural circuits wane absent reinforcement. Across a population, individuals' rationality, or their decision biases, will vary according to the strengths of their neural circuits that, in turn, vary in how often they have been reinforced through experiences and a flow of sensory data. People encounter different experiences with greater or less repetition, producing individual differences in neural circuits and decision making, which suggests that the rational rationality of decisions can be expected to vary across

---

[9] Again, the irreducible noise in neural firing rates may partially affect the changes in people's decisions. Neurons have background stochastic firing rates for reasons that are not well-understood, but may accomplish "housekeeping" tasks that cells need to function properly, and the neurons' stochastic firing rates can, we surmise, give rise to productive exploration of people's sensory landscape about them. Laboratory studies of animals and humans consistently reveal this behavior, and doing the occasional exploration can easily be understood as an evolutionarily adaptive trait (or else we must wonder how or why humans could, as Frank Knight suggested, see so much of life as an "exploration" into the field of alternatives and their values).

people, circumstances, and time (and even within the same person under different circumstances, say, with a full or empty stomach), precisely a hallmark finding in neuroscience research (see, for example, the study on economic decisions with and without serotonin depletion by Crockett et al. 2008). No one should expect, therefore, the rationality of decisions to be the same in one-time laboratory experiments in which subjects are called on to make deliberate decisions with little or no consequences and with little or no experiences with the sensory data presented to them, as that in the real-world settings in which neural circuits have become well established through repetition of experiences, especially, those that come with consequences that justify the energy expended on the honing and maintenance of neural circuits.

Economically Rational Rationality

Many commentators lament the common and mistaken presumption that a prime reason people are no smarter (or no more rational) than they are is that they typically use a minor portion (say, 10 percent) of their mental capacities, as measured by the neurons available for deliberate, conscious thought.[10] A common presumption is that people would be smarter (or learn more or make better decisions) if they engaged a much higher proportion (say, 90 percent) of their mental capacities. Contrary to this presumption, neuroscience research has shown that much of the brain is at work all the time, but with more or less intensity, as determined by the firings of neurons, even when people are asleep and are not engaging (consciously or unconsciously) their brains for decision making, with all parts of the brain serving some function, or multiple functions (Beyerstein 1999; Raichle and Gusnard 2002; Raichle 2006).

Moreover, research also indicates that "60–80 percent of the energy budget of the brain supports communication among neurons and their supporting cells. The additional energy burden associated with momentary demands of the environment may be as little as 0.5–1.0 percent of the total energy budget" (Raichle 2006, p. 1249). Surprisingly, less than 10 percent of the synapses in the visual cortex are actually devoted to carrying sensory data coming from the retinas (Raichle 2006, p. 1249). Surprisingly again, if the research is right, the energy consumption of the brain is fairly constant, varying, perhaps, no more than 5 percent over a twenty-four-hour day – and changes very little when research subjects are specifically asked to make decisions or undertake tasks, as revealed by PET and fMRI scans (Raichle and Gusnard 2002).

One explanation for the constancy in energy consumption is the overwhelming employment of the brain's neural and energy resources to maintain (and predict

---

[10] A summary of the evidence of the myth that humans used only 10 percent of the brain is available at http://faculty.washington.edu/chudler/tenper.html.

future needs of) all bodily systems, including its own (Raichle and Gusnard 2002). This line of research, which implies highly constrained (or more or less fixed) neural and energy resources available for rational (conscious and unconscious) decision making, suggests the likelihood of strong diminishing marginal returns with even minor increases in the processing of sensory data from the external environment. Given the (likely) fixity of the available neural and energy resources in the brain, we should not be surprised if future research shows that the brain, as an evolved economic system, shifts neural resources to the consideration of sensory data and decision making in order of the assessed value in other uses, which suggests increasing marginal cost of dealing with progressively more sensory data. While such a line of argument is necessarily speculative (neuroscientists know little about how the brain's mind works), diminishing returns in the brain certainly have some plausibility, given how everyone can attest to becoming fairly easily confused and frustrated with growing complexity of choice options and, therefore, decisions, to the point of the quality of decision making being undermined (or made worse), a point made in Chap. 7 and documented in some detail by Barry Schwartz (2004a, 2004b). The relative fixity of neural and energy resources available to the brain can also explain why the brain readily shifts unused neural circuits to alternative uses and why forgetfulness is a human plight. The overarching point is straightforward: The brain is likely the scarcest resource involved in economic, rational decision making.

When people are in what has been described as a "flow," in which they are thinking clearly and creating with ease new ideas and extrapolating the relevance of old ideas, they are generally working with a relatively small portion of their neurons engaged (Csíkszentmihályi 1990; Slagter et al. 2007). In research training sessions, subjects are typically focused, which means they have "zoned out" much sensory information that could obstruct the flow of all relevant sensory data. When people are frustrated and anxious over what they are not able to accomplish mentally, they are typically trying to engage a higher percentage of their neural computing capacities. The implication of this line of substantive neurobiological research is that more sensory data considered by the human brain do not always lead to improved decision making, which suggests that beyond some point the marginal improvement in decision making diminishes progressively as more sensory data inflow is allowed. Hence, it is in the interest of both the human, and his or her brain, to curb in a variety of ways the sensory data inflow, which necessarily means that perfect rationality, in the sense of using *all* available information, is no more a viable option for the human brain than perfect environmental quality is a viable option for policymakers in the external physical world of real resources and real diminishing returns in production.

The brain uses some version of the exploit-versus-explore strategy to weigh the value of including more sensory data in decision making. And there are physiological reasons the brain is willing to explore new information, instead of always staying with established neural networks based on past sensory data inflows, considering new information triggers the midbrain dopamine neurons to fire, which is a reinforcement mechanism and which suggests the brain has feedback loops that enables it to learn from and correct errant, even irrational, decisions (Bianca et al. 2008).

There are absolute limits to the amount of work the brain can do. In addition, because of diminishing returns in neural use that set in fairly quickly, the use of available neurons is likely to fall short of that limit. We have already argued that the biology of the brain imposes a limit on information processing, for example, on how many options will be considered and how completely the considered options and their attributes will be evaluated. Many decisions will be made without conscious deliberation, and may not be fully rational. But many of these nonrational decisions will have a quasi-rational foundation. The brain must weigh in some rough and ready form the value of expanding the sensory data inflow and widening the array of options subject to choice, against the alternative physiological and neurological uses for the caloric energy required to acknowledge and absorb the additional sensory data and analyze it. Such decisions often will be rough guesses because sensory data not acknowledged and absorbed necessarily introduce elements of risk and uncertainties into choices (although we hasten to recognize that the brain considers much sensory data at the unconscious level and such unconsciously considered data can predict conscious choices with a high degree of accuracy [Knutson and Bossaerts 2007]).

Economists often treat risk and uncertainties as problems in decision making that are only part and parcel of the external physical world in which their subjects must make their choices. However, risks and uncertainties emerge at least in part from internal mental scarcities and the necessity of ignoring and filtering out lots of sensory data and treating other sensory data with little care. Nevertheless, the brain's decisions on limiting the span and intensity of sensory data inflow can themselves have an element of deliberateness, and as the brain seeks to economize, economic considerations come into play. Not the least of these considerations is the cost of sorting through available real, physical world options and their attributes, and of activating multiple established neural networks. All of this mental activity expends caloric energy that has alternative physiological and neurobiological uses, so it is no wonder that the brain favors established or past decisions and ways of thinking.

Market Prices and Rationality

Of course, the more easily sensory data can be summarized and absorbed, the more decisions will be made with care and the more rational they can be, using both conscious and unconscious neural processes. Given the neurobiology of the human brain, market prices – especially, market prices quoted in money terms – are likely to have economic consequences that extend beyond the purely allocative effects economists attribute to them with little to no effect on buyers' available choice options. Prices can change market equilibriums because of their salience (which can be seen not so much as a mental defect as the brain doing what needs to be done, using its own scarce resource as effectively as possible). If prices capture in summarized and condensed form meaningful information on the relative production costs of various goods, as Hayek (1945) has argued convincingly, then prices contribute to people's internal economizing. As buyers cope with their mental scarcity market prices enable them to consider more purchase options, and more of their attributes, than would otherwise be possible. Because of the omnipresence of prices, buyers can develop well-honed neural circuits devoted to recognition and analysis of prices, which enhances the efficiency of decision making and allocation of resources in more profound ways than economists commonly recognize.

Moreover, to the extent that market prices are determined under competitive market conditions, prices induce producers to minimize their production costs and provide information to buyers on the relative values of goods bought and sold in markets. This means that competitive market prices provide useful information and guidance on relative qualities of goods, which affects buyers' evaluations across goods, market demands across goods and, in a feed-back loop, market-clearing prices themselves.

From the conventional neoclassical perspective of prices, any evaluative effects of prices, whether absolute or relative, are ruled out by assumption. Almost all economics instructors tell their students, "Prices affect the quantity demanded, not consumers' marginal evaluations and their market demands." This is an understandable position, given economists' typical theoretical starting point – perfect rationality. Under such a premise, there is no way that cognitive processing of sensory data can be enhanced by prices or anything else. All decisions are perfect with no room for enhancement. But from the perspective of neuronal scarcity developed here, market prices can impact allocative decisions of the brain, improving decisions over a larger array of options with more attention to their attributes. A recent brain imaging experiment has shown that prices activate regions of the brain associated with pain processing. People find it physiologically and neurobiologically painful when prices rise, with the pain input lessening their desire to purchase goods (Knutson et al. 2007).

The point is that neural limitations imply two levels of economizing – or rational – decision making. The higher level of decision making is the one familiar to economists, conscious and unconscious reflective considerations of relative values of known options (with neurobiological evidence that the brain does have a utility function, or places where evaluations are made, a point to which we will return later in the chapter). At this decision making level, mistakes are expected because of acknowledged risks and uncertainties associated with anything less-than-fully-known options.

The lower or unconscious level involves the brain's efforts to economize on itself with regard to the types and amounts of sensory data that is acknowledged, absorbed, and evaluated at different cognitive levels. There are good evolutionary reasons for the brain to function well at this lower decision-making level, but, of course, there are also good reasons that this lower decision-making level will be replete with mistakes. However, many of these cognitive mistakes will be no less rationally grounded than the mistakes made at higher decision-making levels.

Nevertheless, such a perspective on cognitive decision making leaves much room for decisions (e.g., fight-or-flight decisions) and behaviors (e.g., spontaneous jumps in response to loud noises) that may be construed as nonrational in the sense that they have been automated and are not the result of conscious, deliberate neural processes. Such nonrational processes, however, can enhance the efficiency with which the brain uses its limited resources for conscious and deliberate rational decisions and behavior over and above what would be otherwise possible. All of this is, to say, that human decisions and behaviors must take place within an evolutionarily rational level of rationality – what Vernon Smith calls "ecological rationality" – both in taking in sensory data and in using that data for making conscious and unconscious deliberate decisions and devising behaviors (2008).

The Chemistry of Neural Gains and Pains

In 1738, Daniel Bernoulli suggested the existence of a utility function that mapped rewards into subjective values according to the law of diminishing marginal utility. Such a utility function is the foundation for all modern economic analysis. What we now know from very recent neuroeconomics studies is that the utility function is a real physiologic entity in the human brain (Park and Zak 2007; Knutson et al. 2007; Glimcher et al. 2005; Knutson and Peterson 2005; and Nelson et al. 2004). The physiologic utility function appears to draw on the neural resources in at least four distributed brain regions for the purpose of assessing the relevance, salience, value, and cost of decision options. Utility calculations receive input from the brain's evolutionarily old "wanting" system that processes rewards, as well as the pain-associated cost calculation. Risk aversion, as discussed above, is processed along with visceral states. Perhaps, not surprisingly, patience when waiting for a delayed reward requires substantial resources from the prefrontal cortex, the seat of planning in the brain, an obvious physiological source of a decision bias toward options that offer immediate or near-term gratification or of people's difficulties in properly discounting benefits over time (McClure et al. 2004). It should not be surprising that humans, and indeed all animals, have physiological utility functions. Resource acquisition calculations using explore-versus-exploit decisions require information processing neurons that relate costs to an evaluation of expected benefits. A cow grazing on the pasture with a full stomach has a much different subjective valuation regarding the benefit of additional grass, and thus a decision to move to a different hillock than the cow with an empty stomach. The marginal cost of moving is the same, but the marginal benefit of additional grass is quite different. The hormone leptin signals satiety when the stomach is full, informing the physio-logic utility function. Chronic undernourishment, signaled by elevated levels of the hormone ghrelin, inhibits the ability to make new long-term memories. The animal knows it is hungry only if its brain can make utility calculations.

Such calculations take into account risk (albeit imperfectly), not simply expected marginal benefits, because of the evolutionarily tested survival benefits of weighing dangers and threats to life and limb. Animals are by and large risk averse, as are most people, except during extraordinary circumstances. Taking big risks makes sense, for instance, when one's life is at stake. A hummingbird searches for nectar in tight concentric circles around its nest. But if it does not consume enough calories during the day to satisfy its high metabolic rate, it may not survive a cold night. As a result, when a hummingbird has not consumed enough during the day and the sun begins to set, it will begin to search in highly elliptical patterns that will increase its range. This is a risky strategy because it will be able to return to the safety of its nest only if it is successful at finding food (Bateson 2002). Human beings will display similar behaviors in dire circumstances; for example, "doubling down" when on a losing streak in Las Vegas.

What we know is that the brain has a physiologic utility function that integrates sensory and visceral data on expected benefits and costs, risk aversion, and salience of outcomes. This circuit is distributed throughout the brain, which means that not only are these calculations performed imperfectly as the brain economizes on resources, but interruptions in processing are possible. These interruptions can be due to damage in the connecting fibers (lesions), underdeveloped connections, neurochemical variations, or even crosstalk with other processes the brain is doing that use some parts of this same circuit. Not surprisingly, multitasking increases decision time and reduces decision quality because of the brain's scarce resources. It is all too common for people who shop for groceries on empty stomachs to end up buying more sugary and high carbohydrate foods than they otherwise would (given their long-term weight goals), given that 20 percent of grocery shoppers purchases are unplanned.[11] The distributed physiologic utility function directly produces rational rationality.

To the extent that sensory data is not acknowledged, the array of potential decision options subject to evaluation and choice must be constricted. The sensory data absorbed on the options considered can also be incomplete. Shoppers might notice only a few of the available cuts of beef, or they might consider only the redness of beef and overlook the price and expiration date, or consider the price without noticing the freshness. In any shopping experience, a substantial majority of the available products will not be given any attention.

Shoppers do not take notice of many products because they have no need to do so. Their shopping goals are often narrow and their desired ends fairly well honed. Nevertheless, shoppers must limit their sensory data inflow simply because, again, they do not have the time or mental capacity to take in all potential sensory data, even for products they might, in some sense, want if the products' features and benefits were clearly known. Additionally, shoppers understand that beyond some point consideration of additional products and their additional attributes can make for confused decisions, decisions that are impaired in multiple ways, or outright

---

[11] As reported in "Not on the List? The Truth about Impulse Purchases" at Knowledge Wharton, accessed March 6, 2009 at http://knowledge.wharton.upenn.edu/article.cfm?articleid=2132.

decision inertia. Indeed, research shows that having more options from which to choose lowers subjects' expressed satisfaction in their choices (Schwartz 2004b).

Problems in dealing with choice options are founded on the neurobiological construction of the brain. Decision inertia can occur for two reasons: first, localized brain damage to the orbital-frontal cortex (for example, lesions from accidents, tumors, drug abuse), which is an area of the brain that integrates sensory information with cognitive deliberations, can impede decisions; and second, the chemical milieu of the brain may lead the physiologic utility function to function improperly. For example, patients with schizophrenia may experience decision paralysis as they are unable to properly filter information, leading to a sensory overload and associated apathy. Schizophrenia is associated with a dysfunction in the neurotransmitter dopamine. When schizophrenics are given medicine to normalize their dopamine levels, their apathy and decision inertia abates. Similarly, as already noted, depleting the neurotransmitter serotonin in healthy adults has been shown to change decisions in the Ultimatum Game so that unfair offers are more likely to be accepted (Crockett et al. 2008). Human neurochemistry is dynamic and this, along with biases due to learning how to make related decisions, may cause decision inconsistencies over time. These inconsistencies may nonetheless be rationally rational.

Rationality and Research Findings

The way that the brain learns and recalls information explains many of the research findings of psychologists and behavioral economists. As reviewed in Chap. 7, psychologists and behavioral economists argue, with support from laboratory findings, that the way questions or problems are framed affects decision making (Kahneman and Tversky 1979; Tversky and Kahneman 1981; Kahneman and Tversky 2000; and Kachelmeier and Shehata 1992). The brain acknowledges, absorbs, stores, recalls, and uses sensory data in context, and the context – or the frame – of sensory data can be no less important and useful to decisions than the data itself. The brain is simply not equipped to evaluate sensory data independent of the setting.

The same can be said for people's decisions being affected by relative prices and incomes, but not absolute prices and incomes (Leclerc et al. 1995; Kahneman and Tversky 2000; and Thaler 2001). This is not to say that people give no attention to absolute prices (and incomes), but it does say that people's attention to *relative* values is, perhaps, distorted by more than would be the case if memories were not so firmly grounded in the context of events, or if storage and recall of sensory data were not more heavily processed through specific addresses. But then, although anything is evolutionarily possible, it is hard to imagine an evolutionary process in which the brain developed to give sensory data specific neural locations when the senses have not developed the capacity to digitize the information received and when some sort of biological "transistors" has never emerged. The imposed limitations on sensory data inflow and the contextual nature of stored memories, the force of which is dependent upon repeated experiences, also can help to explain why research subjects are more willing to make a drive to save five dollars when the five dollars represents a higher percentage savings than when it is a lower percentage saving (Kahneman and Tversky 2000a ; Pratt et al. 1979). When memories and neural circuits are contextual, the percentage savings can bias decisions. With restrictions on sensory data inflows, it is altogether natural that many subjects might evaluate the savings in terms of opportunity cost of the driving time. Opportunity cost probably does not carry the same salience as prices that are specified in the experiments. Indeed, many economists have to go on at length in their classes just to impress on their students that many products bought, especially education, have substantial time, or opportunity, costs. Perhaps, if subjects in experiments were explicitly told the prices and the opportunity cost of their driving time to make various purchases, the distribution of the subjects' responses could be quite different. By explicitly stating product prices and making no mention of opportunity costs, researchers have biased the responses by degrading the salience of opportunity costs relative to prices. This problem is, especially, important in laboratory experiments when the rewards for subjects to expand the range of attributes of the choice options and assess opportunity costs might not be sufficient to justify the energy expenditure, which could be used for other neuronal and physiological purposes. The subjects could, indeed, have been more rational than the researchers assumed because they were engaging in cost–benefit assessments that the researchers overlooked.

The workings of the brain can help explain why medical researchers have found that the recuperative effects patients report from placebos pills is positively associated with the fictional price of the supposed pills (Ariely 2008): the higher the price, the greater the reported placebo effect. Patients use their well-developed neural circuits concerning market prices to interpret the stated prices for placebo pills, working from the rationally developed heuristic that "higher priced goods generally carry higher qualities than lower priced goods." This rule might well be invoked when people-as-patients have little experience assessing the medicinal effects of pills, especially, those that are declared effective because their effects pass the scientific test of statistical significance. Put another way, patients can readily use the neural circuits devised for prices in general to interpret what they are told about the placebo prices by researchers. Patients can understand this heuristic – "prices are a good basis for judging product qualities" – as being what, as noted earlier, Knight characterized as a "relatively absolute," meaning the pricing heuristic will be used as a pretty good working decision rule until evidence mounts that it is misleading. Thus, medical researchers would be expected to find that the placebo effect of the fabricated prices dissipates as the medical experiments are repeated time and again with the same patients and the patients gain reason to doubt the validity of their working heuristic and lay down a new neural circuit based on their accumulated experiences.

Understandably, as noted earlier in Chap. 6, researchers have found that the salience of options and their attributes will affect decisions. In marketing terms, the salience of products (those that are on the end of isles of grocery stores, for example) or their attributes (color and design, for example) will significantly, if not substantially, affect purchases. Stores display the after-rebate price in large and bold fonts, noting the posted full price and rebate value in smaller regular fonts, for the purpose of making the after-rebate price salient, knowing that all buyers do not have the time and mental capacities to absorb sensory data on all products and their attributes (McKenzie 2008, Chaps. 10 and 11). Even then, when facing diminishing returns in the engagement of their mental capacities, it is altogether rational for buyers not to consider additional products and their attributes even when they have neurons that have not been engaged at all, or not fully engaged. The improvement in decisions cannot, beyond some point, justify the energy used by the brain. We repeat for purposes of making our point salient that the brain evolved under conditions of scarcity of energy sources in the external physical world and of scarcity of energy within the entire body, meaning there is a likely biological bias toward conservation of energy in decision making. The need of consumers to screen out and filter some product information is an economizing mental process. This helps to explain behavioral findings showing that salience is crucial to buying decisions or, more specifically, why so many prices end in "9," as in $3.99. Consumers consider only the digits to the left of the decimal place to restrict the intake of price data. This also helps to explain why rebates are commonly used (consumers consider only the prominently displayed after-rebate price and might consider the before-rebate price only as an anchor) (McKenzie 2008).

The biology of the brain's learning capacity is such that sensory data the brain uses in decisions from its own energy storehouse will depend, in varying degrees, on past familiarity of the problems requiring a decision. To conserve energy, the brain can be expected to harbor a bias, *ceteris paribus*, toward the familiar, or decision conditions that utilize well-honed circuits. Consequently, the brain's well-documented status-quo bias shows up in examples of people stuck in habits and routine patterns of daily behavior or even in a failure to change their retirement portfolio allocations among assets (Samuelson and Zeckhauser 1988). Thaler and Sunstein report one study that found the median number of times professors changed their financial allocations in their TIAA-CREF pension plans was zero, which they see as confirming the status-quo bias and as a form of irrationality (2008, p. 34). They do not consider the prospect that the status-quo bias can have a rational foundation in the brain itself.

Research showing that many people do not disregard sunk costs in their decisions is also understandable from the biological structure of the human brain (Kahneman and Tversky 2000a). Decisions that are taken seriously, which means they are founded on a nontrivial amount of thought, or consideration of the assessed value of alternatives, are bound to result in establishing or activating neural circuits that literally change the biological structure of the brain. A person who makes a mental commitment to a certain behavior can incur costs beyond the time the initial decision-making costs are incurred. Breaking the commitment to a course of action can have its own evaluative costs. In individual cases, a person might be able to justify breaking the commitment, but mental commitments can be seen as a grouping of costs (as well as trigger tit-for-tat responses from others). Without question, when sunk costs are clearly understood as such, which means they have no chance of relieving future costs, then the person should ignore them. But in evaluating a grouping of costs – some of which can relieve future costs but most of which will not – a person may have difficulty determining which costs are truly sunk and which are not. Under such choice circumstances, a person might follow the heuristic that he or she should hold to the commitments associated with all or most incurred costs, which to outside observers might be mistakenly construed as totally sunk. Doing anything other than holding to commitments implied in incurred costs can waste a lot of mental energy that has cognitive, if not physiological, costs. Again, in a world of internal neurobiological scarcity, heuristics relating to a series of the so-called sunk costs can make economic and cognitive sense that is not evident to external observers who might only be able to observe the separate out-of-pocket expenditures.

Decision conditions that require new neural circuits will likely require more energy than decision conditions that simply employ established circuits, which is to say that there are cognitive and physiological opportunity costs for everything the brain does. Accordingly, the brain must assess the impact that dealing with new sensory data has on the body's ability to handle the energy drain and even to replace the energy. Of course, given that so much potential sensory data is new and unknown, the brain is bound to make what in retrospect might be construed as miscalculations because of its inability to consider all potential sensory data and its inability to assess new sensory data.

Similarly, many research studies show that decision making is contaminated by inertia in thinking, revealed in a reluctance of people to give up well-honed views and lines of argument. People are predisposed to ideologies and cognitive dissonance, given that new sensory data that require new assessments is shunned in favor of well-established, perhaps entrenched, neural circuitry. This is because, to repeat a point made earlier, the brain uses less energy to deal with established neural circuits than to consider new sensory data and to lay down new circuits whose long-term usefulness might be highly uncertain because of lack of repeated experience. The brain's biology also supports the many studies showing that people often have difficulty recalling memories with exactitude or can be led with ease to adopt improbable and even false memories simply by manipulating through suggestions the thought-to-be context of the original experience (Loftus 1997).

Behavioral psychologists' and behavioral economists' experimental techniques, which purport to show that people exhibit an array of irrationalities, may play directly to frailties in brain function. The human brain is not well adapted to cope, much less deal rationally, with one-shot experiments or survey questions with which they are particularly unfamiliar. Many subjects may not have the experientially embedded, well-honed neural circuits to analyze laboratory decision tasks presented to them, and others may not see adequate incentive to expend the energy to activate the neural circuits that they do have to allow them to make decisions that researchers would deem rational. These kinds of research problems are particularly acute when we consider the brain's built-in bias in dealing with one-time sensory input at the emotional level, because the primitive part of the brain is often the initial screen on much sensory data.[12]

Behavioral economists and psychologists might very well have a point when they stress that in external physical world decisions, out-of-pocket expenditures of a given amount are more highly valued than opportunity costs of the same dollar value (Becker et al. 1974). The energy the brain uses in decisions can be construed as, more or less, an "out-of-pocket expenditure." Unconsidered options and their attributes can be construed as foregone, largely unknown, opportunities, which the brain dismisses in favor of familiar options and their salient attributes. Besides, the brain could very well understand that if options are expanded for choice purposes, the risk of making wrong choices will remain. Unknown options have less of a chance of eliciting the emotional pain of regret or cognitive dissonance, both of which have been found to be powerful motivating forces behind much consumer behavior. Any expanded array of recognized choices (or more detailed consideration of the attributes of options) can increase the potential for buyers' feelings of regret and cognitive dissonance, which means that some level of buyer ignorance can have a quasi-rational foundation (Schwartz 2004b).

Concluding Comments

Someone (no one seems to know who) once wisely quipped, "If the human brain would be so simple that we could understand it, we would be so simple that we could not." That quip is pregnant with caution on what people can know about how much they can know via the human brain. Although neurobiologists and neuroeconomists have learned much during the past half century about how the human brain functions, there is still much that is unknown. What exactly "consciousness" is remains elusive. Exactly how subjective evaluations are formed are equally elusive neurobiological phenomena, apart from their descriptions as chemical/electrical processes. We humans "think," and even think about thinking, but it is hard to say what we are doing physiologically when we think beyond describing how various parts of the brain light up on scans or what chemicals are released during the process. This knowledge offers limited satisfaction. Perhaps, as suggested by the anonymous quote above, we could not have evolved to be able to understand in some totally satisfying way how the brain works. The ability of the brain to know itself could be truncated by its own abilities to understand anything.

To summarize, the neurobiology of the brain has important implications for the extent to which people can be expected to be "rational" with respect to choices in the external physical world. Foremost, the human brain cannot be expected to fully

---

[12] Andreoni et al. (2003) have shown that half of contributions in public goods games are due to confusion and half due to "warm glow," or wanting to benefit others. However, over time people get more selfish; i.e., learn they can exploit the system, presumably as they gain experience with the task and engage brain circuits to fully evaluate options.

process all sensory data. The vast majority of sensory data is filtered out of decision processes, which can mean that for many decisions some unknown range of potential choice options will not be considered. Memories will be incompletely and imperfectly stored, and they can be recalled with additional flaws.

The human brain's basic problem is that it can face circuit overload and must devise, through evolutionary processes, heuristics for use of its own resources. The brain processes sensory data in an efficient manner that conserves energy to achieve other physiological and neurological goals while also looking for ways to reduce the cost of processing sensory data from an expanded range of options.

The neuroeconomics of the human brain, indeed, confirms what critics of the perfect rationality premise contend: people's mental limitations rule out the kind of perfect rationality economists assume. However, people's limited rational capacity can, paradoxically, help to make the case for economists presuming, for theoretical purposes, that people are more rational than they really are. Economists (as well as their students and the broader public) have their own limited faculties. As they try to do deductive science, mental limitations can necessitate a simplifying of theoretical models, narrowing variables to those most important, and crystallizing in exacting terms how people assess options and make decisions. Much can be learned by observing how people actually behave as they go about making a living and enjoying, or just coping with, life, as behavioral psychologists and economists have demonstrated.[13] Such a concession, however, does not rule out the prospect that additional, perhaps complementary insights can be garnered through strictly logical, deductive means. Lessons learned from theoretical physics, evolutionary biology, and economics support this point, which we elaborate on in the next three chapters as we build a defense of the assumption of rational behavior in economics. Behavioral economists and psychologists must surely agree that, no matter how broad their findings of human irrationalities, people have some rational capacity. Otherwise, they would not work so hard to make the case for human irrationalities. Behavioralists charge that neoclassical economists have a limited and defective way of viewing human behavior, because behavior is seen only through the prism of perfect rationality. Granted, such may be the case for many economists. By the same token, by their apparent and sometimes exclusive focus on people's irrationalities, as they define them, with no attention to people's rational capacities and inclinations (evident in behavioralists' insistence on rational discussions of people's irrationalities), the behavioralists espouse their own limited and incomplete view of decision making, with their laboratory experiments and surveys narrowing further their partial view of human decision making. Perhaps, given the way the human brain works, it is best for behavioralists and neoclassical economists to recognize the necessarily complementary nature of their approaches to doing science. Both groups press a partial view of decision making, and life itself.

---

[13] For example, neuroeconomists have found brain processes that produce empathy and motivate other regarding behaviors, as well as the utility function already acknowledged (Zak et al. 2007).

Chapter 9
Economic Defenses for Rational Behavior in Economics

The various historical and disciplinary analyses of rational behavior in this book lead inextricably to an overarching conclusion: Perfect rational behavior, the type widely presumed in neoclassical economics – a decision making process in which people flawlessly (with impeccable consistency and transitivity) make choices among *known* alternatives with *known* resources at their disposable – is not, and cannot be, descriptive of the full scope of the human predicament. Frank Knight's observations regarding "scientific economics" is key to understanding the limits of rational behavior for people and the limits of economics as a means of understanding human behavior: "The first question in regard to scientific economics is the question of how far life is rational, how far its problems reduce to the form of using given means to achieve given ends.....[L]ife is at bottom an exploration in the field of values, an attempt to discover values, rather than on the knowledge of them to produce and enjoy them to the greatest possible extent" (1935, p. 105).

Nevertheless, there can be a rationality of a sort – and an economics of a sort – so far as wants are determined and to the extent that people can and do contemplate the relative merits of alternative courses of production and consumption. Behavioral psychologists and economists have more recently documented many imperfections in human rationality, and its derivatives, decision making, and behaviors (see Chap. 6), but neoclassical economists should neither consider such findings unexpected nor deny them. Oddly, as will be seen in Chaps. 10 and 11, the behaviorals' findings should even be welcomed as a *reason d'être* for the economics as a course of study and method for thinking and deducing insights about real-world human behavior.

The standard defense of perfect rationality in economics is Milton Friedman's statement: In order to make testable predictions, we must abstract from the real world the models of behavior. Assuming complex forms of rationality, or just less than perfect rationality, can complicate thinking with no necessary improvement in the "fruitfulness" of the theory. There are four other major lines of defense for continued use of rationality as a theoretical tool of analysis.

- First, economics – or, for that matter, any other discipline – necessarily provides a partial view of life because of the sheer complexity of life especially, at the

R.B. McKenzie, *Predictably Rational?*,
DOI 10.1007/978-3-642-01586-1_9, © Springer-Verlag Berlin Heidelberg 2010

sophisticated levels of modern humans with the great diversity of human motivations and with their enormous opportunities for self-improvements.

- Second, in matters of drawing up contracts and constitutions, an assumption of perfect rationality on the part of people – or an assumption of people leading lives of *homo economics* – can provide institutional protections against some people's worst inclinations.
- Third, the premise of perfect rationality can be productively used as a means of improving business and consumer decision making.
- Fourth, because people's thinking and rational decision making are less than perfect as well as complex, the premise of perfect rationality makes economic analysis possible.

The review of the expected limitations on people's rationality of the last three chapters puts these defenses in perspective. This chapter focuses on the defenses of rationality marshaled by Frank Knight, James Buchanan and Geoffrey Brennan, and Milton Friedman. I include my own assessments of modern critiques of rationality in economics in the next chapter.

Economics as a Partial View of Life

As we have seen in the views among economics' luminaries, from Adam Smith to Milton Friedman, few credible economists have ever really endorsed perfect rationality as a true, full-fledged, fully accurate *description* of human decision making. All seem to agree with Knight that economics, as a science, provides only a "limited and partial view" of life (1936, p. 105), and most fully acknowledge various bounds on rational human decision making that can have evolutionary and moral roots. Smith imposed all kinds of constraints on people's abilities to pursue their own self-interest, not the least of which was the impartial spectator. Surely, he would agree that the effective working of the market's invisible hand itself would undermine people's ability to make welfare-maximizing choices among *known* wants, using *known* resources. The invisible hand will, with some regularity, make wants and resources that are known at any point in time in the market obsolete precisely because, in Smith's view, markets achieve ends (in the process of raising incomes and wealth) that market participants could not possibly imagine in the initial stages of markets' evolutionary processes. Even Milton Friedman would not hold to a premise of perfect rationality as an accurate description of much human behavior.

Any defense of continued use of the premise of full or perfect rationality must be organized around a clear distinction between the way people behave in real life and the way they can be viewed – indeed, must be viewed – as behaving in theory, with theory imposing a set of methodological requirements that stand apart from the requirements of decision making in real-world settings. After all, the way economists (or any other group of scholars) must think about how people live necessarily stands apart from how people must live, because all that is involved in living cannot be captured in thinking about living. Thinking at the scholarly level and living are simply different endeavors, even with different goals. Science is simply a means of coming to terms with the complexity of life, and doubly so in complex social matters, or as Albert Einstein pressed that point:

> One of the strongest motives that lead men to art and science is escape from everyday life with its painful crudity and hopeless dreariness, from the fetters of one's own ever-shifting desires. A finely tempered nature longs to escape from the personal life into the world of objective perception and thought. With this negative motive goes a positive one. Man seeks to form for himself, in whatever manner is suitable for him, a simplified and lucid image of the world, and so to overcome the world of experience by striving to replace it to some extent by this image. This is what the painter does, and the poet, the speculative philosopher, the natural scientist, each in his own way. Into this image and its formation, he places the center of gravity of his emotional life, in order to attain the peace and serenity that he cannot find within the narrow confines of swirling personal experience. (As quoted in Rene Dubos, *The Professor, the Institute, and DNA* [1976] and John M. Barry, *The Great Influenza* [2004]).

The limitations on conscious, deliberate decision making that behavioral psychologists and economists have found necessarily constrain economic analysis itself. If people were not heavily constrained on all sides in their ability to think – if they were far more capable, if not more rational, than they are – then an assumed level of irrationality for subjects of analysis would be far more attractive for theoretical purposes than it is. Theorists themselves could, then, deal with the greater complexity in theory that an assumption of constrained rationality, or prevalent irrationalities, imposes. However, real constraints on people's rational capacities require an underlying premise to deductive theory that assumes people to be more rational than economists actually know them to be. This is especially true when forces in market processes press people to become more rational than they would resign themselves to being in their natural state, without the feedback corrective pressures in markets.

Besides, an assumption of perfect rationality can be a means by which methods for improving people's rationality can be deduced. In this regard, and to the extent to which rationality can be improved, economic theory as a way of thinking can upgrade the rationality of decision making over and above what it would otherwise be. We will use this point of departure in an effort to lay out the various defenses of perfect rationality premise in economic theory.

Buchanan and Brennan's Defense of the Perfect Rationality Premise

As noted in Chap. 5, critics of so much strained economic analysis direct their hostility toward the assumption of full rationality. But James Buchanan and Geoffrey Brennan (1985) defended – indeed, advocated – the use of the narrowly directed model of the exclusively self-interested *homo economicus* in matters of constitutional design under which alternative constraints on people and government are considered (with *homo economicus* not necessarily exhibiting the full consistency and transitivity of fully rational people). Their argument was straightforward, and drew on a fundamental observation James Madison made in defense of the U.S. Constitution: No government would be needed if all men were angels. *Homo angelicas* would do their duty, and would not violate the interests of others, or would not do harm to them through the exploitation of governmental powers in pursuit of private gain. *Homo angelicas'* inherent nature or moral code of conduct would more than adequately constrain their inherent nature. People do not need to protect themselves from the angels in their midst in matters of contracts and constitutional design.

In constitutional design, the framers of constitutions must protect themselves and the members of the polity against the people who see *homo economicus* as the directing model for behavior. The point is that constitutional restrictions are designed for protection from bad people who might abuse the powers of government for their own narrowly conceived self-interest. Constitutional restrictions also protect people from themselves because the pursuit of people's strictly private, selfish ends through government has the potential for *le grande* tragedy of the governmental commons, with everyone getting more government intrusions in the form of programs, regulations, and taxes in the aggregate than anyone would deem desirable or optimal.

Perhaps, it would be desirable for the framers to assume some better, more real-world, descriptive view of the median citizen (or median voter). For constitutional design for small groups for short-time periods, such an effort might be reasonably productive. Small groups can be selective and homogeneous, and those who reveal themselves as having *homo economicus* leanings can be banished from the group. Indeed, for small groups, there can be a constitutional provision for expulsion of those who violate constitutional rules or who engage in opportunistic behavior through government.

Large groups – especially, those groups that are national in scope – are another matter altogether. Exclusion from such large groups can be impractical, if general acceptance of the constitution is to be achieved in the first place. The diversity of the population can, accordingly, be considerable. The framers can know little about which and how many people in the group might rightfully be modeled as *homo economicus*. The guesswork involved is, especially, acute when the constitution is expected to be in force for a long time, extending through multiple future generations with the particulars of private and political circumstances continuing to evolve.

Theorists can reason that the framers of the constitution are acting behind some form of a Rawlsian "veil of ignorance" (which blocks their knowledge of how the selected constitutional constraints will affect their own or others' future welfare) when they assume that a large polity will exclusively seek their own narrow self-interest, just as would *homo economicus*. Such a presumption of *homo economicus* might enlist broader support, if we could imagine (for purposes of argument) that future citizens would have a say regarding the behavioral premises underlying constitutional strictures, choosing those that have the greatest chance of maximizing human welfare through time. Future generations could have a more powerful stake in containing the exploitations of governmental power by any would-be *homo economicus* of the world than the actual framers. The exploitation of governmental powers can do damage in the short term, but even more damage in the long term as more and more people exploit governmental powers and as the effects of time-period-specific exploitations accumulate and are compounded. This might be the case, say, when super-optimal taxes are imposed on capital and economic growth is impaired.

Hence, the Buchanan and Brennan defense of perfect rationality – or as-if perfect rationality or the more restrictive *homo economicus* – need not be in any sense justified on the grounds that such a premise matches with the reality of how people, in general, behave. Indeed, Buchanan and Brennan would be the first to admit to the premise's descriptive failures for most people. They justify the premise only on the grounds that constitutions are designed to protect people from unknown and *prospective* others for whom the perfectly rational behavioral premise – or the *homo economicus* caricature of people's behavior – is a reasonable approximation of how they should be expected to behave. But, again, their goal is to provide constitutional protections against would-be current or future *homo economicus*. Even if no one's behavioral motivations in a collective matches the *homo economicus* caricature, use of such a behavioral premise will afford opportunities for devising constitutional protections *just in case* they are needed in some future time period and environment, the details of which cannot be known with precision at the time of any constitution's construction. Buchanan and Brennan might readily agree that the emergence of self-serving tyrants might be a very rare event in Western cultures, but the dictates of collectively inspired constitutional protections and the reality of tyrants (including Joseph Stalin, Adolph Hitler, and Saddam Hussein) and the enormous harm they (and far more common, rent seekers) can do easily justify constitutional protections against tyranny. The danger of assuming perfect rationality or *homo economicus* in developing constitutional provisions is that the constraints on governments can be excessively tight, which means that government might be too small. Such an outcome, however, might not be objectionable at all for government minimalists (among whom Buchanan and Brennan might count themselves). Indeed, overly constrained governments might be desirable for them. Others (especially, people in future generations) with an interest in a more expansive government might find the constrained size of government objectionable, but still an improvement on the excessive size of an unconstrained government. And there is no reason that having deduced appropriate constraints for a polity made up of *homo economicus*, the constitutional framers could not decide, at the framing, to moderate the constraints. At the very least, having deduced the implications of an assumption of *homo economicus,* they can make such accommodations with knowledge of the risks they are taking.

To summarize, the extent of the Buchanan and Brennan defense of a strident rationality premise in constitutional matters, use of *homo economicus* can be educational and protective, in that the playing out of the logic can suggest how some people might naturally think or might be pressed to think by others who adopt *homo economicus* as a prescription for behavior. The real tragedy in tragedy of the commons of unconstrained government can be the end-game in which people adopt the thinking proclivities of *homo economicus* for strictly offensive and defensive purposes. Use of *homo economicus* as a founding premise can be a means of coming up with constraints on people's *homo economicus* proclivities, to the benefit of all, which suggests that use of *homo economicus* can be defended on the grounds that it reduces the prevalence of *homo economicus* thinking.

For similar reasons, people wishing to protect themselves from prospects of opportunistic behavior on the part of people, whom they do not know but with whom they must deal, might assume, as a matter or ordinary contractual negotiations, that people take on the worst forms of *homo economicus* because that is the type of people from whom they seek protection. Again, the premise of *homo economicus* can be educational and protective, given that it can suggest contract provisions that protect against "holdups" and other forms of opportunism that allow people to exploit their economic positions that come with parties making upfront investments that cannot be recouped either partially or in full. That is, as Paul Rubin and other economists interested in organizational economics have shown can be done, *homo economicus* can suggest ways to managers and lawyers involved in structuring contracts (for example, making them self-enforcing), incorporating incentive systems that ameliorate opportunistic behaviors in markets (Rubin 1993). In this regard, a premise of *homo economicus*, or just full rationality, can lead to greater profitability for firms and greater efficiency in the operations of markets than otherwise.

Friedman's Defense of the Perfect Rationality Premise

Milton Friedman starts his defense for grounding microeconomic theory on the premise of perfect rationality – or the premise that people are assumed to behave *as if* they are rational – by noting John Neville Keynes' distinction between positive and normative science and, by implication, economics as a science: Positive science is, in Keynes' words, a "body of systematized knowledge concerning what is," while normative science is a "body of knowledge of discussing criteria of what ought to be" (Friedman 1953, citing Keynes 1891, pp. 34–35 and 46). Both Keynes and Friedman, of course, seek to admonish their professional colleagues to adopt a very normative methodological position, that economics should be pursued as a positive science of what is, not what ought to be, regarding human behavior as it unfolds in real life, not in theory.

Friedman then dares to recommend a methodological approach grounded on something akin to perfect rationality that, at least on the surface, stands at odds with how he must have known (or, should I say actually, knew) people make decisions and conduct their economic affairs. He surely must have understood people's rationality, as well as their decisions and/or behaviors, could not possibly attain perfection.[1] As we have argued, and as Friedman would surely have conceded if pressed to do so, perfect rationality, decisions, and behaviors necessarily stand at odds with a presumption that people must make choices in a world presumed to be full of scarcities of everything. Perfection, simply, does not make economic sense in the world in which the subjects of economic analysis must operate. And Friedman does indeed stress the imperfections in human decision making are acknowledged at the descriptive level, but not for the methodological level (1953, pp. 14–22).

Tools of Analysis

Still, people's actual decision making and their assumed decision making are literally worlds apart, because they are different enterprises with radically different goals, although they both are tied to how people make decisions, according to Friedman. People's actual decision making is bounded by constraints of resources in the real world and inside the brain. People's assumed decision making is designed to improve economists' thinking about their subjects' actual real-world decision making, and is not designed to improve economists' understandings of the trifling details of decision making.

Perfection at the premise level can make imminent sense when economists' analytical skills and abilities to cope with the full complexity of reality are as limited, or are as scarce, as the analytical abilities of their subjects. A key reason for such a simplifying, if not sterilizing, assumption, which introduces an element of unreality to economic theory, is given by the critics and advocates of the perfect rationality premise, as reviewed in Chaps. 6–8. In fact, critics inadvertently fortify the case for a simplifying, sterilizing economics behavioral premise: The human brain is limited, as well as defective, in accomplishing all that is required of it, precisely because it is an evolved kluge. Reading between Friedman's lines on the complexity of individual behavioral and social/market forces, he must have been arguing that economists can – and indeed must – distinguish themselves from their subjects not so much in terms of their starting raw mental and physical abilities (the full swath of economists might not be, on average, much better than their subjects in terms of raw mental horsepower) but in terms of how they seek to come to terms with their own mental and physical limitations in honing and enhancing their analytical skills and in understanding their subjects' behavior.

More directly to the point, economists seek the development of mental techniques or tools, which are, to one degree or another, figments of creative imagination

---

[1] After all, Friedman's book *Free to Choose* (1980) with his economist wife Rose Friedman is replete with discussions that relate to the pat quip there is no such thing as a free lunch, suggesting that the world abounds with choices that require optimization of outcomes, not perfect outcomes.

that facilitate thinking about decision making and institutional and policy consequences, enabling them to go beyond their subjects in understanding the world in
which they and their subjects operate. The premises of perfect rationality and
maximization of interests permits the construction of equilibrium, which is a
methodological tool insofar as it permits an abstract reference point in the flow of
logic from which the directional changes in key variables can be deduced when
social and market conditions vary. Equilibrium may never exist in reality, given the
constant, complex fluctuations in the multitude of variables in the real world, but
there is no reason it need exist in reality. All that is required is that equilibrium can
be conceived as a mental construct and that changes in key variables can be
deduced from given changes in environmental conditions. Given the constant
fluctuations in complex reality, and the absence of any fixed starting or ending
equilibrium, there is no way that the magnitude of changes can be predicted in
theory. The most that can be predicted is the directional change, which is why
economists spend so much of their econometric energies highlighting the sign and
statistical significance of key coefficients in regression equations with only scant
and infrequent concern for the magnitude of the coefficients. Indeed, it is the
econometrics that establishes the magnitude of changes (with varying exactness),
not the theory.

Economics in Economic Theory

Economic theory must be judged by what it is intended to do, which is to allow
economists to go beyond the bounds of their innate mental limitations to cope with
complex reality. Underneath the rationality premise are the more fundamental
premises undergirding the pursuit of science, which borders on points of faith.
The first premise is that reasoning has merit. The second is that abstract deductive
reasoning, combined with empirical tests, can elevate understanding of complex
reality beyond what could be understood if ever more descriptive or realistic, which
can imply ever more complex, models of the world were employed. (As we saw in
Chap. 5, Ludwig Von Mises accepted both premises, other than contesting the
added value of empirical tests.)

  This is to say, Friedman's defense of perfect rationality starts with these two
premises. Beyond that, his defense of adding a premise of perfect rationality must
be seen as a practical one, imbued with a heavy dose of economic thinking in itself.
No theory, not even those of the behavioralists, can be completely and accurately
descriptive. An assumption of perfect rationality is acceptable only because
economic theory must abstract, as must any deductive theory, from the great
complexity of the world under study and focus on, to use Friedman's words, the
"essential features of complex reality," if it is to fulfill its function as a "filing
system" and a means of generating hypotheses that yield "valid and meaningful (not
truistic) predictions about phenomena not yet observed" (1953, p. 7). The only way
economists, or even natural scientists in experimental, inductive, laboratory

settings, can hope to cope with complex reality is to take the world into theory in reduced form. Again, completeness in any meaningful sense in modeling economic phenomena is simply impossible. Full replication of reality in behavioralists' laboratory is neither possible nor intended, precisely because the isolation of "essential features" of reality is at the core of the scientific method, especially, when applied to complex human behavior. Friedman never mentions economists' neurobiological limitations, discussed in the previous chapter, but such limitations are surely implied in his many passing comments on complex reality juxtaposed against comments about the need to abstract. Otherwise, why did he focus so much of his methodological essay on focusing on "essential features" or, for that matter, justifying his emphasis on the as-if rationality premise's ability to yield testable hypotheses?

Friedman would certainly acknowledge for purposes of argument that descriptive accuracy of complex behavior might be an admiral goal for economic theory. But his economics permeated his methodology to the point of recognizing descriptive accuracy for what it is – a theoretical pipedream. A theory's complexity can add to the cost of using it, as might be expected in a world of pervasive scarcity. That is, theoretical complexity, grounded in descriptive accuracy, can add to the costs of generating insights and predictions with little to no improvement in insights gained and in accuracy of predictions, at least beyond some point as the theory's descriptive accuracy is improved (1953, p. 18). Besides, Friedman argues that the process of science elevates the importance of "simplicity" (the less initial knowledge needed to make predictions, the better) and "fruitfulness" (the more productive the theory is in making precise and empirically testable predictions and suggesting additional lines of inquiry, the better) in evaluating the merits of any theory. He was obviously willing to seek some balance between the goals of simplicity and fruitfulness and was willing to pursue theoretical simplicity to the limit if achievement of the goal of fruitfulness were not undercut (1953, p. 10).

Why not simplify a theory so long as its fruitfulness remains unaffected or is enhanced? For that matter, why not increase the complexity of the theory in the interest of descriptive realism if the theory's fruitfulness more than compensates for the lack of simplicity? For that matter, why not balance descriptive realism and fruitfulness of theory in the same way, or by the same rule, recommended for all welfare and profit maximizing decision making, that is by equating at the margin, to the extent possible, the two implied functions?

My reading of Friedman suggests to me that for Friedman theoretical devices in economics can be something on the order of tools for gardeners. Gardeners want to devise tools that improve their productivity. Consider the garden hoe. No gardener will seek perfection of any tool, and certainly not a hoe. Beyond some point, the perfection of the hoe (in terms of design and/or materials used for any given, narrow purpose) becomes too costly, given marginal gains in productivity (and, perhaps, the loss of usefulness of the hoe for other purposes). The hoe does not do all that is desired and can take only so much wear, but it improves output over a variety of tasks in a garden. Outside observers might find fault with the hoe as designed, because the observers are not gardeners and do not have the requisite gardening experience to judge the tool appropriately or have needs (uprooting trees, for example) for which a given tool may be of little use.

Neoclassical economists are, in a loose manner of speaking, "gardeners" in the business of generating good ideas, which for Friedman meant almost exclusively, testable hypotheses that are not proven wrong. Behavioral economists and psychologists are also gardeners but with different objectives and other tool needs. They do not seem to fully appreciate the economics behind Friedman's methodological perspective and approach. Their attention has been on what the approach does not and cannot do, not on what it has done and can do.

The Importance of Predictions

Friedman surely appreciated the importance of theory in explaining the evolution of events as they could be observed in broad pattern of outcomes (Friedman had great admiration for the methods and political economy of Friedrich Hayek, and he was also a champion of the importance of markets to human progress), but he clearly accepted, as a part of his academic value system, the importance of predictions for economics as science. This is itself a constraint on what is construed as acceptable knowledge to a community of scientists (including economists) and, thus, offers theorists an opportunity to relax the reality of the assumptions undergirding their theories. Accordingly, a theory's "performance is to be judged by the precision, scope, and conformity with experience of the predictions it yields" (1953, p. 4), which is clearly a normative position about positive science. But such is a concession that is required by moves to make the founding premises less descriptive and complete, but, at the same time, to make the theory more productive, or more fruitful.

Clearly, in making such statements, Friedman was willing to set aside the concerns that Knight, Hayek, and Mises had relating to the usefulness of empirical data as proxies for the subjective ends people pursue, which are far from easily measured, as distinguished from the goods they buy in markets, which are easily measured but not necessarily the objects of what people ultimately seek. But then, as much of a positivist as Friedman was, he was willing to acknowledge that much of economics as science is a form of artistry, founded on economists' experience with data and empirical techniques of scientists, as previously noted (1953, p. 25). Friedman was a scientist, but hardly one who failed to recognize the need to make concessions on the inexactness or roughness of data series for testing the implications of theory. In the end, for Friedman, a community of scholars had to scrutinize and hold acceptable both the theory and empirical tests in order for their work to have the force of reputable science (1953, p. 25).

As somewhat of an aside, my reading of Friedman suggests a test of reasonableness of insights and hypotheses by a community of scholars before rigorous empirical tests of hypotheses are made. When the insight or hypothesis is formed from abstract theory, scholars can immediately ask whether the insight or hypothesis makes sense in more complex real-world setting of less than perfectly rational actors. In the case of theorizing about the effects of a minimum-wage hike, one might deduce that employers will be pressed to reduce fringe benefits and/or increase work demands. In the case of theorizing about the household production, one might conclude that an increase in wage rates can lead to fewer home-produced meals. In the complex world of imperfect people, such deductions can be seen to be reasonable by a community of scholars, which can lead them to concur that rigorous empirical tests should follow to ensure that their sense of reasonableness is supported by scientific methods.

However, all such deductions, grounded in neoclassical modeling, may not always pass the test of reasonableness. For example, in the 1970s, an economist published an article in a top journal in which he proved with intense mathematical rigor that people's welfare could be enhanced if all were bisexual. The math was intense, but the point was simple: Bisexuals have a greater choice set, which increases their prospects of securing a higher valued combination of sexual partners. Such a deduction does not pass the test of reasonableness (or the "smell test"), at least not to my way of thinking (and, I have to presume, Friedman's). Such an insight can be doubted simply because, as explained in Chap. 6, greater choices need not always lead to greater welfare (and beyond some point can undercut people's welfare), but there is even a greater problem with the theory. It assumes what people want, or could want. We could just as well develop a theory, assuming that people viewed rocks as food. If they did, then they could move to a higher utility level. But why submit the deduction on the welfare value of bisexualism to rigorous empirical test when it is grounded on a utility function not broadly shared by real people in complex society? (But then critics of neoclassical economics have a legitimate concern about the economic way of thinking and doing science when they can point to articles, such as the one on bisexualism, that are given the light of publication, wrongly).

To Friedman, the logical completeness and consistency of theory are not wholly irrelevant, but do play a decidedly "subsidiary role" (1953, p. 10): "Truly important and significant hypotheses will be found to have 'assumptions' that are wildly inaccurate descriptive representations of reality, and, in general, the more significant the theory, the more unrealistic the assumptions," a claim Friedman justifies on what are essentially economic grounds: "A hypothesis is important if it 'explains' much by little, that is, if it abstracts the common and crucial elements from the mass of complex and detailed circumstances surrounding the phenomena to be explained and permits valid predictions on the basis of them alone. To be considered important, therefore, *a hypothesis must be descriptively false in its assumptions at some level*" (1953, p. 14, emphasis added). Of course, to be able to abstract "common and crucial elements," it must be presumed that economists possess some initial knowledge from intuition, introspection, and experience of that part of the social world they seek to understand. This knowledge can stand apart from that garnered by drawing out the implications of theory and by subjecting generated hypotheses to empirical tests. It is the kind of knowledge that Knight might have had in mind when he talked about knowledge ordinary people gain through common sense (1935, p. 109).

Friedman uses various analogies to make his point that basic assumptions of theory are nothing more than crystallized statements about the essential features of an environment (1953, p. 24). All that is necessary, or economical, is for the model to be "taken to be an *adequate* representation of the real world" and to specify "the correspondence between the variables or entities in the model and observable phenomena" (1953, p. 24, emphasis added). How leaves form on trees can be specified with various levels of precision, depending on the amount of sunshine they receive, for example. However, Friedman suggests that for some theoretical purposes, "the statement that leaves seek to maximize the sunlight each receives" is sufficient or "adequate" (1953, p. 24).

Friedman points to billiard players who may know little to nothing about mathematics, yet their shots might well be predicted on the assumption that they make their shots *as if* they fully understand the "complicated mathematical formulas that would give the optimum directions of travel, could estimate accurately by eye the angles, etc., describing the location of the balls, could make lightning calculations from the formulas, and could then make the balls travel in the direction indicated by the formulas" (1953, p. 21). He then suggests that "it is only a short step from these examples to the economic hypothesis that, under a wide range of circumstances, individual firms behave *as if* they were seeking rationally to maximize their expected returns.....and had full knowledge of the data needed to succeed in this attempt" (1953, p. 21, emphasis in the original). He concedes that few business people make (or even can make or would make, if they could) the required calculations (or consult the type of complicated graphics and equations economists employ) based on a full knowledge of the cost and demand functions, but the assumption that they make the required calculations promotes Friedman's goal of simplicity in theory and thinking. The fact that actual behavior deviates from strict rational precepts does not necessarily undercut the Friedman's goal of fruitfulness, or the conformity of the predictions of the theory and empirically grounded experience (1953, p. 22).

Besides, as Gerd Gigerenzer has stressed over his career (with colleagues), pool players can make decisions more efficiently and to better effect by not even trying to do all the complicated calculations required in the game of pool, or even in baseball games in which outfielders have to catch fly balls on the run: Outfielders can develop heuristics that get the job done reasonably well and reasonably efficiently, given people's time constraints and mental limitations, and heuristics can make people "smarter" than they would otherwise be able to be (Gigerenzer et al. 1999; Gigerenzer 2008). For example, outfielders catch fly balls on the run not by making the required calculations regarding the parabola the ball will follow so that they can be where the ball comes down (they actually cannot make the calculations with precisions, because of the many variables involved, such as the varying wind speed the ball encounters on its flight). Rather, they can frequently catch the ball by following the simple rule of getting a sight fixed on the ball, starting to run in the direction of the ball, and maintaining the angle of the "gaze" by varying their running speed. Such a rule can mean that they will be under the ball at the spot where they can catch it (Gigerenzer 2008, pp. 21–23, citing McLeod and Dienes 1996).

Granted, heuristics might work well for people, but it is not always easy to determine a priori what heuristics people use, and the heuristics used can vary across circumstances and people (baseball players use several heuristics to catch balls). People also adjust their heuristics based on feedback from their environments (Rieskamp and Otto 2006), which, of course, makes deductive reasoning difficult, to say the least. If, however, heuristics make people smarter than they would otherwise be (and the heuristics are developed and refined as people interact, behind static analysis), then assuming a level of rationality that is greater than we know people to be in some natural state has more merit than behavioralists might be inclined to think from their research that shows people are, in fixed and noninteractive laboratory contexts, full of decision-making biases and irrationalities.

When mathematics is employed to crystallize the assumed relationships and goals of supposed subjects, the logical consistency and completeness of the model can be checked with improved efficiency and the implications can be explored: "There is no place in the model for, and no function to be served by, vagueness, maybe's, or approximations" (1953, p. 24). Moreover, "the rules for using the model......cannot possibly be abstract (meaning vague) and complete. They must be concrete and in consequence incomplete – completeness is possible only in a conceptual world, not in the 'real world,' however, that may be interpreted" (1953, p. 25). He presumably had in mind the limitations imposed on thinking through model building by the human brain, by mathematics, and by econometrics.

If theories are necessarily incomplete, but can be made more or less complete in their assumptions, how does the theorist know when the theory is adequate for the purposes at hand? Friedman has an answer that is grounded in what I see as a form of methodological artistry:

> The capacity to judge that these (features of the environment) are or are not to be disregarded, that they should or should not affect what observable phenomena are to be identified with what entities in the model, is something that cannot be taught; it can be learned but only by experience and exposure in the "right" scientific atmosphere, not by rote. It is at this point that the "amateur" is separated from the "professional" in all sciences and that the thin line is drawn which distinguishes the "crackpot" from the scientist (1953, p. 25).

Friedman is widely recognized – and criticized – for taking the same position on rational behavior for firms and consumers as can be taken for tree leaves and billiard players. People in their roles as firm decision makers and as consumers can be assumed to act *as if* they are fully rational (if not *fully* rational, then Friedman surely had something close to full rationality in mind):

> It is only a short step from these examples to the economic hypothesis that under a wide range of circumstances individuals firms behave *as if* they were seeking rationally to maximize their expected returns......and had full knowledge of the data needed to succeed in this attempt; *as if*, that is, they knew the relevant cost and demand functions, calculated marginal cost and marginal revenue from all actions open to them, and pushed each line of

action to the point at which the relevant marginal cost and marginal revenue were equal (1953, pp. 21–22; emphasis in the original).

And Friedman makes clear that firms do not really seek to solve the implied "system of simultaneous equations" (1953, p. 22). The important issue for Friedman is whether or not the deduced predictions bear predictive fruit, not whether the assumptions themselves are fully descriptive. (For mental efficiency purposes, assumptions are not designed to be fully descriptive). This is not to say, however, that economists can be loose cannons in their choice of behavioral assumptions, that any as-if assumption is as good as any other. After all, theory has to be grounded in "essential features" of the real-world environment in which people reveal their behaviors, whether they are founded on "habitual reaction, random chance, or whatnot" (1953, p. 22).

In Friedman's methodology, static, equilibrium-based microeconomic analysis requires the as-if assumption of perfect rationality as a theoretical short-cut. For example, competitive market process dynamics may be features of the economic actors' environment under study that are not explicitly treated in theory simply because they can, for many purposes, be assumed to work themselves out as, say, the market shifts from one equilibrium state to another. In addition, the chief concern of the scientific/predictive endeavor might be only the directional shift in key equilibrium values, such as price and quantity. The competitive market dynamics, hidden totally by the static, timeless nature of the analytics, will ensure (in many environments) that market participants, in equilibrium, exhibit a level of rationality in outcomes that may not have been a part of their initial intent or ability, simply because markets exhibit a powerful evolutionary form of natural selection, as well as ample opportunities with powerful incentives for corrections of misguided decisions (calculated mistakes or even irrationalities). In Friedman's words,

> Whenever the determinant (or behavior) happens to lead to behavior consistent with rational and informed maximization of returns, the business will prosper and acquire resources with which to expand; whenever it does not, the business will tend to lose resources and can be kept in existence only by the addition of resources from outside. The process of "natural selection" thus helps to validate the hypothesis – or, rather, given natural selection, acceptance of the hypothesis can be based largely on the judgment that it summarizes appropriately the conditions of survival (1953, p. 22).

Friedman's confidence in the continued use of the as-if fully rational behavior assumption was bolstered, no doubt, at the time he was penning his *Methodology of Positive Economics* by the record of economic investigations made up to that point: "[T]he failure of any coherent, self-consistent alternative to be developed and be widely accepted, is strong indirect testimony to its worth" (1953, p. 23), a stance he reiterated in his Nobel lecture with the addition that the process of science was always one of replacing one tentative hypothesis with better ones, or ones that dealt with "troublesome" phenomena that was not adequately explained by the original hypothesis (1976, pp. 267–269).

Perfect rationality combined with perfect competition leads inextricably to perfect efficiency in the allocation of resources. There is in such a world no need for a competitive *process*; static analysis is fully satisfactory. If people are in reality less than perfectly rational, with some or all of their misguided decision making, or irrationalities, eventually corrected by competitive market pressures, then markets cannot be as efficient as neoclassical models suggest. There will be ever-present waste of resources in errant, irrational decisions in the competitive process. But, there is the ever-present prospect of externally imposed corrections on decisions. Of course, such a conclusion must be a guarded one on all sides, because those who would impose the corrections (regulators, for example) would also be inflicted with decision-making biases and irrationalities, which means that imposed corrections could still worsen outcomes, just as Friedman and other neoclassical economists suggest using standard static models of markets.

Theoretical Premises vs. Predictions

Friedman's position seems to suggest that he was predisposed to concede his methodological position on the scope of its applications, if mounting evidence warranted retrenchment or containment. But then, behavioral economists and psychologists seem to be convinced that Friedman should have been prepared to concede that the missing "coherent, self-consistent alternative" methodological approach has been developed, and this approach is direct testimony to the conceptual precariousness of the traditional positive economics Friedman espoused. Behavioralists insist with some force that a growing body of credible research findings point to an unavoidable conclusion: People are systematically and predictably irrational, to use the title of a popular book on behavioral economics noted in Chap. 7 (Ariely 2008), so much so that the core of microeconomic theory needs to be jettisoned to rebuild a microeconomics grounded on the way real people actually behave, not on how they are assumed to behave.

We are now left to speculate on how Friedman would react to the professional ground the behavioralists have gained. Very likely, he would go back to one of his major methodological theses, that theory should be judged by what it is intended to accomplish, which is generate insights, implications, and predictions that can be subject to empirical tests. He would likely stress that in revealing an array of people's observed irrationalities, behavioral economists and behavioral psychologists have returned once again to judging microeconomic theory by the descriptive validity of its underlying assumptions rather than the validity of its predictions. Friedman might also argue that the findings of behavioralists make empirical tests of predictions from the theory all the more necessary, and subjected to even more careful professional scrutiny.

In response, behavioral economists very likely would point out that they have tested predictions of theory when, for example, they found that people treat gains of a given dollar amount differently from losses of the same dollar amount or treat out-of-pocket expenditures differently than opportunity costs. They might also point to research on stock and housing market bubbles that contradicts the efficient-market hypothesis, founded on a form of investor hyperrational behavior that, as noted in Chap. 6, came to dominate financial research in the last fourth or third of the twentieth century.

Yet, in the main, the kinds of predictions Friedman has in mind were the directional changes in outcomes though market processes, whether these outcomes were reached through deliberate rational intention or the corrective processes of natural selection in markets (1953, pp. 23–30). The behavioralists' evidence would likely leave Friedman largely unmoved because so much of it is of questionable merit and simply off target (a subject considered with more care in the following chapter), or in Friedman's words:

> The evidence cited to support this assertion [that real-world behavior stands at odds with the underlying theoretical assumptions] is generally taken from the answers given by businessmen to questions about the factors affecting their decisions – a procedure for testing economic theories that is about on par with test theories on longevity by asking octogenarians how they account for their long lives – or from descriptive studies of the decision-making activities of individual firms. Little if any evidence is ever cited on the conformity of businessmen's actual market behavior – what they do rather than what they say they do – with the implications of the hypothesis being criticized, on the one hand, and of an alternative hypothesis, on the other (1953, p. 31).

A great deal of behavioral research (at least the major components surveyed in Chap. 6) tests the efficacy of decision making in laboratory settings or on surveys that often make no provision for dynamic, feedback mechanisms either within actors' brains or within markets. That is, the laboratory controls, by design, rule out corrections founded on incentives that emerge when misdirected, irrational decisions are rampant.

One-shot survey evidence on decisions under artificial laboratory and classroom settings that often do not give subjects information on the choices that all subjects make, much less allow for little or no feedback loops to elevate the rewards for correcting errant decision making, might be interesting and suggestive but are hardly convincing proof, at least not proof enough to jettison the full corpus of the neoclassical approach that, in many areas, has proven so fruitful, in spite of its acknowledged simplicity and lack of realism. From Friedman's perspective (or at least from a sympathetic reading of his perspective), people with limited rational capacities can be pressed in markets or other social, interactive settings with competitive pressures to increase their rationality, improve the cost–benefit precision of their decisions, and eventually achieve outcomes that would supersede their innate initial rational inclinations, absence competitive pressures. Outcomes for Friedman, as for Adam Smith, are critically dependent upon the interaction of people's innate rational proclivities *and* the institutional settings within which decisions and behaviors evolve toward some equilibrium in which net beneficial opportunities are exploited. Then, as supply-side cost conditions or demand-side evaluations change, evolution toward another equilibrium begins, all with pressure on people to adjust along the way the rationality of their decisions.

The Importance of Market Pressures

Friedman would surely add that the utility of the as-if perfect rational-behavior premise depends upon the nature of the competitive market setting, or the competitive pressures on all market participants, which can be founded on at least some, but not all, market participants making tolerably rational decisions. More competitive pressures from whatever source (especially, from freedom of entry into and exit from markets), would be expected to generate more corrections in the decisions of some participants, with the elimination of many persistently errant decision makers – and an evolutionary process toward more (not necessarily perfect) rational decisions than would be expected from less pressure.[2]

This methodological perspective does not mean that market predictions involving monopoly power are unproductive, or not "fruitful." Absent competitive market pressures, owners and managers indeed may have little incentive to increase their alertness to sensory data and to make careful cost–benefit comparisons of alternative courses of production and distribution. If so, monopoly can have inefficiency consequences that go beyond curbs on production to raise price and profits. Predictions of monopoly behavior in response to, for example, taxes might be impaired.

However, even monopolists can face substantial competitive pressures from the struggle among investors for corporate control, or from the entrepreneurs who seek to take profitable advantage of wayward, irrational, and less than cost-effective decisions. That is, owners and managers of monopolies might not be initially predisposed to engage in the type of decision making that the as-if perfect rational premise assumes. However, pressures from corporate raiders or the threat of unknown new future competitors can press corporate managers and owners to pay more attention to key market data, cost minimization, and value maximization, including equating at the margin, ignoring sunk costs, and treating opportunity costs on par with out-of-pocket expenditures. Granted, raiders themselves can be beset with irrational inclinations resulting in their bidding for unprofitable monopolies. The question is whether such inefficient takeovers can be systemic and long lasting, since the raiders would be constrained by their own financial resources, dissipated through irrational misadventures, and by their need to return to financial markets for takeover funds.

On the other hand, the external financial markets might be filled with equally irrational investors. If irrationality were so widespread, without market means of correction, behavioral economists and psychologists might have a right to be pessimistic about corrections in decision biases coming from markets. There might be little hope for improvement in the rationality of decision makers and market outcomes, but there would likely be even less hope that the behavioralists'

---

[2] A premise of perfect rationality does not require a perfect record of empirical confirmation. Predictions founded on as-if perfect rationality can achieve a greater frequency of confirmation under competitive pressures than less competitive pressures and can do better in making confirmable predictions than the next best alternative theory.

proposed decision-making improvements from non-market agendas (for example, Robert Shiller's proposed regulations of financial instruments and markets considered in Chap. 10) would be to improve matters, since such agendas would have to be devised with the cooperation of pervasive market participants who are, supposedly, deeply irrational and incapable of responding to incentives that mount with any growing pervasiveness of irrational decision making. One has to wonder how market actors can be expected to respond to behavioralists' favored nudges if they cannot respond effectively to market incentives that can build with the mounting of irrationalities.

Potential Concessions to Behavioralists

As I read Friedman, he would have surely responded that he was well aware that people are not always and everywhere rational; he acknowledged as much in his essay. The issue is whether, after market dynamics – grounded either in competitive or monopoly market environments – have been at work, decision making has been sufficiently augmented that the as-if premise works sufficiently well or better than the next best alternative in predicting directional equilibrium changes. Acknowledging that behavioral economists have rocked confidence in the perfect rationality premise, Friedman also might very well conclude that economists must undertake their empirical tests with greater care, with higher standards for confirmation of hypotheses, and with greater scrutiny from peers to distinguish "amateurs" from "professionals."

Friedman might also concede that a number of behavioral finance studies have raised legitimate concerns about the fruitfulness of the efficient-market hypothesis in some behavioral environments, but such demonstrations do not necessarily mean that a premise of as-if full rational behavior in financial markets everywhere cannot continue to be used in some environments. And, neither has the inadequacy of the behavioral outcomes in a few instances proved that some form of the efficient-market hypothesis cannot be widely successful in other human environments. After all, what is important about any theory, as a necessarily imperfect and artificial tool of analysis, is its batting average (relative to the batting averages of alternative theories), not whether it fails in particular uses in some identified time periods. Theorists might aspire to devise a theory that is always validated (or, rather, never falsified) by empirical tests, but such a result is no more likely to be realized than perfection in rational decision making, or anything else in a world of pervasive scarcity, both internal mental resources and external physical resources.

Friedman would surely insist that in methodological debates, we should not lose sight of a core concern of economists, which is to assess the unseen, as well as seen, consequences of institutional and policy changes. People differ in ideology and political persuasion, obviously, but he maintains that so many differences among people come from their predictions on the consequences of institutional and policy changes. He explained in his Nobel lecture,

> Positive scientific knowledge that enables us to predict the consequences of a possible course of action is clearly a prerequisite for the normative judgment whether that course is desirable. The Road to Hell is paved with good intentions, precisely because of the neglect of this rather obvious point.....Many countries around the world are today experiencing socially destructive inflation, abnormally high unemployment, misuse of economic resources, and, in some cases, the suppression of economic freedom not because evil men deliberately sought to achieve these results, nor because of differences in values among their citizens, but because of erroneous judgments about the consequences of government measures: errors that at least in principle are capable of being corrected by the progress of positive economics (1976, p. 268).

Behavioralists' Caricatures of Friedman's Position

In making such points, the two sides to the methodological debate are sometimes talking past one another, partially because they have different conceptions of what constitutes the proper test of a theory. One side favors tests of the underlying behavioral assumptions and the other side favors tests of the predictions deduced from theory. Friedman saw theory as a *necessary* guide for interpreting reality through identification of its essential features of complex reality and as a tool of analysis, albeit an imperfect one. I can deduce only that he would have no problem with adding to the descriptive accuracy of the founding premise, so long as someone can show that such a shift makes economic and methodological sense for the type of scientific work that he and other mainstream economists want to undertake.

The behavioralists have great confidence that they have the more defensible approach, likely agreeing with Richard Thaler that analysis is on far firmer methodological grounds when it is founded on behavioral premises that are "messy and vaguely right," not on behavioral premises that are "elegant and precisely wrong" (1991, p. 198). But then the behavioralists' criticisms seem to be organized around the presumption that Friedman and his neoclassical colleagues have truly believed all along that perfect rationality is, in fact, perfectly descriptive of human conditions. Behavioral economist Dan Ariely, for example, asserts that "most economists" hold to the presumption that people in real life (not just in theory) "make the right decisions" with their "reasoning abilities" being "perfect" (2008, p. xix). Maybe "most economists" do hold such a position, although Ariely, while elevating the importance of empirical, laboratory research in all matters economic, provides no laboratory or survey data to support his claim. As we have seen, this claim could not be more wrong about Friedman's methodological position.

In a profession as large and diverse as economics, there are bound to be any number of economists who conduct their work as if they subscribe, or who do indeed subscribe, to the claim that perfect rationality is perfectly descriptive of human motivation for behavior, as Ariely and other behavioralists have insisted.

But, clearly many notable economists are far more sophisticated in their methodology for this caricature to ring true.

Behavioral economists and psychologists may fail to recognize that Friedman and others have realized that the extent to which behavioral outcomes are rational depends on the interplay of people's actual behavioral impulses and the institutional setting in which they are expected to behave. Friedman would surely find congenial points made by Law and economics Professor Ronald Coase, because his points are an echo of Friedman's own:

> I have often wondered why economists, with these absurdities all around them, so easily adopt the view that men act rationally. This may be because they study an economic system in which the discipline of the market ensures that, in a business setting, decisions are more or less rational. The employee of a corporation who buys something for $10 and sells it for $8 is not likely to do so for long. Someone who, in a family setting, does much the same thing may make his wife and children miserable throughout his life. A politician who wastes his country's resources on a grand scale may have a successful career (1998, p. 577).

Friedman made a considerable public reputation as an economist pressing the argument that behavioral outcomes in governmental settings would frequently be less efficient – and less rational – than behavioral outcomes in market settings, precisely because markets provide initiatives to use information that are absent or are weaker in the public sphere. Market settings have the pressures of residual claimants who can press firm managers to operate cost effectively so that they – the residual claimants – can claim the added profits. The interests of taxpayers are not nearly so direct, clear, and strong. Moreover, market settings incorporate strong feedback mechanisms that correct and guide behavior toward outcomes that have the markings of being tolerably rational, as Vernon Smith and a host of experimental economists have documented (2008, citing a vast literature covered in his book's bibliography).

While acknowledging the Friedman/Coase point on the corrective power of market forces, Ariely manages, nonetheless, to sterilize and mischaracterize their point by asking, "What if we make a mistake and do something irrational?" Ariely's answer shows how he believes traditional economists (Friedman and Coase included, I can only suppose) would respond in a knee-jerk manner: "Market forces will sweep down on us and swiftly set us back on the path of righteousness and rationality" (2008, p. xx). No, not really. Thinking mainstream economists would surely pull up short of where Ariely puts them and insist that the true point of mainstream economics is that market forces make outcomes more rational than people, as a group, might be inclined to be, with the equilibrium outcomes more rational, efficient, and welfare enhancing than individual market participants might imagine absent market pressures. After all, followers of Friedman are fully aware of the workings of Adam Smith's invisible hand and would readily concede a point repeated several times in this book that in the real world, perfection – even in decision-making and behavioral outcomes – is not a viable option when scarcity in the external physical world and the internal mental world abound.

Ariely and other behavioralists also seem to forget the intended purpose of the presumption of perfect rationality – to conceptualize equilibrium as a reference condition; such a reference condition permits improved understandings of the directional changes in essential features in, for example, prices and quantities. Whether equilibrium is even established, or reestablished, is beside the point.

The Economics of Empirical Tests

Friedman's methodology is founded on the argument that deductions based on behavioral premises must be subjected to empirical tests to follow the dictates of science, to ensure that economists are not misled by their behavioral premises, and to convince others of the (tentative) validity of the deductions that emerge from reduced-form models of complex human behavior. Given that Friedman's approach is everywhere grounded in cost–benefit analysis, Friedman might not argue (or maybe should not argue, just for sake of consistency) that all hypotheses must be subjected to rigorous empirical tests. The reason flows from his economics: As empirical tests are extended, beyond some point, the benefits of additional tests are bound to decline and the costs of additional tests can raise – in at least some research endeavors. Even if the marginal costs of additional tests remain unchanged as tests are extended, there can be some point in testing beyond which the added value is of little consequence and exceeds the added costs, no matter how low.

An obvious example for making the point of the optimizing testing hypothesis is the law of demand, the most general and forceful proposition economists can offer (or so I argue). That is, from rational choice theory in its most sterile form, economists might deduce that demand curves slope downward. Surely, that hypothesis needs some level of rigorous testing for, say, oranges – and maybe tangerines and apples. However, there surely is a point in the expansion of the rigorous, econometrics-based tests of the hypothesis on various fruits in which the price variable is always negative that additional tests will add little or nothing to economists' confidence in the law of demand, at least when applied to fruit. Beyond some point, the law of demand can be taken as one of Frank Knight's "relatively absolute absolutes," or statements that are adopted as being valid until evidence mounts that shakes economists' confidence in the proposition and that once again require formal econometric testing. Indeed, the value of economics can derive from the fact that the process of generating hypotheses and undertaking tests can generate tolerably general understandings about the complex world we live in, which economists can treat as relatively absolute, which explains why economists, Friedman included, have so often spoken in public with confidence about the impact of proposed hikes in tariffs and minimum wages without having recently undertaken rigorous empirical tests of the effects of the proposed hikes (which cannot be done anyway, since "proposed hikes" will, at the time they are proposed, have unrecorded effects). In short, for consistency, it would appear that the Friedman approach to positive economics would itself be constrained by its own internal economic logic.

Concluding Comments

In summary, to understand Friedman's defense of perfect or as-if perfect rationality, his broader methodological position needs to be appreciated. He was persistent in pressing for testing hypotheses with real-world data to maintain some constraint on the selection of simplifying assumptions and to ensure at least some (albeit tenuous) connection between the assumptions and real-world decision making and behavior.

Friedman recognized the importance of judgment and experience in the scientific process, but he was unwilling to accept Knight's position that common sense should be, or could be, the only test of the value of theory. Friedman surely had his doubts about economists' abilities to perceive truth at the intuitive level in complex social settings where a multitude of variables are at work, perhaps, because he understood people's mental limitations. He was aware of the limitations of data in testing hypotheses that involved the kind of human actions that von Mises considered central to economic analysis, but then he exuded confidence that economists as scientists could, with experience, use judgment to good effect. Friedman was unwilling to allow common sense, or people's intuitive powers, to be the final arbiter of truth, because intuition can be distorted by the particulars of circumstances under which people make everyday observations, as well as prior beliefs of those doing the theorizing. He recognized that empirical analysis can be very useful when there is disagreement over what is the truth of reality, so long as people can agree on appropriate empirical tests.

Friedman extended economizing behavior to the development of deductive theory (or so it seems from my reading of his work). His first principle of economic theory was clearly on the order of economy in first premises and principles. In Friedman's methodological world view, there is a form of artistry in the selection of the simplifying premises, as well as in assessments of the fruitfulness of theory rooted in the theoretical and empirical experience and situation of the theorists. This constraint on what constitutes acceptable science is, especially, important when judging the appropriateness of inserting identified real-world goods in utility and production functions and when choosing empirical proxies for testing hypotheses. Take economists out of a community setting in which integrity and the honest search for truth are paramount, and economics can become excessively unconstrained and lose its value as a deductive, scientific process.

Finally, Friedman would likely dispute the challenges of much of the work of behavioralists on the grounds that they (like many other scholars before them) have been testing not the implications of theory, but the descriptive accuracy of the rationality premise, which, Friedman explicitly insisted, is not intended to be fully descriptive. For example, when subjects are asked to choose between a sure-thing option and a gamble or between opportunity costs and out-of-pocket expenditures of a project, the test is of a static implication of the premise, not a test of the theory's prediction. The latter would involve a change in essential features that can give rise to a shift in (market) equilibrium. Such a test would presuppose a market process and an interaction between the decisions of all market participants constrained by market institutions. Such a prediction might be derived from a presumption that the relative values of the sure thing and gamble are variables, subject to change by endogenous and exogenous forces.

What is crucial to understanding Friedman's methodological framework is that his rationality premise presupposes some process under which people are pressured to set aside or overcome their decision-making biases, with irrationalities in decisions and behaviors suppressed sufficiently to make his theory tolerably fruitful. The rationality premise and the adjustment pressures are subsumed to go hand in hand; neither can be had without the other, except with lost fruitfulness. This suggests a sobering thought for behavioralists. As neoclassical economists have moved from focusing their attention on market topics, or "the ordinary business of life," to use Alfred Marshall's phrase, where corrective pressures on decision making can be everywhere intense, to applying their methods to an ever-widening range of topics in social and political settings where corrective pressures can be less intense, the fruitfulness of the theory might, indeed, be expected to dissipate.

It is hard for me to see how the behavioralists would quibble with Buchanan's and Brennan's use of the rationality premise, or just *homo economicus*, as they have extended the premise to matters of constitutional design. After all, they take a sterilized view of motivations and decision making for exclusively protective purposes, or devising constitutional provisions that contain the misuse of governmental powers for narrowly defined self-serving ends of some people. The behavioralists, however, might have a stronger case with the economic analyses of economists in the Stigler/Becker variant of the Chicago school whose work involves economic arenas where corrective competitive (or other feedback) pressures may be weak.

Chapter 10
Problems with Behavioral Economics

Behavioral economists and psychologists feel confident, if not cocky, that they have substantively undermined the methodological approach to neoclassical economics identified in modern times with the two branches of the Chicago school associated with Milton Friedman and, more pointedly, Gary Becker. Certainly, the behavioralists have contributed to our understanding of people's decision-making abilities, especially their limits, and have caused neoclassical economists (including me) to rethink their (my) methodologies. This in turn has led me to a new understanding of the role of the rationality premise in economics and of a budding economic theory of the human brain. There are, however, several good reasons for caution in siding with the behavioralists on all critical fronts, even if their research findings on people's decision biases and irrationalities are confirmed time and again. Let me count the ways.

The Perfect Rationality Caricature

In a growing number of books, behavioral economists and psychologists follow what has become a fairly well-worn format for argument, starting with a caricature of perfect rationality's function in economic theory. Richard Thaler and Cass Sunstein assert that economists assume that "homo economicus can think like Albert Einstein, store as much memory as IBM's Big Blue, and exercise the will power of Mahatma Gandhi" (2008, p. 7), with the none-too-subtle suggestion that neoclassical economists who base their theory on *homo economicus* – or, more broadly, perfect rationality – must believe their premise is descriptively accurate in its full details. This is because they presume that one could not expect reliable insights from a theory founded on a patently false premise. Thaler and Sunstein add that modern mainstream economics is founded on the "false assumption" that people either almost always make the best decisions, or make better decisions than could be made by someone else: "We claim that this assumption is false – indeed, obviously false. In fact, we do not think that anyone believes it on

R.B. McKenzie, *Predictably Rational?*,
DOI 10.1007/978-3-642-01586-1_10, © Springer-Verlag Berlin Heidelberg 2010

reflection" (2008, p. 9). They are certainly right on one point: Probably no economist truly believes – and certainly Friedman did not (and never used the phrase "perfect rationality") – the Thaler/Sunstein characterization of perfection in human decision making as a descriptive proposition.

One of the problems in using Einstein as the paragon of human thinking is that while Einstein was brilliant in thinking through tough physics questions, he was remarkably inept when it came to thinking through much more complex economic and social issues, at least as judged by the standards of modern microeconomics. He had a feeble understanding of how markets worked, which largely explains why he consistently and unabashedly and with vigor advocated socialists solutions for the major economic ills of his era, all points I have developed at length elsewhere (McKenzie 1982). At any rate, as we have noted, Gerd Gigerenzer and his colleagues (Gigerenzer, et al. 1999; Gigerzenger 2008) have shown how people can make themselves smarter than they are innately, simply by devising heuristics that sidestep the need to make the kind of complicated calculations implicit in rational decision making (in pool or baseball, for examples). The rationality premise itself can be construed as a heuristic that makes economists at least appear smarter than economists know themselves to be, simply because the premise allows them to work within their own mental limitations. Again, the important constraints on economists doing deductive (or inductive) science are not the constraints facing their subjects as they try to allocate resources efficiently in a world with pervasive scarcity. Rather, economists' more pressing constraints are likely to be those of their own limited mental abilities as they try to understand vastly complex human interactions in markets and other social settings.

Otherwise, Thaler and Sunstein do not seem to appreciate in such pronouncements the important distinction between perfect rationality (or some close approximation) as a *description* of the foundation of human decision making and behavior, and perfect rationality as a *premise* devised for strictly deductive, theoretical purposes – or in other words, as an imperfect tool of analysis, which has still proven productive (and for that reason alone many neoclassical economists are not likely to jettison it readily). As noted, Friedman advocated use of the rationality assumption, but only so long as it lowered the complexity and cost of doing theory without undermining the intent of theory, which is to generate insights and testable predictions. Friedman and other neoclassical economists have insisted all along that people do have some rational capacity, which means the premise of rationality is not completely arbitrary and makes for a connection between how people are believed to make decisions and can press people to be more rational than they might naturally be inclined to be. And as noted in Chap. 7, a rational capacity at some level could be justified on evolutionary grounds. As noted in Chap. 8, neuroeconomists have found that the human brain does include a utility function, which supports a presumption of some rational capacity.

As noted in Chap. 5, Friedrich Hayek did indeed argue directly that he and other Austrian economists (who share at least some methodological, pedagogical, and ideological affinities with neoclassical economists of the Chicago price theory schools) advocated delegating choices to individuals not because they always make the best decisions, but because it is hard to say who else could make better the numerous daily choices individuals have to make other than the individuals themselves. Hayek and many other Austrians recognized that the voluntary advice of others could and does guide many people in their decisions toward higher welfare levels. Frank Knight believed that communications among people were an underrated source of information for ends that should be pursued individually and collectively and for goods and services that could be bought to achieve those ends. Indeed, in Chap. 7, I describe how people's sociality is very likely an evolutionary successful human trait because congregate living served the function for early humans of providing greater predator detection for all, given that groups provide more eyes and ears to survey safety perimeters. For humans with highly developed communication skills, congregate living allows for conserving and focusing the brains' limited neurons as some group members specialize in the sensory information flows absorbed, consider the data with care and communicate the value of the information to others in the group, points elaborated in Chap. 8 with the help of Paul Zak and Jessica Turner.

What Hayek and Knight – and Friedman and Becker – have disputed giving some self-appointed or collectively appointed experts the authority and power to impose their values and decisions on others in such detailed matters of daily life as designating exactly what personal ends individuals should pursue and the consumer goods that should be bought to achieve those ends – as if the experts have the research techniques and the intuitive powers to divine the subjective ends of all others as well as to know when other people's decisions are truly wrong. Experts might know something of what their relatively small number of laboratory subjects want, but they can hardly know the minute details of people's wants, especially, over stretches of time for multitudes of diversely situated people. Moreover, experts' decision powers can be as defective – formed with decision biases and filled with irrationalities – as anyone else's. Hayek, Knight, and others would likely worry that the decisions of behavioralist experts would be as "predictably irrational" as the people they study, mainly because the behavioralist experts doing the so-called nudging of other's behaviors must be drawn from the human population, all of whom suffer the same evolutionary history and have many, if not all, of the same rational limitations. They would also worry that the delegation of nudge powers to self-acclaimed experts could magnify the influence of decision frailties and irrationalities because they could affect large numbers of people. The grant of such powers could also suppress experimentation, which is crucial to the advancement of human welfare improvement precisely because people have limited rational capacities.

Granted, behavioralists as experts might be better able than their subjects to discern right decisions from wrong ones, but should we not worry that the experts' own rational limitations will show up in areas they have not studied, not the least of which is the exact and varying implications of their proposed nudges on different people over time? Will their nudges take out experimentation that could lead to better nudges, and more rational decision making, over time for different people? Such questions must remain a concern because even minor and gentle nudges can give rise to sequences of decisions, behaviors, and interactions of decisions and behaviors, all with feedback loops that could not possibly be known to the experts when they initiate any agenda of decision reforms. The derivative decisions that people may make several decision sequences removed from the original nudges may never have been studied in their full complexity over extended real-world populations and over extended time periods during which irrationalities can be corrected to one degree or another through feedback mechanisms, most notably experiential learning and the communication of lessons among a very large number of people. My point here is separate from an obvious problem with so much behavioralist research: The great majority of laboratory subjects in past studies have been undergraduate or graduate students who, by virtue of their being in universities and volunteers, are biased samples, perhaps unrepresentative in their values and sensitivities of the great wash of humanity across a nation or the globe.

The behavioralist experts' decisions could be further flawed if they are based on defective research techniques that overlook essential features of decision environments. Real life decision environments are far more varied across large numbers of people and are ever changing through time. Behavioralists themselves insist that human decisions are critically dependent upon the way in which choices are framed, yet choices can be framed in innumerable ways. If framing is as strong a force as behavioralists claim, then is it even possible for generalizations to be expected to be reliable over a long time for a large portion of the human population? At what point can research be stopped and reform agendas be confidently developed? There is reason for skepticism about the application of knowledge of human behavior from the behaviorist research program, a point that will be fortified as we go through the arguments in this chapter.

Then, there is the nontrivial concern that behavioralists can become unjustifiably enthralled with their newfound sense of judging other people's decisions, so much so that they recommend nudges that generalize their principles, applying them to situations and people where they need not and should not be applied. Employing resources to nudge those people who make right or rational decisions in the behavioralists' research would surely be a waste.

In short, Austrian and mainstream economists would have a healthy skepticism for any proposal that delegates the power of making personal choices for others to Richard Thaler, Cass Sunstein, or Dan Ariely, no matter how expert they and their admiring followers see themselves. First and foremost, to reiterate, behavioralists have found that not all of their subjects have made wrong or irrational decisions (even by the behavioralists chosen criteria of rationality). In laboratory experiments, some subjects (often a nontrivial minority of all subjects) did choose the higher expected value gamble over a lower valued sure thing, an important fact that often is set aside as later reports of the experiments include loose talk about how subjects are collectively irrational with little to no attention to how the minority can be an important force in changing the decisions and behaviors over time of those making wrong or irrational decisions.

Then, there is no reason to believe that the sure-thing option was in any sense wrong or irrational, given the role variance can play in people's evaluations. In a widely cited experiment, some subjects treated projects involving out-of-pocket expenditure as less preferred than similar projects of equal dollar value involving only opportunity costs. As noted in Chap. 6, Richard Thaler concluded, "the students systematically preferred the project with the opportunity cost" (2000b, p. 274). Those who chose the opportunity-cost projects may have imagined some hidden benefit to the projects that the researchers, for a good reason, did not observe – these types of evaluations are necessarily subjective. Even if there is a true decision bias among business people for opportunity-cost projects, not all subjects suffered from the identified bias. Some subjects treated the projects as equals, or may have exhibited a bias in favor of out-of-pocket-expenditure projects. If there is a right decision, those who made it can cause, with appropriate learning and feedback loops, a shift in the distribution of right and wrong decisions over time (which is more likely in the real world than in laboratory settings).

There is also the consequential problem I have encountered: I repeated (as best I could) Thaler's experiment with my MBA students, giving my students two ways of pursuing a business venture that required a $1 million investment: (A) through the use of firm resources devoted to other projects (or involving an opportunity cost) or (B) through the raising of outside equity funds or through borrowing (which could be construed as requiring out-of-pocket expenditures). The overwhelming majority (upwards of 75 percent) in the two separate classes chose option B (the out-of-pocket expenditure). When I made option B the use of the firm's cash reserves in one class, 87 percent chose option B. (Of course, the use of cash reserves involves an opportunity cost, but the use of cash might be expected to be seen as more of an out-of-pocket expenditure than option A, given Thaler's use of out-of-pocket expenditure. The cash might have been seen as a more explicit or salient cost). But, perhaps, my class experiment was framed differently than Thaler's. If so, my point remains: Generalizing about decision biases from the experiments framed in particular ways is fraught with inherent risks that are rarely acknowledged because there is essentially no limit to the details of the "frames" for experiments.

Sure, give Thaler, Sunstein, Ariely and everyone else in the behavioralist camp all the opportunities they desire to present their arguments in books, articles, and classes, and to solicit (paid and/or unpaid) consulting jobs, but such a concession is a far cry from giving them or other experts the power to impose supposedly correct decisions on all (or even a few) others, no matter if they made the right choices. Power can be misused, and while those in the behavioral camp might be able to make more rational decisions for themselves than the average of all others, there is no guarantee that their decisions, based on their own assessments, for others in fact will be more rational for others, even if they could divine the ends of others. They just might be inclined to infuse their decisions for others with their own value systems, perhaps, affected by principles of decision making they have deduced from, say, mean scores in their research findings (a form of valuation through group think), which likely will have little chance of improving the decisions of a large number of people scattered about the mean.

One could go through the "irrationalities" listed by behavioral economists to explain reoccurring phenomena such as asset (stock market and housing) bubbles. For example, part of the problem with bubbles, behavioralists tell us, is that market participants engage in "herding," which is claimed to be irrational because people do not look to the fundamental data to make their decisions, but rather look to what others are doing (Shiller 2005, 2008). Richard Posner makes a strong argument that herding is not necessarily irrational, and can be quite rational: "It is risky but not irrational to follow the herd. (It is also risky to abandon the safety of the herd – ask any wildebeest.)" (2009, p. 84). When uncertainties abound, following the herd can be a good working heuristic because other members of the herd can have information individuals do not have and cannot obtain. And herding works well in so many areas of life, especially, those relating to use of language, culture, social norms, and morality.

Besides, when a bubble is expanding, knowing when to get out of the asset market is hard to determine because the peak can only be known in retrospect. And, Posner reminds us that the expected value of staying in assets in the midst of a bubble can be greater, given the unlimited upside gain, than the expected losses that will be incurred when or if the bubble bursts, given that the downside losses for individual participants is truncated by the size of their investments. Nevertheless, the result of individual rationality can be a "collective irrationality." Put another way, individual irrationality cannot be deduced from collective irrationality (Posner 2009, p. 106). When economists talk about public goods, they recognize that individuals behaving rationally and individually will underproduce the good. Competitive prices are a form of collective irrationality for sellers. Economists do not ascribe irrationality to market participants, but rather use individual rationality as a way of explaining (or predicting) the underproduction in the case of public goods and equilibrium prices in the case of competitive markets. Posner effectively argues that bubbles can be treated in, essentially, the same way that public goods and competitive markets are treated (Posner 2009, Chap. 3).

Reliance on Constrained Laboratory Studies

The behavioralists argue that research demonstrates how human beings are less rational and exhibit more irrationalities than people – especially, economists – assume: "Hundreds of studies confirm that human forecasts are flawed and biased. Human decision making is not so great either" (Thaler and Sunstein 2008, p. 7). In the process, the behavioralists point to a varying collection of decision deficiencies or biases (availability bias, optimism bias, status quo bias or inertia bias, representativeness bias, relativity bias, loss-aversion bias, anchoring bias, planning bias, and the list goes on) and recite findings of a series of studies demonstrating that people's decisions and behaviors do not match the presumption of perfect rationality, as indicated by the high proportion of subjects who gave what the behavioralists deemed wrong – equated with irrational – responses to constructed choices. Along the way, the behavioralists might acknowledge, as Ariely does, that "life is complex, with multiple forces simultaneously exerting their influences on us, and this complexity makes it difficult to figure out exactly how each of these forces shapes our behavior" (Ariely 2008, p. xxi), with complexity being the reason d'être for carefully crafted laboratory experiments (Thaler and Sunstein 2008, p. 7), which are the "microscopes and strobes lights" used by economists and others in their roles as social *scientists* (Ariely 2008, p. xxi). "They [the experiments] help us slow down human behavior to a frame-by-frame narration of events, isolate individual forces, and examine those forces carefully and in more detail. They let us test directly and unambiguously what makes us tick" (Ariely 2008, p. xxi).

Never mind that any admission that "life is complex, with multiple forces simultaneously exerting their influences on us" necessarily draws into question the usefulness of applying the results of laboratory experiments, which can entail gross simplifications, to the broader and ever-changing complexities of real life (the kind of charge behavioralists make against neoclassical economists for their simplifying premise of perfect rationality). Moreover, behind the setup of laboratory experiments, which are designed to select and isolate a few variables (often among innumerable social and physical forces) must be some sterilized premise of decision making and behaviors so that the simplified experiments can be devised in the first place. How else might researchers select and isolate essential features of complex real-world environments for study in laboratory settings? The behavioralists' guiding theory seems to be a negative one: Behavior cannot be perfectly rational – with which Friedman and other neoclassical economists might agree without going to the trouble of proving the point with expensive laboratory research. After all, as we have seen, perfect rationality has always been touted as a simplifying assumption, an imperfect methodological means of easing the cost of thinking.

We also should not ignore the fact that behavioralists' careful research often amounts to nothing more than the tabulation of subjects' responses to surveys completed in classes or laboratory settings where the subjects have few, if any, meaningful incentives to make and report accurately the required calculations and evaluations before making their choices and where there are no feedback loops on decisions, whether right or wrong, either within the brain or among the subjects and between the subjects and the external environment. Hence, there are few opportunities to correct errant decisions and behaviors, as the focus in classroom and laboratory settings is generally on the decisions and behaviors themselves isolated from their consequences and from any interaction among the subjects or between the subjects and institutional settings. Sure, lots of wrong decisions can be expected if the potential for corrections is ruled out, especially, when there are no or few incentives (much less growing incentives as decision-making errors mount) for subjects to detect errors and to take the time and resources to make corrections.

And it needs to be noted that there is a substantial experimental literature that indicates that people's decisions in real-world settings (or some approximation of such settings) are significantly different than in laboratory settings where subjects may be inclined to give the researchers what they want and where their decisions may be under scrutiny by others, as reviewed by economists Steven Levitt and John List (2007). For example, subjects were asked to allocate sports trading cards among other subjects who gave different prices for cards. The subjects tended to give higher "quality" cards to those offering the higher prices. However, in real-world settings in which "confederates" approached real-world card traders, different prices, the tie between the buy price and quality was weak at best (List 2006). In another study, subjects who had never given to charities gave 60 percent of their allocated endowment in their laboratory setting to what they were told was charity (Benz and Meier 2006). When subjects in a dictator game in a laboratory experiment knew they were being monitored, 46 percent of the subjects donated at least $3 of their $10 laboratory endowment. When the subjects were given complete anonymity, less that 16 percent donated at least $3 (Hoffman, McCabe, Shachat, and Smith 1994). Subjects who show a high tendency to contribute to public goods in laboratory settings have a low tendency of contributing to a real public good (urban tree-planting for a nonprofit) in the outside world (Laury and Taylor 2006).

The Human Brain's Internal Inclination to Correct Errant Decisions

Presumably, within the behavioralists' methodology, the brain is nothing more than a black box that makes decisions and has little, if any, internal interest in adjusting to feedback sensory data that emerge from decisions. That is, wrong decisions, and the sensory data that are bound to emerge from them, are not cause enough for the brain to adjust decisions to the scope of the external data considered, the ways in which external data are recombined with already stored data, or the extent to which decisions are shifted from the primitive and limbic system to the frontal cortex. No matter how serious the flaws in past decisions, behavioralists often overlook ways in which people – through their brains – can adjust past decisions, the reported errant decisions are the end of the surveys or experiments. The unstated presumption is that the brain has no interest in correcting its own mistakes and is perfectly content to continue to systematically make all identified errors, even when the brain learns that it and the body it inhabits would be better off if corrections were made.

The presumption seems to be that the only economizing behavior is in the external world. There is no recognition that, consciously and unconsciously, the brain is constantly filtering sensory data inflows, and changing the assessments of various components of the inflows, given what is decided. This reality of how the brain works means there are reasons to expect at least some feedback loops embedded in the process by which the brain interacts with the external world, especially, if the consequences for its errant decisions and behaviors mount with time.

There is also no recognition that the brain itself must economize, or has any independent interest in economizing, on its own energy and neuronal resources and can suffer in the achievement of its own goals (which can be in full synchronization with the goals of decision makers themselves for whom it is a dutiful agent) when it makes errant decisions. Surely, errant decisions – especially when consequential, systemic, and predictable enough for behavioralists to pay attention to them – will affect the brain's internal workings as new and more solid neuro-networks are laid down through those decisions and their consequential experiences.

If the human brain has an interest in securing energy resources for its own functions and those of the body, which the brain manages, but yet it has evolved to fear a scarcity of such resources, then certainly the brain would have an interest in correcting errant decisions to some degree even absent external pressures to do so, at least, again, beyond some point as the consequences of its errors mount. If behavioralists' brains can deem other people's decisions and behaviors errant, then should not the brains of the decision makers themselves, who necessarily have more details of the decisions' circumstances and must suffer their consequences, be able to detect at least some of the errant, irrational consequential errors, at least at some level?

Okay, the brains of the decision makers might not be able to detect, or have an interest in detecting, the full error of their ways (especially, in artificially constructed laboratory settings), but so long as they can detect some degree of error of consequence, then feedback loops within the brain are created with the potential for correcting decisions over time. These corrections then combine with the brain's sensory data inflow, and potentially may be absorbed and used by other decision makers because of external pressures the corrections impose. These external pressures, the exact nature of which depends on the institutional environment, may affect only the speed and degree to which corrections are made, but there should nonetheless be pressures for corrections if the errors are truly consequential for the prosperity of people and their brains and if they mount, or are made more consequential as others make right decisions and, in turn, others correct the errors of their ways.

The point worth stressing here is that established irrationalities set up their own feedback loops within the brain, at least to some degree, especially when the irrationalities are deemed consequential. Such feedback loops, both conscious and automatic, are part and parcel of the human brain's evolved construction. One cannot deny the prospects of such loops and potential correction without assuming away what the brain is designed to do, which is constantly to assess and reassess internal and external sensory data, including the sensory data that errant decisions elicit.

But then, behavioralists' research may involve only administering surveys on some choice circumstance, the full results of which for all subjects in the experiments are known only to the administrators. That is, the subjects themselves are not made privy to the data on the choices of all other subjects until later, after the experiment has been terminated and the reports on the experiments are filed or published. The errant decisions, and their subsequent consequences, cannot then be sensory data that the subjects' brains can employ in feedback loops for reassessment and correction of errant decisions. No wonder in such research paradigms people's observed rationality falls far short of perfection. Human decision making as a *process* is often denied (or is severely constricted).

The critical point missed in survey findings is that the subjects are not given opportunities to adjust to their own and others' decision experiences. In real life, interactive processes, some real or supposed irrationality can be presumed to abate, or else we must worry that the irrationalities are not really consequential or that the brain does not do what we think it does, which is to think and, in some way, economize on its own limited resources. As stressed in Chap. 8, we have to wonder how the brain could have evolved to do anything other than economize on itself, given the body's evolved physiological constraints and the brain's own neurobiological constraints, as well as energy constraints faced by both body and mind.

We also might wonder how only the behavioralists are capable of understanding errant decisions and recommending corrections. If corrections at some level are not naturally forthcoming, then surely behavioralists' notifications of people's irrationalities should provide new and useful data to people to correct their own decisions, at least to the degree that their evolved mental constraints will allow. Perhaps, behavioralists might retort that people are too captured by decision-making biases to correct their ways in the normal courses of their lives, but should such be the case if the errant decisions were truly consequential, or as powerfully important and widespread and predictable, as behavioralists suggest? If so, then how have the behavioralists escaped the bounds of their own irrationalities, if others cannot do the same? But then, the behavioralists could be the ones who are incorrectly assessing the irrationalities of all others. Any number of behavioralists have certainly fallen in the trap of obtaining evidence of a majority of subjects making wrong decisions and then talking with ease about how people, in general, are irrational or harbor decision-making biases, when their own evidence does not warrant the generalization that individuals are so thoroughly irrational that they are so thoroughly and predictably irrational (Ariely 2008). Researchers from the behavioralist school do seem to suffer a generalization bias, as well as myopic focus on irrational decision making since they so rarely report subjects' rationalities. Indeed, in their books Ariely (2008) and Thaler and Sunstein (2008) focus so completely (if not exclusively) on subjects' irrationalities, their readers must wonder how they can expect to carry on rational discussions with readers about people's pervasive irrationalities.

Ecologically Adaptive Environments

In any number of the behavioralists' decision surveys, there is little external competitive market pressure on subjects to induce them to ratchet up their rational inclinations in decisions, to expand the intake of sensory data beyond that which is noted in the experimental survey or to shift consideration of sensory data to more deliberate and calculating levels of the brain. The surveys capture decisions in snapshot form, without allowing time for processes of adjustment to kick in. Moreover, the given survey instruments and laboratory settings are specifically designed to restrict relevant sensory data for the choices that are made. Laboratory settings are environments that the investigators define, which means that the settings are not defined by the subjects themselves in some ecologically adaptive manner. In such artificial environments, subjects might be expected to make more mistaken, irrational decisions than they would in more natural, evolved, real-world environments that accommodate the subjects' rational limitations and the errant decisions people are inclined to make. Research settings typically have few to no opportunities for subjects to correct their own errant decisions or to respond to the correct and errant decisions of other subjects, and subjects typically have no control over the research environment or the experimental programs of the researchers.

Subjects' Overall Rationality

In their reviews of laboratory and survey findings, the behavioralists also do not seek to assess the relative merits or consequences of irrational *and* rational decisions. Perhaps, such can be expected when behavioralists use perfect rationality as their standard for judgment, which makes fully rational decisions rare, if not impossible, and when the intent may be only to expose anomalies in decision making that undermine neoclassical economists' premise of perfect rationality and encourage support for behavioral economists' recommendations for other people's decisions and behaviors. Yet, subjects' tolerably rational decisions made in real-world settings or under circumstances not considered in the laboratories could be of greater frequency and of greater consequence than their irrational decisions made in laboratory experiments and surveys. We are left to wonder about what the limited research findings show when the universe of decisions is so vast, a basic concern with all inductive reasoning that is no less problematic than the premise of perfect rationality is for deductive reasoning. To repeat, this issue is particularly troublesome since behavioralists themselves insist that decisions depend crucially on the particulars of how choices are framed, which suggests possible inexhaustible ways in which choices can be posed to subjects, which, in turn, suggests an endless research agenda with increasing difficulties in drawing out generalities, other than that which decisions depend on the exact conditions under which they are made – not a particularly impressive insight with added value.

Might the behavioralists' framing of their reviews give a distorted impression of the extent of people's irrationalities, or errant decisions? Subjects in laboratory settings could make many errant decisions, but still be deemed reasonably rational overall (especially, outside of laboratory settings), because they make far more correct decisions than errant ones or because their rational decisions are more consequential than their irrational ones. We can never know for certain people's overall rationality, and surely not with the confidence that the behavioralists suggest from identifying only irrational decisions and weighing down their research reviews with only those findings. We must presume, contrary to any impression left from the behavioralists' reviews of their findings, that behavioralists still hold that people are capable of being rational (a point that seems apparent in their favored use of "bounded rationality" [Simon 1982] and "quasi rationality"

[Thaler 1991]). After all, they do seem intent on having a rational discussion with their readers and broader audiences about people's irrationalities and proposals for corrections.

The question again is how much stock can be placed on evidence that comes in snap-shot form and from artificial environments devoid of internal and external feedback loops, and representing a limited segment of potential experiences – especially, when the surveys and experiments are not guided by a general deductive theory of behavior, other than that everything affects decisions, or perfect rationality is wrong on its face. Without a general deductive theory, there seems to be little or no basis for selecting the essential features to incorporate into the research surveys and the laboratory settings. Laboratory settings can be fruitful, but the construction of the settings must have some guiding theory, openly described, that includes subjects' motivations, or we have to wonder how irrationalities can be identified.

To clarify the point at issue, let us reconsider the type of experiment widely touted as providing evidence of irrationality (as noted in Chap. 6). Daniel Kahneman and Amos Tversky (2000a) posed a choice to their subjects between a sure-thing payoff of $800 and a prospect with an outcome of either $1,000 or nothing, and an expected payoff of $850, given that the subjects had an 85 percent chance of receiving $1,000. A reported substantial majority of the subjects took the sure-thing payoff, which Kahneman and Tversky and other behavioralists contend (wrongly, I suggest) is contrary to the dictates of rationality. Rational subjects would have taken the option with the higher expected payoff, the gamble, according to the behavioralists' determination of the rational decisions. Note that there was nothing in the choice environment for repeats of the choice. In one sense, Kahneman and Tversky have validated what economists have long known: Variance of outcomes matters in people's subjective assessments of options (again, see Lee 1969). And economic theory, founded on rationality, is at its best when used to assess the directional changes in decisions when essential features of the environment, like variance, are altered.

If the same subjects were allowed to play the game repeatedly and the game were truly fair as stated (85 percent of the draws yielded $1,000), we might reasonably expect the percentage of (rational) subjects taking the higher-valued gamble would tend to rise. This can be expected to happen because as the game is repeated, the variance of outcomes would fall, which would cause the subjects' assessed value of the gamble to gravitate toward – if not reach – its expected value of $850. To prove the methodological value of the perfect rationality premise, not all subjects need to choose the gamble when the choice is repeated, say, numerous times. Again, all that economists can predict (and maybe seek to predict) is the *directional* change on the margin: As the count of repeated plays is increased, the percentage of subjects taking the gamble can be expected to rise, at least up to some count of repeated plays.

Similarly, if a large number of subjects could agree to share their drawings equally, then the subjective value that individual choosers place on the prospect option would also begin to approach the expected value, $850. Again, the variance in outcomes for individual subjects would begin to narrow. We would thus expect that the percentage of people choosing the lower-valued sure thing would likely fall.

Also, the larger the number of choosers who share their drawings, the lower the expected variance in outcomes, or the closer the average drawing would approximate the expected value, $850, which suggests that the larger the number of choosers who pool their drawings, the greater the percentage of subjects who would be expected to choose the gamble.

And it follows that, given a fixed variance in outcomes for the gamble, any growth in the dollar gap between the sure thing (originally set at $800) and the gamble (set with an expected value of $850) would be expected to cause the percentage of the subjects taking the gamble to rise. For example, if the expected value of the gamble is held at $850 and the value of the sure thing were gradually dropped toward, say, $500, then, at the very least, beyond some point, the percentage of subjects taking the gamble would be expected to rise, if the payoffs were real payoffs and not just hypothetical laboratory choices. If the percentage of subjects taking the gamble did not rise under repeated plays of the game, then the Kahneman/Tversky claim of subject irrationality would be all the stronger. On the other hand, if the percentage of the subjects taking the gamble did not rise or even decreased, Kahneman/Tversky's claim of irrationality (or flaw in economic theory) would be weakened, if not discredited.

The implied hypotheses in the foregoing discussion are the kind of testable predictions neoclassical economists surely have in mind in their deductive methodology based on some variant of the rationality premise. Again, Friedman was perfectly willing to concede that some people might make what observers view as irrational choices in a given one-shot choice situation. Accordingly, the use of perfect rationality as the standard for assessing the presence of irrationality is something of a methodological straw man, which is bound to be proven flawed. Again, the testable predictions Friedman had in mind were of the sort that some essential feature in the environment changed, which could give rise to an expected directional change in choices and in behavior on the margin, not to a prediction of any given level of behaviors, including irrational behaviors (for example, in consuming apples or taking gambles). After all, rational tenets by themselves allow economists to deduce that demand curves slope downward, not where they will actually be positioned on a graph.

Kahneman and Tversky (2000b) report an experiment that supports, albeit indirectly and without intent, the prediction that if choosers are given more than one chance of choosing a gamble with an expected value greater than the sure thing and then receive the mean payouts from all drawings, the percentage of people taking that higher expected-valued gamble would increase, again because of the decline in the variance. In one of their experiments, subjects were given a choice between a 25 percent chance of receiving $6,000, with an expected value of $1,500, and a 25 percent chance of receiving $4,000 plus a second 25 percent chance of receiving $2,000, the combined expected value of which is also $1,500. Although the expected values were the same, 82 percent of the subjects chose the second option (Kahneman and Tversky 2000b, p. 33). Kahneman and Tversky's findings support my point: In choices involving prospects (gambles), choosers will tend to attribute some subjective negative value to the variance of outcomes (Lee 1969).

The lower the variance, the greater the likelihood that the strict expected value would dominate people's choices. The fact that the second gamble had a lower variance made it relatively more attractive to more subjects.

To test my point about the impact of narrowing variance on choices, I undertook a set of experiments in which I gave one hundred and seventy-four executive and fully employed MBA students in my 2006 microeconomics classes two options, all before the students were told anything about behavioral economics. I posed this problem:

Experiment I

Suppose you are given a choice of drawing from two barrels, A and B. You cannot choose to draw from both barrels. Barrel A has only one coupon in it that is worth $800. You have only one draw from Barrel A. Barrel B has 100 coupons in it, 85 percent of which are worth on redemption $1,000. The rest are worth zero. You have only one draw from Barrel B. Which option do you choose?

As expected from the review of the behavioral economic literature discussed in Chap. 6, a substantial majority, 72 percent, of the MBA students chose Barrel A. I then gave the same students the following set of options, involving a change in option B only.

Experiment II

Suppose you are given a choice of drawing from two barrels, A and B. You cannot choose to draw from both barrels. Barrel A has only one coupon in it and that one coupon is worth $800. You have only one draw from Barrel A. Barrel B has 1,000 coupons in it, 85 percent of which are worth $10 each. The remaining 15 percent have a zero value. You can draw 100 (and only 100) coupons. All coupons in the barrel are thoroughly mixed, and you cannot see the coupons before you pull them out. A computer will do the random drawing for you and will total the coupons drawn at no cost to you. Which option do you take?

As expected, the percentage of the students taking option A (55 percent) in experiment II was a quarter below the percentage taking option A in experiment I. To my way of thinking, behavioral economists are right: The option taken depends on how you frame the choices. In my classroom experiments, increasing the number of draws – and reducing the potential variance of outcomes around the expected value – substantially decreased the percentage of subjects who chose the sure-thing option.

In a follow-up run of the experiment, the subjects were given a prospect of having a thousand draws from a barrel in which 85 percent of the coupons were worth $1 and the rest zero (the expected value remained at $850); the percentage of students choosing the sure-thing option declined again, but only to 51 percent (revealing, perhaps, declining marginal utility to declining variance).

Of course, in such classroom experiments, the fact that subjects do not have to calculate the value of the sure thing distorts the percentage of subjects making that choice. Subjects do have to calculate the value of the gamble. Some subjects might choose the sure thing because they are unsettled by the time constraint, which can impose calculating mistakes that they would not make in more real-world environments where they can take their time and look to other's experiences with the choices. The subjects in class may also have had little incentive (and they had no real monetary incentive) to make the required calculations to make what outside observers might consider the right choice. There is a cost of thinking after all.

In my initial test of the above experiment in 2005, I confess to making a mistake in devising the sure-thing and gamble options for the first trial, which was serendipitously revealing. Instead of the coupons in Barrel B being worth $1,000, I mistakenly set them worth $850. The paragraph read as follows:

> Suppose you are given a choice of drawing from two barrels, A and B. You cannot choose to draw from both barrels. Barrel A has only one coupon in it that is worth $800. You have only one draw from Barrel A. Barrel B has 100 coupons in it, 85 percent of which are worth $850. The rest are worth zero. You have only one draw from Barrel B. Which option do you choose?

Twelve percent of the students actually chose the gamble, option B, in spite of its expected value being $722.50, 10 percent below the value of the sure thing. Either those students were risk-loving, in which case their choices were not irrational, or they simply did not make the required calculations because they had no real incentive to do so, which suggests again that their wrong choices cannot be construed as irrational, except by the imposed standard of outside observers. But, such serendipitous findings do make one wonder how many subjects made the wrong choice by mistake or simple mental laziness in all such experiments.

Errant Decisions, Entrepreneurs, and Market Pressures

In the Kahneman/Tversky study, no attention was given to the possibility that entrepreneurs could emerge who would be alert to the unexploited profitable opportunities available in the errant decisions and behaviors and orchestrate corrections, if the subjects themselves were not willing to correct the errors of their ways.

Laboratory experiments often provide no prospect for the accumulation of errant decisions and behaviors to affect the value of unexploited opportunities and for the growing value induced by errant decisions to affect the subjects' tendency to be more rational (or less irrational) in their selections. The behavioralists-experimenters could see the subjects' errant decisions and behaviors and could devise corrective decisions (Thaler and Sunstein 2008; Ariely 2008). Mysteriously, the subjects could not do the same, not even those who were intimately integrated into the social processes in which the errant decisions and behaviors emerged and pervaded the group. They simply were not given the chance. This is understandable: in laboratory experiments, only the experimenters are privy to the full sweep of errant decisions. They are the ones who collect and hold the data. Again, the behavioralists do not, in reporting their findings, recognize a role for decision entrepreneurs, other than themselves. Perhaps, subjects in the laboratory-experimental process are deemed too irrational, or too captured by the process, to be capable of being entrepreneurs' intent on profiting from errant decisions, or just intent on setting the decisions of others straight. Maybe giving subjects some leeway for entrepreneurial work has not occurred to behavioralists.

One has to wonder why it is that behavioralists see their methodological approach as the more credible, if not the only, means of detecting broad irrationalities and devising corrective solutions. They have criticized neoclassical economists for sterilizing their economic analyses, but are not behavioralists doing the same? Behavioralists seldom consider how the prevalence of profitable opportunities embedded in the distribution of the irrational choices, as determined by subjects' responses on surveys, can affect with time the relative value of, say, the sure-thing option and the prospect option. The division of the subjects' choices between the two options is treated as a given with no implication for future choices, even if the subjects in the experiment knew that the vast majority of the subjects made wrong choices. Presumably, the minority of subjects who made the right choices are not deemed sufficiently rational, intelligent, or creative to take advantage of all the subjects who made the wrong choices.

In short, laboratory experiments do not allow people to be tolerably rational; that is, to take in new revealed sensory data on wrong choices in their environments, to make cost–benefit assessments, and to reconstruct their decisions with the intent of advancing their welfares through the exploitation of profitable and welfare-maximizing opportunities that are bound to emerge from the wrong choices of so many others.

To assess the validity of the line of argument being developed here, I reframed the options in the Kahneman/Tversky experiment noted above. On the first day of class in 2008, without any discussion of microeconomics, I gave my one hundred and fifty-six first-year executive and fully employed MBA students a choice between two options, A and B:

> **Option A:** There is a business venture A that is a sure thing, giving the owner/owners a guaranteed profit of $800 a year on the one product that is produced.
> **Option B:** There is a another business venture B that is something of a gamble: the owner/owners have an 85 percent chance of receiving a profit of $1,000 a year and a 15 percent chance of receiving a profit of zero.
>   Which do you take? (You cannot take both).

Again, behavioralists are right in that how people choose between the two options depends on the framing of the options. In this case, options A and B were identified as "business ventures," a slight change of words that, no doubt, redirected the students' frame of reference toward expected payoffs from the options, which might help explain why the students' choices were far more evenly split between the two options. Fifty-four percent of the MBA students chose business venture A and the remainder chose business venture B.

I then told them about earlier experiments in which 70 percent or more of the students took option A, and I also assigned them a short paper in which they were asked to take the earlier data as valid, and to consider the way the choice split would affect the relative prices of the two business ventures, and thus their relative rates of return. I then asked the students in their teams to come up with ways of making money off the choices that had been revealed (with the teams ranging from five to seven students). The students had no trouble recognizing that the expected value of business venture B was greater than business venture A and that the division of the choices would affect the relative prices of the ventures, and the relative rates of return on their investments. Several teams noted in their papers that as the number of people who chose A grew, its rate of return would likely fall for any number of good economic reasons (not the least of which is that the price of buying into venture A could increase with its market demand), which means it would not necessarily have the sure-thing payoff that was advertised (or that might be thought from the given payoff set in the option at $800). Seventy-plus percent of the teams came up with ways by which money could be made off the (supposedly) risk-averse students who chose venture A.

- Several teams came up with a strictly cooperative strategy – getting all students to choose venture B and dividing the total take, which, they reasoned (correctly), would likely increase the average payoff. Their cooperative solution also reduced the variance problem in the process.
- More ingeniously, several teams noted that they, individually or as teams, could go into the business of offering those who chose A a sure-thing payoff of, say, $801 to choose B and hand over the payoff. Several students even recognized that competing entrepreneurs would bid up the price offered to choosers of A, with the competition increasing the number of subjects choosing B.
- Several teams suggested that they would offer those inclined to choose A insurance that would mitigate the risk associated with choosing venture B, at a price, of course.
- Several teams indicated that they would, if allowed, select venture B multiple times (just as many companies do when they introduce multiple products, for example, books and toys).

More to the point, when told about the division of choices between the given options and when allowed time to think about how money might have been left on the table in the classroom experiment and about how money could be made from a redistribution of choices, the seasoned business people/students in my classes demonstrated far more rationality (and less outright stupidity) than behavioralists have found from framing the options in narrow and one-shot terms with no potential for entrepreneurial corrections. I surmise that the students, when told of the methods their classmates proposed to use to pick up the dollars left on the table by those who chose venture A, could be induced to replicate those methods with little hesitation.[1]

The influence of the emergence of feedback loops on initial decisions and on entrepreneurs engaged in corrective activity to profit from mistaken decisions of others can be relevant to other behavioral findings. Behavioral economists and psychologists have found that a majority of their subjects (mistakenly) treat sunk costs as relevant costs (see Chap. 6). They have also found, it must be stressed, that some minority of subjects treat sunk costs the way rational people can be expected to treat them, as costs that have already been incurred and cannot be re-incurred and are, therefore, irrelevant for current decisions. And this minority can be far more important to ongoing market outcomes (as opposed to one-shot laboratory outcomes) than their numbers might suggest, because their decisions can induce others to correct their behavior or suffer the economic consequences of their misjudgments. The minority of rational decision makers on sunk costs in laboratory settings can approach a majority in market processes, perhaps, reversing the behavioralists' general assessments of people's predictable irrationality. Those market participants who are sufficiently rational to ignore sunk costs will have a pricing advantage over those who treat them as relevant costs. Those who ignore sunk costs will also put competitive pressure on those who do not, forcing those who are imbued with what we might call the "sunk-cost decision bias" to change altogether their cost calculations and to set sunk costs aside (when, in fact, sunk costs are truly sunk with no associated commitment).

Similarly, many producers may, indeed, have a decision bias (grounded in, say, evolutionary forces that have shaped human physiology and neurobiology) for projects with opportunity costs rather than those with out-of-pocket expenditures of equal dollar investment, suggesting that they can be inclined during any initial time period to accept too many projects with opportunity costs higher than projects with out-of-pocket expenditures. If such is the case, those producers will have a higher than necessary cost structure, and producers without a preference for projects with opportunity costs will have a competitive pricing advantage and, therefore, greater access to financial capital for expansion. In turn, producers with a bias for opportunity-cost projects will see their market share contract, if they do not correct the error of their ways. Some (maybe not all) errant decision makers can be expected to correct their ways and, in the process, increase the pressures on others to do the same.

These kinds of competitive market pressures will tend to correct consequential errant decisions. The pressures might not press market outcomes to achieve some sort of competitive ideal in terms of welfare, but then achievement of some competitive ideal in the real world through the playing out of market forces is beside the point

---

[1] Indeed, they might come to hope that there would be more students choosing A so that there would be more money to be made, but then with some thought and experience with the options, they might expect fewer of their classmates to choose A.

of neoclassical analytics, as is the achievement of elusive equilibriums. Equilibriums will never likely exist in the real world because market, social, and physical environmental forces are always in motion and because market processes themselves, which are necessarily affecting people's rational tendencies and their opportunity sets, make equilibrium and any competitive ideal outcome moving targets. But, still, equilibrium-based analysis can remain useful for thinking purposes.

But, we should not be too harsh on the behavioralists. Abstractions from complex reality are required in any scientific endeavor. Reality is simply too complex; the mind is too limited – familiar themes from past chapters. The problem that the behavioralists' arguments highlight is obscured beneath their claims regarding the distribution of errant decisions: Behavioralists impugn deductive neoclassical theory for abstracting from reality through the sterilization of the rationality premise, but they do not seem to recognize that they are doing the same thing in their sterilized laboratory settings, although in an inductive methodological way. Behavioralists employ grossly simplistic environments – devised out of experimental necessity – to take issue with what they see as a grossly simplistic behavioral premise at the foundation of neoclassical theory, a classic case of an old adage at work, the kettle calling the pot black. However, the late Kenneth Boulding, who was as much a philosopher as an economist and who is credited with founding the subdiscipline of evolutionary economics, once quipped incisively: "It is a fundamental principle indeed that knowledge is always gained by the orderly loss of information; that is, by condensing and abstracting and indexing the great buzzing confusion of information that comes from the world around us into a form we can appreciate and comprehend" (1970, p. 2). That is, some form of sterilization of the real world is absolutely essential to advance science, or just thinking, a point that should be a friendly reminder to neoclassical and behavioral economists alike. And for theory to have scientific value, it must represent a partial view of reality, simply because any theory that can explain everything can be devoid of predictive value (which can be the case for utility theory absent any constraints on what motivates people or what they want).

The Rational Emergence of Choice Options

Of course, choice options should not be expected to magically appear in real-life market settings in the way they do in the classroom and laboratory settings, at the will and direction of behavioralists-experimentalists (or even neoclassical economists). In the real world, there has to be at least some rudimentary economic foundation for available options, which have economic value (at least if the options are to be viable for some stretch of time). Options in the real world generally have histories, which means providers and choosers in real life are likely to have more experience with the available options than the enlisted research subjects who have choice options presented to them in experimental settings more or less out of the blue, so to speak. Experience with options is important because experience can affect choices, if for no other reason than experience can affect the existence and efficiency of the brain's neuro-networks, as discussed in Chap. 8. If options emerge from an entrepreneurial process that influences their values and if people at any point in time overwhelmingly make the wrong or irrational choices, then surely their choice sets will change, giving rise to at least some alterations in options taken and the relative values of those options with time and repeated interactions.

Experimental evidence from a large number of laboratory studies involving subject interactions through time and repeated plays of games, which allow at least some feedback loops, reveal three major conclusions:

- First, the existence of the so-called endowment effect is mixed, especially, in market settings (Franciosi, Kujal, Michelitsch, Smith, and Deng, 1996).
- Second, if the endowment effect exists, consumer experience in buying goods can affect the actual endowment–effect gap, possibly eliminating it altogether when subjects realize the gains to be had from the gap. As neoclassical economists, but not behavioral economists, might have expected, John List found market field data that suggests that inexperienced consumers exhibited an endowment effect consistent with behavioral theory. Experienced consumers, on the other hand, found ways of overcoming any endowment effect they might have initially exhibited (2003 and 2004).
- Third, subjects in hundreds of experiments, even when they have highly incomplete information on what others will do and even when they are few in number, can make adjustments, find mutually beneficial trades, and achieve more or less all gains from potential trades (V. Smith 2008, citing V. Smith 1962 and 1982; Davis and Holt 1993; Kagel and Roth 1995; Plott 1988 and 2001).

Vernon Smith, a founding force behind experimental economics, observes "that an important component of the emergent observed order in these isolated single-product market experiments derives from the institution, not merely from the presumed rationality of the individuals. Efficiency is necessarily a joint product of the rules of the institution and the behavior of the agents" (2008, p. 64, citing Gode and Sundar 1993 and Sundar 2004). What is remarkable is, as experiments have shown, even robots with no intelligence and much less rationality can achieve most of the known gains from trading, suggesting again that the rationality and efficiency of outcomes is necessarily related in a consequential way to the interactions of subjects with all others and the institutional constraints under which they make and revise their decisions (2008, pp. 64–65, citing Sundar 2004).

The Irony of Nudges

The behavioralists note that neurobiological considerations founded in evolutionary forces can predictably "sway" human decisions and behaviors. Accordingly, changes in the environment that behavioralists have found to be effective can nudge decisions and behaviors toward what they and others consider improvement. Thaler and Sunstein define a nudge as "any factor that significantly alters the behavior of humans even though they would be ignored by Econs" (2008, p. 8, with "Econs" being Thaler and Sunstein's derogatory name for the subjects of neoclassical economics). Ariely stresses, "whether we are acting as consumers, businesspeople, or policy makers, understanding how we are predictably irrational provides a starting point for improving our decision making and changing the way we live for the better" (2008, p. xx).

Thaler and Sunstein reason that economists have traditionally focused on the role of incentives in guiding people's decisions and behaviors to the virtual exclusion of nudges (all nonincentive influences on decisions and behaviors) that "improve our ability to improve people's lives, and help solve many of society's major problems. And we can do so while still insisting on everyone's freedom to choose" (2008, p. 8). The nudges Thaler and Sunstein recommend include the following sample of a rather extensive and varied list:

- If schools want to alter the combination of healthy and unhealthy foods chosen by students in cafeterias, cafeteria workers can place the healthy foods at eye level and toward the start of the lines (2008, p. 2). They ask, "would anyone object to putting the fruit and salad before the deserts at an elementary school cafeteria if the result were to induce kids to eat more apples and fewer twinkies? Is the question fundamentally different if the customers are teenagers, or even adults?" (2008, p. 11).
- If businesses want to reduce the splatter from men relieving themselves in public restroom urinals, then maintenance departments should place something for men to aim at (a small plastic spider, for example) (2008, p. 4).
- Because people's decisions are subject to inertia, firms can encourage payroll-based savings by not returning monthly payroll deductions for saving to zero at the start of a new fiscal year, unless workers specify otherwise. Rather, the default option should be that workers are automatically enrolled in company-based saving plans (especially, when companies match their workers' savings) and from then on workers' savings are held to their past levels (2008, p. 10). Better yet, firms should encourage workers to commit to boost their savings with future raises on the grounds that the loss in future consumption will seem less onerous in the present than it may in the future when raises are awarded. Moreover, when the future arrives, workers will again be reluctant to change their future saving level because of the status-quo or inertia bias (Chap. 6). Firms can also encourage saving by paying workers biweekly instead of monthly (2008, p. 10).
- If charitable organizations want to raise more contributions, then they should recognize that suggested starting points – or anchors – for people's contributions can affect how much they give. Charities that have suggested contribution levels of "$50, $75, $100, and $150 can increase their total contributions by increasing the suggested amounts to $100, $250, $1,000, and $5,000" (2008, p. 24).

- Because people are subjected to the availability bias, which is to say that their decisions are distorted by recent information, they may inaccurately judge the probabilities of future bad events occurring. Reminding people of bad outcomes may nudge their assessed probabilities back in the direction of true probabilities and improve their decisions. To increase their optimism, remind them of good outcomes (2008, p. 26).
- To increase the availability of transplantable human organs, the default option would no longer be that citizens must select the donation option on, say, their driver's licenses, which people infrequently do because (supposedly) of their inertia bias. Instead, "all citizens would be presumed to be consenting donors," but would retain the option of easily opting out of the donor category (2008, p. 177), all with the expectation that no more people would opt out of being presumed organ donors than would opt in to being organ donors.
- To make people's mortgage decisions less grounded in irrationalities, forged by a host of decision-making biases, lenders would be given a list of new information disclosure mandates on lending fees and interest rates that would be totaled into a "single salient number" (pp. 135–136) and would be required to simplify the confusing variety of mortgages (2008, p. 136). Similarly, to make students better borrowers in the student-loan market, which is distorted by "sleazy" lender practices (2008, p. 140), loan applications should be simplified with fewer questions and made uniform for all federal and private loan sources (2008, p. 141).
- To curb misuse of credit cards, "credit card companies should be required to send an annual statement, both hard copy and electronic, that lists and totals all fees that have been incurred over the course of the year," which can be expected to cause cardholders to shop for better deals and to be more conservative on, say, their expenditures on trips abroad (pp. 142–144).
- To improve the environment, the government should build on the success it has had with mandates that require tobacco companies to disclose the health effects of cigarettes and that require drug companies to list the drug risks on labels. Thaler and Sunstein's proposed "low-cost nudge" would be to have the government "create a greenhouse gas inventory, requiring disclosure by the most significant emitters," which would enable people to track the behaviors of the worst offenders and to pressure them to improve their ways (2008, p. 191).

Ariely does not use the word nudge as a way of describing his embedded suggestions on how people's irrational behaviors can be made less irrational, given their decision-making biases. Nonetheless, he offers, albeit indirectly, a catalogue of means by which people's behaviors can be improved, only a few of which need be noted:

- People have great difficulty appraising the value of different products isolated from one another (just as the assessed size of a darkened circle can change with the sizes of other surrounding circles (2008, p. 7)). Because of people's relativity bias, sellers of products should place their products for sale in the context of similar options in a product line. Also, when given a choice among three options – say, different size television sets with their prices rising with their screen size – buyers tend to buy the option in the middle, both in features and price. Retailers such as Sam's Wholesale Clubs can increase the sales of its favored, supposedly most profitable, product by offering three alternatives and pricing the favored product in the middle. Restaurants owners can increase the orders of their favored upscale meal by inserting on the menu a higher priced meal that they do not expect to be ordered with any frequency precisely because patrons will scan the menu for lower-priced meals. However, the mere placement of the higher priced meal on the menu will move customers from low-price menu options to the restaurants' favored upscale, but now middle-priced menu option (2008, pp. 2–6).

- Because of their relativity bias, people who want to buy houses or cars should restrict their searches to a range of options they can easily afford. By including options that are out of their price range, they can lead themselves to buy more house and car than they should, given their incomes and wealth (2008, p. 19).
- People often behave like goslings (because of the brain's imposed requirement for arbitrary coherence), with first impressions counting unduly and acting as anchors against which all other options are judged. Hence, people's decisions can be controlled by their initial experiences. The prices people say they are willing to pay for something can be heavily influenced by the price of the first product and price (or anchor) they see. For that matter, the prices the buyers say, that they will pay for a product, can be affected by buyers doing nothing more than writing down the last two digits of their social security numbers (or the outside temperature). Hence, sellers can influence sales and can increase the actual selling price by listing a manufacturer's suggested retail price (MSRP) for no other purpose than to take advantage of buyers' arbitrary coherence, which means that buyers will be inclined to see any other discounted price being a better bargain than if no higher MSRP were indicated. Such pricing strategies can work because "that is the way we are – goslings, after all," Ariely adds (2008, p. 28). Needless to say, a variety of product promotions work only because we are irrational and predictably so (2008, p. 45).
- How much people pay for anything depends on their anchors, which includes how the deal is framed. After reading a selection of poetry in class, Ariely (2008) reports asking one group of students to indicate how much they would pay him to undertake poetry readings of various lengths later. He asked another group of students how much they would have to be paid to listen to readings of various lengths. With the anchors set, the first students group volunteered actual payments they would make for the readings. The second volunteered prices they would have to be paid, again suggesting that anchoring and framing are important for decisions and should be exploited.
- People will respond unduly to the word "free." When a 30-cent truffle was offered to students at fifteen cents and a two-cent Hershey Kiss was offered to students for a penny, 73 percent bought the truffle and 27 percent bought the Kiss. But, when the prices of both chocolates were lowered by a penny – making

the Kiss free – 69 percent chose the Kiss. Ariely suggests that his research explains why free is frequently used in product promotions and why he advocates its greater use, as in products being sold with a free second copy added or with free shipping.[2] To induce large numbers of people to buy electric cars, do not just lower their prices; give them away. To get more people to adopt preventative medicine, eliminate any co-pay for doctor visits (2008, p. 62). The word free in itself provides an "emotional surge," perhaps, "because humans are intrinsically afraid of loss" (2008, p. 54).

- "Market norms," which allow for explicit money payments, work well in business, but not so well in family and social settings where "social norms" involving the rule of tit-for-tat govern. When social norms are controlling, explicit money payments should not be used. Even in business settings, employers can often get more work out of their employees when they are asked to work for causes other than money. Payments can have the exact opposite effect of the one intended. When an Israeli daycare center started charging parents who picked up their children late, late pick-ups increased, according to Ariely, because the parents felt justified in arriving late since they were paying for the extended care service (2008, pp. 76–77). Ariely adds, "indeed, just thinking about money (in social settings) makes us behave as most economists believe we behave – and less like the social animals we are in our daily lives" (2008, p. 75).
- Similarly, paying students and teachers for more learning (or just higher test scores) can shift education from social to market norms, reducing the inclination of students or teachers to perform for the sake of goals other than money. Ariely advises that "money, as it turns out, is often the most expensive way to motivate people. Social norms are not only cheaper, but often are more effective as well" (2008, p. 86).
- A male's state of sexual arousal can influence the quality of his decisions (a surprising research finding!), which suggests that males should make decisions about birth control or AIDS prevention prior to their being sexually aroused (2008, Chap. 5).
- Because people are inclined to procrastinate, strict deadlines for completion of course assignments can improve student performance (2008, p. 114–115), and those people – students included – who admit their procrastination "are in a

---

[2] Ariely's research on candy prices needs to be considered with some skepticism for two reasons. First, he doesn't say whether the group of subjects remains the same when the prices of the chocolates are lowered by a penny. Because he undertook his candy sales on a college campus, I suspect that percentages are for different groups of students. Second, Ariely doesn't give the number of students in the two samples. It could be that few people switched from buying the truffle to buying the kiss when both goods' prices were lowered by a penny. There could have been simply far more people picking up the kiss when its price was lower, leading to a higher percentage. After all, when the kiss was priced at zero, people did not have to spend time searching for change or waiting for change to "buy" one. "Free" might still have an effect, but the point is that the effect might not have been for the reasons Ariely suggests.

better position to utilize available tools for precommitment......" (2008, p. 116). Similarly, doctors can overcome their patients' procrastination in getting medical tests by demanding up-front payments of $100, which will be refunded only when patients show up on time for the tests (2008, p. 119).

- Americans' "overdependence" on credit cards can be curbed through a "smart credit card" that the consumer programs with governors to control spending over time and under "particular conditions" (2008, pp. 124–125).
- Because of the endowment effect, consumers should be leery of trial offers of products and money-back guarantees. Ariely recommends viewing transactions as "nonowners, putting some distance between (one's self) and the item of interest" (2008, pp. 136–138).

Of course, Ariely, Thaler, and Sunstein do not appear to have serious qualms with setting themselves up as the arbiters of improved decisions and outcomes that "are for the better." They see no apparent conflict between deploying behavioral-directing nudges and maintaining true freedom of choice and insist that they favor "nudges over commands, requirements, and prohibitions" because of the risk that such powers of telling people what to do can be misused (Thaler and Sunstein 2008, p. 10). And after all is said and done, Thaler and Sunstein are convinced that their recommendations amount to nothing more than "gentle nudges" (2008, p. 14), although such a category seems to include government mandates and fairly harsh social pressures that could be brought to bear on people and firms for not giving way to the "nudge." Yet their nudge recommendations seem to be at odds with the explicit and strong statement earlier in their book opposing "commands, mandates, and prohibitions" (2008, p. 10) and their advocacy of "libertarian paternalism," which means their proposals, they insist, would be "liberty-preserving" (2008, p. 5).

Why make the case for nudges that they do? Thaler and Sunstein assert, "The paternalistic aspect (of libertarian paternalism) lies in the claim that it is legitimate for choice architects (those who design nudges) to try to influence people's behavior in order to make their lives longer, healthier, and better" (2008, p. 5), a comment made on the belief that all beyond the walls of classrooms and laboratories want what researchers say they want and that all can agree on what constitutes "longer, healthier, and better."

Behavioral economists do not seem to be able to acknowledge that neoclassical economists see the premise of perfect rationality as a means of doing in their theoretical arguments what behavioralists seek to do, which, paraphrasing Ariely, amounts to the "slowing down of human behavior to a frame-by-frame narration of events, isolating individual forces, and examining those forces carefully and in more detail" (2008, p. xxi). By focusing on equilibria, neoclassical economists are able to set frame against frame to see how key variables move in response to changes in essential features in the environment, assuming some process is set afoot through given changes in the essential features.

There is no such process of adjustment in behavioral economics. People just make poor, or rather irrational, decisions in response to set choices. There is no endogenous mechanism embedded in behavioral analysis for the subjects themselves to correct their decisions, aside from discovering their poor decisions through the behavioralists' findings. If any adjustment is permitted, it is the behavioralists themselves who assume the role of choice architects for all others, proposing changes in the environment for their research subjects (and, by extension, everyone else) so that decisions can be nudged more correctly in one way or another, as the behavioralists themselves deem desirable (or the behavioralists themselves believe that the subjects deem desirable). Never mind that defined and pressed nudges can impose a uniformity in decisions and behavioral outcomes that is at odds with the great variety of human needs, desires, and aspirations, as well as at odds with almost all forms of libertarianism that I can imagine (and I must confess to seeing libertarian paternalism as a total oxymoron) and ignore the value of varied experimentation, with the experimentation more or less ensuring bad, maybe irrational decisions on reflection (or when compared with better decisions).

For example, Thaler and Sunstein argue that employers can increase workers' participation in company-sponsored savings plans by making the plans the default option on employment (2008). Even if they were correct on the facts of worker participation, the Thaler/Sunstein nudge of mandatory savings plans is not without problems. Some unknown number of firms and worker groups might simply prefer the full libertarian position of making "opt-in" the default option because they have found a better incentive for increasing participation or because greater participation may increase the firms' costs of the plans and cause them to reduce their contributions for every worker who contributes, or lower worker wages (and Thaler and Sunstein say nothing about potential interactions of nudges and worker wages and benefits unrelated to the nudges, and neoclassical economics does indicate that there should be interactions if the nudges have the advertised consequential effects).

Again, in behavioral research settings, irrationalities do not have built-in feedback loops that can give rise to corrections. People would, presumably, have to have some rationality for that to happen, which suggests they must be able to see, or be pressured to see, the errors of their ways. And if we concede everyone's rationality, then the behavioralists' self-assumed guiding, corrective role would surely be diminished, if not called into question altogether. The built-in feedback loops, founded on some residual rationality, could very easily lead with time to corrections of misjudgments and irrationalities that could be superior – at least in theory – to the nudges (and their interactive consequences) the behavioralists recommend, because the subjects might know of detailed, essential, and varying environmental conditions that were unknown to the behavioralists-experimentalists as they designed their laboratory experiments and drew out their findings. The subjects might know better what constitutes improvement in outcomes, knowledge that the behavioralists-experimentalists cannot know to the degree that they, the behavioralists, suggest – a point that many Austrian and neoclassical economists have stressed when considering the consequences of fettered markets.

Moreover, the behavioralists would have to concede that they, also having flawed decision-making capacities and beset with irrationalities, could recommend errant nudges, simply because their recommendations will be based on laboratory experiments that do not replicate the real world in all its complexity, that are at odds with the findings of others.[3] If people harbor no rationality, they cannot see the errors of their ways, which means there would be no internal feedback loops, other than, perhaps, in the form of other nudges from other behavioralists. Nothing in the behavioralists' methodology would suggest that a sequence of nudges devised and imposed would lead with time to equilibrium in the nudge process that represents true improvement, not for everyone at least.

Hayek might rightfully worry that the behavioralists' methodology can lead to its own form of road to serfdom. Of course, behavioralists exude confidence that they *know* where people go wrong in their decisions and they *know* what constitutes corrections in decisions and behaviors. Hayek would surely worry that such a position is itself grossly errant, given that nudges are necessarily based on limited survey and laboratory information on what people want and how people will respond to nudges and respond to people's responses to nudges.

I can only suppose that behavioralists are willing to adopt their methodology and to elevate the importance of nudges because they imagine that their research has already shown where decisions makers go wrong and what corrections are needed or that they themselves will be chosen to do the research required to see where the decisions of others are errant and to devise corrective nudges. However, no one should be so confident. The decision to orchestrate nudges can be separated from the decision of who will be anointed with the powers of investigation and of the development of nudges. The behavioralists might not be among those chosen as choice architects even when such decisions are made with the interest of the public at heart. However, a system of nudges that has any depth and breadth will likely be grounded in disagreements over exactly what nudges, and combinations of nudges that can have interacting effects, should be imposed and orchestrated, and any given set of nudges will likely affect people differently.

Accordingly, if the nudges are of any consequence, political interest groups will likely be forces in the selection process, which means that behavioralists themselves might fear the development of such a process because they very well might not be selected as choice architects and might not want to endure others' possibly errant nudges devised to correct the errant decisions and behaviors of people, in general. After all, bookstore shelves are lined with advocates – scholars, ministers, self-appointed self-help gurus, and charlatans alike – for whole agendas of nudges that will correct people's errant decisions and behaviors. If people are as beset with decision-making flaws as behavioralists suggest, it is hard to know how behavioralists would provide assurance that the vast majority of heavily irrational people would not select choice architects who are themselves heavily irrational or, in other ways, would not be inclined to select nudges through irrational, counter-productive means.

---

[3] Consider the findings from other experiments, my own and others reported above, that are at odds with the findings of behavioralists, and that do not mirror the incentives that may emerge when the nudges are applied to the real world.

Why would the selected choice architects be expected to provide the definitive improvements in people choices that the behavioralists believe should be provided? That question at the heart of the behavioralists' reform agenda is never addressed, and for good reasons: It has no good answer, or not one as clear as behavioralists imagine, assuming they are not among the nudgers. The advocates of nudges are not just advocating reforms in the broad institutional framework of society, as James Buchanan and Geoffrey Brennan propose (see Chap. 9), within which people can do as they please. Rather, the advocates of nudges want to manipulate the details of people's decisions and behaviors based on the kinds of (limited) research the behavioralists conduct. Indeed, if so many economists (and their public policy followers) can be led astray with (supposedly) the kind of misguided theory, neoclassical economists have employed for so long, as behavioralists insist has been the case, one has to wonder how the behavioralists can be so cock-sure now, after only a few decades of behavioral research, that their own theoretical and empirical research is any less defective and misleading.

Of course, behavioralists might retort that they do not harbor any interests in having a system of forced nudges through, say, governments. Although Thaler and Sunstein concede that their phrase "libertarian paternalism" might appear self-contradictory, they write: "The libertarian aspect of our strategies lies in the straightforward insistence that, in general, people should be free to do as they like – and to opt out of undesirable arrangements if they want to do so" (2008, p. 5). They see their agenda as liberty-preserving and choice expanding: "Libertarian paternalists want to make it easy for people to go their own way; they do not want to burden those who want to exercise their freedom" (2008, p. 5). But then they have no compunction against setting themselves up as choice architects who "influence people's behaviors to make them live longer, healthier, and better" and "steer people's choices in directions that will improve their lives," all of which is set in motion by the belief that concepts like improvement and better off are what people want but do not achieve because "individuals make pretty bad decisions – decisions that they would not have made if they had paid full attention and possessed complete information, unlimited cognitive abilities, and complete self-control" (2008, p. 5).

The embedded ironies in the behavioralists' argument should be self-evident. Behavioralists insist that all of the decision-making biases are not simple surface defects in every now-and-then decisions; rather they are deeply engrained, perhaps, by evolutionary forces. But, how can people recognize their wayward decisions if they are as irrational, or so thoroughly deficient in rational skills, as Thaler and Sunstein and other behavioralists believe them to be? If they cannot make good decisions, how can they judge any more effectively the quality of their decisions after being nudged by behavioralists? Might we not expect people's bad judgments to extend to assessing the quality of their decisions after the decisions have been made? How would they know they are better off when their decisions have been altered by the judgment calls of behavioralists acting as choice architects?

Behavioralists might insist that they can be guides to improved decision making, but the behavioralists will hardly be alone in wanting to guide and to correct others' decisions, especially, when the standard for judging the correct decisions is as elusive and debatable as improvement is bound to be. Surely, the personal interests of those competing advocates of nudges can infect the decisions on how to define improvement.

From Nudges to Mandates: The Slippery Slope

Then, there is the deeper problem of devising corrections for what the behavioralists hold to be pervasive irrationalities in people's decision making – behavioralists (or their intellectual descendants) succumbing to the temptations to move from relatively minor, "gentle" behavioral nudges that are more or less voluntary to major governmental mandates that take the pretense of libertarianism out of libertarian paternalism. In Chap. 6, we recounted Yale University behavioral economist and finance professor Robert Shiller's explanation for the irrational exuberance in the stock market in the 1990s and in the housing market in the early 2000s, all organized around good stories that gave rise to bubble thinking that, in turn, led to expansion of the bubbles to unsustainable levels. The stock market bubble did burst as the first edition of Shiller's *Irrational Exuberance* was published in March 2000. The second edition came out with an added chapter on the emerging housing price bubble in 2005, the year in which housing prices peaked (Shiller 2005). The burst of the housing market bubble had morphed into the gravest financial panic since the Great Depression within months of the publication of Shiller's *The Subprime Solution* (2008). Shiller concluded that current and future economic conditions were so dire and systemic and founded on pervasive irrational thinking that the "subprime solution" would require policy and institutional changes every bit as sweeping and aggressive as the New Deal of the Franklin Roosevelt era. In general, the solution for the short-term required massive government bailouts (in a variety of forms) for lenders and borrowers. Shiller recognized the inherent moral hazards of bailouts – they would encourage flawed loans negotiated irresponsibly in the future – but maintained that the short-run gains from abating a worse credit crisis would exceed any long-run harm from additional irresponsible use of credit, a claim for which Shiller (2008, Chap. 5) makes no attempt to provide supporting evidence beyond repeated references to the success of Great Depression policies in averting the fall of capitalism and the rise of communism (an assessment of the effects of New Deal policies that is strongly disputed by any number of economists, the most aggressive of whom is Powell 2004).

The long-run solution to the credit crisis required, generally, "democratizing finance – extending the application of sound financial principles to larger and larger segments of society, and using all the modern technology at our disposal to achieve that goal" (Shiller 2008, p. 115). The net effect would be to "stress-proof the whole economy, building greater ballast into the institutional framework so that buyers and sellers are better able to conduct business with confidence rather than through speculative moves" (Shiller 2008, p. 121). Thus, he strongly proposed the following institutional reforms that are far removed from the gentle and simple nudges proposed by his behavioral cohorts Thaler and Sunstein:

- Strengthen the nation's information infrastructure, making more financial information readily available to the populace with the goal of "altering the social contagion and information cascades that underlie the formation of bubbles" (Shiller 2008, p. 121).
- Create a national, government-subsidized system for distributing financial advice to everyone, not just the wealthy, with the advisors' fees set by the hour (to avoid conflicts of interest) that would serve to fend off the public bad of individuals' poor financial decisions (Shiller 2008, pp. 123–126).
- Establish a new financial product safety commission to protect investors from new financial products that may be unsafe to their financial health, in the same way that the consumer product safety commission protects consumers (Shiller 2008, p. 129).
- Provide required automatic enrollment in employers' savings plans, with an opt-out option, and induce employees to devote some portion of their future salary increases to company-based saving plans, which would increase saving as people are unlikely to change a default option (Shiller 2008, pp. 131–132).
- Devise standard boilerplate terms for common contracts such as mortgages (2008, p. 133) with the attendant "requirement that every mortgage borrower have the assistance of a professional akin to a civil law notary" (Shiller 2008, p. 134).
- Require borrowers and lenders alike to disclose more data on their incomes and finances, which would be fed into national financial databases (which, of course, Shiller assures his readers, would come with privacy protections) (Shiller 2008, pp. 134–138).
- Create a new unit of account called *baskets* (a price index of a basket of goods) and quote prices in baskets as opposed to dollars, the value of which is subject to erosion from unexpected inflation rates (Shiller 2008, pp. 140–148).

Problems abound with even his more modest reform agendas, as noted earlier in this chapter. Here, we simply have to wonder whether his diagnosis of the disease – a looming second great depression – and his assessments of the causes of the Great Depression and the success of New Deal reforms could not themselves be the product of herding mentality, given the number of people worldwide who held at the time doom-and-gloom views of mankind's future during the crisis that emerged in 2008. Prominent scholars in the past have certainly misjudged the causes of economic troubles and have recommended misguided policies, most notably those developed for the original Great Depression. Shiller's assessment could also be nothing more than another good new-era story that could very well eventually be proved wrong (for example, political pressures and errant monetary policies were at the root of the 2008 financial mess), but providing all the justification political activists need in the meantime to expand greatly the reach of government into the nation's information infrastructure and financial markets. The theoretical and factual foundation of his new-era story is, at this writing, no more firmly grounded than the bubble thinking of the people Shiller criticizes, including, most notably, former Federal Reserve Chairman Alan Greenspan.

Shiller develops a line of argument that runs something like this: People – on both sides of credit markets – are prone to irrational decision making. A variety of government regulatory authorities, including the Federal Reserve, failed to recognize and avert the financial bubbles of the 1990s and 2000s. Indeed, government only aggravated the bubbles with misguided policies relating to the lack of regulation of the securitization of mortgages and limits of mortgage guarantees. Hence, the solution is more of the same, a line of argument that surely Hayek (1944) once again would worry, for good reason, would push the country further down the road to serfdom, contrary to what Shiller professes to want.

We would have to wonder if Shiller has real confidence that if Congress were to accept the challenge of devising a "new informational infrastructure," it would follow his recommendations exactly, or something much worse. We have to wonder if other behavioralists, interested only in nudges, would want anyone to take up their own or Shiller's agenda, given the likely disagreement among the behavioralists on the diagnosis of the country's economic troubles and cures.

The Bailout Bubble

As this writing, Robert Shiller looked to be the most prescient finance professor in the country (and world), perhaps, one of a handful of people who accurately forecast the collapse of both stock market and housing bubbles, and the timing of Shiller's written assessments and predictions of the country's and world's dire financial and economic troubles could not have been more on target. The American stock markets were in full panic mode, with the Dow Jones Industrial average having fallen by 23 percent during the previous week (with a rebound of 11 percent the following Monday) and by 45 percent during the prior calendar year. Congress had given the Treasury the authorization to buy $700 billion in troubled assets of financial institutions – and practically anyone else deemed necessary – in the interest of stabilizing the financial markets and the national economy. Other governments around the world passed plans for bailouts and nationalization of financial institutions (Cimilluca et.al. 2008). The Treasury belatedly followed suit and announced plans to take $250 billion in equity stakes (nonvoting preferred stock) in the country's nine largest banks as a part of the bailout plan, with equity stakes in smaller banks to be undertaken later (Soloman and Paletta 2008; Landler 2008).

Talking heads appeared, and continue to appear, on all the major American television news programs supporting the proposed bailout plan championed by Treasury Secretary Henry Paulsen and Federal Reserve Chairman Ben Bernanke. Many prominent economic thinkers, from Nobel Laureate Gary Becker (2008) to the editors of *The Wall Street Journal* (Editors 2008a), had set aside their free-market proclivities and endorsed the view that a massive bailout was necessary, even if the bailout created equally massive moral-hazard problems for the economy going forward. Anchors of major news channels seemed confident that a massive bailout of the nation's financial sector was the only prudent course.[4]

A form of bubble policy thinking seemed to have taken hold. Both 2008 presidential candidates, Barack Obama and John McCain, endorsed without reservation the then recently passed and enacted bailout plan. Commentators of all political persuasion focused their attention on the dire consequences for the national economy, if not the world economy, if a massive bailout program were not enacted, with scant attention to the downside to the bailout program that, at this writing, could take on a life of its own. The urgency of the calls for bailouts, and more bailouts, gave policymakers little time for careful consideration of what they were doing. Nonetheless, practically everyone exuded confidence that the bailout policy course – which initially meant the Treasury's purchase of banks, "toxic mortgage-backed securities" – enacted was *the* only viable political and economic option for the country. Shiller's "social contagion" and an unchecked "bailout bubble" seemed to be growing in policy circles through late 2008, as policymakers and commentators took positions that seemed to be founded on what all relevant others were saying about the need for a bailout.

A bailout of some constrained size might have been appropriate, and something both Shiller and I could agree upon. However, various interest groups – not the least of which was the domestic automobile manufacturers – started lining up for their own bailout once Congress showed any interest at all, in bailing out the financial sector. As this chapter was being finalized, calls could also be heard for a regime of greatly expanded regulations of the financial sectors from all points on the political spectrum on the grounds that the free market had clearly failed. It was not clear, at the time of this writing, that the collection of policies that would be passed would, in the end, represent a reform agenda that even Shiller could endorse. There was some evidence that Paulsen and Bernanke really had no clear idea of the cause or the solution for the country's and world's financial and other economic problems. They both had testified before Congress in September that the Treasury's purchase of toxic mortgage-backed securities was urgent and the only viable option to unfreeze the thought-to-be frozen credit markets. By early November, Paulsen had set such plans aside in favor of the Treasury's purchase of equity stakes in financial institutions. The stock market was still on a highly volatile downswing, in spite of the open monetary faucet at the Federal Reserve and the mounting support the enactment of ever growing stimulus package. But to follow the details of the

---

[4] For example, a reporter for *The New York Times* editorialized in a news report in a matter of fact manner, "If nothing were done, the banking system could collapse, and bring down much of the economy with it. That's what happened in the Great Depression, when a shortage of money led to a steep downward spiral of wages and production. But that episode taught a clear lesson: Governments have a responsibility to keep the financial system going" (Hadas, October 13, 2008).

developing policy course is beyond the scope of this book.[5] The one policy course that seemed totally off the table was to allow the housing and financial markets to find their own bottoms. In this regard, the debate between behavioralists and neo-classical economists about the rationality premise appeared to be inconsequential.

Concluding Comments

Thaler, Sunstein, Ariely, Shiller, and almost all other behavioral economists and psychologists argue that people make some "pretty bad decisions"; however, they use perfect rationality as the standard of comparison, concluding that people make "decisions that they would not have made if they had paid full attention and possess complete information, unlimited cognitive abilities, and complete self-control" (Thaler and Sunstein 2008, p. 5). But why should behavioralists use such a standard for judging decisions if they are convinced that the standard is descriptively untenable? If the standard for judgment is relaxed to reflect real-world conditions of scarcity in both the external physical world and the internal mental world, then many decisions people make might not be judged to be so bad after all – and might not need nearly so many nudges toward improvement as the behavioralists propose.

---

[5] Bernanke made the case for the aggressive fiscal actions the federal government had taken through the bailouts in a column for *The Wall Street Journal*: "History teaches us that government engagement in times of severe financial crisis often arrives very late, usually at the point at which most financial institutions are insolvent or nearly so. In these conditions, the consequences and costs of inertia and inaction can be staggering. Fortunately, that has not been the situation we face today." Bernanke goes on to assure readers, "Americans can be confident that every resource is being brought to bear: historical understanding, technical expertise, economic analysis and political leadership" (Bernanke 2008). Perhaps understandably, he made no mention of possible downside to the policy course he was helping to direct.

The House of Representatives turned down solidly the first bailout proposal, surprisingly to many. Subsequently, the original $700-billion bailout proposal quickly became a political Christmas tree, covered with bailout ornaments – tax cuts and a variety of bailouts for other past bad credit decisions (for example, $25 billion for bad car loans and billions more federal funding for Hurricane Katrina) – all designed to achieve the requisite number of votes. The bailout bill as passed had at least $140 billion of bailout "sweeteners" that benefited specific congressional districts (McClam 2008).

There appeared at this writing to be truly no natural or political limit to the expansion of "bailout thinking," which totally denied or set aside the downside risk to expanded bailouts, or the "bailout bubble." The fact of the matter is that the proponents of the bailout really could not be as confident as they seemed that the bailout would work as advertised, or even that the bailout will not make the country's economic problems worse, which no one had even hinted at. The moral hazards the country will face in the future because of the current likely escalating growth in bailouts to an ever-expanding circle of economic sectors could be real and substantial, and those future problems could be captured in people's current expectations about the future health of the country, thus undercutting the country's economic vitality today, and worsening today's financial mess. But then, Shiller's "social contagion" in policy thinking seems to have taken hold, with the bailout becoming the proverbial "free lunch." This future burden from bad decisions could throttle current economic incentives and, thus, the economic recovery in the short term, a point that the bailout advocates have never acknowledged at this point, to my knowledge.

In this chapter, I have described three levels of weakness in the methodological approach embedded in behavioral economics:

- First, the behavioralists are inconsistent in their argument when they challenge neoclassical economics for assuming as-if perfect rationality in making testable predictions, but then use a form of perfect rationality as the benchmark to determine the breadth and depth of irrational decisions. They then, in turn, use this information to construct nudges and mandates, many of which could be as off the mark as they believe the behavioral implications drawn from strict neoclassical economics to be. Many proposed nudges might be unnecessary or unproductive if people are inclined to adjust their rationality through time as their errors become apparent. The errors people make in decisions can elicit new sensory data and improved decisions. Decision-making errors by some (or most) people can lead to cost disadvantages, cause adjustments in the relative values of choice options, and impose competitive market pressures for corrections through time. This can be, especially, true when not all people are prone to make the same decision errors and see exploited profitable opportunities in the wrong and irrational decisions of others, as the behavioralists have always found in their surveys and experiments. As noted in the chapter, it was not at all difficult for my MBA students to find profitable ways of correcting for many wrong choices made in reaction to an initial set of options – a sure-thing payoff and gamble payoff – from which they could choose.
- Second, behavioralists seem to harbor no appreciation for the idea that many supposed irrationalities can have a rational foundation (but then such a position might be implied in their attention to decision biases). This is, especially, problematic because the abundance of rational irrationalities depends upon the exact nature of the real-world institutional settings in which people make real decisions and adjust subsequent decisions according to the consequences of their own and other people's errant choices. That is, the persistence of irrationalities depends on the absence of corrective feedback loops infused throughout people's own internal mental hardwiring and the external institutional settings.
- Third, behavioralists exhibit little concern for how their proposed corrective nudges and mandates can change the institutional settings, or can have derivative effects (not inconsequentially on the political front) that cannot be anticipated. The behavioralists cannot anticipate such changes because they cannot foretell how people will interact after the nudge and mandate process is installed as nudges, and mandates can give rise to reactions that in turn give rise to other actions and reactions. The chain of actions and reactions cannot be known with precision beforehand because of the evolutionary nature of human interactions through time, maybe long stretches of time.

No one should expect people's real-world behaviors – even when markets are in equilibrium – to always be devoid of irrationalities of one sort or another. There is no reason to believe that Friedman or Stigler or Becker would have had such an expectation. All markets (or any other institutional setting) can do is to mitigate the frequency and distorting the influence of irrationalities. This is for two basic reasons. First, perfect efficiency – including, perhaps, perfect eradication of irra-tionalities – in competitive markets is a useful theoretical construct for discussions in economics but perfection in reality is simply not optimal, and not even an option. Second, the human brain is simply not constructed to make all decisions, and all behavioral responses, rational in the sense that all costs and benefits of all options are carefully and accurately weighed. The infinite regress lurking behind cost–benefit calculations rules out perfectly rational decisions.

As argued in Chap. 8, the higher brain simply does not contain enough neurons to accomplish a goal of perfection in decision making. The human brain does not always have the time and energy to engage precisely in more rational, deliberate decision making. Many decisions and behavioral responses are reflexive and emotional ones that are made with split-second speed, with limited sensory data and without conscious, exacting contemplation of alternatives, and thus are fre-quently mistake-ridden. But still, such mistake-ridden decision processes can be, on balance, efficiency and welfare enhancing. This is to say, if automated and emo-tional, irrationality-laden responses were ruled out, or could be (for sake of argu-ment) totally suppressed by nudges and mandates, there is good reason to expect that people would be less well off than they are, with their decisions and behaviors likely even more infiltrated with misjudgments, irrationalities, or nonrational and emotional responses. In the development of their nudges, behavioralists do not appreciate the extent to which their proposed nudges and mandates can undermine the efficiency of defective decision making.

People must first be able to economize on the limited resources in their brains before they can hope to economize on the use of real resources in the external physical world. As part and parcel of decision-making processes, irrationalities can be welfare enhancing for the same reason that mistakes in judgments and behaviors are inextricably bound up in social and market process that are welfare enhancing. A fundamental issue is whether given institutional settings improve decision making and, hence, the welfare of people, sufficiently that a theoretical premise of rationality – even perfect rationality – can lead to fruitful insights about behavior that can be validated, at some level by intuition, common sense observations, and real-world experience, if not by scientific inquiry that relies on extensive and detailed data bases and sophisticated statistical techniques for assessing the validity of hypotheses.

In a perfect decision-making world, nudges and mandates can be deemed good, or Pareto optimal. However, in a world of external and internal scarcity, such is not likely always the case. The proposed nudges and mandates can easily generate suboptimal outcomes because they seek to eliminate or modulate the impact of some bad decisions, deemed to be such based on an implied standard of perfect decision making which can generate decisions that they would not have made if they had paid full attention and with complete information, unlimited cognitive abilities, and complete self-control. The nudges and mandates themselves can carry development and imposition costs, but they can also eliminate bad decisions that were good for the welfare of the decision makers in the same sense that mistakes in a world of risk and uncertainty can reflect mental-economizing behavior.

As noted throughout this book, markets *improve* decision making simply by summarizing a lot of data on products into prices that enable people to economize on their rational capacities, by weeding out decision makers who persistently make bad (or irrational, net-gain destroying) market decisions, and by pressuring market participants to correct their decisions. The culling of bad decision makers can, of course, cause others to correct their own errant decision making by inducing them to be more rational than they would be absent the culling pressure. People can become more rational through a conscious decision to transfer many decisions from their reflexive and emotional systems in their brains to the more deliberate reflective systems.

The core issue that behavioralists leave largely unaddressed is whether the market processes that Friedman held dear and that are indispensable to neoclassical economics are able to correct people's tendencies to make irrational decisions to any significant degree, even when an assumption of perfect rationality makes those processes invisible in the analytics. Behavioral economists have compiled findings of human irrationalities when snapshots of their controlled behaviors are taken. However, any number of experimental economists have found from laboratory experiments that market processes often do quite well in guiding market outcomes toward equilibrium states that the experimentalists know to be the welfare-maximizing outcomes, despite the fact that the subjects' mistaken decisions might infect the processes along the way (V. Smith 2008a). Moreover, experimentalists have found that welfare-maximizing outcomes of the laboratory market processes can be approximated even when the subjects have far less than complete information, or when they know only information particular to themselves, say, the price at which they can buy or sell a given quantity. Competitive equilibrium also has been approximated (if not exactly achieved) when the count of buyers and/or sellers are far from numerous, the thought-to-be required condition for achievement of perfectly competitive output levels and net welfare gains for market participants (V. Smith 1962).

Finally, the methodological criticisms of rational behavior contain an inherent contradiction. The critics seem to believe that people's behavior is everywhere irrational, so much so that natural selection and corrective dynamics cannot be counted on to generate anything approaching rational, efficient outcomes. At the same time, they seemed convinced that they can engage their readers or listeners in a meaningful, rational discussion of people's pervasive irrationalities, all with the intent of nudging people into corrective changes toward improved behaviors for the great swath of people outside their own academic camp and relatively small groups of subjects. One can only wonder how pervasively irrational people can engage in rational discourse with the goal of lasting improvements in behavior. Do the critics of neoclassical economics believe that they and their readers and listeners stand apart from all irrational people? If critics believe that they and their readers can, with the aid of laboratory and survey research findings, improve their decision making, why cannot the decision making of others be improved by themselves once they (errant decision makers) see the data on errant decisions and/or through feedback loops in market settings? Markets might do a better job of nudging people toward enhanced welfare than a system of potentially ill-conceived and difficult-to-adjust nudges and mandates based on snapshot surveys of decisions inside laboratory settings devoid of feedback loops.

Then again, in pointing out people's decision-making limitations, biases, and failures, behavioralists could improve the feedback loops within markets and increase the pressure on people to correct their decision-making ways. Because of what they learn from behavioral economics and psychology, more market participants than otherwise might be made aware of the decision errors and biases of others, and the unexploited opportunities in their decisions, sooner than otherwise, which means that the behavioralists findings could increase (marginally, if not structurally) competitive market pressures to correct errant decision-making ways, which can give rise to more rational decisions and less waste of resources. That is, the research findings themselves could be the most important nudge the behavioralists have devised, especially, since such a nudge is fully consistent with libertarian paternalism as people are allowed to decide for themselves what to do with the research findings.

Chapter 11
Rationality and Economic Education

Economists have long prided themselves on the positive intent of their work as researchers and teachers. That is, as scientists, economists insist that their goal has always been largely directed toward understanding the world as it is, not as they would will it to be or as it "ought to be," to draw again on John Neville Keynes' words.

Thus, Milton Friedman contends that "positive economics is, in principle, independent of any particular ethical position or normative judgments" (1953, p. 4). As did Friedman in his seminal methodological essay (1953), many economists are willing to acknowledge the existence of normative economics, or the imposition of personal values – their own or others' – into the selection of institutional and policy options. But, economists often hasten to add that their personal values should not be given any special consideration because economists' professional skills lie in analyzing and empirically assessing the effects of proposed changes in institutional and policy options, not in judging their relative merits. Any instructional intention of the rationality premise has been limited to exploring the logic of how rational people, intent on maximizing their personal welfares as they themselves individually define their personal welfares, can be expected to behave, given changes in the "essential features" of their environment, not how they should behave or are advised to behave.

Interestingly, behavioral economists show little hesitation to use their research to offer advice on how people should behave or to assume the role of "choice architect" (Richard Thaler and Cass Sunstein's phrase 2008) and induce people to change their behaviors through "nudges" (or even mandates) for changes in behavioral outcomes selected not by economic actors but by choice architects (including the behavioral economists themselves) as discussed in Chaps. 6 and 10.

Neoclassical economists' scientific work can, say, determine the effects of an imposed minimum wage on the employment opportunities and fringe benefits of covered workers. Although positive analyses might consistently reveal negative effects of minimum-wage laws, economists-qua-scientists attest that they must remain objective on the moral or policy implications of such laws, at least as scientists (especially, when journal publication of their theoretical and econometric

R.B. McKenzie, *Predictably Rational?*,
DOI 10.1007/978-3-642-01586-1_11, © Springer-Verlag Berlin Heidelberg 2010

works is at stake). Moreover, economists studiously refrain from using their supply-and-demand-framed analysis of minimum-wage laws to explain how employers should react (or would be advised to react) on employment and fringe benefit fronts when a minimum wage is mandated. Rather, they limit their analysis to drawing only testable hypotheses on how employers can be expected to react, and what the employment and fringe benefit effects will be. When economists express policy preferences, they speak not as economists acting in their scientific roles but only as policy advocates, perhaps, assuming the role of public intellectuals (although many economists obviously confuse the two roles).

This reluctance to make normative judgments may be because neoclassical economists like George Stigler and Gary Becker (1977) tend to agree with Friedman that people generally share basic values and part ways primarily in terms of "different predictions about the economic consequences of taking action," such as imposing a minimum wage (Friedman 1953, p. 5). If economists and others have the same basic values, then disputes about public policies will be resolved by factual evidence on the effects of policies. Hence, neoclassical economics, as practiced by Friedman, Stigler, and Becker (to take only three cases), has an embedded positive hypothesis relating to political outcomes, that "progress in positive economics" can be expected to lead to greater agreement on policies (Friedman 1953, p. 5).

So, an intentional professional breach is, generally, maintained between positive and normative economics. Normative economics is generally treated as moral philosophy, politics, or just academic musings that mistakenly and surreptitiously can infect the real work of economists as detached observers/analysts/scientists. Perhaps, the breach (or the pretense of a breach) is useful because entangling personal values with professional assessments of the effects of policies can inadvertently corrupt the scientific process, one of Friedman's expressed concerns, since "the investigator is himself part of the subject matter being investigated in a more intimate sense than in the physical sciences" (Friedman 1953, p. 4). Even though he was a lifelong advocate of various free-market policies and highly constrained government, Friedman always insisted on keeping his science and policy advocacy as distinctly separate career pursuits (although the credibility of his public policy pronouncements was obviously bolstered because of his scientific work).

If economists have a professed reluctance to deal with what ought or ought not to be in human affairs, then it may seem strange that they have no trouble-modeling human behavior as they seemingly want it to be – perfectly rational (or some reasonable approximation) – which may seem to imply that economists expect people to be perfectly rational or that they should behave as if they are (which we have already seen is a mistaken interpretation of Friedman's expressed position). Yet, economists know that people cannot be expected to behave with perfect rationality and would not even want them to behave that way, assuming the prevalence of scarcity of external real-world resources. I have described one defense of the perfect rationality premise that Friedman and his followers have used: An assumption of perfect rationality enables economists to develop testable predictions by simplifying the analysis and easing the costs of thinking. The perfect rationality premise has predictive, not descriptive or prescriptive, value in neoclassical economics.

In this chapter, I break dramatically with professional convention, arguing that an assumption of perfect rationality is also useful because it allows economists to give people guidance on how people should behave (under some conditions) if they want to maximize their welfares and/or firm profits, especially, under competitive market pressures. Economic instruction founded on the perfect rationality premise can be used as a pedagogical device for devising principles of economics – heuristics – that can enable people, if they choose, to be more rational than they would otherwise be inclined to be, and thus can reduce the waste of resources that mount when people persist for some time in making irrational decisions, or generally ignoring their decision-making biases (which behavioral economists and psychologists have documented). Economic education itself can add to competitive market pressures for people to behave rationally that, in turn, can elevate human welfare and lubricate the workings of the invisible hand, a deduction the normative content of which is not unlike the normative content of the usual deduction that competitive markets improve allocative efficiency, given known wants and known resources. The imagined efficiency in my deduction is at two levels, first in the form of the clarity, facility, and efficiency of thinking and second in the form of an improved allocation of resources due to the elimination of resources wasted on misdirected decisions that will be corrected by competitive pressures. People (students included) can reject both deductions for their normative content, as many people do. And they can be hostile toward economic education, as many people are, precisely because of its effects on their rationality and the resulting greater pressure to heed market forces. Of course, if it is conceded that people are not actually perfectively rational and that economics helps people deal with their less-than-perfect rationality with more cost-effective ways of thinking, then the benefits of economics instructions must surely extend beyond the efficiency gains achieved through competitive markets when wants and resources (and production and consumption technologies) are given.

As we will see, neoclassical economics, founded on perfect rationality, is replete with proposed decision-making and behavioral nudges, an outcome of economic education that behavioral economists have, for the most part, missed in their myopic focus on their self-assumed role as choice architects bent on changing people's irrationalities.[1]

---

[1] As noted in Chap. 6, Thaler does recognize the prescriptive content of neoclassical economics: "Setting price so that marginal cost equals marginal revenue is the right answer to the problem of how to maximize profits. Whether firms *do* that is another matter. I try to teach my MBA students that they should avoid the winner's curse and equate opportunity costs to out-of-pocket costs, but I also teach them that most people don't" (Thaler 1992, p. 197, emphasis in the original).

The Economic Rationality of General Education

If people were perfectly rational at all times throughout their lives, the case for compulsory or subsidized education of any kind would be undermined (but hardly destroyed). This is the case because a major justification for compulsory and subsidized education is founded on the proposition that people – or, rather, parents, but especially children – do not always know what is good for them. Perfectly rational people – even children – would correctly assess (either from their own investigations or by asking informed others) the personal costs and benefits of all forms of education, buying that level of education that would optimize their long-term personal welfares.

Perfectly rational people, however, would also assess with complete accuracy the externalities of education, separating them from their assessed personal costs and benefits. They also would understand how everyone else would make similar calculations, with the result being that everyone would achieve education levels that were suboptimal for everyone, to the extent that education truly involves externalities and the group setting is sufficiently large.

Perfectly rational people would be eternally frustrated in large group settings because they would understand with full clarity the gap between their and others' achieved education levels and the social optimum that everyone would want, given externalities. However, they would also understand that all perfectly rational people in large-group settings would be free riders in political efforts to remove the education gap through compulsory and/or subsidized education. They would understand, again with clarity, that their political efforts, rationally determined, would require them to incur organizational costs while having no consequential effects in motivating others to devise policies to remove the educational shortfall, given the prevalence and tenacity of free riding among perfectly rational others. Perfectly rational people, in the case of education and other issues involving consequential externalities, would not want people to adhere strictly to the *homo economicus* or perfect rationality behavioral models, for this rationality implies that people have no room in their utility functions for their own individual provision of collective goods in large-group settings.

However, there is an embedded paradox in a premise of perfect rationality, the resolution of which suggests that perfectly rational people would choose to be less than perfectly rational. Perfectly rational people would understand, again with clarity, the scarcity of their mental resources, the omnipresent prospect of sensory data overload within the human brain, and the brain's need to economize on its own resources by limiting selectively and imperfectly the data inflows (see Chap. 9). They would recognize the potential value of education to enable people (and their brains) to choose more cost effectively among the potential inflows of sensory data, causing some data inflows to be less valued and others more valued, thereby making more mental resources available for careful, deliberate processing of accepted sensory-data inflows and for the development of automated, unconscious rationality-grounded decision-making processes.[2] Of course, as already noted, people can object to economic education precisely because of such embedded normative intent, but such is what much economic education does and such is why many professors, the National Council of Economic Education (and its networks of Centers of Economic Education), and the Association for Private Enterprise Education are such intense boosters of economic education. Surely, some of their support of economic education is founded on the goal of giving people the tools to devise testable hypotheses, but some must certainly be directed toward changing the way people think about the world, absent any effort at empirical tests. This is, especially, true for students at all levels of education below graduate school (from elementary school to university) who will never employ their economics training to empirically test in any remotely rigorous way the deduced hypotheses. Many can be expected to forget many of the findings from empirical studies that speak to the policy implications of theory (because of the public goods nature of education designed to boost economic literacy on public policies, a point I developed decades ago [McKenzie 1977]).

Perfectly rational people will understand that education can offer valued guidance from others who have gained experience with a broader array of sensory-data inflows. The guidance from teachers (broadly defined) will not likely be flawless in a world of scarcities of external real-world resources and internal mental resources, but the guidance can offer the prospect of *improvement* in the mental processing abilities of students (broadly defined), which is all perfectly rational people will seek. Education (in the form of courses) in music, art, history, and even cooking can provide cost-effective guidance on how students can better discriminate among a broader range of competing sensory-data inflows.

Perfectly rational people will also understand that education can serve another important function, that of providing techniques, skills, and methods of thinking, which are often captured in arrays of heuristics distinguishable by disciplines that students might not otherwise devise on their own or with the same clarity and force in affecting decisions. These methodologies and skills can enhance the brain's efficiency in processing sensory-data inflows, freeing up the brain's neural resources for processing a wider array of relevant sensory-data inflows and enabling people to be more rational, at the conscious and unconscious levels, than they would otherwise be – a thought that suggests that embedded in any perfect rationality premise is the presumption that perfectly rational people will not likely be, in reality, perfectly rational at all times and under all circumstances. An assumption of perfect rationality implies a need for some room for *improvement*, including improvement in people's rationality. Courses in reading and composition, mathematics, and economics can be a means to enhance people's ability to process sensory-data inflows so that perfect rationality can be more nearly approached.

---

[2]Some education can allow the brain to treat some sensory data inflows with less needed deliberation such as that what happens when people learn to read, do math, and play music.

Perfectly rational people would also understand that education can literally change the brain's neural networks by discarding, or making irrelevant, many neural networks that education shows to be flawed and then building and fortifying other neural networks, all of which can enhance the efficiency with which future sensory-data inflows can be handled. Along the way, evaluations of recognized options can be changed and improved, which in turn can improve the achievement of more rational decisions.

Again, I note the internal contradiction between an assumption of perfect rationality and any improvement in rationality. Improvement in rationality is not strictly possible under conditions of perfect rationality, which suggests that any perfect rationality premise must serve the purpose of a useful methodological device for understanding what people would want and would do to achieve their ultimate goals, which is an achievement I have dubbed rational rationality. A premise of perfect rationality is a mental device that expedites thinking about complex issues of choice at the intersection of external real-world scarcity and internal mental scarcity. In doing so, the premise itself lays down neural networks of its own and harbors the potential of making other neural networks more efficient. With improvement in rationality allowed, then economic instruction founded on the (perfect) rationality premise assumes normative intent and normative outcomes, captured in the concept of *improvement* in decision-making.

Rationality and Economic Education

Economic education can be thought of as doing no more than what many neoclassical economists propose, that of explaining to students how the behavior of individuals, firms, and markets can be modeled for the purpose of devising testable hypotheses, all founded on the premise of perfect rationality. In this regard, again, economic education has strictly positive intent and effect. That is all it can do, given the starting position of perfect rationality.

If people were, indeed, perfectly rational, economic education would not be needed, or so it would seem. Perfectly rational people would not need to be told that they were perfectly rational. They surely would know that fact, if they could make all the detailed, precise, and completely accurate decisions perfectly rational people would be able to make. Furthermore, perfectly rational people would be able to formulate on their own all the implications of perfect rationality, or so it would seem, given all else they can do with such ease (sometimes without costs) in economic, consumer-choice models. Principles of economics would come naturally to them.

Economic education need not be limited to developing testable hypotheses, provided economic educators understand that students' real-world behavior falls short of the dictates of the discipline's underlying behavioral premise of perfect rationality. If students' rationality is seen as less than perfect, then there is room for *improvement* in their rationality, which can come from students considering a different, and perhaps expanded, array of sensory data inflows – economic in nature – and being able to process them more efficiently. The heuristics – principles – explained in economics courses and training courses provided can help the students to lay down new neural networks and fortify other neural networks that can ease thinking when students are no longer in the classroom.

Economic education, thus, can have two normative, even paternalistic goals (perhaps, consistent with the "libertarian paternalism" that Thaler and Sunstein espouse, which are covered in Chaps. 6 and 10). First, economic education can expose potentially relevant sensory data inflows that students, otherwise, might not have considered with welfare-enhancing attentiveness (as the students define welfare enhancing). Economists as educators can, for example, point to the prevalence of scarcity in the external real world, a point that can lead to the heuristic useful for many thinking purposes: All choices have costs, many of which can be hidden or nonobvious, as is so often true of opportunity costs.

Similarly, economists can point out the interdependency of imports and exports. The law of comparative advantage is (in a Frank Knight sense) a relatively absolute heuristic that can enable students to see points they might not otherwise recognize, given their limited range of sensory data inflow prior to their economic education: International trade can be mutually beneficial even when one might least expect it to be so, when one trading partner is more efficient in everything. Indeed, the content of economics textbooks and courses can guide students to discriminate more precisely among sensory data in the world around them such as personal observations of others' behavior as well as actual numerical data series that can be tabulated, graphed, and analyzed with statistical methods for insights on choices that would improve their thinking about the world and their welfare.

Second, economic education can inform students about how they should (or how they would be advised) to make decisions and how they should behave if, or when, they want and seek to maximize their individual welfares or their firms' profits. Examples of principles and heuristics – perhaps on par with, if not better than, behavioralists' nudges – embedded in economics courses that can be voluntarily adopted (or rejected) by students and, if adopted, can guide decision-making are many – are listed below. Surely, these principles or heuristics can be grouped under the best form of "libertarian paternalism," since no behaviors are dictated. They represent only recommended guides for saving resources when imperfect decision making is conducted under market pressures. Most such listings of recommended nudges for thinking would surely include (but would not be limited to) the following principles or heuristics, all assuming goals of personal welfare and profit maximization: all future streams of costs and benefits should be discounted for time and risk.

- Marginal costs and benefits should be assessed and should be equated in determining the optimum, welfare-maximizing consumption level.

- Costs should be minimized and production should be optimized, which implies equating at the margin.
- Firms should produce where marginal revenue equals marginal cost if maximum profits are to be obtained.
- Sunk costs should be ignored.
- Firms should price their products on the relatively absolute presumption that demand curves slope downward, and if a firm's product demand is inelastic, then it *should* raise its price.
- A monopolist should always raise its price until its elasticity coefficient is greater than 1.
- People should override, as best they can, any natural inclination to consider only salient features of resource and product purchases.
- People should treat opportunity costs on par with out-of-pocket-expenditures.

At the policy level, students can be taught common heuristics that fall out of supply-and-demand analytics and the presumption of profit maximization.

- Employers should cut jobs and lower the fringe benefits of the remaining workers when a minimum wage is imposed.
- Landlords should reduce maintenance when rent is controlled.

Economics instruction could be founded on a behavioral premise of any level of less-than-perfect rationality, but an assumption of perfect rationality is sufficient and, perhaps, cost-effective for developing any number of relatively absolute principles or heuristics. For example, if welfare or profit maximization is to be approached, all costs – out-of-pocket and opportunity costs – must be considered on an equal footing, not differently because some costs might be more salient (or because students might have a hard-wired mental bias toward projects with less salient opportunity costs). Another example could be that curbs on imports can curb exports, as well as the welfares of the trading parties.

Granted, behavioral economists could well be right that an array of decision-making biases may encumber people, causing them to make many decisions inconsistent with those expected from perfectly rationally people. But such observations can serve only to fortify the potential value of economic education as a normative endeavor, that of telling students what they should *consider* doing to improve their welfares and policy outcomes, helping them to overcome their decision-making biases. Indeed, such decision-making biases can give less-than-perfectly rational students reason to want, and to pay for, economic guidance on the sensory data to which they should be attentive and on decision-making rules that they should follow in their personal and business lives, *if* they want to approach perfect rationality and its implied welfare and profit enhancements. Succinctly, an assumption of perfect rationality (or even the more restrictive presumption embedded in the *homo economicus* model) can be, and perhaps should be, seen as a methodological device for ferreting out normative, relatively absolute heuristics for improved welfare and profit maximization.

Competitive Market Pressures and the Perfect Rationality Premise

In the last chapter, I noted how competitive market pressures could cause market participants to become more rational than the participants would otherwise be. Market participants who systematically incur unnecessarily high costs (because of any combination of decision-making biases) and who make decisions for which the costs are higher than the benefits will lose access to resources compared with market participants who are more rational, or less irrational (or have less encumbered decision-making biases that impair their welfares). In business, firms led by managers who make systematically irrational decisions will fail outright or will have to struggle in their resource and product markets. Such firms will have to pay higher prices for capital and labor because of their relatively high risk of failure. Such firms will also have to charge relatively high product prices because of their relatively higher costs. Under pressure from market forces, managers of many such firms can be expected to correct the errors of their decision-making ways, eliminating at least some, if not all, of their decision-making biases.

Firms that have fewer decision-making biases and thus lower cost structures, lower product prices, and higher prospects of survival and profitability errors can be expected to take over firms in which managers do not correct their decision making. Again, there is a tendency for error-prone producers to be replaced by less-error-prone, if not close-to-error-free, producers. Competitive market pressures, thus, can cause people to move toward the standard of perfectly rational decision-making, or, better yet, the more reasonable standard of rational rationality.

It follows that competitive pressure can be expected to do more than enlist greater economic efficiency from a reallocation of given and known resources among given and known uses. Competitive pressure can also enhance the extent to which market participants adjust consideration of sensory data inflows and change the care and precision with which they evaluate costs and benefits (both at the conscious and unconscious levels).

Economic education could make competitive markets more efficient by upgrading people's decision making (but, of course, only if the education is provided cost effectively). The inefficiency derived from irrational decision making must be consequential or just greater than the cost of the economic education. As the relatively more rational decision makers gain competitive advantage in their markets, the pressure for other decision makers in other firms to improve their decision making can escalate, causing progressively more economic pain for irrational decisions and causing more less-than-fully-rational decision makers to improve the rationality of their decisions. Again, the improvements can be expected because of the economizing behavior of the human brain that settles on an optimum, rational level of rationality in the use of its own energy and neural resources. With the escalating pain from irrational decisions and competitive pressures, the brain can be expected to justify devoting more energy and more neurons to making decisions more carefully and based less on initial, perhaps, innate decision-making biases.

The end result of the competitive market process is that any initial (even substantial) majority of irrational decision makers can be expected to recede toward a much smaller portion of the covered population of decision makers, perhaps, with rational decision makers comprising a substantial majority in the end, when (conceptually speaking) a new equilibrium is reached. Again, economic education can be seen as a means of informing prospective market participants – students – about the prospect of innate decision-making biases. Using an assumption of perfect rationality, students can be shown the logic of correct general decision-making heuristics. Such heuristics drawn from economic instructions on how competitive markets work can save neural and real-world resources and enhance welfare and firm profits because the embedded message can be: "Ignore these principles and your competitive position, if not survival, could be in jeopardy as others make more rational decisions either because they are so naturally predisposed or because they correct their decision-making ways – or learn early in economics (or other) courses the principles for welfare-enhancing and profit-maximizing." In this regard, perfect rationality can be used in economics instruction to show students how they can think better and operate more competitively in competitive markets. This is to say, premise of perfect rationality can serve the same instructive and protective purpose that the premise of *homo economicus* served in James Buchanan and Geoffrey Brennan's search for protective constitutional precepts.

Such normative economic principles of decision making are every bit applicable to managers of would-be monopolies, so long as resources are scarce and there is a healthy competitive market for ownership of monopolies. If managers of monopolies err in decisions by succumbing to decision-making biases, then they will have unnecessarily high production costs and will be less profitable than they could be, with their impaired profitability captured in their depressed stock prices. Hence, more rationally inclined prospective owners can buy control of erring monopolies, replace the erring managers, and improve the monopolies' decision making. The new owners can then capitalize the cost savings and revenue increases in the price of their firms' stock. As relatively more rational investors/management decision makers take over poorly run firms, causing economic pain for the affected managers in the firms taken over, the less-than-fully-rational managers of other firms not yet subject to takeover will feel the growing economic pressure to make their decision making more rational.

Of course, continual irrational, nonrational or even thoughtless decision making will cause economic waste, but that waste will abate as if by an invisible hand as the competitive pressures for corporate control escalates, causing decision makers in yet-to-be-taken-over firms to correct their errors as more rational decision makers replace less rational decision makers, with the rationality of outcomes surpassing, perhaps, decision makers' rational inclinations.

Economic education, then, not only can have a normative, didactic intent, for the individual student, but also can reduce the waste of resources associated with more or less natural and irrational, biased decision making, perhaps, set as mental proclivities through long-ago evolutionary forces. Assuming people also have some capacity to override their decision-making proclivities, economic education can add to competitive market pressures because students trained in the "economic way of thinking" can make more rational decisions sooner than they would naturally be inclined to make, putting pressure on untrained others to improve the rationality of their decision making – which, in turn, can impose feedback competitive pressures on students trained in economics to take their training even more seriously.

Furthermore, competitive market pressure for the benefits of economic education can lead to an even greater demand for such education. But then such points must assume that economic education is provided in a cost-effective manner and is organized at least in part with normative intent, meaning that the instruction is designed to explain to students how they can – or should (or would be advised to) – behave, and even must think and behave, to cope with competitive pressures. Economics instruction founded on a premise of perfect rationality can be such a cost-effective methodology and pedagogy precisely because it abstracts from the full complexity of human decision making and behavior, introduces a major element of simplicity into model building, and eases the costs of thinking, freeing up some neural resources for learning and more deliberate consideration of choices.

Variable Rationality and Efficiency

Efficiency in the allocation of resources in conventional neoclassical economics, founded on perfect rationality, is a well-defined theoretical construct. Optimum production and consumption levels can be precisely identified graphically and mathematically and market participants' aggregate welfare gains can be precisely identified (with the precision in outcomes one methodological reason for the perfect rationality premise). Great analytical precision is possible because resources and wants (or goods) are known and given to the analytics. Market participants' rationality is also given and is not a variable. People are assumed to make all decisions with perfect rationality, which does not allow for even the possibility of improvement in decision making and which does not open the analytics to changes in the range of resources and goods, or their evaluations, that are considered for optimization or in the perceived quality of the various features of any given array of resources and goods considered for optimization. Hence, the improvement from, say, markets is strictly limited to the gains from the reallocation of known resources from known low-valued uses to known higher-valued uses and from the reallocation of known goods from those people who value them less to those who value them more, with the values on the resources and goods also known with precision to market participants and with those values remaining stable for purposes of conceptualizing equilibrium.

When market participants are recognized for being less than perfectly rational, or are acknowledged to be imbued with extensive innate irrational tendencies, efficiency becomes something of an elusive, if not a mushy, theoretical construct. This is because resources and goods, as well as their values, are no longer precisely given and known everywhere by everyone and at all times as the market process unfolds and moves toward equilibrium. Efficiency, under such a process, loses its precision because people's rationality is potentially variable, and an endogenous variable at that, subject to upgrading or degrading. Individuals' perceived well-being is also subject to change in character and depends on the exact nature of market pressures, which, in turn, can be affected by the exact institutional features (the extent to which property rights are enforced, for example), the count of market participants, the extent and consequences of market participants' decision-making biases, the plasticity with which the human brain can adjust its neural memory and decision-making networks, as well as people's inclination and willingness to correct their decision-making biases and move toward more rational decision making and behaviors. As people adjust the rationality of their decision making, the array of sensory data inflows acknowledged and considered in decisions can change. Hence, the array of goods can change, and evaluations of features of any collection of goods can be expected to change. The care and precision with which the costs and benefits of goods are considered can also be expected to change. Accordingly, efficiency can no longer be grounded in welfare gains achieved from given and known resources and goods, since they all are moving targets.

Such deductions do not mean that the concept of individual and aggregate welfare improvement or efficiency must be abandoned. On the contrary, all that is required is that welfare improvement, if not maximization, must be moved back or disconnected from identified goods at any moment in time. Welfare improvement must be associated with broader *ends* that alternative collections of resources and goods can serve.

Gary Becker is widely recognized for having focused neoclassical analytics on household production, with things bought in markets (meats and vegetables, for example) considered as inputs that are combined with householders' labor to produce final products (family dinners, for example). Here, I am proposing that in their search for welfare improvements, people can consider goods bought in markets and produced in households as being subject to recombination as people discover new and improved sensory data inflows and methods for considering with greater cost-effectiveness the sensory data inflows. In such a setting, efficiency can still have meaning so long as the *ends* of what people do are more fundamental and tolerably stable because of evolutionarily settled physiological and mental constraints that guide and direct the consideration of sensory data inflows.

For example, in conventional neoclassical economics, the goods subject to optimization can be identified as meats and vegetables that go into family meals, or the family meals themselves. I suggest here that the more stable ends subject to maximization can be quality family life, reproductive success, survival, or even a happy (and meaningful) life. The goods (meals, trips, home theater systems, and numerous other things people can buy or do) that go into the achievement of such ends can be switched in and out of people's utility functions in much the same way that resources are switched in and out of firm's production processes, given changes in their relative prices and productivities (and awareness of their relative prices and productivities).

As the ends people seek are broadened and their rationality is allowed to vary with competitive pressures, economic analysis can be opened to the prospect of greater economic gains from markets than is recognized by conventional neoclassical economics. This expansion is possible because the gains can come from better, or more highly valued, collections of recognized and considered resources and goods and because decision making can be improved through market pressures that guide people, as if by an invisible hand, toward eliminating their decision-making biases (irrationalities) and achieving cost-effective productions of goods that serve the broader ends that people consciously and subconsciously seek with welfare gains literally on the mind.[3]

Having made these points, I hasten to add that this construction of improvement may provide an understanding of why market processes are not always appreciated with the uniformity that might be expected from conventional neoclassical economics. Not all market participants will likely appreciate to the same degree the pressures to make their decisions more rational, mainly because such pressures can impose thinking costs that can differ among people with varying mental capacities and inclinations. Just as competitive pressures may push producers in a given product market to lower their prices and upgrade their product's quality by more than would be profit maximizing under monopoly conditions, many market participants may be pressed to be more rational than they might like. That is, some people may spurn competitive markets (and economics courses) precisely because market pressures guide them to a level of rationality that they would prefer not to achieve.

For similar reasons, some people might be expected to harbor a hostility toward economic education (and business education more generally) – especially the type that is heavily weighted toward explicating the consequences of free or open or unconstrained competitive markets (especially, where there are no guiding behavioral norms of ethics, the kind that Adam Smith felt were crucial to welfare improvement through markets, as developed in Chap. 3). This can be the case precisely because economic education in the neoclassical tradition, founded on a premise of perfect rationality and combined with an assumption of the perfectly competitive model, can suggest that free markets are more efficient than critics believe they can actually be. Critics of neoclassical economics might fear that all debate over societal institutions and public policies is effectively rigged by undetectable mathematical and graphical models and by claims that models are intended only to deduce testable hypotheses, with empirical tests mistakenly interpreted as validating the perfect rationality premise. In neoclassical theory, market

---

[3] I remind readers of a point made in Chap. 8: The achievement of welfare improvement need not always be deliberate, as in conscious comparisons of the costs and benefits of various courses of action. As noted in Chap. 8, the relegation of some (or many) decisions to subconscious mental routines can improve the overall efficiency of the human brain, even when mistakes or irrationalities at times creep into decisions. When the ends of human action are fundamentally conceived, the only relevant issue is whether or not the combination of conscious and subconscious decision making – both of which contribute to human rationality – improves welfare as broadly conceived.

participants never make mistakes other than those that are rationally determined, all of which might suggest undue reliance on free markets, and a proclivity to spurn government solutions to observed social ills. Either the government solutions are likely unneeded once markets are able to work their magic of eliminating the waste from temporary irrational decisions of market participants and/or the government policies are likely to be ill-conceived because policymakers can have all the decision-making limitations that behavioralists and others have identified and because they can be disproportionately influenced by special interests in the political process.

The findings of behavioral economics are reminders of the unavoidable sources of decision-making frictions in market processes that move decision makers toward any given conceptualized equilibrium. Any number of their so-called nudges can be interpreted as efforts to reduce the decision-making frictions, just as deduced principles of economics can be seen as nudges for improved thinking, decision making, and behavior.

Economic education might also engender hostility because it can provide useful heuristics that can make the students and prospective business people more rational, and more competitive, than they would naturally be inclined to be, adding to market pressures for all market participants to improve their rationality. The hostility toward economic education, and markets, emerges with, perhaps, greater strength when goods and broader ends sought are "positional," as can be the case when people judge their welfares by, say, the relative sizes of their houses or by their reproductive success. Any enhancement in people's rationality can, under such conditions, lead to expenditures of greater energies with little to no effect on aggregate welfare, or with the gains in welfare of some offset by the losses of others. Those who gain in relative position on the totem poles of positional goods might look favorably on their economic education and on markets. Those who lose in relative position might, of course, harbor different assessments.

Moreover, not all economic education can be expected to be efficiency enhancing, even when it upgrades people's rationality and competitive market pressures. By explaining to students the logic of free riding as group sizes grow to the point of being large, economic educators uncover a fundamental logical force that works against competitors successfully colluding with the intent of curbing their collective market supply for the purpose of raising their market prices and profits. As is conventional, individual competitors can be expected to reason that his or her output will not materially affect aggregate market production and market price, which suggests that individual competitors cannot justify time devoted to the development of cartels and, if a cartel is formed, to ignore the cartel's production curbs. They can be expected to free ride. Or put another way, free riding among all competitors is a cause of competitive pressures and market efficiency (so long as there are no externalities). Therefore, economic education can lead to greater free riding.

Where external costs prevail, free riding, which gives rise to competitive pressures, can result in maximum external costs. The logic of free riding can suggest to students another heuristic that is not necessarily innate, in the sense that it is engrained from evolutionary forces: Free riding in large groups is welfare enhancing at the personal level (or is more enhancing than they might have been naturally inclined to believe, given decision-making biases that evolved in small-group settings and transferred to large-group settings, as discussed in Chap. 7). If students are taught that all rational people can be expected to free ride, especially in large groups, each can begin to believe that other students will adopt the free-riding heuristic because they also begin to think that rational people will be inclined to free ride, an understandably natural implication of the perfect rationality premise and economics education. Then, goods with external costs will be overproduced more than would otherwise be the case, and goods with external benefits will be underproduced more than otherwise. All the (learned) free riding can be expected to add to competitive market pressures and even more free riding, with more people more inclined to adopt some variant of the *homo economicus* model for personal behavior. And economic education does appear to promote behaviors that many might see as "antisocial," especially, when decision making on the margin seems to be press as a prescription without regard to social norms or prior personal commitment. Public choice economists Gerald Marwell and Ruth Ames (1981) have found that economics majors tend to be less inclined toward cooperative efforts than other majors, given that many economics majors have taken to heart core tenets of their discipline, undercutting the collective gains from cooperation grounded in irrationalities (or tendency to act from evolutionary-grounded tendencies to cooperate and share, maybe out of engrained tit-for-tat decision strategies).

Public choice economics is widely recognized for a positive argument: Given the inconsequential probability that an individual's vote will count in determining the outcome of any large-group election, many voters can be expected never to go to the polls and to remain uninformed about many election issues when they cast their vote. For the overwhelming majority of voters, the expected discounted payoff from voting and from becoming informed on election issues and the candidate's positions is bound to be lower than the costs of voting, and certainly lower than the even greater costs of becoming informed voters (Tullock 1967). The normative heuristic that many students can take from such analysis is none-too-subtle: Do not vote. Or if voting is done for, say, reputational purposes, remain uninformed on election issues (or vote in fewer elections and then vote less informed).

Concluding Comment

Behavioral psychologists and behavioral economists have done neoclassical economists a favor. They have reminded them of the extent to which perfect rationality is a caricature of how people really are. In doing that, however, they have, perhaps inadvertently, expanded the welfare-enhancing potential of markets, as well as help free neoclassical economists from strict prohibitions on undertaking normative economics. Competitive pressures, whether in markets for resources, products, or corporate control, *can* reduce errant decision making and, thus, *can* upgrade people's rationality and improve the welfare of market participants (although we have noted how enhanced rationality on the part of market participants can, under some conditions, also have negative consequences).

Having established an array of decision-making biases, the behavioralists have not been reserved in devising ways – through nudges – for decisions and welfare to be improved. In the process, they have exposed neoclassical economics for what so many economists attest the discipline really is: a way of thinking – and a means of improving thinking, if the goal is individual and collective welfare maximization and firm profit maximization – that stands in sharp methodological contrast to behavioral economics. That is, as argued in this chapter, neoclassical economics is a means of deducing testable hypotheses and thinking nudges, with the latter clearly giving the discipline a normative, as well as positive, foundation – although strict neoclassical economists might continue to protest that role for their discipline. Behavioral economists have presented a competitive challenge to mainstream economics in that the behavioralists have recommended behavioral nudges, which many people (budding majors and PhDs) might find attractive because of the practical value of the behavioralists' approach (which has shown up in the substantial sales of the behavioralists' books and expansion of their research agendas and publication records).

Fortunately, as argued in this chapter, there is a way for mainstream, neoclassical economists to respond to the competitive challenge, which is to recognize that their analytical models, based on the perfect rationality premise, can also generate, in addition to testable hypotheses, any number of welfare-enhancing and profit-maximizing thinking nudges, fully consistent with libertarian paternalism, with emphasis on "libertarian," or the voluntary adoption of the thinking nudges at the individual level. The chief difference between the nudges the behavioralists propose and those I propose, suggested by neoclassical economics, is that the behavioralists in the Thaler/Sunstein/Ariely tradition often have specific behaviors – more purchases of fruits and greater savings – in mind. My nudges, by contrast, relate to how people think about the things they – not choice architects – want to accomplish. Certainly, in my role as an economic educator, I am more interested in suggesting methods for patterns of thinking, no matter the various specific objectives people have, rather than recommending the detailed content of students' behaviors, given the method of thinking (to play on a distinction in analytics Hayek pressed). Admittedly, there is a paternalistic element to my proposed thinking nudges, but only a slight one, if people/students voluntarily seek economics instructions to improve their ability to maximize utility and profits. In this regard, my interest, here, in pushing thinking nudges stands apart from goals for economic education typically advocated by the economic education industry, which is to make students of the subject "better citizens," which I am inclined to see as a weak reed on which to found economics courses, because of the public-goods nature of such a goal, which suggests fleeting benefits, which George Stigler (1963) suggested was likely long ago.

This is not to say that the behavioralists do not have useful advice in their proposed nudges – and advice that can add to competitive pressures. It is to say, however, that some behavioralists want to change behavior by first assessing how people actually do behave, often only in laboratory settings that often do nothing more than provide snapshot views of decision making without corrective pressures. Here, I make a defense of perfect rationality in economics as a means of changing the way people think.

Bibliography

Aiello, Leslie and Peter Wheeler. 1995. The expensive tissue hypothesis. *Current Anthropology* 36:199–211.

Akerlof, George. 1970. The market for lemons: Quality Uncertainties and the Market Mechanism. *Quarterly Journal of Economics* 84:488–500.

Allais, M. 1953. Le comportement del'homme rationnel devant le risqué, critique des postulats et axioms de l'ecole Americaine. *Econometrics* 21:503–546.

Anderson, Jenny, Vikas Bajaj, and Leslie Wayne. 2008. Democrats set conditions as Treasury chief rallies support for bailout plan: Big fanciers Start Lobbying for wider aid. *New York Times*, September 22, p. A1.

Anderson, John R. and Robert Milson. 1989. Human memory: An adaptive perspective. *Psychological Review* 96(4):703–719.

Andreoni, James, William T. Harbaugh, and Lise Vesterlund. 2003. The carrot or the stick: Rewards, punishments and cooperation. *American Economic Review* 93(3, June):893–902.

Andrews, Edmund L. 2008. Bush officials urge swift on broad recue powers. *New York Times*, September 20, p. A1.

Ariely, Dan. 2008. *Predictably Irrational: The Hidden Forces that Shape Our Decisions*. New York: HarperCollins Publishers.

Arkes, Hal R. and Catherine Blumer. 1985. The psychology of sunk cost. *Organizational Behavior and Human Decision Processes* 35 (February):124–140.

Aronson, E. and J. Mills. 1959. The effects of the severity of the initiation on liking for a group. *Journal of Abnormal and Social Psychology* 59:177–181.

Axelrod, Robert. 1984. *The Evolution of Cooperation*. New York: Basic Books.

Axelrod, Robert and W. D. Hamilton. 1987. The evolution of cooperation. *Science* 211: 1390–1396.

Bajaj, Vikas. 2008. Wall street goliath teeters amid fears of widening crisis. *New York Times*. September 14, A1.

Banerjee, Abhijit V. 1992. A simple model of herb behavior. *Quarterly Journal of Economics* 107(3):797–817.

Banyas, C. A. 1999. Revolution and phylogenetic history of the frontal lobes. *The Human frontal Lobes*, ed. by B. L. Miller and J. L. Cummings. New York: Guilford Press, pp. 83–106.

Bardo, M. T., R. L. Donohew, and N. G. Harrington. 1996. Psychobiology of novelty seeking and drug seeking behavior. *Behavioral Brain Research* 77(1–2):23–43.

Bastiat, Frederic. 1850. *Economic Harmonies*. Irvington-on-Hudson, NY: The Foundation for Economic Education, Inc., trans. W. Hayden Boyers, ed. by George B. de Huszar, 1996, accessed December 22, 2007 from http://www.econlib.org/library/Bastiat/basHar2.html.

Bateson, Melissa. 2002. Recent advances in our understanding of risk-sensitive foraging preferences, *Proceedings of the Nutrition Society* 61:509–516.

Becker, Gary S. 1962. Irrational behavior and economic theory. *Journal of Political Economy* 70(1, February):1–13.

Becker, Gary S. 1963. Rational action and economic theory: A reply to I. Kirzner. *Journal of Political Economy* 71(1, February):82–83.

Becker, Gary S. 1965. A theory of the allocation of time. *Economic Journal* 75(299):493–517.

Becker, Gary S. 1971a. *Economic Theory*. New York: Alfred A. Knopf.

Becker, Gary S. 1971b. *The Economics of Discrimination*. Chicago: University of Chicago Press (originally published in 1957).

Becker, Gary S. 1976. *The Economic Approach to Human Behavior*. Chicago: University of Chicago Press.

Becker, Gary S. 1993. *A Treatise on the Family*, expanded edition. Cambridge, Mass.: Harvard University Press.

Becker, Gary S. 1994. *Human Capital: A Theoretical and Empirical Approach*. Chicago: University of Chicago Press.

Becker, Gary S. 1996. *Accounting for Tastes*. Cambridge, Mass.: Harvard University Press.

Becker, Gary S. 1997. *The Economics of Life*. Chicago: University of Chicago Press.

Becker, Gary S. 2008. We're not heading for a depression. *Wall Street Journal*, October 7, p. 27.

Becker, Gary S. and Guity Nashat Becker. 1997. *The Economics of Life*. New York: McGraw-Hill.

Becker, Gary S. and Kevin M. Murphy. 1988. A theory of rational addiction. *Journal of Political Economy* 96(4):675–700.

Becker, Jo, Sheryl Gay Stolberg, and Stephen Labaton. 2008. White House philosophy stoked mortgage bonfire. *New York Times*, December 21, p. A1.

Becker, W. J. Ronen and G. H. Sorter. 1974. Opportunity costs: An experimental approach. *Journal of Accounting Research* (Autumn):317–329.

Beigel, H. G. 1954. Body height in mate selection. *Journal of Social Psychology* 39:257–268.

Bensinger, Ben. 2009. For GM, bad gets worse. *Los Angeles Times*. February 27, p. C1.

Bentham, Jeremy. 1781. *An Introduction to the Principles of Morals and Legislation*. Oxford: Clarendon Press, 1907, accessed December 26, 2007 from http://www.econlib.org/library/Bentham/bnthPML1.html.

Benz, Matthias and Stephen Meier. 2006. Do people behave in experiments as in real life? Evidence from donations. Zurich: University of Zurich, Institute for Empirical Research in Economics, working paper 248.

Berg, J., J. Dickhaut, and K. McCabe. 2005. Rick preference Instability across institutions: A dilemma. *Proceedings National Academy of Sciences* 102:4209–4214.

Bernanke, Ben S. 2008. We're laying the groundwork for recovery. *Wall Street Journal*, October 14, p. A21.

Beyerstein, B. 1999. Whence cometh the myth that we only use ten percent of our brains? In *Mindmyths: Exploring Everyday Mysteries of the Mind and Brain*, ed. by Sergio Della Sala. New York: Wiley.

Bianca C. Wittmann, Nathaniel D. Daw, Ben Seymour, and Raymond J. Dolan. 2008. Striatal activity underlies novelty-based choice in humans. *Neuron* 58:967–973.

Bikhchandani, S. D., David Hirshleifer, and Ivo Welch. 1992. A theory of fashion, social custom and social change. *Journal of Political Economy* 81:637–654.

Bjork, J. M., B. Knutson, G. W. Fong, D. M. Caggiano, S. M. Bennett, and D. Hommer. 2004. Incentive-elicited brain activation in adolescents: Similarities and differences from young adults. *Journal of Neuroscience* 24:1793–1802.

Blair, Claire, David P, Baker, David A. Gamson, Steven Thorne. 2005. Rising mean IQ: Cognitive demand of mathematics education for young children, population exposure to formal schooling, and the neurobiology of the refrontal cortex. *Intelligence* 33(1):2005.

Boulding, Kenneth E. 1970. *Economics As a Science*. New York: McGraw-Hill.

Bowles, Samuel and Herbert Gintis. 2001. The Evolution of Strong Reciprocity. Amherst, Mass.: Department of Economics, University of Massachusetts.

Boyer, Pascal. 2001. *Religion Explained: The Evolutionary Origins of Religious Thought*. New York: Basic Books.

Brennan, Geoffrey and James M. Buchanan. 1985. *The Power to Tax: Analytic Foundations of a Fiscal Constitution*. Cambridge, U.K.: Cambridge University Press.

Brown, Donald E. 1991. *Human Universals*. New York: McGraw-Hill.

Browne, Kingsley R. 1995. Sex and temperament in modern society: A Darwinian view of the glass ceiling and the gender gap. *Arizona Law Review* 37 (winter):971.

Browne, Kingsley R. 1998. *Divided Labours: An Evolutionary View of Women at Work*. New Haven, Conn.: Yale University Press.

Browne, Kingsley R. 2002. *Biology at Work: Rethinking Sexual Equality*. New Brunswick, N.J.: Rutgers University Press.

Bruel-Jungerman, E., S. Davis, and S. Laroche. 2007. Brain plasticity mechanisms and memory: a party of four. *Neuroscientist* 13(5):492–505.

Buchanan, James M. 1969a. *Cost and Choice: An Inquiry in Economic Theory*. New Haven, Conn.: Markham Publishing.

Buchanan, James M. 1969b. Is economics a science of choice? In *Roads to Freedom: Essays in Honour of Friedrich A. von Hayek*, ed. by Erich Streissler. London: Routledge & Kegan, pp. 47–64.

Buchanan, James M. 1975. *The Limits of Liberty: Between Anarchy and Leviathan*. Chicago: University of Chicago Press.

Buchanan, James M. 1994a. The return to increasing returns: An introductory summary. *The Redrun to Increase Returns*, eds. James M. Buchanan and Yong J. Yoon. Ann Arbor, Mich.: University of Michigan Press, pp. 3–13.

Buchanan, James M. 1994b. The supply of labor and the extent of the market. *The Redrun to Increase Returns*, ed. by James M. Buchanan and Yong J. Yoon. Ann Arbor, Mich.: University of Michigan Press, pp. 331–356.

Buchanan, James M. and Gordon Tullock. 1962. *The Calculus of Consent: The Logical Foundations of Constitutional Democracy*. Ann Arbor, Mich.: University of Michigan Press.

Burnham, Terry and Jay Phelan. 2000. *Mean Genes*. Cambridge, Mass.: Perseus Publishing Group.

Bush, George W. 2008. Excerpts from President Bush's speech to the nation on the economy. *New York Times*, September 25, p. A24.

Buss, David M. 1986. Human mate selection. *American Scientist* 73:47–51.

Buss, David M. 1988. The evolution of human sexual competition: Tactics of mate attraction. *Journal of Personality and Social Psychology* 54:616–628.

Buss, David M. 1989. Sex differences in human mate preferences: Evolutionary hypotheses tested in 37 cultures. *Behavioral and Brain Sciences* 12:1–14.

Buss, David M. 2003. *The Evolution of Desire: Strategies of Human Mating*. New York: Basic Books.

Buss, David M. and Michael F. Barnes. 1986. Preferences in human mate selection. *Journal of Personality and Social Psychology* 50:559–570.

Buss, David M., et al. 1990. International preferences in selecting mates: A study of 37 societies. *Journal of Cross-Cultural Psychology* 21:5–47.

Calomiris, Charles W. and Peter J. Wallison. 2008. Blame Fannie Mae and Congress for the credit mess. *Wall Street Journal*. September 23, p. A29.

Camerer, Colin F. 2003. *Behavioral Game Theory: Experiments in Strategic Interaction*. Princeton, N.J.: Princeton University Press.

Camerer, Colin and R. M. Hogarth. 1999. The effects of financial incentives in experiments: A review and capital-labor-production framework. *Journal of Risks and Uncertainty* 19:7–42.

Camerer, Colin F. and George Loewenstein. 2004. Behavioral economics: Past, present, and future. *Advances in Behavioral Economics*, ed. by Colin F. Camerer, George Loewenstein, and Matthew Rabin. Princeton, N.J.: Princeton University Press.

Cameron, C., P. S. Oskamp, and W. Sparks. 1978. Courtship American style: Newspaper advertisements. *Family Coordinator* 26:27–30.

Cantillon, Richard. 1755 (first extant ed.). *Essay on the Nature of Trade in General*. London: Frank Cass and Company, translated by Henry Higgs, 1959, as accessed on January 25, 2008 from http://www.econlib.org/library/NPDBooks/Cantillon/cntNT0.html.

Caplan, Bryan. 2007. *The Myth of the Rational Voter: Why democracies Choose Bad Policies*. Princeton, N.J.: Princeton University Press.

Carstensen, Laura L., Joseph A. Mikels, Mara Mather. 2006. Aging and the intersection of cognition, motivation, and emotion. *Handbook on the Psychology of Aging*. San Diego, Calif.: Academic Press.

Castro, J. M. Bermu dez de M. Martino n-Tores, S. Sarmiento, M. Lozano, J. L. Arsuaga, and E. Carbonell. 2003. Rates of anterior tooth wear in middle Pleistocene hominines from Sima de Los Huesos (Sierra de Atapuerca, Spain), *PNAS* 100(21, October 14), accessed on April 10, 2008 at http://www.pnas.org/cgi/reprint/2034879100v1.pdf

Christiansen, Charlotte, Jesper Rangvid, and Juanna Schroter Joensen. 2006.Gender, Marriage, and the Decision to Invest in Stocks and Bonds: Do Single Women Invest More in Less Risky Assets?, as accessed October 24, 2008 from http://papers.ssrn.com/sol3/papers.cfm?abstract_id=948164.

Cimilluca, Dana, Carrick Mollenkamp, Alistair MacDonald, and Marcus Walker. 2008. Europe raises stakes in bank bailout race. *Wall Street Journal*, October 13, 2008, p. A1.

Clark, Gregory. 2007. *A Farewell to Alms: A brief History of the World*. Princeton, N.J.: Princeton University Press.

Coase, Ronald. 1998. Comment on Thomas W. Hazlett: Assigning property rights to radio spectrum users: Why did FCC license auctions take 67 years? *Journal of Law and Economics* 41(2):577–80.

Coleman, Major, Michael LaCour-Little, and Kerry D. Vandell. 2008. Subprime lending and the housing bubble: Tail wags dog? *Journal of Housing Economics* 4 (October):1–19.

Conde, Jessica R. and Wolfgang J. Streit. 2006. Microglia in the aging brain. *Journal of Neuropathology and Experimental Neurology* 65(3):199–203.

Cosmides, Leda and John Tooby. 1992. Cognitive adaptation for social exchange. *The Adaptive Mind*, ed. by Jerome H. Barkow, Leda Cosmides, and John Tooby. New York: Oxford University Press, pp. 163–228.

Cosmides, Leda and John Tooby. 1994. Better than rational: Evolutionary psychology and the invisible hand. *American Economic Review* 50(2, May):327–332.

Cosmides, Leda, John Tooby, and Jerome H. Barkow. 1992. Introduction: Evolutionary psychology and conceptual integration, in *The Adapted Mind: Evolutionary Psychology and the Generation of Culture*, ed. by Jerome H. Barkow, Leda Cosmides, and John Tooby. New York: Oxford University Press, pp. 3–18.

Cowen, Tyler. 2007. *Discover Your Inner Economist: Use Incentives to Fall in Love, Survive Your Next Meeting, and Motivate Your Dentist*. New York: Dutton.

Cowen, Tyler. 2008. Three trends and a train wreck. *New York Times*, October 19, p. BU6.

Cowles, Alfred and H. Jones. 1937. Some a posteriori probabilitis in stock market action. *Econometrica* 5:280–294.

Crockett, M. J., L. Clark, G. Tabibnia, M. D. Lieberman, and T. W. Robbins. 2008. Serotonin modulates behavioral reactions to unfairness. *Science* 320:1739.

Crockett, S., Vernon V. Smith, B. Wilson. 2006. Specialization and Exchange as a Discovery Process. Fairfax, Va.: Interdisciplinary Center for Economic Science, George Mason University, working paper.

Csíkszentmihályi, Mihály. 1990. *Flow: The Psychology of Optimal Experience*. New York: Harper and Row.

Daly, Martin and Margo Wilson. 1988. *Homoside*. New York: Aldine de Gruyter.

Darwin, Charles. 1859. *The Origins of the Species*. New York: Signet Classics, reissued in 2003.

Dash, Eric. 2009. U.S. is said to agree to raise stake in Citigroup. *New York Times*. February 27, as accessed February 27, 2008 at http://dealbook.blogs.nytimes.com/2009/02/27/us-is-said-to-agree-to-raise-stake-in-citigroup/.

Davis, D. and Charles Holt. 1993. *Experimental Economics*. Princeton, N.J.: Princeton University Press.

Dawkins, Richard. 1976. *The Selfish Gene*. New York: Oxford University Press.

de Vries, Jan. 1994. The Industrial Revolution and the industrious revolution. *Journal of Economic History* 54 (June, 2):249–270.

Deck, C. and B. Wilson. 2004. Economics at the pump. *Regulation* 1:22–29.

Dennett, Daniel C. 2003. *Freedom Evolves*. New York: Viking Adult.

Duhigg, Charles. 2008. Pressured to take more risk, Fannie reached tipping point. *New York Times*, October 5, 2008, p. A1.

Dunbar, Robin. 1998. The social brain hypothesis. *Evolutionary Anthropology* 6:178–190.

Editors. 2008. Bailout for billionaires (editorial). *Wall Street Journal*, September 11, p. A14.

Elder, Glen H. 1969. Appearance and education in marriage mobility. *American Sociological Review* 34(4):519–533.

Elster, Jon. 1990. When rationality fails. *The Limits of Rationality*, ed. by Karen Schweers Cook and Margaret Levi. Chicago: University of Chicago Press, pp. 19–46.

Evans, Lisa H., N. S. Gray, and Robert. J. Snowden. 2007. Reduced P50 suppression is associated with the cognitive disorganization dimension of schizotypy. *Schizophrenia Research* 97(1-3):152–162.

Fama, Eugene F. 1965a. The behavior of stock market prices. *Journal of Business* 38:34–105.

Fama, Eugene F. 1965b. Random walks in stock market prices *Financial Analysts Journal* 21 (5):55–59.

Finkelstein, Eric A and Laura Zuckerman. 2008. *The Fattening of America*. New York: Wiley.

Fischhoff, B., Slovic, P., and Lichtenstein, S. 1980. Knowing what you want: Measuring labile values. *Cognitive Processes in Choice and Decision Behavior*, ed. by T. S. Wallsten. Hillsdale, N.J.: Erlbaum, pp. 117–141.

Flynn, J. R. 1999. Searching for justice: The discovery of IQ gains over time. *American Psychologist* 54:5–20.

Foley, Robert. 1995. *Humans Before Humanity*. Cambridge, Mass.: Blackwell.

Ford, Clellan Stearns and Frank A. Beach. 1951. *Patterns of Sexual Behavior*. New York: Harper and Row.

Fouraker, L. and S. Siegel. 1963. *Bargaining Behavior*. New York: McGraw-Hill.

Franciosi, R., Kujal, P., Michelitsch, R., Smith, V., and Deng, G. 1996. Experimental tests of the endowment effect. Journal Economic and Behavior Organization. 30:213–226.

Frank, Robert. 1987. If *Homo Economicus* could choose his own utility function, would he want one with a conscience? *American Economic Review* 77(September):593–605.

Frank, Robert H. 2007. *The Economic Naturalist: In Search of Explanations for Everyday Enigmas*. New York: Basic Books.

Frank, Steven A. 2009. Evolutionary foundations of cooperation and group cohesion *Games, Groups, and the Global Good*, ed. by Simon A. Levin. Heidelbery, Germany: Springer (in press, page numbers in text refer the prepublication manuscript version).

Frank, Steven and Richard B. McKenzie. 2008. The male-female pay gap driven by coupling between labor markets and mating markets, *Journal of Bioeconomics* 8:269–274.

Fraser, Hunter B., Philipp Khaitovich, Joshua B. Plotkin, Svante Pääbo, and Michael B. Eisen. 2005. Aging and gene expression in the primate brain. *PLOS Biology* 3(9):e274.

Friedman, Milton. 1953. The methodology of positive economics. *Essays in Positive Economics*. Chicago: University of Chicago Press, pp. 3–46.

Friedman, M. 1962 (republished in 2007). *Price Theory: A Provisional Text*. New Brunswick, N.J.: Transactions.

Friedman, Milton. 1976. Inflation and unemployment. *Nobel Memorial Lecture, December 13*, as accessed on December 17, 2008 from http://nobelprize.org/nobel_prizes/economics/laureates/1976/friedman-lecture.pdf.

Friedman, Milton. 1980. *Free to Choose*, a PBS television documentary. Erie, Penn." Idea Channel (http://www.ideachannel.tv/).

Friedman, Milton and Rose Friedman. 1980. *Free to Choose: A Personal Statement*. New York: Harcourt Brace Jovanovich.

Gazzaniga, Michael S. 1992. *Nature's Mind: The Biological roots of Thinking, Emotions, Sexuality, Language, and Intelligence*. New York: Basic Books.

Geary, David C. 1998. *Male, Female: The Evolution of Human Sex Differences*. Washington, D.C.: American Psychological Association.

Genesove, David and Christopher Mayer. 2001. Loss aversion and seller behavior: Evidence from the housing market. *Quarterly Journal of Economics* 116(4, November):1233–1260.

Gerard, H. B. and G. C. Mathewson. 1966. The effects of severity of initiation on liking for a group: A replication. *Journal of Experimental Social Psychology* 2 (July):278–287.

Ghiselin, Michael T. 1974. *The Economy of Nature and the Evolution of Sex*. Berkeley, Calif.: University of California Press.

Gigerenzer, Gerd. 2008. *Rationality for Mortals: How People Cope with Uncertainty*. New York: Oxford University Press.

Gigerenzer, G, P. M. Todd, and the ABC Research Group, editors. 1999a. *Simple Heuristics That Make Us Smart*. Oxford, U.K.: Oxford University Press.

Gigerenzer, Gerd and Peter M. Todd. 1999b. Fast and frugal heuristics: The adaptive toolbox, *Simple Heuristics That Make Us Smart*, ed. by Gigerenzer, Gerd, Peter M. Todd, and the ABC Research Group. Oxford, U.K.: Oxford University Press, pp. 1–18.

Gilbert, Daniel. 2006. *Stumbling on Happiness*. New York: Alfred A. Knopf and Random House, Inc.

Gillis, John S. 1982. *Too Tall, Too Small*. Champaign, Ill.: Institute for Personality and Ability Testing.

Gillis, John S. and Walter E. Avis. 1980. The male-taller norm in mate selection. *Personality and Social Psychology Bulletin* 6:396–401.

Glimcher, P. W., M. C. Dorris, and H. M. Bayer. 2005. Physiological utility theory and the neuroeconomics of choice. *Games and Economic Behavior* 52:213–256.

Gode, D. and S. Sundar. 1993. Allocative efficiency of markets with zero intelligence traders: Markets as a partial substitute for individual rationality. *Journal of Political Economy* 101:603-630.

Gosselin, Peter G. and Maura Reynolds. 2008. Bailout tab: $700,000,000,000. *Los Angeles Times*, September 21, p. A1.

Gould, Stephen Jay. 1990. *Wonderful Life: Burgess Shale and the Nature of History*. New York: W. W. Norton.

Gourville, John T. and Dilip Soman. 1998. Payment depreciation: The effects of temporally separating payments from consumption. *Journal of Consumer Research* 25(September): 160-174.

Green, Susan, Dale R. Buchanan, and Shiela Heuer. 1984. Winners, losers, and choosers: A field investigation of dating initiation. *Personality and Social Psychology Bulletin* 10:502–512.

Gregersen, Edgar. 1982. *Sexual Practices: The Story of Human Sexuality*. New York: F Watts.

Guala, F. 2005. *The Methodology of Experimental Economics*. Cambridge, U.K.: Cambridge University Press.

Hadas, Edward. 2008. Crisis is milder outside finance. *New York Times*, October 13, p. B2.

Hall, Doug. n.d. *Jump Start Your Marketing Brain*, as accessed October 24, 2008 at http://books.google.com/books?id=eCUcQ1WiHAIC&pg=PA58&lpg=PA58&dq=%22flavors+of+jam%22+twenty+three&source=web&ots=AFrfh7hPdi&sig=DX0pNlRUGOuBhHV3PFHIwz_Piqk&hl=en&sa=X&oi=book_result&resnum=1&ct=result#PPP1,M1.

Hamburger, Tom, and William Heisel. 2008. Heavily invested in outcomes: Financial firms are big donors to both parties. *Los Angeles Times*, September 23m p. A1.

Hamermesh, Daniel S, and Jeff E. Biddle. 1994. Beauty and the labor market. *American Economic Review* 84(December, 5):1174–1194.

Hamilton, William D. 1964. The genetical evolution of social behaviour. *Journal of Theoretical Biology* 7:1–52.

Hardin, Garrett. 1968. The tragedy of the commons. *Science* 162:1243–1248.

Harford, Tim. 2008. *The Logic of Life: The Rational Economics of an Irrational World*. New York: Random House.

Harrison, Albert A. and Laila Saeed. 1977. Let's make a deal: An analysis of revelations and stipulations in lonely hearts advertisements. *Journal of Personality and Social Psychology* 35:257–264.

Hayek, F. A. 1944. *The Road to Serfdom*, Chicago: University of Chicago Press.

Hayek, Friedrich A. 1945. The use of knowledge in society. *American Economic Review* 35(4, September):519–530, accessed March 9, 2007 at http: //www.econlib.org/Library/ Essays/hykKnw1.html.

Hayek, Friedrich A. 1952. *The Counter-Revolution of Science.* Chicago: University of Chicago Press.

Hayek, Friedrich A. 1967. *Studies in Philosophy, Politics and Economics.* Chicago: University of Chicago Press.

Hayek, Friedrich A. 1973 (vol. 1), 1976 (vol. 2), and 1979 (vol. 3). *Law, Legislation, and Liberty.* Chicago: University of Chicago Press.

Henrich, J. 2000. Does culture matter in economics? Ultimatum game bargaining among the Machiguenga of the Peruvian Amazon. *American Economic Review* 90(4):973–979.

Henrich, J. R. Boyd, Colin Camerer, E. Fehr, H. Gintis. R. McElreath, M Alvard, A. Barr, J. Ensminger, N. Henrich, K. Hill, F. Gil-White, M. Gurven, F. Marlowe, J. Patton, Herszenhorn, David M. 2008. Bailout plan wins approval; Democrats vow tighter rules. *New York Times*, October 4, p. A1.

Herszenhorn, David M., Stephen Labaton, and Mark Landler. 2008. Democrats set conditions as Treasury chief rallies support for bailout plan: Oversight is issue. *New York Times*, September 22, p. A1.

Hertwig, R. and A. Ortmann. 2001. Experimental practices in economics: A methodological challenge for psychologists. *Behavioral and Brain Sciences* 24(3):383–403.

Hirshleifer, Jack. 1982. Evolutionary models in economics and law: Cooperation versus conflict strategies. *Research in Law and Economics* 4:1–60.

Hirshleifer, Jack. 1984. On the emotions as guarantors of threats and promises. Los Angeles: Department of Economics, University of California, Los Angeles, working paper 337 (August), downloadable from http://www.econ.ucla.edu/workingpapers/wp337.pdf.

Hirshleifer, Jack. 1993. The affection and the passions: Their economic logic. *Rationality and Society* 5(2):185–202.

Hitt, Greg and Deborah Solomon. 2008. Historic bailout passes as economy slips further. *Wall Street Journal.* October 4–5, p. A1.

Hitt, Greg, Deborah Solomon, and Damilan Paletta. 2008. Bailout pact gains momentum amid push for tough controls. *Wall Street Journal*, September 25, p. A1.

Hitt, Greg, Deborah Solomon, and Michael M. Phillips. 2008. Treasury relents on key points. *Wall Street Journal*, September 23, p. A3.

Hobbes, Thomas. 1642. *De Cive.* New York: Appleton-Century-Crofts , reissued 1949.

Hoffman, Elizabeth, Kevin McCabe, Keith Shachat, and Vernon L. Smith. 1994. Preferences, property rights and anonymity in bargaining games. *Games and Economic Behavior* 7(3, November):346–380.

Hollis, Martin and Edward J. Nell. 1975. *Rational Economic Man: A Philosophical Critique of Neo-Classical Economics.* London: Cambridge University Press.

Holmes, Steven A. 2008Fannie Mae eases credit to aid mortgage lending. *New York Times*, September 30, as accessed October 20, 2008 from http://query.nytimes.com/gst/fullpage. html?res=9C0DE7DB153EF933A0575AC0A96F958260.

Hoyland, A., C. L. Lawton, and L. Dye. 2008. Acute effects of macronutrient manipulations on cognitive test performance in healthy young adults: a systematic research review. *Neuroscience and Biobehavioral Reviews* 32(1):72–85.

Isaac, R. Mark and D. James. 2000. Just who are you calling risk averse. *Journal of Risk and Uncertainty* 20:177–187.

Isaac, R. Mark, James M. Walker, and Susan H. Thomas. 1984. Divergent evidence on free riding: An experimental examination and possible explanation. *Public Choice* 43:113–149.

Isaac, R. Mark, Kenneth F. McCue, and Charles Plott. 1985. Public goods provision in an experimental environment. *Journal of Public Economics* 26:51–74.

Jessup, Kathy. 2008. Cell-phone distractions are causing more traffic accidents. *Kalamazoo Gazette*, July 30, as accessed March 6, 2009 from http://blog.mlive.com/kzgazette/2008/07/cellphone_distractions_are_cau.html.

Jevons, William Stanley. 1871. *The Theory of Political Economy*, 5th edn. New York: Augustus M. Kelley, pp. 1965.

Jones, Philip and John Cullis. 2000. "Individual failure": and the analytics of social policy. *Journal of Social Policy* 29(1):73–93.

Kachelmeier, Stephen J. and Mohamed Shehata. 1992. Examining risk preferences under high monetary incentives: Experimental evidence from the People's Republic of China. *American Economic Review* 82(5):1120–1141.

Kagel, John H. and Alvin E. Roth. 1995. *The Handbook of Experimental Economics*. Princeton, N.J.: Princeton University Press.

Kahneman, Daniel. 1994. New challenges to the rationality assumption. *Journal of Institutional and Theoretical Economics* 150:18–36.

Kahneman, Daniel. 2002. Interview on the Nobel Prize in Economics, Nobelprize,org, accessed March 15, 2009 from http://nobelprize.org/nobel_prizes/economics/laureates/2002/kahneman-interview.html

Kahneman, Daniel and Amos Tversky. 1979. Prospect theory: An analysis of decisions under risk. *Econometrica* 47:313–327.

Kahneman, Daniel and Amos Tversky. 2000a. Choices, values, and frames, as reprinted in *Choices, Values, and Frames*. Daniel Kahneman and Amos Tversky, eds. Cambridge, U.K.: Cambridge University Press, pp. 1–16.

Kahneman, Daniel and Amos Tversky. 2000b. Prospect theory: An Analysis of Decision under Risk, as reprinted in *Choices, Values, and Frames*, ed. by Daniel Kahneman and Amos Tversky. Cambridge, U.K.: Cambridge University Press, pp. 17–43.

Kahneman, Daniel, J. Knetsch and Richard H. Thaler. 1990. Experimental tests of the endowment and the Coase Theorem. *Journal of Political Economy* 98(6):1325–1348.

Kandel, E. R. 2007. *In Search of Memory: The Emergence of a New Science of Mind.* New York: W.W. Norton & Company.

Kaplan, Hillard, Kim Hill, Jane Lancaster, and A. Magdelana Hurtado. 2000. A theory of human life history evolution: Diet, intelligence, and longevity. *Evolutionary Anthropology* 9:156–185.

Keeley, Lawrence H. 1996 *War Before Civilization.* New York: Oxford University Press.

Kelly, Robert C. 1995. *The Foraging Spectrum: Diversity in Hunter-Gatherer Lifeways.* Washington, D.C.: Smithsonian Institution Press.

Kessler, Andy. 2008. The Paulsen plan will make money for taxpayers. *Wall Street Journal*, September, p. A21.

Keynes, John Maynard. 1963. *Essays in Biography.* New York: W.W. Norton.

Keynes, John Neville. 1891. *The Scope and Method of Political Economy.* London: Macmillan & Co.

Kim, Oliver and Mark Walker. 1984. The free rider problem: Experimental evidence. *Public Choice* 43:3–24.

Kirtzner, Israel M. 1962. Rational behavior and economic theory. *Journal of Political Economy* 70(4, August):380–385.

Kirtzner, Israel M. 1963. Rational behavior and economic theory: Rejoinder. *Journal of Political Economy* 71(1, February):84–85.

Kirzner, Israel M. 1973. *Competition and Entrepreneurship. Chicago: University of Chicago Press.*

Klein, Richard G. 2000. Archeology and the evolution of human behavior. *Current Anthropology* 9:17–36.

Knauft, Bruce. 1991. Violence and sociability in human evolution. *Current Anthropology* 32: 391–428.

Knight, Frank H. 1921. *Risk, Uncertainty, and Profit.* Boston, Mass.: Hart Schaffner; Houghton Mifflin, as accessed on February 4, 2008 at http://www.econlib.org/library/Knight/knRUP.html,

Knight, Frank H. 1924. The limitations of the scientific method in economics, *The Trend of Economics,* ed. by Rexford Tugwell. New York: Alfred A. Knopf, pp. 229–267.

Knight, Frank H. 1933. *The Economic Organization.* Chicago: University of Chicago.

Knight, Frank H. 1935. *The Ethics of Competition, And Other Essays.* Chicago: University of Chicago Press, reissued in 1976.

Knight, Frank H. 1947. *Freedom and Reform: Essays in Economics and Social Philosophy,* Port Washington, N.Y.: Kennikat Press, reissued in 1969.

Knutson, B. and P. Bossaerts. 2007. Neural antecedents of financial decisions. *Journal of Neuroscience* 27:8174–8177.

Knutson, B. and R. Peterson. 2005. Neurally reconstructing expected utility. *Games and Economic Behavior* 52:305–315

Knutson, B., S. Rick, G. E.Wimmer, D. Prelec, G. Loewenstein. 2007. Neural predictors of purchases. *Neuron* 53:147–157.

Krebs, Dennis L and Kathy Denton. 1997. Social illusions and self-deception: The evolution of biases in person perception. In *Evolutionary Social Psychology,* ed. by Jeffrey A. Simpson and Douglas T. Kenrick. Mahwah, N.J.: Lawrence Erlbaum Associates.

Krugman, Paul. 2008. *The Return of Depression Era Economics and the Crisis of 2008.* New York: W. W. Norton.

Krugman, Paul. 2009. The Obama gap. *New York Times,* January 8, as accessed February 27, 2008 from http://www.nytimes.com/2009/01/09/opinion/09krugman.html?em.

Laffer, Arthur B. 2004. The Laffer curve: Past, present, and future. *Backgrounder.* Washington, D.C.: Heritage Foundation, policy paper #1765 (June 1).

Landler, Mark and Eric Dash. 2008. Drama behind a banking deal. *New York Times,* October 15, p. A1.

Landsburg, Steven E. 1995. *Armchair Economist: Economics and Everyday Life.* New York: Free Press.

Landsburg, Steven E. 2007. *More Sex means Safer Sex: The Unconventional Wisdom of Economics.* New York: Free Press.

Laury, Susan and Laura O. Taylor. 2006. Altruism spillovers: Are behaviors in context-free experiments predictive of altruism toward a naturally occurring public good? *Journal of Economic Behavior and Organization* 65(1, January):9–29.

Leclerc, France, Berndt Schmitt, and Laurette Dubé. 1995. Is time like money?: Decision making and waiting time. *Journal of Consumer Research* 22:110–119.

Lee, Dwight. 1969. Utility analysis and repetitive gambling. *American Economist* 13 (fall, 2): 87–91.

Lehrer, Jonah. 2009. *How We Decide.* New York: Houghton-Mifflin.

Levitan, Daniel J. 2006. *This Is Your Brain on Music.* New York: Dutton Books.

Levitt, Steven D. and Stephen Dubner. 2005. *Freakonomics: A Rogue Economist Explores the Hidden Side of Everything.* New York: William Morrow.

Levitt, Steven D. and John A. List. 2007. What do laboratory experiments measuring social preferences reveal about the real world? *Journal of Economic Perspective* 21(2, spring): 153–174.

Levy, David M. and Sandra J. Peart. 2001. The secret history of the dismal science. Part I. Economics, religion and race in the 19th century. *The Library of Economics and Liberty January 22,* as accessed on November 13, 2008 from http://www.econlib.org/library/Columns/LevyPeartdismal.html.

Lewis, Kenneth D. 2008. Main street needs the Treasury plan. *Wall Street Journal,* September, p. A19.

Li, Ching Chun. 1967. Fundamental theorem of natural selection. *Nature* 214:505–506.

List, John A. 2003. Does market experience eliminate market anomalies? *Quarterly Journal of Economics* 118(1):41–71.

List, John A. 2004. Neoclassical theory versus prospect theory: Evidence from the marketplace. *Econometrica* 72:615–625.

List, John A. 2006. The behavioralists meet the market: Measuring social preferences and reputational effects in actual transactions. *Journal of Political Economy* 114(1):1–37.

Loewenstein, George and Nachum Sicherman. 1989. Do workers prefer increasing wage profiles? *Journal of Labor Economics* 9(1, February):67–84.

Loewenstein, George and Nachum Sicherman. 1991. Do workers prefer increasing wage profiles? *Journal of Labor Economics* 9(1):67–84.

Loftus, Elizabeth F. 1997. Creating false memories. *Scientific American* 277:70–75.

Lott, John R., Jr. 2007. Driving the lemon myth off the lot. Fox Business News, accessed on March 12, 2008 at http://foxbusiness/latest-news/article/driving-lemon-myth-lot_290898_1.html.

Lynn, Michael and B. A. Shurgot. 1984. Responses to lonely hearts advertisements: Effects of reported physical attractiveness, physique, and colorization. *Personality and Social Psychology Bulletin* 10:349–357.

Malthus, Thomas Robert. 1798. *An Essay on the Principle of Population*. London: J. Johnson, 1798, accessed December 20, 2007 at http://www.econlib.org/library/Malthus/malPop1.html.

Manson, Joseph H. and Richard W. Wrangham. 1991. Intergroup aggression in chimpanzees and humans. *Current Anthropology* 32:369–390.

Marcus, Gary. 2008. *Kluge: The Haphazard Evolution of the Human Mind*. Boston: Mariner Books.

Marlowe, Frank, Coren Apicella, and Dorian Reed. 2005. Men's preferences for women's profile waist-to-hip ratio in two societies. *Evolution and Human Behavior* 26:458–468.

Marr, D. 1982. *Vision: A Computational Investigation into the Human Representation and processing of Visual Information*. San Francisco: Freeman [finalize reference].

Marshall, Alfred. 1890. *Principles of Economics*. London: Macmillan and Co., Ltd, 1920, accessed January 24, 2008 from http://www.econlib.org/library/Marshall/marP1.html.

Marshall, Alfred. 1890. *Principles of Economics* New York: Cosimo, Inc., originally published in 1890.

Marwell, Gerald and Ruth Ames. 1981. Economists free ride: Does anyone else? *Journal of Public Economics*.15:295–310.

Marx, Karl. 1848. *The Communist Manifesto*. Chicago: Henry Regnery Co., reissued in 1954.

McClam, Erin. 2008. Trillion: It's now the new billion. *Los Angeles Times*, October 13, p. C3.

McClure, Samuel M., David Laibson, George Loewenstein, and Jonathan D. Cohen. 2004. Separate neural systems value immediate and delayed monetary reward. *Science* 306:503–507.

McGaugh, J. L. 2004. The amygdale modulates the consolidation of memories of emotionally arousing experiences. *Annual Review of Neuroscience* 27:1–28.

McKenzie, Richard B. 1977. Where is the economics in economic education? *Journal of Economic Education* 3 (Fall):5–13.

McKenzie, Richard B. 1982. *The Limits of Economic Science: Essays in Methodology*. Boston: Kluwer Nijhoff.

McKenzie, Richard B. 1995. *Times Change: The New York Times and the Minimum Wage*. San Francisco: Pacific Institute for Public Policy Research.

McKenzie, Richard B. 2000. *Trust on Trial: How the Microsoft Case Is Reframing the Rules of Competition*. Boston: Perseus Books.

McKenzie, Richard B. 2008. *Why Popcorn Costs So Much at the Movies, and Other Pricing Puzzles*. Heidelberg, Germany: Springer Publishers.

McKenzie, Richard B. and Dwight R. Lee. 1991. *Quicksilver Capital: How the Rapid Movement of Wealth Has Changed the World*. New York: Free Press, Inc.

McKenzie, Richard B. and Dwight R. Lee. 2008. *In Defense of Monopoly: How Market Power Fosters Creative Production*. Ann Arbor, Mich.: University of Michigan Press.

McKenzie, Richard B. and Gordon Tullock. 1976. *The New World of Economics: Explorations into Human behavior*. Homewood, Ill.: Richard D. Irvin (reissued in revised versions, 1978, 1981, 1989, and 1994).

McLeod, P. and Z. Dienes. Do fielders know where to catch the ball or only how to get there? *Journal of Experimental Psychology: Human perception and Performance* 22:531–543

Medema, Steven G. 2008. Chicago price theory and Chicago law and economics. Denver, Colo.: Economics Department, University of Colorado, Denver, working paper, September.

Menger, Carl. 1871. *Principles of Economics*, translated by James Dingwall and Bert F. Augustus. New York: New York University Press, 1976.

Mill, John Stuart. 1848. *Principles of Political Economy*. London: Longmans, Green and Co., ed. by William James Ashley, 1909. [Online] available from http://www.econlib.org/library/Mill/mlP1.html; accessed 24 January 2008; Internet.

Miller, Geoffrey. 2001. *The Mating Mind: How Sexual Choice Shaped the Evolution of Human Nature*. New York: Vintage..

Mises, Ludwig von. 1949. *Human Action*. Irvington-on-Hudson, NY: Foundation for Economic Education, Inc., reissued 1996, as accessed on February 8, 2008 from http://www.econlib.org/library/Mises/HmA/msHmA2.html.

Mises, Ludwig von. 1951 (English edition; originally published in German in 1922). *Socialism*. Indianapolis, Ind: Liberty Fund, Inc.. 1981, trans. J. Kahane, reissued 1981, accessed on February 8, 2008 from http://www.econlib.org/library/Mises/msS1.html.

Mises Ludwig von. 1962. *The Ultimate Foundation of Economic Science: An Essay on Method*. Princeton, N.J.: D. Van Nostrand.

Mollenkamp, Carrick, Susanne Craig, Serena Ng, and Aaron Lucchetti. 2008. Crisis on Wall Street as Lehman totters, Merrill is sold, AIG seeks to raise cash. *Wall Street Journal*, September 15, p. A1.

Nelson, A. J., D. J. Heeger, K. McCabe, D. Houser, P. J. Zak, P. W. Glimcher. 2004. Expected utility provides a model for choice behavior and brain activation in humans. *Society for Neuroscience*, Program No. 20:12.

Nettelbeck, T., & Wilson, C. 2004. The Flynn effect: Smarter not faster. *Intelligence* 32:85–93.

Norris, Floyd and Vikas Bajaj. 2008. Financial crisis reshapes Wall Street's landscape. *New York Time*, September 15, p. A1.

Nuñez, Angel and Eduardo Malmiera. 2007. *Corticofugal Modulation of Sensory Information*. Heidelberg, Germany: Springer.

Odean, Terrance. 1998. Are investors reluctant to realize their losses? *Journal of Finance* 53 (5):1775–1798.

Oliphant, James and Richard Simon. 2008. Vying for a piece of the stimulus pie. *Los Angeles Times*, December 14, p. A19.

Olson, Mancur. 1965. *The Logic of Collective Action: Public Goods and the Theory of Groups*. Cambridge, Mass.: Harvard University Press.

Park, J. W. and Zak, P. J. 2007. Neuroeconomics studies. *Analyse & Kritik* 29(1):47–59.

Pezdek, K. and I. Blandon-Gitlin. 2005. When is an intervening lineup most likely to affect eyewitness identification accuracy? *Legal and Criminological Psychology* 10(2, September):247–263

Philipson, Tomas J. and Richard A. Posner. 2003. The long-run growth in obesity as a function of technological change. *Perspectives in Biology and Medicine* 46(3, Summer supplement):S87–S107.

Pigou, A. C. and C. R. Fay. 1926. Memorials to Alfred Marshall. *American Economic Review* 16 (March, 1):81–87.

Pindyck, Robert S. and Daniel L. Rubinfeld. 2004. *Microeconomics*, 6th edn. Upper Saddle River, N.J. Prentice Hall, Inc.

Pinker, Stephen. 1997. *How the Mind Works*. New York: W. W. Norton & Company.

Plott, Charles. 1988. Research in Pricing in a Gas Transportation Network. Technical Report No. 88-2 Washington, D.C.: Federal Energy Regulatory Commission, office of Economic Policy.

Plott, Charles. 2001. Equilibrium, Equilibration, Information, and Multiple Markets: From Basic Science to Institutional design. Paper presented to the Nobel Symposium, Behavioral and Experimental Economics, Stickholm, December 4–6.

Plott, Charles R. and G. Agha. 1983. Intertemporal speculation with a random in: An experimental market, in *Aspiration Levels in Bargaining and Economic Decision Making*, ed. by R. Tietz. Berlin, Germany: Springer-Verlag.

Plott, Charles R. and T. Turocy. 1996. Intertemporal speculation under uncertain future demand, in *Understanding Strategic Interaction: Essays in Honor of Reinhard Seten*, ed. by W. Albers, W. Guth, P. Hammerstein, and E. van Damme. Berlin, Germany: Springer-Verlag, pp. 475–493.

Plott, Charles and K. Zeiler. 2005. The willingness to pay/willingness to accept gap, the "endowment effect." Subject misconceptions and experimental procedures for eliciting valuations. *American Economic Review* 95(3):530–545.

Pomeranz, Kenneth. 2000. *The Great Divergence: China, Europe, and the Making of the Modern World Economy*. Princeton, N.J.: Princeton University Press.

Posner, Richard A. 2009. *A Failure of Capitalism: The crisis of '08 and the Descent into Depression*. Cambridge, Mass.: Harvard University Press.

Powell, Jim. 2004. *FDR's Folly: How Roosevelt and His New Deal Prolonged the Great Depression*. New York: Three Rivers Press.

Pratt, J. W., D. A. Wise, and R. Zeckhauser. 1979. Price differences in almost competitive markets. *Quarterly Journal of Economics* 93(2):189–211.

Price, George R. 1970. Selection and covariance. *Nature* 227:520–521.

Puzzanghera, Jim. 2009. Cost of bailout could double. *Los Angeles Times*. February 27, p. C1.

Radner, Roy. 1998. Economic survival, in *Frontiers of Research in Economic Theory: The Nancy Schwartz Memorial Lectures, 1983–1997*, ed. by Donald P. Jacobs, Ehud Kalai, and Morton I. Kamien. Cambridge, U.K.: Cambridge University Press, pp. 183–209.

Raichle, Marcus E. 2006. The brain's dark energy. *Science* 314 (November 24):1249–1250.

Raichle, Marcus E. and Debra A. Gusnard. 2002. Appraising the brain's energy budget. *PNAS* 99 (16, August 6):10237–10239.

Reiskamp, J. and P. E. Otto. 2006. A theory of how people learn to select strategies. *Journal of Experimental Psychology: General* 135:207–236.

Reiss, Steven. 2000. *Who Am I? The 16 Basic desires That Motivate Our Actions and Define Our Personalities*. New York: Tarcher/Putnam.

Reynolds, Maura. 2008. Fed's moves fail to calm markets. *Los Angeles Times*, October 8, p. A1.

Reynolds, Maura and Peter Nicolas. 2009. Obama $3.55 trillion stand. *Los Angeles Times*. February 29, p. A1.

Reynolds, Maura, Richard Simon, and Peter G. Gosselin. 2008. Congress balks at bailout plan. *Los Angeles Times*. September 24, p. A1.

Ricardo, David. 1817. *On the Principles of Political Economy and Taxation*. London: John Murray, 1821, accessed December 20, 2007 from http://www.econlib.org/library/Ricardo/ricP1.html.

Ridley, Matt. 1996. *The Origins of Virtue: Human Instincts and the Evolution of Cooperation*. New York: Viking Press.

Robbins, Lionel. 1932. Introduction, in Phillip H. Wicksteed. 1910. *The Commonsense of Political Economy, Including a Study of the Human Basis of Economic Law*. London: Macmillan, 1910, pp. i-xxiii.

Robertson, Alan. 1966. A mathematical model of the culling process in dairy cattle. *Animal Reproduction* 8:95–108.

Rode, Catrin and X. T. Wang. 2000. Risk-sensitive decision making examined within an evolutionary framework. *American Behavioral Scientist* 43:926–939.

Rogers, Alan. 1994. Evolution of time preference by natural selection. *American Economic Review* 84:460–481.

Rose, Michael R. 1998. *Darwin's Spectre: Evolutionary Biology in the Modern World*. Princeton, N.J.: Princeton University Press.

Roth, A. and M. Sotomayer. 1990. *Two-Sided Matching: A Study of Game Theoretic Modeling and Analysis*. Cambridge, U.K.: Cambridge University Press.

Rothschild M. and Joseph Stiglitz. 1976. Equilibrium in competitive insurance markets: An essay on the economics of imperfect information. *Quarterly Journal of Economics* 90:629–649.

Rubin, Paul H. 1993. *Managing Business Transactions*. New York: Free Press.

Rubin, Paul H. 2002. *Darwinian Politics: The Evolutionary Origin of Freedom*. New Brunswick, N.J.: Rutgers University Press.

Rubin, Paul H. and Chris Paul. 1979. An evolutionary model of taste for risk. *Economic Inquiry* 17:585–596.

Sadalla, E. K., D. T. Kenrick, and B. Vershure. 1987. Dominance and heterosexual attraction. *Journal of Personality and Social Psychology* 52:730–738.

Samuelson, William and Richard Zeckhauser. 1988. Status quo bias in decision making. *Journal of Risk and Uncertainty* 1(1):7–59.

Sargent, Thomas J. 1993. *Bounded Rationality in Macroeconomics.* Oxford, U.K.: Oxford University Press.

Say, Jean-Baptiste. 1855. *A Treatise on Political Economy.* Philadelphia: Lippincott, Grambo & Co.. 1855, translated by C. R. Prinsep, ed. by Clement C. Biddle, as accessed on January 25, 2008 from http://www.econlib.org/library/Say/sayT1.html.

Scholey, A. B., S. Harper, and D. O. Kennedy. 2001. Cognitive demand and blood glucose. *Physiological Behavior.* 73(4):585–592.

Schumpeter, Joseph A. 1942. *Capitalism, Socialism and Democracy.* New York: Harper.

Schumpeter, Joseph A. 1954. *History of Economic Analysis.* Oxford, U.K: Oxford University Press.

Schwartz, Barry. 2004a. The tyranny of choice. *Scientific American* 290(April):70–76.

Schwartz, Barry. 2004b. *The Paradox of Choice: Why More Is Less.* New York: Harper Collins

Sharot, Tali, Elizabeth A. Martorella, Mauricio R. Delgado, and Elizabeth A. Phelps. 2006. How personal experience modulates the neural circuitry of memories of September 11. *Proceedings of the National Academies of Sciences, December 20, as access online on September 17, 2008 from http://www.pnas.org/content/104/1/389.abstract.*

Shiller, Robert J. 2003. From efficient markets theory to behavioral finance. *Journal of Economic Perspective* 17(1, Winter):83–104.

Shiller, Robert J. 2005. *Irrational Exuberance*, 2nd edn. Princeton, N.J.: Princeton University Press.

Shiller, Robert J. 2008. *The Subprime Solution: How Today's Global Financial Crisis Happened and What to Do about It.* Princeton, N.J.: Princeton University Press.

Simon, Herbert. 1956. Rational choice and the structure of the environment. *Psychological Review* 63:129–138.

Simon, Herbert. 1957. *Models of Man.* New York: John Wiley & Co.

Simon, Herbert A. 1982. *Models of Bounded Rationality*, 3 vols. Cambridge, Mass.: MIT Press

Simon, Richard and Nicole Gaouette. 2008. Approval of bailout comes amide signs that s steep recession is just beginning. *Los Angeles Times*, October 4, p. A1.

Simons, Daniel J. and Christopher F. Chabris. 1999. Gorillas in our midst: Sustained inattentional blindness for dynamic events. *Perception* 28:1059–1074, accessed on May 5, 2008 from http://www.cnbc.cmu.edu/~behrmann/dlpapers/Simons_Chabris.pdf.

Simons, Daniel J. and D. T. Levin. 1997. Change blindness. *Trends in Cognitive Sciences* 1: 261–267.

Simons Daniel J. and D. T. Levin. 1998. Failure to detect changes to people in a real-world interaction. *Psychonomic Bulletin and Review* 5:644–649

Singh, Devendra. 1993. Adaptive significance of waist-to-hip ratio and female physical attractiveness. *Journal of Personality and Social Psychology* 65:293–307.

Singh, Devendra. 1994. Is thin really beautiful and good: Relationship between waist-to-hip ration (WHR) and female attractiveness. *Personality and Individual Differences* 16:123–132.

Skouras, Thanos, George J. Avlonitis, and Kostis A. Indounas. 2005. Economics and marketing on pricing: How and why do they differ. *Journal of Product and Brand Management* 14(6):362–374.

Slagter, H. A., A. Lutz, L. L. Greischar, A. D. Francis, S. Nieuwenhuis, J. M. Davis, and R. J. Davidson. 2007. Mental training affects use of limited brain resources. *PLoS Biology* 5(6):e138 doi:10.1371/journal.pbio.0050138.

Smith, Adam. 1759 (republished in 1790). *The Theory of Moral Sentiments.* A. Millar. Indianapolis, Ind.: Library of Economics and Liberty, accessed September 17, 2007 and any number of dates from http://www.econlib.org/library/Smith/smMS1.html>.

Smith, Adam. 1776 (republished in 1904). *An Inquiry into the Nature and Causes of the Wealth of Nations,* ed. by Edwin Cannan. Methuen and Co. Library of Economics and Liberty, accessed September 17, 2007 and many other dates from <http://www.econlib.org/library/Smith/smWN1.html>.

Smith, John Maynard. 1982. *Evolution and the Theory of Games.* Cambridge, U.K.: Cambridge University Press.

Smith, Vernon L. 1962. An experimental study of competitive market behavior. *Journal of Political Economy* 70:111–137.

Smith, Vernon L. 1976. Experimental economics: Induced value theory. *American Economic Review* 66:274–279.

Smith, Vernon L. 1980. Relevance of laboratory experiments to testing resource allocation theory. *Evaluation of Econometric Models,* J. Kmenta and J. B. Ramsey, eds. San Diego, Calif.: Academic Press, pp. 345–377.

Smith, Vernon L. 1982. Microeconomic systems as experimental science. *American Economic Review* 72:923–955.

Smith, Vernon L. 2008a. *Rationality in Economics: Constructivist and Ecological Forms.* Cambridge, U.K.: Cambridge University Press.

Smith, Vernon L. 2008b. There's no easy way out of the bubble. *Wall Street Journal,* October 9, p. A17.

Smith, Vernon L. and J. Walker. 1993a. Monetary rewards and decision cost in experimental economics. *Economic Inquiry* April:245–261.

Smith, Vernon L. and J. Walker. 1993b. Rewards, experience and decision costs in first price auctions. *Economic Inquiry* 31(2, April):245–261.

Sober, Elliott and David Sloan Wilson. 1998. *Unto Others: The Evolution and Psychology of Unselfish Behavior.* Cambridge, Mass.: Harvard University Press.

Solomon, Deborah and Damien Paletta. 2008a. Treasury hones next rescue tool. *Wall Street Journal,* October 13, p. A3.

Solomon, Deborah and Damien Paletta. 2008b. U.S. bailout plan calms markets, but struggle looms over details. *Wall Street Journal,* September 20–21, p. A1.

Sorkin, G. M. 2008. Speeds hat in hand to treasury. *New York Times,* October 28, p. B1.

Sowell, Elizabeth R., Paul M. Thompson, and Arthur W. Toga. 2004. Mapping changes in the human cortex throughout the span of life. *Neuroscientist* 10(4):372–392.

Spence, A Michael. 1973. Job market signaling. *Quarterly Journal of Economics* 87:355–374.

Squire, L. R. 1986. Mechanisms of Memory. *Science* 232(4758):1612–1619.

Stigler, George J. 1951. The division of labor is limited by the extent of the market. *Journal of Political Economy* 59(3, June):185–193.

Stigler, George J. 1952. *The Theory of Price,* rev. ed. New York: Macmillan Company (last reised edition 1987).

Stigler, George J. 1962. The economics of information. *Journal of Political Economy* 69 (June):213–225.

Stigler, George J. 1963. Elementary economic education. *American Economic Review* 53 2, May):653–659.

Stigler, George J. 1966. *The Theory of Price,* rev. ed. New York: Macmillan Company.

Stigler, George J. 1987. *The Theory of Price,* 4th edn. New York: Macmillan Company.

Stigler, George J. 1975. *Citizen and the State: Essays on Regulation.* Chicago: University of Chicago Press..

Stigler, George J. and Gary S. Becker. 1977. *De gustibus non est disputandum. American Economic Review* 67(2, March):76–90.

Stiner, Mary C., Natalie D. Munro, Todd A. Surovell, Eitan Tchernov, and Ofer Bar-Yosef. 1998. Paleolithic population growth pulses evidenced by small animal exploitation. *Science* (September 25), accessed on March 23, 2008 hppt://www.sciencemag.org.

Streitfeld, David and Gretchen Morgensom. 2008. Building flawed American dreams. *New York Times,* October 19, p. A1.

Sundar, S. 2004. Markets as artifacts: Aggregate efficiency from zero-intelligence traders. In M. Augier and J. March, eds., *Models of Man: Essays in Memory of Herbert A. Simon*. Cambridge, Mass.: MIT Press.

Sutherland, Stuart. 2007. *Irrationality*. New York: Printer & Martin (first published in 1992).

Taylor, P. A. and N. D. Glenn. 1976. The utility of education and attractiveness for female status attainment through marriage. *American Sociological Review* 41:484–498.

Thaler, Richard H. 1991a. *Quasi Rational Economics*. New York: Russell Sage Foundation.

Thaler, Richard H. 1991b. Toward a Positive Theory of Consumer Choice, as reprinted in *Quasi Rational Economics*. New York: Russell Sage Foundation, pp. 3–24.

Thaler, Richard H. 1992. *The Winner's Curse: Paradoxes and Anomalies of Economic Life*. New York, Free Press.

Thaler, Richard H., ed. 1993. *Advances in Behavioral Finance*. New York: Russell Sage Foundation.

Thaler, Richard H. 2000a. Mental accounting matters. As reprinted in *Choices, Values, and Frames*, ed. by Daniel Kahneman and Amos Tversky. Cambridge, U.K: Cambridge University Press, 2000, pp. 241–268.

Thaler, Richard H. 2000b. Toward a positive theory of consumer choice, as reprinted in *Choices, Values, and Frames*, ed. by Daniel Kahneman and Amos Tversky. Cambridge, U.K.: Cambridge University Press, 2000, pp. 269–287.

Thaler, Richard H. 2001. Anomalies. *Journal of Economic Perspective* 15(1):219–232.

Thaler, Richard H., ed. 2005. *Advances in Behavioral Finance*. Princeton, N.J.: Princeton University Press.

Thaler, Richard H. and Cass R. Sunstein. 2008. *Nudge: Improving Decisions About Health, Wealth, and Happiness*. New Haven, Conn.: Yale University Press.

Tooby, John and Leda Cosmides. 1990a. On the Universality of Human Nature and the Uniqueness of the Individual: The Role of Genetics and Adaptation. *Journal of Personality* 58(1):17–67.

Tooby, John and Leda Cosmides. 1990b. The past explains the present: Emotional adaptations and the structure of ancestral environments. *Ethology and Sociobiology* 11:375–424.

Townsend, John Marshall. 1987. Sex differences in sexuality among medical students: Effects of increasing socioeconomic status. *Archives of Sexual Behavior* 16:425–441.

Townsend, John Marshall and Gary D. Levy. 1990a. Effects of potential partners' physical attractiveness and socioeconomic status on sexuality and partner selection. *Archives of Sexual Behavior* 19:149–164.

Townsend, John Marshall and Gary D. Levy. 1990b. Effects of potential partners' costumes and physical attractiveness on sexuality and partner selection. *Journal of Psychology* 124:371–389.

Tracer, David P. 2005. "Economic man" in cross-cultural perspective: Behavioral experiments in 15 small-scale societies. *Behavioral and brain Sciences* 28(6):795–815.

Treue, S. and J. H. Maunsell. 1996. Attentional modulation of visual motion processing in cortical areas MT and MST. *Nature* 382(August):539–541.

Trivers, Robert. L. 1985. *Social Evolution*. Menlo Park, Calif.: Benjamin-Cummings.

Tullock, Gordon. 1967. *Toward a Mathematics of Politics*. Ann Arbor, Mich. University of Michigan Press.

Tullock, Gordon. 1992. *Economic Hierarchies, Organization, and the Structure of Production*. Heidelberg, Germany: Springer.

Tullock, Gordon. 1994. *The Economics of Non-Human Societies*. Tucson, Arizona: Pallas Press.

Tversky, Amos. 1972. Elimination by aspects: A theory of choice. *Psychological Review* 79:281–299.

Tversky, Amos and Daniel Kahneman. 1981. The framing of decisions and the psychology of choice. *Science* 211(4481):453–458.

Tversky, Amos and Daniel Kahneman. 2000. Advances in prospect theory: Cumulative representation of uncertainty. As reprinted in *Choices, Values, and Frames*, ed. by Kahneman, Daniel and Amos Tversky. Cambridge, U.K.: Cambridge University Press, pp. 44–65.

Udry, J. Richard. and Bruce K. Eckland. 1984. Benefits of being attractive: Differential payoffs for men and women. *Psychological Reports* 54:47–56.

Wade, Nicholas. 2007. *Before the Dawn: Discovering the Lost History of Our Ancestors.* New York: Penguin.

Walras, Leon. 1874. *Elements of Pure Economics.* Homewood, Ill.: Richard D. Irwin, 1954.

Wanniski, Jude. 1978. Taxes, revenues, and the "Laffer curve." *The Public Interest* (winter): 3–16.

Weber, Martin and Colin F. Camerer. 1998. The disposition effect in securities trading: An experimental analysis. *Journal of Economic Behavior and Organization* 33(2):167–184.

Weiss, Yoram, Arden Hall, and Fred Dong. 1980. The effect of price and income in the investment in schooling: Evidence from the Seattle-Denver NIT experiment. *Journal of Human Resources* 15(4):611–640.

Wicker, Bruno, Christian Keysers, Jane Plailly, and Jean-Pierre Royet. 2003. Both of us disgusted in My Insula: The Common Neural Basis of Seeing and Feeling Disgust. *Neuron* 40(3):655–664.

Wicksteed, Philip H. 1888. *Alphabet of Economic Science.* New York: Kelley & Millman, reprinted in 1955.

Wicksteed, Phillip H. 1910. *The Commonsense of Political Economy, Including a Study of the Human Basis of Economic Law.* London: Macmillan, accessed January 4, 2008 from http://oll. libertyfund.org/title/1415.

Wicksteed, Philip H. 1914. The scope and method of political economy in the light of the "marginal" theory of value and of distribution. *Economic Journal* 24 (March, 93):1–23, presidential address to Section F of the British Association, 1913.

Wilson, James Q. 1993. *The Moral Sense.* New York: Free Press.

Wrangham, Richard W. and Dale Peterson. 1996. *Demonic Males: Apes and the Origins of Human Violence.* New York: Houghton Mifflin.

Wright, Robert. 1999. *Nonzero: The Logic of Human Destiny.* New York: Pantheeon.

Young, Allyn. 1928. Increasing returns and economic progress. *Economic Journal* 38(152, December):527–540.

Zahavi, Amotz, Avishag Zahavi, Ma'ama Ely, Melvin Patrick Ely, Amir Balaban. 1999. *The Handicap Principle: A Missing Piece of Darwin's Puzzle.* New York: Oxford University Press.

Zak, Paul J. 2004. Neuroeconomics. *Philosophical Transactions of the Royal Society B* 359:1737–1748.

Zak, Paul J. and Arthur Denzau. 2001. Economics is an evolutionary science. In *Evolutionary Approaches in the Behavioral Sciences: Toward a better Understanding of Human Nature*, ed. by Albert Somit. Greenwich, Conn.: JAI Press.

Zak, Paul J. and Kwang Woo Park. 2002. Population genetics and economic growth. *Journal of Bioeconomics* 4(1):1–37.

Zak. Paul J., A. A. Stanton, and S. Ahmadi. 2007. Oxytocin increases generosity in humans. *Public Library of Science ONE* 2(11), accessed on date from url: e1128. doi:10.1371/journal. pone.0001128.

Zimmer, Carl. 2008. Lots of animals learn, but smarter isn't better. *New York Times*, May6, p. D1, as accessed October 30, 2008 from http://www.nytimes.com/2008/05/06/science/06dumb. html?pagewanted=print.

Index